This book is due on the last date stamped below.
Failure to return books on the date due may result
in assessment of overdue fees.

FINES	.50 per day	

Nixon at the Movies

NIX0N
AT THE MOVIES

A BOOK ABOUT BELIEF **Mark Feeney**

The University of Chicago Press
Chicago + London

MARK FEENEY is a staff writer for the *Boston Globe*.

The University of Chicago Press, Chicago 60637
The University of Chicago Press, Ltd., London
© 2004 by The University of Chicago Press
All rights reserved. Published 2004
Printed in the United States of America

13 12 11 10 09 08 07 06 05 04   1 2 3 4 5
ISBN: 0-226-23968-3

Feeney, Mark.
    Nixon at the movies : a book about belief / Mark Feeney.
        p. cm.
    Includes bibliographical references and index.
    ISBN 0-226-23968-3 (alk. paper)
        1. Nixon, Richard M. (Richard Milhous), 1913– 2. Nixon, Richard M.
(Richard Milhous), 1913– —Views on motion pictures. 3. Nixon, Richard M.
(Richard Milhous), 1913– —Psychology. 4. Presidents—United States—
Biography. 5. Motion pictures—Social aspects—United States. 6. Motion
pictures—United States—Psychological aspects. 7. Motion pictures—
United States—History—20th century. I. Title.
    E856.F435 2004
    973.924'092—dc22   2004004964

A portion of chapter 8 appeared in *The American Scholar* 70, no. 1 (Winter
2001).

Photo on page 2 is courtesy of the Wisconsin Center for Film and Theater
Research.

Contents

. . . He will not feed the people on movie-star daydreams . . .

GARRY WILLS, *Nixon Agonistes*

:: :: ::

Despite all the polls and all the rest, I think there are still a hell of a lot of people out there, and from what I've seen they're—you know, they, they want to believe, that's the point, isn't it?

RICHARD NIXON TO H. R. HALDEMAN, APRIL 25, 1973

Introduction

He would have made a fantastic tragic figure in a Bergman film, if only he were a better actor. LIV ULLMANN, AFTER SITTING NEAR RICHARD NIXON AT A STATE DINNER

In 1956, when [Tricia Nixon] was ten years old, she was taking piano lessons and I was trying not too successfully to convince her how important it was to practice. She finally turned to me and said, "Daddy, you should have practiced more when you were a little boy. If you had, you might have become famous and gone to Hollywood and they would have buried you in a special place." RICHARD NIXON, *In the Arena*

In a century of celebrity, it was inevitable that the most powerful man in the world and the most alluring medium of mass communication should find themselves frequently intertwined. William McKinley was the first president to be filmed. Woodrow Wilson gave *The Birth of a Nation* (1915) what remains the most memorable blurb any motion picture has ever received—"It is like writing history with Lightning," he allegedly said—an endorsement D. W. Griffith himself couldn't have bettered. In 1928 the nation's First Family, the Coolidges, had the nation's First Couple, Mary Pickford and Douglas Fairbanks, to lunch at the White House. Louis B. Mayer, the second "M" in MGM, cherished a friendship with Herbert Hoover. They "are practically sleeping in the same bed," Marie Dressler, one of Mayer's most popular stars, complained when he forbade anyone on the studio's payroll from attending a rally for Franklin D. Roosevelt at the Los Angeles Coliseum in 1932.

Mayer may have loved Hoover, but it was Roosevelt the rest of Hollywood loved. FDR loved Hollywood right back, and they were a perfect match. As he once told Orson Welles, "You and I are the two best actors in America." Harry Truman didn't much like movies—though he was such a big fan of Frank Capra's *State of the Union* (1948) that a Hollywood trade paper called him "a one-man sales-staff" for the political comedy—and Dwight Eisenhower cared only for Westerns. John F. Kennedy changed the equation even more than FDR had. He was the biggest star in America. The son of a man who bankrolled studios and slept with movie stars, he was the first candidate to explicitly utilize star power, both his own and that of such friends as Frank Sinatra. Other presidents have had their movie connections. Two decades after posing for a Hollywood studio portraitist, Lyndon Johnson saw his trusted aide Jack Valenti become president of the Motion Picture Association of America. Gerald Ford included among his Palm Springs golf partners Capra and Bob Hope. Bill Clinton was so starstruck he sat through *Air Force One* (1997) twice. Looking in the mirror the morning after, did he see Harrison Ford? As for George W. Bush, he did his best Tom Cruise imitation landing in that navy carrier jet on the USS *Abraham Lincoln*. Kennedy's special genius, though, was to have the movies associate with *him*. Only Ronald Reagan, of course, has surpassed him in this regard—Reagan actually *was* a movie star and owed his political career to his association with Hollywood.

When Jack Warner heard that his former contract player was going to run against Pat Brown, the mogul is said to have reacted with consternation. "No, no: Jimmy Stewart for governor—Ronnie Reagan for best friend!" So, too, with the title of this book: Nixon at the movies rather than Reagan or any of the rest? The casting seems all wrong. Nixon's is far from the first name that comes to mind for the protagonist of a book that refracts themes and incidents in a president's life through various films and film genres (and vice versa). Yet that it should be *Nixon* at the movies rather than Reagan or any of the rest let there be no doubt.

It is the fundamental premise of this book that no other political figure so well typifies what Stanley Cavell has referred to as "America's special involvement in film, from the talent drawn to Hollywood in making them to the participation of society as a whole in viewing them."[1] The phrase "at the movies" pertains, after all, to those watching the screen rather than those appearing on it. The moviegoer's fundamental yearning and loneliness—why else sit for two hours in the dark if not in pursuit of yearning's fulfillment and loneliness' abolition?—find an unmistakable embodiment in Nixon. Growing up hard by Hollywood as Hollywood itself grew up, he added a particularly vivid strand to the pattern of outsiderdom that would define him all his life: indeed, it was a pattern that helped elevate him to the White House and then remove him from it. The standard road to political success is to ape the lineaments of stardom: glamour, grace, assurance. However unwittingly, Nixon followed another route: representing the rest of us—drab, clumsy, anxious—the great silent majority of moviegoers who don't decorate the screen but stare at it.

"Nixon must always be thinking about who he is," Kennedy remarked once to John Kenneth Galbraith. "That is a strain. I can be myself."[2] True enough: there were all those "new Nixons" so painfully emerging from a man who had to keep reinventing himself. Yet fatiguing though such an internal process must be, its searchful unease and attraction to novelty more nearly approximate the condition of the moviegoer, the eager fantasist for whom such questions as *Who am I? Whom can I identify with? What lives might I lead?* can be answered (for a couple of hours, anyway) by nothing more demanding than the purchase of a ticket. Jack Kennedy was no stranger to such internal urges as he read John Buchan and Ian Fleming novels or David Cecil biographies, casting himself in his mind's eye as Richard Hannay or James Bond or Lord Melbourne. No, JFK didn't need movie fantasies (he'd had movie realities: sleeping with Gene Tierney, with Marilyn Monroe). He could afford the more rarefied projections of the page. Little wonder that, as Arthur M. Schlesinger Jr. reports, he "was not a great movie fan and tended, unless the film was unusually gripping, to walk out after the first twenty or thirty minutes."[3] Such an act, as we shall see, was unthinkable for Richard Nixon.

In May 1967, on a fact-finding trip to Latin America, Nixon visited Rio de Janeiro. He had long ago learned the value of spontaneous encounters with average citizens during foreign visits. Such meetings were often informative and always well publicized. Walking through the Rio slums, he came upon a pregnant woman with three children in tow. Nixon's attempt to strike up a conversation proved awkward, at best. (When he inquired, "What do you most need to improve your life?" the woman answered, "Money.") After Nixon had moved on in search of someone more promising, reporters asked the woman if she had recognized the world-famous figure to whom she'd been speaking. "I think he's connected with the movies," she replied.[4]

That woman spoke with more wisdom than she ever could have imagined. No president has had a more charged relationship with the media than Nixon—and none has had a more peculiar relationship with the most glamorous medium, motion pictures. He married a woman who once worked as a Hollywood extra—and he enjoyed one of his greatest political triumphs matched against a woman who once worked as a Hollywood actress. He drew upon entertainment executives for major financial backing and served on the House Committee on Un-American Activities at the time of the Hollywood Ten hearings. He demonstrated with the Hollywood-friendly provisions of the Revenue Act of 1971 that, as the MCA/Universal executive Taft Schreiber wrote him at the time, "No President before you has shown such concern for this industry."[5] A dedicated filmgoer, he had well over five hundred motion pictures screened at the White House, Camp David, and his various vacation homes during his presidency—the most notorious instance being *Patton* (1970), which he saw three times before and during the invasion of Cambodia.

Nixon's fascination with motion pictures has long been reciprocated. Well before Oliver Stone and Anthony Hopkins assayed him, Nixon (or Nixon-like characters) had been portrayed onscreen by Cliff Robertson, Rip Torn, Jason Robards, Peter Riegert, and even Glenda Jackson. He has fascinated filmmakers as diverse as Robert Altman, whose *Secret Honor* (1984) brought to the screen a one-man play about Nixon; and Jean-Luc Godard, who gives a killer the name "Richard Nixon" in his existentialist noir *Made in U.S.A.* (1966) and who later requested an interview with Nixon so that he and Norman Mailer might discuss the subject of power with him for a segment in the filmmaker's *King Lear* (1987). In what was surely art's loss, and just as surely Nixon's gain, the former president found that the demands of his schedule precluded such a meeting.[6]

Nixon has figured in various ways in a surprising range of films: from *Shampoo* (1975), which takes place on Election Day 1968; to *The Ice Storm* (1997), set in that autumn of the president, the fall of 1973; to the original *Star Wars* trilogy (1977–83), whose evil emperor George Lucas has said he based on Nixon. More significant, his presence can be felt throughout the period of moviemaking that coincided with his presidency, Hollywood's Silver Age. Nixon was that age's tutelary deity, as FDR was of Hollywood's Golden Age. The darkness, paranoia, and distrust of authority on display in such films as *Five Easy Pieces* (1970), *Klute* (1971), *The Candidate* (1972), the first two *Godfather* films (1972, 1974), *Chinatown* (1974), *The Parallax View* (1974), *The Conversation* (1974), *Nashville* (1975), and *All the President's Men* (1976), to cite just the most obvious examples, are, in their way, as much monuments of the Nixon era as American flag lapel pins and eighteen-and-a-half-minute gaps in presidential conversations.

"Nixon does not need to be a great artist," the Shakespeare scholar Gary Taylor has written, "as long as he is a great *subject*."[7] Watching certain movies and certain lives without as well as within movies, we can discern in parallel his greatness as a subject—even, in a sense, his greatness of artistry. Ronald Reagan, Fred MacMurray's Walter Neff in *Double Indemnity* (1944), Henry Fonda in *Mister Roberts* (1955), Tony Curtis's Sidney Falco in *Sweet Smell of Success* (1957), James Stewart in *Mr. Smith Goes to Washington* (1939), Gene Hackman's Harry Caul in *The Conversation*, even certain aspects of Henry Kissinger and (yes) Elvis Presley: they are a series of "alternate Nixons," the character and image of each refracting and illuminating who Richard Nixon was and is in the American imagination. Just as in watching the movies he could help shape himself, so can watching the movies help how *we* shape *him*. "Isn't that a hell of a thing," he once remarked to Garry Wills, "that the fate of a great country can depend on camera angles?"[8] The fate of an almost great man, too.

In the end, though, the man himself, as he should and must be, is the star *Nixon at the Movies* steers by, his furtive centrality to the second half of the twentieth century in America being mirrored in this book. "The study of Richard Nixon," writes John Osborne, one of his keenest students, "requires a steadfast clinging to the fact that he is human."[9] Looking at him in terms of the movies helps us cling to that humanity, makes us better appreciate—perhaps even feel some guilty affection for—what Murray Kempton, the most acute of all Nixonologists, saw as the man's "insinuating ungainliness."[10] For me, the movies and Nixon connect at a single compelling point: where a man trapped in loneliness enjoys an experience that assumes it. Sitting in the dark and staring straight ahead was a perfectly natural thing for Richard Nixon to do, for he was a man who loved screens: those that conceal as well as those that show.

Finally, a word about the title: the nouns are symmetrical in weight. Just as Richard Nixon's career tells us so much about the fears and aspirations of the nation he led, so do the movies tell us even more. Looking at Nixon in terms of the movies is a way to get a fresh angle of approach on his life and career. Conversely, looking at the movies in terms of Nixon is meant to do the same for them. Like the man himself, the title *Nixon at the Movies* is an exercise in incongruity; but—again, not unlike Richard Nixon—the incongruity masks deeper, darker, more revealing unities as it reminds us of "the degree to which," as Kissinger writes, "the romantic and real merged in his mind."[11] The movies and this man are both surpassingly (even, at times, sublimely) American phenomena. It is my hope that, in bringing together such seeming incommensurables and investigating what they have meant to each other, we might learn a little more about what they have meant to us.

Nixon at the Movies

Bette Davis and Ronald Reagan

DARK VICTORY

■-■

You see I too live in a world of make believe . . .
RICHARD NIXON, IN A LETTER TO PATRICIA RYAN, 1938

He never learned where his home was.
HENRY KISSINGER, *Years of Upheaval*

He was born on the wrong side of Hollywood, both the Hollywood
that was and the Hollywood that soon would be Incorporated
only ten years before, it was as yet, in 1913, the year of his birth,
just another obscure small town: sunnier and drier than most, but
otherwise utterly undistinguished. The idea of such a place coming to dominate the imagination of much of the planet was as
unthinkable then as it seems inevitable now. Yet that same year
witnessed the making of the first motion picture there, a Cecil B.
DeMille Western, *The Squaw Man*, its production the start of an astonishing train of events that would see a collection of empty
fields and parched hills transformed into a metonymy for wealth

and fancy such as to shame Xanadu or Versailles: Hollywood, the world's preferred purveyor of dreams. No, that was no place for Richard Nixon.

He was born to the east, away from ocean breezes and elevated vistas—and that much further from wealth and fancy. He was born amid the thirsty citrus groves, out where people *worked* (and worked hard) making things grow rather than making things up: selling dusty produce, not tinselly dreams. Eventually, he, too, would retail dreams, doing so as tirelessly—and, for a time, as successfully—as any studio executive. The only difference was studio executives called their dreams "movies"; he called his "America."

"I was born in a house my father built": with that austere, almost biblical sentence, Nixon begins his memoirs, *RN*. The house was in Yorba Linda, which had been founded just five years before—still so new that his was the first birth recorded there. His second cousin, the novelist Jessamyn West, who grew up in a house on the other side of an irrigation ditch from the Nixons', could have been speaking for her relative when she writes of her own Yorba Linda childhood: "Though Hollywood is only twenty-five miles away, it is as remote to me as Africa. . . ."[1]

In *RN*, Nixon describes Yorba Linda as an "idyllic" setting for a child. That statement comes no later than the fourth sentence, thus giving it pride of place among the many arguable propositions set forth in that book's more than one thousand pages. For at best, Yorba Linda was an idyll in progress. A town of barely two hundred inhabitants, with as yet no paved streets, it comprised semi-arid rangeland little better than desert. "No grass, no nothing except dust" was how one Nixon neighbor described the town's appearance during the second decade of the last century. "You could hear the rocks hitting the side of the house when the wind would blow. . . . If you laid by the east wall when you'd go to bed, then next morning your hair would be white with dust when we had those winds."[2] Coyotes were still common and didn't hesitate to nose around doorways. Theodore Roosevelt once declared that "California is west of the West." Yorba Linda wasn't so much west of the West as beneath it—harsh, baked, demanding—less a purveyor of dreams than (as the Nixons would all too soon discover) an impediment to them.

Such descriptions make it sound as if Yorba Linda could have been at the end of civilization. Actually, it lay at the terminus of a Pacific Electric rail line to downtown Los Angeles; nine times a day a trolley made the fifty-minute-long run. The PE train traversed a distance considerably greater than the route's mileage might indicate, however, and the city's ready accessibility only cast into greater relief the farming community's backwardness. Yorba Linda, a dry town characterized by "the crude Victorianism of a backwoods border country," as a far-from-disaffected West later put it, was a world away from urbanity.[3] The town had no theater, of course. A handful of residents (Nixon's father among them) saw to its having no pool table, either. As for the one café in town, it was closed two or three months for every one it was open. Even the bell donated to the local Quaker meetinghouse remained stored away, West recalls, "until the death of those elderly Quakers who believed that bell ringing was not conducive to godliness."[4] That's the sort of place Richard Nixon's Yorba Linda was: dour in godliness as well as recreation, suspicious even of church bells. "You can't imagine how narrow [people there] were," recalled Mary George Skidmore, Nixon's first-grade teacher half a century later.[5]

It was a drear existence within as well as without. "I suppose I came from a family too unmodern, really," Nixon told a journalist in 1958.[6] Backwoods Victorianism came naturally to Frank and Hannah Nixon. Along with their oldest son, Harold, they had moved to Yorba Linda two years before Richard's birth, coming from Whittier, ten miles to the northwest, the home of Hannah's people, the Milhouses. The house Frank Nixon built stood on a ten-acre plot planted in barley. He bought chickens and a cow, rabbits and a horse, and put in a vegetable garden. These were all subsidiary to his main purpose, though, for Frank had purchased the land as a citrus ranch. He put in lemon trees from his father-in-law's Whittier nursery and tended them during the five years they required to mature and bear fruit. The sweet scent and yellow bounty of lemon trees flowering in the California sun: it's hard to imagine a more beckoning (a more idyllic?) prospect for a trolley motorman from Columbus, Ohio, who'd come to the Southland to ease the pain of frost-bitten feet.

The brochure put out by the town's developers described the land as free of frost, its soil made up of Ramona loam well suited to citrus. That was largely true, but on Nixon's land the topsoil was of insufficient depth for the trees to root. Worse, the stock from his father-in-law was of poor quality and, ignoring the advice of neighbors, Frank avoided the expense of fertilizer by never using it. The trees grew up stunted and bore inferior fruit. By 1919 he abandoned raising lemons and was reduced to seeking roustabout work from Union Oil. Three years later the Nixons moved back to Whittier to open a combination gas station and grocery.

Such a failure was doubly galling to Frank. "I never missed a day's work in my life," he liked to boast, yet here he was with nothing to show for a decade of constant toil.[7] Worse, he was forced to reenter the ambit of the Milhouses. Hannah Nixon's people were birthright Quakers, prosperous and genteel, who'd never altogether disguised the fact that they looked slightly askance at the thumping bluster of their black Irish in-law. Overbearing and pugnacious, Frank Nixon was ever ready to take offense: an easy man to anger, a hard one to appease. "My husband was a stubborn man, and arguments stiffened him," Hannah Nixon recalled after his death.[8] So did failure, and once again having to live among the Milhouses provided a constant reminder of his inability to strike off on his own and succeed.

In her piety and calm, Hannah was worlds removed from Frank. Where he was a fighter, a complainer, her reputation for equanimity assumed near-legendary proportions in local lore: she was impossible to cross—if also, perhaps, impossible to truly please. As a friend once put it, "She was born to endure."[9] That she and Frank loved each other is plain. That their characters profoundly differed is even plainer. Certainly, Frank would never have said to Mary George Skidmore, as Hannah did, "By the way, Miss George, please call my son Richard and never Dick. I named him Richard."[10] Her almost throttling sense of what was and was not seemly extended even to her own family. Nixon writes in his book *In the Arena*: "In her whole life, I never heard her say to me or to anyone else, 'I love you.' She did not need to. Her eyes expressed the love and warmth no words could possibly convey."[11] He means this as a tribute, one as sincerely felt as his notorious declaration in the last speech he delivered as president that "my mother was a saint," but could anything a son might say of his mother be more damning than that first sentence?

Such withholding gave her a tight purchase on her sons—the kind of spiritual force generally limited to, yes, saints—and that purchase stayed intact after her death. While serving as a White House speechwriter, William Safire heard Nixon remark once, "People react to fear not love— they don't teach that in Sunday school, but it's true."[12] Was it Frank speaking or Hannah? The answer is more complicated than one might think. By all accounts, Hannah was a model of tolerance and charity. Yet her goodness would seem to have possessed an almost oppressive quality, radiating light without heat. Frank's temper and occasional cuffings could be taken in stride—so long as you didn't provoke him, he could be gotten along with easily enough—but the constant implied judgment of Hannah's implacable saintliness was a burden more difficult to bear.

One demonstration of just how difficult came in 1974, seven years after her death, with the release of the White House transcripts of conversations Nixon had had taped in the Oval Office and the presidential retreat in the Executive Office Building. Publication of the transcripts proved a disastrous setback in Nixon's battle to stay in office, and the single greatest harm the transcripts did was owing to that now-deathless phrase "expletive deleted." Those two words became inextricably linked to the name of Richard Nixon. The revelation that so stern an advocate of clean living and moral rectitude stooped to gutter language when in private did him grievous harm. Only later was it learned that there had been few Anglo-Saxonisms to expunge, but rather a series of mostly "hell's" and "goddam's." Why did the most powerful man in the world feel he had to conceal his use of language that, however coarse, was so commonly employed? "If my mother ever heard me use words like that she would turn over in her grave," he told White House staffers.[13] Better to look bad in the eyes of the world than suffer the saintly wrath, even when posthumous, of Hannah Milhous Nixon.*

As one might expect, religiosity suffused the Nixon household. Prayer was an important part of their daily routine, and there were four obligations on Sunday—Sunday school, morning service, Christian endeavor in the afternoon, and an evening service—as well as one on Wednesday nights. The church might even be said to have supported the Nixons, literally. "Make not my Father's an house of merchandise," Christ declared. That didn't keep Frank from buying the old structure when the East Whittier Friends Church, the congregation the family belonged to after leaving Yorba Linda, dedicated a new building in 1927, then moving it to his property to house the store.

To go along with Hannah's sanctity, there was her husband's characteristically more voluble faith. No birthright Quaker, Frank took to his new denomination with the classic convert's enthusiasm. In teaching Sunday school, he brought such stem-winding vigor to the classroom that Jessamyn West regarded him as the best religion teacher she ever had. Such preacherly exuberance meant he differed in degree, not kind, from his newfound coreligionists. Quietism little informed Southern California Quakerdom, which differed substantially in both doctrine and demeanor from the religion practiced by the Society of Friends in Philadelphia or even the Quakers in southern Indiana portrayed in West's best-known book, *The Friendly Persuasion*. As she puts it with some asperity,

*The irony is she already knew. As she confessed to readers of *Good Housekeeping* in 1960, "I have never heard him swear, but I am told that sometimes, when he is tense, he will swear like a sailor. . . ." Hannah Nixon, as told to Flora Rheata Schreiber, "A Mother's Story." *Good Housekeeping,* June 1960, p. 208.

"The Quakerism I knew as a child in southern California had little to distinguish it from shouting Methodism."[14] Certainly, the Nixons saw nothing odd in a Quaker family's driving into Los Angeles, as they themselves did, to seek raucous redemption at the hands of an Aimee Semple McPherson or a Fighting Bob Shuler.[15] Then, as now, evangelists and revivalism were no small part of Southern California's religious climate—their attraction extending even to the good folk of refined, sedate Whittier.

Named for John Greenleaf Whittier, it was the most famous Quaker colony in the United States: an outpost of upright living and high-mindedness amidst the boomer mentality of the Southland. As late as 1937, more than half the town's fifteen thousand inhabitants belonged to the Society of Friends. And the rest of its citizens were no less observant than the Quaker majority: in 1932 Whittier boasted some nineteen churches. A member of that religious minority was the young M. F. K. Fisher. In later years the doyenne of American food writing, she accompanied her parents and younger sister to "that tight little fortress of brotherly love" when her father purchased the *Whittier News* in 1912.[16] Fisher made no effort to disguise her genteel loathing for the place. As newcomers, they quickly discovered what a close-knit community it was, its sense of apartness grounded in an atmosphere of inherent superiority. Fisher's parents may have been pillars of the community and she herself impeccably reared and popular with her schoolmates, yet she claims never once to have been invited into a Quaker home. Comity in Whittier was not to be confused with friendship, nor good manners with acceptance.

Fortunately for the Nixons, Hannah's family was prominent and well represented in the community. Frank might be made to feel ill at ease among his in-laws, but being affiliated with the Milhouses bestowed a membership status among the Whittier Friends not otherwise easily obtained. Such things as a sense of belonging and connection mattered there as they rarely did elsewhere in the region. Indeed, the community's weird blend of self-regard and boosterism is evident in a phrase from the *History of Whittier*, which the town produced to celebrate the fiftieth anniversary of its founding: "the privilege, and distinction, of living in this homeyhome [*sic*] city."[17]

This sense of civic self-worth meant that Whittier had less in common with Yorba Linda (for all that the Nixons' previous home had also been a predominantly Quaker community) than it did with, say, Pasadena. Living in Whittier signified a more gracious way of life—or the promise of it, anyway—as the Nixons' previous residence had not. Whittier was obviously far less backward than Yorba Linda (it lies closer to downtown Los Angeles than Santa Monica does) and a far more desirable place to live (on a clear day, one could make out from the Puente Hills breakers along the Pacific shore). The town enjoyed the further distinction of possessing its own college. Whittier may have been "an eddy on the stream of life," as Merton Wray, a year ahead of Nixon at both Whittier High and Whittier College, waspishly recalled.[18] But for most who lived there, their privileged "homeyhome" was a comfortable-enough eddy, and they knew it.

The town's poorer section lay to the east—farther from Los Angeles, closer to the desert—and that was where the Nixons settled. Later on Richard Nixon took a dismayingly patent delight in expounding on how little his family had had when he was growing up. That he luxuriated in tales of economic distress made perfect sense politically, but what was always so striking about his lovingly detailed accounts of early poverty was the emotional satisfaction he derived from them. While it's certainly true that once the Nixons moved to Whittier they had to work extremely hard to do well, the point is they *did* do well. Thanks to the region's expanding population and ever-increasing reliance on the automobile, Frank's business flourished—even during the Depression. "The idea that the key to Nixon was his early poverty is ridiculous," West once observed. "The Nixons had a grocery store, two cars, and sent their son to college. By some they were considered rich."[19]

Their actual economic circumstances were less important, though, than the fact that the Nixons themselves were not among those sumptuary-minded "some." West's observation may be financially accurate, but it overlooks a crucial element in the family's character, one that actually does provide a key to Richard Nixon's later life. That was their embattled quality, their experience of, if not actual poverty, then the *sense* of it. Having failed once, Frank would not fail again. Widely viewed as having married beneath herself, Hannah would not let her household descend any further. Spurred on by their (relative) prosperity, the Nixons worked all the harder. The man who had never missed a day's work in his life now missed barely a waking hour's work: pumping gas, tending the cash register, even baking pies. It was Hannah, though, who was famed for her pies—they became the store's most popular item—and she rose at five each morning to make as many as ten a day.[20]

The boys all worked, too. Richard, whose job it was to oversee the market's produce, would wake every morning at four to ensure he'd make it by five to the Seventh Street wholesale market in Los Angeles. (The night before his first meeting with Nikita Khrushchev during his 1959 "kitchen debate" visit to the Soviet Union, Nixon got up at 5:30 in the morning and, accompanied only by a Secret Service agent, went to Moscow's open-air produce market to see how much it resembled what he'd known in Los Angeles as a boy.)[21] And he maintained this grueling routine while keeping up excellent grades and participating in various extracurricular activities.

The boys' hard work was conditioned on good health. The demands placed upon the Nixons by their religious, social, and financial circumstances, great though they were, were as nothing compared with those made by illness and death. Nixon's younger brother Arthur, the sweetest-tempered of the boys, died in 1923 of tubercular encephalitis; he was only five. At least his death was relatively quick. Harold, the most extroverted and engaging member of the family, spent more than a decade battling tuberculosis before it finally killed him at twenty-three. His struggle with illness not only strained the family's financial resources; it frequently separated Richard, Donald, and Edward (the other surviving brothers) from Hannah, who spent several years caring for Harold at an Arizona sanitorium.

Premature death was more common in the first third of the twentieth century than today, of course. Yet that made it no less painful. Who might begin to comprehend the devastation the young Richard Nixon underwent at the loss of not one but two brothers? That the man was an individual of surpassingly strange emotional makeup was a truth universally acknowledged almost as soon as he arrived on the national scene. If anything, his inherent peculiarity became even more pronounced over the years. Considering his past, though, the truly unnerving thing would have been Richard Nixon's being normal.

Store, classroom, church, the grave: these defined his youth. He did do other things, of course. He played the violin and piano (and rather well). He excelled at debate and oratory. He read a great deal. He played sports with unbounded enthusiasm (and almost no skill). And he even went to the movies. The point isn't that his youth and adolescence were unrelievedly grim—they were not—and limited only to work, school, religion, and an awareness of how fugitive life can be. What *is* true is that he was brought up in a domestic environment that was consistently draining and claustral to a degree unusual for socially aspirant white Americans of the first third of the last century—unusual even for those in somewhat straitened financial circumstances. Again we find that sense of impoverishment, and all the psychic baggage it carried, which did so much to shape the Nixons and how they saw the world.

Another way to put this is to say there was nothing wayward about Richard Nixon's early years. "California is somewhere else," Joan Didion once remarked.[22] Richard Nixon's California—toilsome, unforgiving, death struck—was always right there. He could as easily have been growing up in Kansas, or Oz (the part with Margaret Hamilton in charge), as hard by Hollywood. It comes as no surprise that he should have been such a serious boy. Everyone who knew him in his early years noted his seriousness. The young Nixon "was not as outreaching as many children are," a family friend noted. "He lived more within himself."[23] "He was a very solemn child and rarely ever smiled or laughed," recalled Mary George Skidmore.[24] Roger Ailes, his television consultant during the 1968 campaign, famously lamented the fact that Nixon looked like he "was forty-two years old the day he was born. [Voters] figure other kids got footballs for Christmas, Nixon got a briefcase and he loved it."[25] What Ailes's comment ignores is that Nixon had been the kind of kid who also felt lucky to get anything for Christmas. No, not just that: the kind of kid who also felt lucky still to be alive. Surrounded by the bounty of sunny California, Richard Nixon learned at an early age to take nothing (and no one) for granted.

Is it any wonder that, in his own circumscribed fashion, he sought ways of escape? In the words of Earl Mazo and Stephen Hess, as close to him as any of his biographers, the young Richard Nixon "preferred daydreams to anything else on earth."[26] First there were schoolboy fantasies of becoming a train engineer. A mile or so away from the Nixon house in Yorba Linda ran a Santa Fe Railroad spur line. He would lie awake at night listening; and, he later confessed, "The train whistle was the sweetest music I ever heard." Then there was actual music ("a way of expressing oneself that is perhaps even more fulfilling than writing or speaking"), when he moved to Lindsay, in central California, to live for six months with his mother's sister, a conservatory graduate, to concentrate on his piano and violin lessons.[27] And in both high school and college, there was his notoriously inept devotion to sports—football, above all.

The boy who variously fantasized about a future spent in an engineer's cab or the concert hall or on the gridiron was no stranger to reveries of another sort, the reassuringly two-dimensional destinies projected on a screen. "Once in a while we'd go to a movie," he told an interviewer in 1958, "but that was a luxury."[28] The luxuriousness made it all the more precious a treat, as it did for so many others in the years following the rise of Hollywood. Hadn't the motion picture come of age as he did? Nixon and *The Squaw Man* had arrived in Southern California in the same year, and he had just entered his teens when *The Jazz Singer* (1927) ushered in the Sound Era. He belonged to a generation for whom the movies were simply a part of life, even less of a novelty than radio was (which, after all, hadn't become a part of most people's regular experience until well into the '20s). During the Depression it was the rare young person who never dreamed at least a little of the silver screen. It wasn't even a question of volition. Hollywood was simply in the air then, the way television is now— at once a climate unto itself and a part of the climate of everything else— and its gossamer reach extended even to the Nixon Market on the corner of Whittier Boulevard and Leffingwell Road.

The town's Quaker character did not keep the movies away from Whittier (though it did mean no Sunday screenings). The town's first movie theater, the Berry Grand, was in a converted space below the local Elks hall. That venue was soon superseded by two far grander affairs: Wardman's, across the street from the Hoover Hotel, and the Whittier, on Whittier Boulevard. On Wednesdays they'd alternate a "bank night" drawing for a cash prize.[29]

Frank Nixon was enough of a fan to have favorite stars; and years later, after he and Hannah had retired to a farm in York, Pennsylvania, he paid them jocose homage, naming his cows Dorothy Lamour, Loretta Young, and Gary Cooper.[30] So perhaps Richard Nixon's love of movies, like his competitive nature and quickness to take offense, was inherited from his father. For all that his regimen of school, church, and store left almost no free time, the teenage Nixon still managed to sneak in the occasional movie, usually accompanied by his steady, Ola Florence Welch. Nearly six decades later, he could still recall the impact that seeing *All Quiet on the Western Front* (1930) had on them.[31]

After graduating from Whittier College in 1934, Nixon went east to attend law school, at Duke University. The loss of proximity to Hollywood did nothing to interrupt his moviegoing. If anything, Duke encouraged it. Nixon was on an exceedingly tight budget (he and three other students spent their second year there sharing an unheated room with no electricity or indoor plumbing), and this made the nickel movies the student union screened on Saturday nights all the more attractive as a weekend social option. Among the films he saw were *The Private Life of Henry VIII* (1933), *The 39 Steps* (1935), and *Mutiny on the Bounty* (1935).[32]

The movies remained a staple of his social life after he returned to Whittier to practice law at a small local firm. Inexpensive and readily available, they were very much a part of his courtship of Patricia Ryan. "We were both movie fans," he later recalled, "and we often drove up to the large movie theaters in Hollywood."[33] They continued to go after their marriage, in 1940, and it was coming out of a Sunday matinee that they learned of the bombing of Pearl Harbor.

Pat Nixon had long been a moviegoer, too. Her favorite theater, as a student at the University of Southern California, had been the Paramount (Paramount, the studio of and Marlene Dietrich and Claudette Colbert, was the cynosure of sophistication during the early and middle '30s). In fact, she had helped pay her tuition at USC working as a movie extra, and the knowledge that the pretty redheaded teacher had worked in the movies could only have added to her allure. "I was in quite a number of [movies]," she later recalled. "You would have to hunt real hard to find me, but I made quite a bit of money." She even had a brief walk-on part in *Becky Sharp*, Rouben Mamoulian's 1935 adaptation of Thackeray's *Vanity Fair*. "I did have a line. I can't remember what it was, though, because it was cut before it reached the screen. What I do remember about that movie is that I got $25 for it, rather than the usual $7."[34]

A note Nixon sent Pat the summer before their marriage names four movies he wanted to take her to: *Daughters Courageous*, "Sonja Henie's latest," *Beau Geste*, and *On Borrowed Time*.[35] It was a fair indicator of their tastes then and later: mainstream, partial to big stars and strong entertainment values, not unsophisticated but not especially demanding, either—in a word, escapist. This attitude toward movies Nixon never abandoned. One might have expected him on appropriate occasions to play the serious public man and speak to the responsibilities of the art form. Yet even before a gathering of Hollywood celebrities at his San Clemente home in 1972, he cheerfully declared that, yes, movies "can educate—have a lesson—but don't knock entertainment. People need to laugh, to cry, to dream, to be taken away from the dull lives they lead."[36] These words weren't boilerplate. He truly meant them. He prepared the remarks himself—there are two drafts in his own hand—and they came from personal experience. It had been several decades since his own life had been in any way dull, but the man who had been a boy in Yorba Linda and Whittier and had heard the distant whistle of the Santa Fe understood all too well the need to be transported from one's daily existence.

That was never truer than during the war. Nixon saw movies in the South Pacific, as did Pat back at home. In her letters to him, she often described what she'd gone to see ("Saw *Crossroads* tonight—William Powell and Hedy Lamarr. It was a very good picture").[37] No matter how far apart they might be, the movies were something they could share, something that gave them both great pleasure. This was one of the reasons why, out of the well over five hundred movies he had screened during the sixty-seven months he was president, such a relatively small number were current releases. "The difficulty we have at present is that so many of the movies coming out of Hollywood, not to mention those that come out of Europe, are so inferior that we just don't enjoy them," he wrote to Jane Wyman (the first Mrs. Ronald Reagan, as well as an Academy Award–winning actress) on February 6, 1973. "Consequently, we often on weekends at Camp David search through the catalogs of older movies and have one shown."[38] The pull of older movies wasn't just their presumed superiority or even that they allowed Nixon to avoid the frequent unpleasantnesses—social, linguistic, sexual, even at times political—of seventies cinema. Rather, older films allowed him to revisit his earlier life, a happy portion of which had been spent watching those movies.

They also allowed him to make up for lost time. For all that Nixon so enjoyed older films, fewer than ten of the movies he saw as president predate 1941. John Ford, as we shall see, was his favorite filmmaker. Yet the earliest Ford picture he had screened was *Stagecoach*, from 1939. Other prewar titles include *Rose-Marie* (1936), *The Citadel* (1938), and *Gone with the Wind* (1939). It wasn't as if he didn't like old movies. He certainly did; and, in fact, that's the kind of moviegoer he was: one who not only saw but sought out and savored Nelson Eddy–Jeanette MacDonald musicals. Rather, it was as if while president he was making up for all those years he hadn't been able to go. So many of the movies he saw were from the late '40s, '50s, and early '60s, the period when he first gained national attention and began his pursuit of the presidency. He had little opportunity to indulge even so cherished a leisure-time activity as moviegoing. How could he? He had no leisure. When on Election Day in 1950, waiting for the results of his Senate race against Helen Gahagan Douglas, he confessed to his future biographer Ralph de Toledano how much he'd like to take in a movie,[39] it was a mark not just of how much pressure Nixon had been under during the campaign. That such a rigidly, rigorously disciplined man could admit at such a time to such an ostensibly frivolous desire shows how sorely he missed moviegoing.

It wasn't until moving to New York in 1963 that he and Pat could resume their filmgoing with any regularity. They most often frequented the Cinema I & II on Third Avenue at Sixtieth Street, a short walk from their Fifth Avenue apartment. They also regularly took in the big road-show attractions at Radio City Music Hall. Nixon cited *The Great Escape* and *Charade* as two movies he'd enjoyed that year[40]—enjoyed well enough that he saw them again, as president, by which time his circumstances (access to almost any film he wanted; a private screening room at the White House and projection facilities at Camp David, as well as more rudimentary arrangements at Key Biscayne and San Clemente) allowed for a good deal more watching of movies.

Once he became a politician, Nixon's movie fandom had a further inducement: being alert to the needs of a major local employer. "You are regarded as a staunch friend of the film industry," the publicity chief at RKO wrote him in 1951, "and have many friends here."[41] Schreiber, vice president of MCA/Universal, was one of Nixon's leading financial backers, as was Barney Balaban, for many years the president of Paramount Pictures. Both Darryl Zanuck, the head of 20th Century–Fox, and Jack Warner, of Warner Bros., were major campaign contributors and had inscribed photographs of Nixon prominently displayed in their offices. During the 1952 campaign, Zanuck sent him a five-page single-spaced memorandum on how best to exploit the "new era" that television had created.[42] Nixon's solicitude toward the industry did not cease when he entered the White House. On April 5, 1971, he met with a delegation of studio executives to discuss international copyright protection and the importance of Hollywood as a major American exporter. Two years later he agreed to appear at the presentation of the first American Film Institute Life Achievement Award. The identity of the recipient, John Ford, had something to do with his willingness to appear, but it was also another opportunity to affirm his connection to the Hollywood elite.

Still, he was never one of them, and one wonders how much of Nixon's anti-Semitism owed to his lack of affinity with film executives, the one predominantly Jewish group with whom he had substantial dealings. The very nature of his relationship with Hollywood put him in a doubly inferior position: as a supplicant for money and simply as a fan (even in the White House, he remained unmistakably starry-eyed in the company of movie people). For all that he'd come up in the world—indeed, come up as far as any American could—he remained on the wrong side of Hollywood.

There's no more telling example of the incompatibility between Nixon and Hollywood than his presentation of the Presidential Medal of Freedom to Samuel Goldwyn on March 27, 1971. Bestowing the nation's highest civilian honor on the legendary producer not only acknowledged the most antically quotable career in Hollywood; it allowed Nixon to repay several debts. In 1960, after Nixon had lost to John F. Kennedy, Goldwyn had brought him to lunch at his studio to boost the defeated

candidate's spirits; he'd supported Nixon in the 1962 California gubernatorial race and contributed $15,000 to his presidential campaign in
1968. More generally, the presentation allowed Nixon to demonstrate his
appreciation for Hollywood's leadership class. Goldwyn failed to recip-
rocate. Nixon, after delivering some pro forma introductory remarks,
leaned down to place the medal around the wheelchair-bound producer's neck. The old man whispered, "You'll have to do better than that
if you want to carry California." A flustered Nixon explained to Goldwyn's son, the only other person within earshot, that his father had said,
"I want you to go out there and beat those bastards!"[43]

The Goldwyn incident typifies how problematic dealing with show-biz
types could be for a politician. Politics and entertainment are like enough
to repel, unlike enough to clash, and their mingling can be a recipe for
embarrassment. That being the case, most politicians keep their distance,
except when fund-raising. Then there's the simple matter of time, or
rather its lack. Politics is such an all-consuming vocation as to leave little
room for any outside interest. So it's not just the incongruity of Nixon—
awkward, effortful, uncomfortable Nixon—being a devoted movie fan.
It's the incongruity of any major political figure being so devoted. Tip
O'Neill used to get a laugh by telling about being introduced to Warren
Beatty. "You know, Warren," he told Beatty, "you're handsome enough to
be in the movies." Even when the actor was identified for him afterward,
O'Neill mistook him for Clyde Beatty, the animal trainer.[44] That that is an
extreme, but by no means unusual, example makes all the more excep-
tional Nixon's own interest. Consumed by politics, *defined* by politics, as
perhaps no other president in our history has been (even Lyndon Johnson took the time to amass a fortune and indulge his libido), Nixon
nonetheless found a place for the movies.

Finding a place for the movies was never a problem for Ronald Reagan. The problem for him had been the reverse, finding a place for politics. In fact, Wyman would complain that it was her husband's growing
absorption in politics, in his capacity as president of the Screen Actors
Guild and one of Hollywood's leading liberal activists, that led to their divorce. It was while he was SAG president that Reagan and Nixon first met,
in the spring of 1947, in California, then again when he testified before
the House Committee on Un-American Activities in October. Nixon, a
committee member, asked no questions, but later noted that Reagan
"made a good impression in his testimony."[45]

Reagan supported Helen Gahagan Douglas and made speeches on
her behalf. That was before his political migration to the right, so it was

nothing that Nixon held against him, and he welcomed Reagan's backing ten years later in his race against Kennedy. Reagan thought that was a good time to finally change his registration to Republican, but Nixon demurred. "He said I'd be more effective if I campaigned as a Democrat," Reagan recalls in his memoirs, *An American Life*, "and so I agreed not to change my party affiliation until after the election."[46] He tells the story with so artful a guilelessness that it draws all the more attention to Nixon's own guile. Knowing perfectly well Nixon's image for craftiness and chicanery, Reagan was happy to use his own for accommodating good fellowship to play it up.

Nixon had a thoroughly mixed opinion of his fellow Californian, one equally grounded in admiration and scorn. In most respects, his view mirrored that of most of the electorate during Reagan's presidency. He envied the man his affability and leaderly bearing and respected his sense of determination. "He may be too nice to be President," Nixon said in 1980 shortly after Reagan's election; and eleven years later privately called him "one of the most decent men I have known."[47] Of course, Nixon did not necessarily regard decency as a paramount virtue in a leader. He did, however, value the fact that Reagan solicited his foreign policy advice (even if not always heeding it). He'd come a long way from 1968, when he didn't hesitate to tell the *New York Times* columnist Tom Wicker he'd never consider Reagan as a running mate because the California governor was "a know-nothing in foreign policy. I'd never put him next in line for the presidency."[48] Nixon's circumspection on the retreat from détente during the Reagan presidency—indeed, his embrace of it—was a response not just to events abroad but also a tacit recognition of the incumbent's command of the international scene.

At the same time, Nixon had serious reservations about Reagan's intellect and capacity for hard work and questioned the narrowness of his views. He once told a friend that where Barry Goldwater, for example, "was a reasonable man who scared people by saying things in an unreasonable way; Reagan was an unreasonable man who soothed audiences by saying the same things in a reasonable way."[49] The clearest expression of his dismissal of Reagan's intellectual abilities, as well as an implicit acknowledgment of his own acumen, came during the Iran-Contra scandal. "Reagan will survive," Nixon told John Sears (who had worked as a high-level operative for both men), "because, when all is said and done, he can get up and say, 'I am an idiot and therefore can't be blamed,' and everyone will agree." Nixon paused an instant before saying ("quite wistfully," Sears thought), "I never had that option."[50]

No, empty-headedness was the dark side of Reagan's likability—just as darkness itself was the dark side of Nixon's single-mindedness and drive. Mindless charm and empty sunniness—"That's the Reagan school of politics based on flattery," Nixon complained to an associate in 1992. "Flatter, flatter."[51] Reagan, in Nixon's eyes, was a glad-handing good-timer, "a glamor boy," in the derisive phrase he used to describe him (in private, of course) at the 1968 Republican convention, the very thing Richard Nixon—for better, for worse—most assuredly was not.[52] Yet Nixon was too astute to see all this as wholly insubstantial. He had been in politics more than long enough to learn that soothing and flattery very much had their place in our public life, and in 1968 Nixon paid Reagan the sincerest of all political tributes: co-optation. For it was Reagan (or, rather, fear of his popularity with the conservative wing of the party, Nixon's base in 1960) who inspired the foundation of his campaign, the Southern Strategy, with its backpedaling on race and tough stands on law and order. Reagan, not Nelson Rockefeller or George Romney or anyone else, was the one candidate who could have denied him the nomination that year, a fact no one knew better than Nixon.

Two years earlier Nixon had received a stinging lesson in Reagan's political formidability. In the 1962 California gubernatorial race, Pat Brown, the Democratic incumbent, had handed the former vice president his most humbling electoral defeat. Four years later it was Reagan who crushed Brown's bid for a third term. The political amateur had done what Nixon, America's most prominent active Republican, had so humiliatingly failed to do.

Although Reagan's stunning victory meant an implicit reproach to Nixon, it carried its own rebuke for the winner. He had won a landslide victory, yes, but he hadn't been the leading vote-getter on the GOP ticket. That distinction belonged to Robert Finch, who was elected lieutenant governor while running ahead of Reagan by 100,000 votes. This was the same Robert Finch who for more than a decade had been Nixon's closest political associate, the manager of his 1960 presidential campaign. Nixon would offer Finch the GOP vice-presidential nomination in 1968 and then make him secretary of health, education, and welfare. How sincere Nixon's offer of the second spot on the ticket was remains a subject of debate; nonetheless, the fact of its being made underscores both the closeness of their relationship and the extent of Finch's political appeal.

This was the man who got to run California whenever Reagan was away from the state, the man whose liberal Republican presence called into question the nature of the ostensibly conservative Republican tide that had brought Reagan to the governor's mansion. Finch's presence was an implicit threat to Reagan's control of the state party, a reminder of his political limits, of the fact that while Nixon may have left for New York, he remained the most prominent Californian in U.S. politics. Finch's presence in Sacramento amounted to a political variation on the Kilroy sign: "Nixon is here."

Reagan did little campaigning for the Nixon-Agnew ticket in 1968; and Barry Goldwater noted how Nixon, not surprisingly perhaps, snubbed the Reagans at an inauguration ball.[53] The problematic nature of the two men's relationship was on display a year later at a reception prior to the annual Gridiron Dinner when Reagan introduced Nixon to Lou Cannon, already a respected journalist and later to be the *Washington Post*'s White House correspondent. "He has written a book about me," Reagan explained. "Well, I'll skim it," Nixon replied. "As soon as he got out of earshot," Cannon later recalled, "Reagan turned to me and said, 'Well, Lou, he just took care of you *and* me.'"[54]

It's the two men's personas epitomized: Reagan, genial and self-deprecating; Nixon, graceless and gratuitously blunt. Yet draw back from the anecdote to reflect on the scene and a somewhat altered picture emerges. Nixon was socially obtuse, but he wasn't stupid. The polite thing to say would have been a simple (and meaningless), "How about that" or, even better, "Well, I'll read it." One can be sure that's what Reagan, all smiling enthusiasm, would have said, and all would have been well, with everyone parting happily, each basking in the warm glow of a white lie. Everyone involved would also have known it wasn't true. "How about that" means nothing, and the idea of a president finding the time to read such a book does not bear scrutiny. Of course, a president finding the time to *skim* it, that's just conceivable, and his making a point of doing so would be no small tribute. Nixon's saying what he did might be seen, then, not as arrogant discourtesy but rather that rarest of compliments from the lips of Richard Nixon: the truth. Yet in the retelling, it's just one more instance of his abiding clumsiness—and of Reagan's relaxed good cheer.

Or, another way of saying the same thing, it's but one more instance of Reagan's actorliness. This was a man who, in the Oval Office just as much as on a movie set, always bore in mind three fundamental rules: "You learn your lines; don't bump into the furniture; and in the kissing scenes, you keep your mouth closed." When the camera was on—when the presidential seal was on display—he was on, too. It was a skill Nixon sorely lacked. Even if kissing was never an issue for him and he always got his lines right (Nixon prided himself on not needing a teleprompter), he was, alas, no stranger to bumping into things, figurative or otherwise. When the Great Communicator looked at Nixon, he saw a Great Prevaricator: a president who made it look like acting—unlike himself, an actor who made it look presidential. No, Reagan respected Nixon as a politician and statesman, but as Lou Cannon notes, he "was contemptuous of Nixon's skills as a performer."[55] And this was where they most differed, perhaps: where Nixon disdained Reagan for being a performer, Reagan disdained Nixon for being such a bad one.

The irony is that, for a time, Nixon had far more acting experience than Reagan did. Prior to his first screen test, Reagan had never been on stage. He'd been a sportscaster and done a little modeling, but that was the extent of his performing. Nixon, however, appeared on stage in several productions at Whittier College, and it was while rehearsing for a play with the Whittier Community Players, a local theatrical troupe, that he met Pat. In addition, there was his great success at debate and oratory in both high school and college. Clearly, he was comfortable on stage (as he was not, and never would be, off it) and could make a strong impression on an audience.

No observer is recorded as having predicted Reagan would one day act. At least two saw a thespian's career in Nixon's future. Besides being his longtime girlfriend, Ola Welch played Dido to his Aeneas in a school pageant. "I honestly believe that if he had made the stage into his career instead of studying law," she once said, "he would have developed into a top-notch actor." And Albert Upton, a Whittier English professor who supervised undergraduate theatricals, called him "the easiest person to direct I've ever dealt with." Upton didn't remember Nixon as someone who seemed likely to have a future in politics. "But I wouldn't have been surprised if, after college, he had gone on to New York or Hollywood looking for a job as an actor."[56]

He never pursued an acting career, of course, but he did remain a little stagestruck the rest of his life. He and Pat regularly saw Broadway shows during the mid-'60s; and two decades later he delighted in escorting his grandchildren to the annual Christmas pageant at Radio City Music Hall. What may be the most striking example of his love of the theater took place in 1994, just six weeks before his death. An admiring biographer, the Conservative member of Parliament Jonathan Aitken, has described accompanying him to a London revival of *Carousel*, the Rodgers and Hammerstein musical. Seated beside him, Aitken was stunned to see that Nixon was "word perfect in many of the lines and most of the songs and actually began to cry during 'You'll Never Walk Alone.'"[57] Various factors complicated Nixon's relations with Reagan, but a lack of appreciation for how much skill acting required was not among them.

Nixon was familiar with Reagan's movie career—or at least familiar enough that, in a 1985 *Time* interview, he could throw in a reference to one of his more obscure efforts, playing the Hall of Fame baseball pitcher Grover Cleveland Alexander in *The Winning Team* (1952).[58] Five years later he offered a resoundingly unemphatic endorsement of Reagan's film work. "Pat and I had seen him in the movies and liked him because we preferred movies where the good guys won, and he always played a good guy." Perhaps the clearest evidence of how familiar he was with his former rival's body of work is that, of the fifty-three films Reagan appeared in, Nixon screened only one during his time in the White House, *Dark Victory* (1939).

Reagan always cited *Kings Row* (1942) as the most distinguished title in his filmography. A far stronger argument might be made for *Dark Victory*, which boasts one of Bette Davis's most celebrated performances (it was her personal favorite among her roles) and earned an Academy Award nomination for Best Picture in Hollywood's annus mirabilis. The story of an egocentric socialite who dies young—but only after falling in love with and marrying her doctor (George Brent), who teaches her the value of selflessness—it's one of the classic women's weepers: expertly made, affectingly presented, resolutely shameless.

Dark Victory is a most unlikely screen credit for a paladin of hearty masculine cheer like Ronald Reagan, yet there he is, as an implausibly dissolute playboy smitten with Davis's character, Judith Traherne. His part in *Bedtime for Bonzo* (1951), in which Reagan played straight man to a chimpanzee, is usually singled out as his most embarrassing role; but at least he played the lead—and the laughs he got were intentional. *Dark Victory*'s Alec ("silly old Alec," as Davis's character calls him with rather charitable understatement) is even more risible. Reagan gets fifth billing in a casting against type so ludicrous—the part's better suited to his fellow Warner Bros. contract player Jack Carson, the studio's favorite good-time Charlie—that the struggles of a third-billed Humphrey Bogart, attempting to approximate a brogue in the thankless part of an Irish stable hand, seem dignified by comparison.

Reagan's first line recalls a (very) poor man's Cary Grant—"Judy, Judy, Judy—oh, what a party!"—and it's all downhill from there. The problem isn't just the insubstantiality of the part, the actor's relative inexperience (it was only his third year of acting), or even that the director, Edmund Goulding, wanted him to play the character as a repressed homosexual (Reagan demurred).[59] It's his fundamental unsuitability to play Alec or anyone like him: straight, gay, or otherwise. It's impossible to accept this aw-shucks former sportscaster having a place, drunk or sober, in a world of mink coats and cigarette holders. In a weird way, his anomalousness in *Dark Victory* speaks to his later political success: Ronald Reagan, the future favorite of blue-collar voters and staunch defender of middle-class entitlements, seems as stricken in the company of old money as he in fact was at the thought of playing a gay roué. Ascribe it to his limitations as an actor or to the already considerable proportions of what would prove to be an epically scaled persona, but he had nothing in common with these people or they with him—and it showed.

This was one thing, at least, Reagan had in common with Nixon—but with a key difference. For Reagan, there was nothing personal about it: in life, as on screen, the easy arrogance of encrusted privilege was neither here nor there to him. It was not his style, to be sure, but he had no particular problem with it, either. He was happy to send a son to Yale, to be friends with the likes of William F. Buckley Jr.—even to have George Herbert Walker Bush for a vice president. For Nixon, it was an altogether different matter. Murray Kempton once spoke of "the resentment whose suppression is the great discipline of [Nixon's] life."[60] That observation may come as close to Nixon's essence as we're ever likely to get. Yet when it came to the Eastern establishment, this almost punitively disciplined man allowed himself to relax the rules. For all that many groups drove him to a fury—intellectuals, journalists, Jews, Kennedys, liberals, to cite just four letters of the alphabet—none inflamed him more than those considered better by dint of who they are and where they come from than what they do or how they do it.

"My name is Traherne, Judith Traherne. Or don't names matter?" Davis says, by way of introduction to Brent. To Nixon, the boy who couldn't afford Harvard or Yale, the aspiring lawyer who was snubbed by the white-shoe Wall Street firms, the politician who at various times tangled with the patrician likes of Jerry Voorhis (Yale '23), Alger Hiss (Johns Hopkins '26, Harvard Law '29), Adlai Stevenson (Princeton '22, Northwestern Law '26), Nelson Rockefeller (Dartmouth '30), and John F. Kennedy (Harvard '40), names certainly did matter—but for all the wrong reasons. They were a way of keeping score, for the bearers—and a goad to settling scores, for Frank Nixon's son.

Reagan knew better: he simply didn't care. Why bother about settling scores so long as yours are higher? He'd been a name himself, albeit of a different sort, a movie-star name. And then he recorded the highest score of all, reaching the Oval Office. So did Nixon, of course, but for Nixon it was different. He'd felt his supposed betters' scorn (or certainly believed he had) and suffered their superiority, and that was something he never got over. Resentment became an engine of ascent for him, as dynamic as it was corrosive. "If your anger is deep enough and strong enough," he once confided to an aide, "you learn you can change those attitudes by excellence, personal gut performance, while those who have everything are sitting on their fat butts."[61] A Judith Traherne or silly old Alec knew nothing of personal gut performance, and one can well imagine the blend of disgust and derision Nixon experienced when Davis says to Brent of the shared life she envisions after they marry, "We'll be such useful people in the world."

Usefulness is as usefulness does, and death intervenes before she can demonstrate much, other than planting some ornamental bulbs or bringing her husband the lunch their kitchen staff has prepared for him. Instead, Davis can concentrate on enjoying (that is the correct verb) one of the most radiant demises in screen history. Having gotten the best medical attention money could buy (including no fewer than twelve second opinions), she knows she must die. Yet Davis consoles herself with the knowledge that, as she declares to her secretary-companion, Geraldine Fitzgerald, "When death finally comes, it will come as an old friend, gently and quietly." Richard Nixon, who'd seen premature death at close hand, knew otherwise.

No, Nixon prided himself on being able to see through all the spoiled little rich girls and boys. He never masked his detestation for upper-class wastrels like Alec or someone like Judith Traherne, with her wealthy father who drank himself to death and her mother off in Paris, a twenty-three-year-old who lives, as she freely admits, only "for horses and hats and food." As he told David Frost in 1977, "To me, the unhappiest people in the world are those in the watering places. Like the south coast of France, and Newport, and Palm Springs, and Palm Beach . . . drinking too much, talking too much, thinking too little. . . . They don't know life. Because what makes life mean something is purpose. A goal. The battle. The struggle."[62]

The sole struggle Reagan's character faces is keeping his glass full. His feckless bon vivant appears in just a handful of scenes, yet one can only wonder at the glee Nixon felt as this least gleeful of men watched *Dark Victory* at San Clemente in August 1973. Two months later, as he chose Gerald Ford to replace Spiro Agnew, might he have briefly recalled the sight of a tuxedoed, three-decades-younger Reagan, attempting to look intoxicated as he ordered another champagne cocktail? The congressional Democratic leadership dictated his choice of Ford—Nixon's own preference had been for his former secretary of the treasury John Connally—but the Republican right had plumped for Reagan, who was one of the four finalists Nixon considered. "I concluded that nominating [Reagan or Rockefeller] would split the Republican Party down the middle and result in a bitter partisan fight," Nixon later explained.[63] Surely, though, the chance he might choose either had always been nil. It was unthinkable he would have nominated the rich man's son who exemplified the establishment that Nixon loathed (and envied). It was even more unthinkable that he would have selected the smiling public man who had easily dispatched the opponent Nixon had lost to in 1962—Reagan, whose sunniness and ease embodied the California ethos just as much as the gloom and awkwardness of Nixon, the native son, put the lie to it.

"To understand the spirit of California," Carey McWilliams once wrote, "one really needs a sociology of what is called 'good luck.'"[64] Nixon certainly had his share of it. Marrying Pat; running against an overconfident incumbent in 1946, a landslide Republican year; two years later coming up against Hiss, the perfect foil for Nixon; being from the West and relatively young when the Republicans had someone from the East and old heading their ticket in 1952; having George McGovern for an opponent in 1972. After 1972 his luck rather precipitously ran out, but that is another story. The important point is that he never *felt* lucky—certainly not the way Reagan did. Reagan, who knew he was fortune's fool and gloried in it (good spiritual Californian that he was), had the excellent sense to present himself as the very embodiment of good luck.

Reagan exemplified the state's transparent promise: he was about hope. Nixon exemplified its dark underside: he was about struggle. "I crossed the burning desert," Reagan writes in his book *Where's the Rest of Me?*, "and sundown saw me driving that long stretch between the banked orange trees from San Bernardino to Los Angeles."[65] That long stretch of nowhere was where Nixon came from, an emptiness that Reagan, not even an actor yet, could dismiss as being merely a someplace else to slice through on his way to destiny.

In everything but place of birth, Nixon was Homer Simpson (not *that* Homer Simpson, the other one, from *The Day of the Locust*): an emotionally malformed midwestern grotesque, withering in the sunshine and balm of Southern California. There was always something so emotionally confined about Nixon—so unlike the constitutional expansiveness of Reagan. Reagan, who actually did come from the Midwest, had in the very marrow of his bones the palmy confidence and relaxed attitude of the Golden State. If Nixon was someone out of Nathanael West, Reagan was a latter-day Jack London (California's own) making political art out of easy living and muscular good cheer. Quite simply, he was of California, as Nixon clearly never was.

An adopted son of the West, Reagan was never so happy as when outdoors, cutting brush or atop a horse. He was "appalled" to discover that Nixon—who during his youth had traveled to the ocean on only one or two occasions and never once ventured into the nearby mountains—had had many of the riding trails at Camp David paved over.[66] Nixon was not given to the enjoyment of open-air relaxation, a California ideal, or relaxation of any kind, really. That immense and ongoing democratization of leisure in the years after the war, a process in which California led the way, never quite registered with someone so uninterested in recreation. In that regard, even the Kennedys, with their sailing and touch football and fifty-mile hikes, were more truly of his native state than Nixon was.

Much of what Judith Traherne's money and privilege could obtain for her back East was in California already, there for the taking (if one was white and middle class, anyway). Brent asks Davis, "What do you do with yourself down there on Long Island?" Her reply is meant to suggest just how rarefied her world is. "Oh, horses, dogs, shooting, yachting, travel, parties, gossip, all the pleasures of the station-wagon crowd." In California it wasn't just a crowd but an entire culture. Instead of "station wagons," people called them "woodies." Eventually they became a symbol of surfing culture, but originally they were simply part of the unconfined way of life there. For Nixon, though, the station wagon was a vehicle of utility—literally. The Nixon Library has on display the wood-sided Mercury wagon he used to crisscross the state during the early stages of his 1950 Senate campaign. In a famous photo, he stands beside it somewhere in the San Joaquin Valley, sleeves buttoned, tie knotted, a microphone in his hand, hard at work. For him, a station wagon was about getting ahead, not getting away.

Reagan's Golden State of infinite, shining possibility was one of hard, sometimes-dire necessity for Nixon: a place to seek votes, not surfing beaches. Himself born on the wrong side of Hollywood, Reagan wasted no time driving straight to it and staying there (even when he was in the governor's mansion or the White House, Ronald Reagan never quite left Hollywood). He based his whole adult life, in Christopher Matthews's memorable formulation, on a triune imperative: "dream the dream, live the dream, sell the dream."[67] Nixon also dreamed—recall the haunting keen of that Santa Fe whistle or, not so many years later, how the White House began to beckon—but never did he forget that nightmares are oneiric, too.

No California optimist he, not one ever to take for granted the glow of a rosy-fingered future. Instead, there was always this oddly nostalgic quality to the man—odd because he was so inherently pragmatic, odd because so much of what he had to look back on was far from being all that appealing—for he knew that the slippage had begun, that high noon was past and the American Century had started its slow fade to black. The leader who so desperately wanted to avoid being the first U.S. commander in chief to preside over a lost war knew in his bones that defeat in Vietnam was inescapable. The great, grim antagonist of communism became the architect of détente because he recognized the increasing limits on U.S. global power. The boy whose father had once supported the family by working in the Southern California oilfields grew up to become the president who had to sell arms at bargain-basement prices to a parvenu emperor of Persia so as to ensure a steady supply of petroleum in a post-OPEC world. The fact that, barely five years after his leaving office, that policy would prove as bankrupt as U.S. involvement in Indochina or the then-current state of U.S.-Soviet relations simply demonstrated Nixon's larger point.

The past was so much more reassuring for him because he believed—as neither Roosevelt, say, nor Kennedy nor Reagan ever did—that the future was more threat than opportunity. At various times, Richard Nixon has been called everything from a fascist to the last liberal. Perhaps the aptest assessment comes from Godfrey Hodgson, in his biography of Daniel Patrick Moynihan: Nixon "was a neurotic tangle of conservative instincts and liberal aspirations, wrapped in cynical political calculation that was not so much second as first nature."[68] Yet in Nixon's natural affinity for the past and abiding distrust of the future, one sees revealed the fundamental conservatism of what was otherwise an ideological orientation of almost unrelieved pragmatism.

Indeed, didn't Nixon's essential pessimism, in some sense, undergird ambition as the driving dynamic behind his many comebacks? He always knew he had to do it all himself, that there were no greater forces to carry him forward, no dialectic for him to ride. Nixon held so strongly to the great-man theory of history partly because he so wanted to be considered a great man himself but also because he did not subscribe to any view of history as the mere working out of impersonal forces. (This is why the greatest moment of his life was that first meeting with Mao Tse-tung: *here,* supremely, was history being made—and here, sitting right at the table, was Richard M. Nixon.) He appreciated perfectly well that there was nothing linear or inevitable about his career. Not that there's anything linear or inevitable about anyone's, but in one's own case the temptation is always great to think otherwise. Nixon, the politician laureate of personal gut performance, never bothered to—he knew that that way fat butts and failure lie. To get ahead, one had to keep pushing oneself: motion was what mattered. To stop was to die. Worse, to stop was to lose.

It makes absolute sense that, from the time he graduated from college, he never really settled anywhere—anywhere, that is, other than the empyrean realm of his own ambition. Even after he finally attained the White House, he couldn't stay in one place. Theodore H. White, that master of the presidential superlative, called him "the most peripatetic President in history," and for once he did not exaggerate.[69] It's altogether fitting that the great triumphal moments of his administration occurred thousands of miles from home, in Beijing and Moscow, and that the last fevered gasp of his presidential popularity arose from massed throngs in Egypt in June 1974. Nor did his travels extend only to state visits and campaign swings. He shuttled constantly among Camp David, San Clemente, and Key Biscayne, rarely spending a weekend in Washington. Indeed, he spent nearly a quarter of his first term at either San Clemente or Key Biscayne (195 days at the former, 157 at the latter).[70] That, too, makes perfect sense: a man so uncomfortable with leisure had to constantly work at it.

Nixon grew up in a far more rooted time, which makes the man's sheer restlessness all the more striking, as he followed a trajectory that took him from Yorba Linda to Whittier; then on to North Carolina for law school; back to Whittier; to Washington to work for the Office of Price Administration in the early days of the Second World War; then navy postings in Rhode Island, Iowa, the South Pacific, San Francisco, New York, and Baltimore; back to Whittier; then fourteen years in Washington; barely two years in Los Angeles; New York, to practice law and lick his wounds; Washington again; exiled to San Clemente back to New York; and, finally, to New Jersey's dependably Republican Bergen County, first Saddle River, then Park Ridge.

He was a man who fit in everywhere . . . and nowhere. It was just one more reason for him to detest the *Eastern* establishment. The place-names we hear mentioned in *Dark Victory*—Vermont, Philadelphia, Park Avenue, Long Island (Gatsby's Long Island, not Al D'Amato's)—define a tightly confined constellation of privilege: geography as destiny. So rooted is Judith Traherne in her milieu that her living anywhere else is unthinkable. Nixon's scorn for her kind was born as much of incomprehension as envy. How could someone like him understand people with such a sense of place and belonging? For Richard Nixon, geography was opportunity: so many rungs on a ladder to climb. He told a reporter in 1965, "Someone suggested that I get a house trailer and move around from state to state establishing residence. Then I could pick the best one as my base for 1968. Why not? I've tried everything else." He wasn't entirely joking.[71]

Even if in most every other regard he was an alien graft, Nixon's deracination made him the personification of a salient aspect of Southern California, a land that time forgot, where roots never quite reached. That same rootlessness ensured he was never truly at home there after the Second World War. It is but another mark of Nixon's inherent perversity that during a period when a considerable part of the population of the rest of the Union was moving to California, he was spending nearly all his adult life fleeing it. Of the sixty years remaining to him after his graduation from Whittier, he spent barely a sixth of them living in California. Indeed, one of the reasons Nixon had had such difficulty running against Pat Brown in 1962 was the near-universal recognition of the degree to which he was an outsider in the state he ostensibly wanted to govern (voters had no such problem with Ronald Reagan four years later).

"The transition back to California was, for him, a very difficult one," noted Stephen Hess, his closest aide at the time. "California had become his voting address, but was not spiritually his home any longer."[72] "If ever," one is tempted to add. Both times Nixon resumed California residence after entering politics in 1946, it was for wholly pragmatic reasons: to secure his political base after losing to Kennedy in 1960; then to get as far away from Washington as possible and try to restore his reputation after Watergate. In both instances, he soon realized the unsuitability of Southern California for his purposes and decamped for New York.

The one aspect of the region that did appeal to him was the aspect that had been most decisively denied him at birth. Having been born on the wrong side of Hollywood, he would now make sure to reside on the right side. He had grown up in an environment worlds removed from movie stars and well-manicured lawns. That would now change—so much so that when he moved to Los Angeles in 1961, he rented the house of an honest-to-goodness filmmaker (Walter Lang, the director of *The King and I*—a Nixon family favorite—as well as such less-prestigious offerings as *Snow White and the Three Stooges*) while he waited for his dream home to be built in a posh Beverly Hills development, Trousdale Estates. Besides having seven bathrooms, the new house boasted for neighbors two of the Marx Brothers, Harpo and Groucho. The latter was not shy in making known his unhappiness over having the Nixons in the neighborhood. (Ten years later he'd go so far as to tell an interviewer, "I think the only hope this country has is Nixon's assassination.")[73] Not that Groucho's ire kept Nixon from associating with other movie stars. It was, for example, in the company of Randolph Scott that he shot the only hole in one he ever recorded, at the Bel-Air Country Club, in 1961.

Eight years later Nixon bought the house in San Clemente. It lay deep in Orange County, too far away from Los Angeles to allow for much elbow rubbing with movie stars (John Wayne, though, who lived twenty-five miles up Highway 1, in Newport Beach, was a frequent visitor). Instead, Nixon gave the ten-room, twenty-acre oceanfront estate a grand name to go with its sweeping views, La Casa Pacifica, the House of Peace, as if to imply a rich Spanish provenance it did not in fact possess. Still, suggesting such an association was good for Nixon's ego—it was good for property values—so why not?

Here, too, we see another of the few affinities Nixon had with his native region. An ethic of salesmanship and what might most charitably be called moral complaisance was part and parcel of the Southern California mentality, as indeed of the entire state (wasn't the discovery of gold in 1848 the key formative event in its settling?). The creative use of the truth in the pursuit of financial gain and/or personal advancement was a tradition much observed in the Golden State, and Nixon's experience of it began as far back as Yorba Linda. Alas, he and his parents and brothers had been on the receiving end of the cozening. "The rancher was a liar," he would often bitterly say of his Milhous grandfather, the one who had gotten Frank Nixon to plant his sickly lemon trees in such inhospitable soil.[74] There was a lesson in that, as in the get-rich-quick ethos of California culture generally. It was the golden rule as practiced in the Golden State: Do unto others as they have done unto you, so long as you think you can get away with it. Wanting to get away with it would prove as important an element in his makeup as not belonging or never giving up. It's not too much to say that Richard Nixon, as one California-bred and California-raised, was born not just on the wrong side of Hollywood but on the wrong side of the law, as well.

Fred MacMurray

DOUBLE INDEMNITY

■ ■

To Richard Nixon: the most honorable man this country has ever produced.
ROSE MARY WOODS, OFFERING A TOAST AT A NIXON ADMINISTRATION REUNION
DINNER, 1982

We call it gold. RICHARD NIXON, CORRECTING THEODORE H. WHITE AFTER
WHITE HAD PRAISED THE OVAL OFFICE'S NEW "YELLOW" DECOR, *The Making of the
President, 1972*

The year is 1938, and the place somewhere in Los Angeles County.
A certain man has attracted our attention. Why he has attracted
our attention is hard to say, for he fits in this setting as naturally as
the shadows cast by the Southland sun.

The man has a long rectangular face, with a prominent forehead beneath wavy black hair and above dark, heavy brows. A professional man or in a business of some kind, he communicates an
obvious intelligence—but without being quite so smart as he rather
plainly thinks he is. Even a casual observer might see that this man

has an eye for the main chance, that he is someone who knows how to get things done, though perhaps a little too expeditiously. A furtive affability characterizes him, his humor being a trifle forced, his bonhomie too obviously reflexive. Absolutely correct in his behavior, he is nonetheless vaguely untrustworthy—an impression befitting such an evidently calculating man—and yet he seems surprisingly self-conscious, a little too much so to fit the classic booster profile he would otherwise appear to match (he gives the sense somehow of being overly *anxious*). He has a tendency to perspire, which rather undercuts the mask of smooth confidence he likes to present.

He is a bachelor, and one senses that, at some basic level, he is utterly unaffiliated: wary, apart, and almost painfully his own man. That might not be the best way of putting it, though, for "his own man" suggests someone who is unconventional in behavior as well as unattached in life. That is not the case here, for conformity is how he compensates for his isolation; and his urges, his ambitions and drives, are as commonly shared as the balmy, as-yet-unpolluted breeze that scents the air around him. For that matter, those urges, ambitions, and drives are as burning—as unyielding—as the Santa Ana winds that come and shake that air. Sleek yet uneasy, he is eager for success—for even more success—wanting not just to make it but to make it big. Sameness, not difference, is what defines him. It is also what makes him such an unsettling figure, for he is very much a representative man, unusual in two things only: his relative success (America is still in the Depression, after all) and his willingness to commit criminal acts.

Criminal acts? As it happens, this description applies to either of two men. If the man is a twenty-five-year-old lawyer recently admitted to the California Bar—as Richard Nixon was, returned from Duke University School of Law, "back in Whittier," as he later put it, "with good prospects, but an uncertain future"[1]—the high crimes and misdemeanors for which he will be forced to resign his office lie three decades and more ahead of him. If he is the other man, a thirty-five-year-old insurance agent named Walter Neff, then the crime he is willing to commit is murder and it is about to happen before our eyes—before our eyes, that is, if we are watching the most influential of all film noirs, *Double Indemnity*.

For unlike Nixon, Neff is a fictional character: the protagonist of the 1944 film that Billy Wilder based on James M. Cain's 1936 novella. Cain named the character "Huff." It's important to note that it's Neff we're talking about, not Huff. For what this man looks like—the face we see on the screen, the awkward avidity etched in shadow and light—matters a good deal for our purposes. Not only is Neff's dour appearance an augury of the disgrace that awaits him. It also means that, of the several alternate Nixons moving through these pages, he unquestionably bears the most striking—the most unnerving?—physical resemblance to the actual man. Of them all, he may well be the most consistently congruent with the original: from saturnine looks to geographical location, from arm's-length manner to moral acrobatics, Walter Neff is a remarkably suggestive simulacrum of Nixon the younger: a debased Horatio Alger hero vigorously complicit in his debasement. As played by Fred MacMurray in this, his greatest role and the finest motion picture he ever appeared in, Neff is Nixon as he might have been, a Nixon who had not gone east and then returned home a lawyer: a Nixon who sold policies instead of argued cases. It's all, almost eerily, there: the high forehead, the deep-set eyes, and hint of jowl; the elongated face and cleft chin; the brusque opacity; the sweaty man-on-the-make earnestness; the marriage of cool officiousness with enthusiastic, subcutaneous sleaze; the oddly distancing formality. (As did Nixon, Walter wears a necktie even while bowling.)

For his insurance salesman, Wilder told his biographer Maurice Zolotow, he wanted "a guy who had larceny and lust inside his Rotarian go-getter skin."[2] However fortuitously, Wilder grasped in Walter Neff the kind of man Richard Nixon partook of—grasped such a man right down to brilliantly casting against type to get him. George Raft and Brian Donlevy had turned down the part before a reluctant MacMurray accepted it. Raft, louche and lizardy, would have made Neff into a caricature of amorality, an oil slick masquerading as human. Donlevy, all beefy bluster and muscle-bound charm, would have shown a Walter simultaneously thuggish and ingratiating. Each in his different way would have portrayed a character too bad to be true: too comfortable with his actions—far more damning: too little surprised by them—to be compelling. It is because everything Walter does so goes against the grain of every role MacMurray had previously played that he is so ideal for the part. It is also a key ingredient in making Neff so Nixonian. MacMurray's Walter doesn't mouth bromides as Nixon did or ape the lineaments of a homiletic life. He doesn't have to: it's present in the audience's collective memory, courtesy of the wholesomely negligible screen persona MacMurray had presented during a decade of appearing in cheerful piffle with titles like *Champagne Waltz* (1937), *Invitation to Happiness* (1939), and *Take a Letter, Darling* (1942).

Wilder, who wrote the original script for *Champagne Waltz*, knew just what he was getting in MacMurray: a colorlessly all-American good guy.

It's the sum of what MacMurray stands for added to what Walter does that clinches it. And once the resemblance has been noted, the sense MacMurray conveys of a sort of Nixon is very nearly uncanny. Barbara Stanwyck's* performance opposite him as Phyllis Dietrichson, the femme fatale who leads Neff astray, is a Hollywood touchstone—has sullenness ever seemed so dangerous? ruthlessness so irresistible? Yet the Nixon angle is enough to make even her performance seem ever so slightly suspect. If only Helen Gahagan Douglas had postponed her political career a few more years and remained an actress, think of the Phyllis she could have made: "Can I fix you a drink, Walter? Care for a pink lady, hon?"

Phyllis (or, more precisely, what she embodies) is what most distinguishes the two men's characters. For Neff is something all but impossible to imagine: Nixon with a sex drive, unsublimating and too *little* inhibited, bankrolling his conquests with a shoeshine and a leer. In his early days as a lawyer, Nixon had to take the occasional divorce case and later liked to tell the story on himself of how he "turned fifteen colors of the rainbow" hearing one wife's detailed account of conjugal difficulties.[3] Neff, in similar circumstances, would have seen it as an opportunity— comforting the afflicted can offer rewards money simply *cannot* buy— rather than any cause for embarrassment. He is, after all, a salesman first and foremost; and like any salesman, the top-of-the-line item he has to offer is himself.

Unleashed libido aside, neither man would have had much trouble recognizing himself in the other. They might even have found themselves, fighting off boredom, at some of the same social functions. For Nixon followed the standard route to small-town success for an aspiring professional in need of clients: as he once explained, "Young lawyers trying to get business for their firms are expected to join local clubs."[4] Thus this most unclubbable of men forced himself to become a joiner, seeking contacts in a variety of organizational settings, using conviviality as a means of advancement. He belonged to the La Habra Kiwanis and Chamber of Commerce, the Whittier and Duke alumni clubs, the University Club, the Los Angeles and local bar associations, and the 20-30 Club, a service group for young adults that the Rotary Club sponsored. He was program chairman of the Whittier Kiwanis, president of the Orange County Association of Cities, and, of course, there was the local theater group where he was introduced to Thelma Patricia Ryan.

*Stanwyck was a Nixon admirer, dating back to 1946, when she and her husband, Robert Taylor, endorsed him in his race against Jerry Voorhis for Congress.

In such settings, a young lawyer got an opportunity to meet people, to present himself—to display his steadiness, his competence, his know-how—and so, over time, perhaps get his firm some new business. Brilliance in the courtroom was all well and good, but a lawyer needed someone to represent before he could go into the courtroom. So this was what a small-town lawyer did to get ahead—and if meeting so many people helped pave the way to a political career as well, why, so much the better. And, in fact, Nixon served as deputy city attorney for both Whittier and La Habra and came close to running for an assembly seat in 1940. The way to advancement for a young professional living on the periphery of Los Angeles County—perhaps then even more than now—consisted of untold luncheons and fund drives and smokers. Though we never see Walter Neff at such events in *Double Indemnity*, we can be sure he attended his share. Or so one might gather from his pace-setting sales record—that, and the dullness in his eyes.

It's what a salesman has to do if he wants to prosper, and make no mistake: an associate or junior partner in a small-town law firm is as much a salesman as a senior agent in a big-city insurance company. Either man must speak the language of salesmanship. Selling, along with the duplicities it so easily lends itself to, is what makes both Neff and Nixon such potent expressions of their region. It could seem at times, even during the Depression, as if all of Southern California carried a for-sale sign. "There's nothing, by God, but real estate offices and hot-dog stands," Ronald Reagan's father noted with amazement on his first visit there in the late '30s.[5] Carey McWilliams, California's foremost journalist-chronicler echoed Jack Reagan a few years later, noting that "Los Angeles has always been the city of phony business opportunities, the city of swaps and trades, the city of auctions."[6] James M. Cain went even further, arguing that hucksterism had lodged itself so deeply in the Southern California psyche that it affected the very language spoken there, "the glib chatter of habitual salesmanship"[7] having become the region's common tongue. Small wonder that a leader of the Los Angeles County Republican Committee, seeking to promote Nixon's suitability as a candidate for Congress in 1946, might consider especially complimentary a description of him as "saleable merchandise."[8]

Walter Neff is familiar with such talk (we see him employing it, to ultimately disastrous effect, in *Double Indemnity*). Less obviously, so was Richard Nixon. He knew how to sell as well as how to be sold. Although he downplayed his talent for salesmanship—"I have no difficulty at all in speaking to a large audience, or to millions over television," he once told a sympathetic biographer, but "I am perhaps the worst salesman in the country"[9]—his personal experience argues otherwise. As a boy, he sold newspaper and magazine subscriptions; and as a teenager, he even worked two summers as a carnival barker in Prescott, Arizona (in 1929 his Wheel of Fortune earned more money than any other concession on the midway).[10] It was a useful preparation for his postwar career. Any successful politician is a form of salesman, and Nixon offers a signal example of that fact. For nearly two decades, he was his party's foremost pitchman: heading its ticket three times; twice carrying the GOP's banner in off-year elections as Dwight Eisenhower's political surrogate—Nixon's "platform manner is that of a sales promotion manager pepping up his sales force,"[11] one observer wrote of his performance during the '58 campaign —and again in the wake of the 1964 debacle. During the '64 campaign itself, he "worked harder than any one person for the ticket," as no less an authority than Barry Goldwater put it. In 1965 alone, Nixon "logged 127,000 miles visiting forty states to speak before more than 40 groups" and raising "more than $4 million in contributions to the party."[12] Southern California–born and Southern California–bred, Nixon understood the language of selling.

In a get-rich-quick scheme whose ambitious reach Neff might have envied, Nixon began an effort in 1938 to unite the fruits of his native region with its retail ethic. More than a salesman, Nixon became an entrepreneur: the president and counsel of Citra-Frost, a company formed to freeze orange juice and ship it to the rest of the country. A group of local citrus growers "convinced Dick that they could all make a fortune," Thomas Bewley, Nixon's senior law partner, later recalled. As Charles Fletcher Lummis, the laureate of Southern California boosterism, noted at the turn of the century, the orange "is not only a fruit but a romance."[13] Nixon found himself smitten. Maybe money really did grow on trees. Nixon's father had thought so. But just as Frank Nixon's lemon groves failed, so did his son's juice-freezing system. He had quickly succeeded in getting investors to back the scheme, putting in some money himself, and worked unstintingly in his free time to make the enterprise work. For eighteen months he tried, with growing desperation, a variety of packaging materials: metal, glass, paper, cellophane. The problem was that Citra-Frost tried to freeze the juice in its entirety, rather than just the concentrate. In the end, the entire investment was lost. Nearly four decades later Wingert & Bewley, Nixon's old law firm, continued to carry Citra-Frost losses on its books.[14]

Just as the young Nixon's weakness wasn't sex, neither was it money. Citra-Frost was his sole attempt to try to make a financial killing. Easy money didn't really interest him. His ambition took the form of getting ahead, not getting rich. And once he finally gained elective office, a professed uninterest in financial gain turned into a professional asset: a way of maintaining not only a claim to personal honesty but also political purity. This salesman sought votes, not money. For Nixon, good product that he was of the great wide-open market of Southern California, crookedness was coextensive with money, and corruption limited to graft. If it doesn't involve money, then it's okay. That power itself might corrupt simply didn't enter into his ethical calculus. Personal gain was wrong, no argument there; but political gain, and the means used to get it, that was a different matter. Politics isn't beanbag; it's hardball—played for keeps and played to win—and to the tougher man goes the spoils. There's nothing dishonest about that—so long as you win and keep your hand out of the public till. As Alexander Haig once recalled, "Nixon always said to me—and he took great pride in it—'Al, I never took a dollar; I had somebody else do it.'"[15]

It was a position Nixon would maintain throughout his adult life. Having to make public his personal holdings during the 1952 presidential campaign, with the Checkers speech, may have been mortifying, but it was an inescapable corollary to Nixon's double-entry view of what did, or did not, constitute ethical behavior. He was still maintaining such a view ten years later, when Howard Hughes's 1956 loan to his brother Donald became an issue in the California gubernatorial race. "Now it is time to have this out," an indignant Nixon told reporters. "I was in government for fourteen years. I went to Washington with a car and a house and a mortgage. I have made mistakes, but I am an honest man."[16]

Even Watergate, which should have finally put paid to any such image of himself, found Nixon maintaining this interpretation of what was politically allowable. "There had been no thievery or venality,' he writes in *RN* of his view of the scandal at the time of James McCord's letter to Judge Sirica in March 1973.[17] Seventeen months later, barely two hours before giving up the presidency, he clutched at this defense even more tenaciously. A third of the way into his farewell speech to the White House staff—his last public words as president—he declared, "No man or no woman came into this Administration and left it with more of this world's goods than when he came to it. No man or no woman ever profited at the public's expense or the public till. . . . Mistakes, yes. But for personal gain, never." It wasn't the strongest of reeds, but he clung to it for the rest of his life. Two months before his death, Nixon used a discussion of the Clintons' Whitewater difficulties to sound the theme once again: "The point has to be made that unlike this situation, no one ever profited in Watergate."[18]

Profit was, in fact, a sensitive issue for Nixon during his presidency. It was true that as a member of Congress and then as vice president he had been far from being a wealthy man—this despite the fact that, in the words of Bobby Baker, who knew all too much about congressmen and cash, "Getting elected to the House or Senate gave a man a good leg up on getting about half rich."[19] Instead, it was after Nixon left Washington, when he returned to California in 1961, that he began to get that good leg up. He joined a high-powered Los Angeles law firm, Adams, Duque and Hazeltine, earning nearly three times his vice-presidential salary, and signed a lucrative contract for the book that would become *Six Crises* (his royalties eventually amounted to some $250,000). The Beverly Hills development where he bought his house had for its advertising slogan "If you can afford to live where you please you belong in Trousdale Estates—California's most exclusive community."[20] In early 1962 he told a journalist that he'd made more in his first fourteen months back in California than during all his fourteen years in elected office. Between the time he moved to Los Angeles in 1961 and began his presidential campaign in 1968, Nixon's personal assets grew nearly ninefold, to $858,190.[21] For too many years he'd seen too many men who were his inferiors in ability and intelligence, in power and repute, nonetheless be his financial betters. That would now change.

More than anything else, it was the move back East—where temptation was so much more variegated and complex than in California, where temptation was so much more *tempting*—that encouraged him, in what he did if not in what he said, to tame and attenuate his views of the importance of money and its corrupting effects. In a place where the language of salesmanship is not considered common parlance, it's appreciably easier to overlook the fact that what one is doing is cutting deals. So Nixon went from Main Street to Wall Street (almost literally: the offices of the Manhattan law firm he joined were at 20 Broad Street, in the heart of the financial district). His annual salary now a quarter of a million dollars; he regularly associated with men who were wealthy as well as powerful—Donald Kendall, of Pepsi-Cola; Elmer Bobst, of Warner-Lambert Pharmaceutical, the man who got Nixon his partnership at the law firm; Walter Annenberg, of Triangle Publications; Roger Blough, of U.S. Steel; Hobart Lewis, the editor in chief of *Reader's Digest*; and, of course, his two closest friends, Robert Abplanalp and Bebe Rebozo. Inevitably, he began to share their attitudes and assumptions about money and (what one might call) the innocence of uncomplicated affluence. The good life was no longer just good; it had become, for a man like himself, necessary. A validation of importance and demonstration of worth, it served as an outward and visible sign of inward and material grace.

What's so remarkable isn't that Nixon was finally making it, but that he wanted it *known* he was making it. His official campaign biography in 1968 pointedly included the fact of Nixon's belonging "to impressive in-town clubs—Metropolitan, Links, Recess—and fashionable country clubs—Blind Brook in Westchester, Baltusrol in New Jersey."[22] Now the last thing a Republican candidate for president, let alone a Republican candidate for president in an increasingly tight race, should want to seem is one of *them* rather than one of *us*. Yet Nixon was so pleased at having at long last clearly arrived that he put personal pride before political advancement. Winning the highest office in the land was all well and good, but Nixon, who had presided over Cabinet meetings and Senate sessions and been a single (famously feeble) heartbeat away from the presidency, wanted people to know that he'd won at another game, too, one that was in some ways even harder to succeed at. Really, when you stopped to think about it, anyone could be president—Harding, for heaven's sake! Truman!—but you had to be someone special to tee off at the seventeenth hole at Baltusrol.

As Nixon's appreciation for the good life grew, so did his willingness to compromise himself in pursuit of its attainment—no, of its furtherance—and that came to dog him after he became president. Ostentation—and what ostentation requires for its maintenance, money—now mattered to him and mattered a great deal. The man who had signally boasted of his wife's having only a cloth coat had less than two decades later become the president who fitted out the White House police in comic-operetta uniforms. The vice president who had lived in a seven-room house so cozy his wife had needed to cover a living-room wall with a mirror "to create the illusion of spaciousness"[23] was now a president who, despite residing in the White House and having regular use of Camp David, also required not one but two vacation homes. Such airs were indicative of the way he had changed—and the change did not go unnoticed.

The uniforms, which almost immediately disappeared, subjected him to ridicule. Richard Nixon shrank from ridicule even more than most men do, but it was the houses that proved incalculably more damaging.

Along with Nixon's presidential tax returns—the precedent of financial disclosure he had created with the Checkers speech returning to haunt him—the houses called into question his carefully cultivated reputation for financial probity. In a very real sense, the most harmful Watergate revelations (most harmful politically, anyway) had nothing to do with the break-in or cover-up. They had nothing to do with matters so abstract or rarefied as conspiracy or obstruction of justice or withholding evidence. What hit home with the public was the series of revelations in the fall of 1973 concerning Nixon's tax deductions and the expenditure of government funds on improvements to the houses at San Clemente and Key Biscayne.

From a legal, let alone constitutional, point of view, these were trivial matters. Indeed, from the point of view of criminality, they proved quite insubstantial. Nixon deeded his vice-presidential papers to the government in return for a substantial tax write-off. Because of a change in the tax code, the papers had to have been contributed by July 25, 1969, to qualify for the deduction. Though Nixon had decided to donate his papers months before that, his lawyers missed the filing date and later backdated the contribution (apparently, without Nixon's knowledge). He ended up paying a penalty of nearly half a million dollars. Even more harmful to Nixon's image was the discovery that the $1.2 million spent by the General Services Administration on improvements to the San Clemente and Key Biscayne properties had not gone exclusively for security measures, nor had they all been done at the behest of the Secret Service. Nixon himself had requested much of the work, and it extended to such questionable items as landscaping, a shuffleboard court, and a gazebo.

Padding your deductions, getting free work on your house: these were matters any taxpayer, any home owner, could relate to—could see through. The question of illegality was ambiguous, at best. The point is, whether justified or not, the charges stuck to Nixon. It didn't come as a surprise to people that he should have tried to pull a fast one, to cut corners, to profit at the government's expense. It wasn't even that Nixon was perceived as being greedy so much as being naturally attuned to getting away with something. And it was precisely these revelations that lay behind what may have been an even more shocking declaration than "I shall resign the presidency," those five equally unprecedented words for a chief executive of the United States to utter: "Well, I'm not a crook."

That's what Nixon said: not "I am not a crook." People always get the quote wrong. The way Nixon actually put it, it's conversational, that Reaganesque "well" and the informality of the contraction working to make the sentence sound matter-of-fact, casual, no big deal—in the way people express things they consider to be unassailably true ("Well, it's very hot today") or so obvious that one barely sees the need to state them ("Well, I'm leaving," said the man as he put his coat on). Stresses fall throughout the sentence evenly, and the emphasis could as easily lie on "well" as on "crook" or "not." "I am not a crook" sounds altogether different. The rhythm is staccato, calling attention to the gathering consonantal harshness of the *t, cr,* and *k.* The words seem less like a disavowal than a slogan—admittedly, a peculiar slogan, but it has that emphatic calling-attention-to-itself quality one expects to find on a billboard or bumper sticker. The sentence may not persuade, but neither is it easily forgotten. It has this additional quality of an advertisement: one simply takes for granted its tendentiousness. "Well, I'm not a crook" tries to tell us something. "I am not a crook" tries to sell us something. That it's the latter we commonly—incorrectly—remember Nixon as having said reveals something about our fundamental assumptions concerning him.

"I made my mistakes," Nixon announced, "but in all of my years of public life, I have never profited, never profited from public service—I have earned every cent. . . . And I think, too, that I could say that in my years of public life, that I welcome this kind of examination, because people have got to know whether or not their President is a crook. Well, I'm not a crook. I have earned everything I have got." By the time he got to the end, he could barely contain his anger. What he said may or may not have been true—it depends on how one defines "earned"—but it was truly felt.

As Stephen Ambrose points out, Nixon's "crook" remark is uncomfortably "reminiscent of his 1952 Checkers speech."[24] That speech remains the locus classicus of Nixon's difficulties with personal honesty: at one and the same time the origin of public questions about his financial dealings and the most stirring declaration of his personal blamelessness. It created a template for both how he viewed himself (as honest and embattled) and for public doubts about him (as shifty and shameless). What he described as "the most scarring personal crisis of my life" was also the defining crisis.[25] Forever after, he managed to seem simultaneously sanctimonious and unsavory—a sort of televangelist before his time—embarrassingly naked to his enemies, insufferably superior to his peers. The violation visited upon him Nixon never forgot. The violation he visited upon himself he chose never to recall.

A sense of Nixon as man on the make fed into as well as off of the events leading to the Checkers speech. The three other men on the national tickets that year had also engaged in questionable financial dealings—Adlai Stevenson had his own slush fund (with more money in it than Nixon's); Dwight Eisenhower had benefited from a special tax break on the royalties from his memoir, *Crusade in Europe*; John Sparkman, the Democratic vice-presidential nominee, employed his wife in his congressional office—but none of *them* had to mortify himself on television. No, people somehow expected such behavior of Nixon; it agreed with their sense of him. Anyone capable of such self-righteousness and cant cried out for investigation.

"The fund speech" he always called it. The $18,000 fund collected for political purposes from private contributors was what it was about, after all. "The Checkers speech" reduced it to a piece of melodrama, a bit of sleeve pulling, something undignified and mawkish: an address about a dog. And just as there were two names for it, there were two diametrically opposed interpretations. What *Variety* dismissed as "a slick production parlaying all the schmaltz and human interest of the 'Just Plain Bill'–'Our Gal Sunday' genre of weepers," Darryl Zanuck hailed as "the most tremendous performance I've ever seen."[26] Whichever view one took—and they need not be mutually exclusive—there had never been anything like it. Ike had told Nixon he needed to be as "clean as a hound's tooth," an impossible task for any successful politician. Yet hadn't he done it? In his eyes, the astounding success of the speech simply *proved* how honest he was. In his critics' eyes, it simply proved the opposite. It's not just that he protested too much. It's that he protested too . . . egregiously. "That must be the most demeaning experience my country has ever had to bear," Walter Lippmann told a friend after the broadcast.[27] Anyone who could give a performance like that must have *something* to hide and, more to the point, was clearly capable of anything. Where would such a man draw the line?

Well, it wouldn't be at debasing himself on national television twenty-one years later, protesting his innocence in words that might have sounded more appropriate—if equally unconvincing—coming from Edward G. Robinson or James Cagney in a Warner Bros. gangster movie. What other president would ever have dreamed of making such a declaration—let alone actually saying such a thing? (Bill Clinton, perhaps, though he would do it in such a round of hugs and choked-back tears that it would be more benediction than self-exoneration.) Worse, what other president would ever do it with such premeditation? "This was not a spur-of-the-moment statement," Nixon later said of his declaration, made at the 1973 convention of the Associated Press Managing Editors.

"The attacks on my personal integrity were more disturbing for me and my family than all the other attacks put together."[28] "I am not a crook" has come to be seen as a kind of shorthand response to the Watergate scandal generally. In fact, as we have seen, it was the allegations concerning his tax returns and the GSA improvements that he was addressing—that, not any constitutional issue or matter of national security, was what had outraged him. It so offended Nixon because nothing less than his self-image was at stake, and looking at a videotape of the question-and-answer session, one is struck by how far he goes out of his way to bring up the issue of his honesty. In fact, he is the one who raises the matter of his financial record. "Some of you might be too polite to ask such an embarrassing question," he tells the editors. He *wants* to give this answer, so he provides the opportunity to do so. It's the president who elicits the notorious response—Nixon himself, not any interlocutor, puts him on the spot—oblivious to how much the act of denial serves as self-indictment when no denial has been sought.

"Well, I'm not a crook." What's startling about this is how familiar it sounds—the defensiveness, the sense of personal violation, and, in the sentences preceding it, the lawyerly qualifications, the assumption that unethical behavior is coterminous with financial gain. Substitute "congressman" or "senator" or "vice president" for "President" and these sentences could have come at any point during the previous twenty-seven years of Nixon's political career. Yet at the same time, it was a culmination of that career, an accretion of resentments. "Well, I'm not a crook": within these five monosyllables one can hear Frank Nixon's truculence; the hostility toward the press; the decades of embitteredness; the sense of endless offense and (what went with it) the yearning for respect from his betters; the pain of so many never-healed wounds.

Is it any wonder Nixon felt as he did? His immediate predecessor actually *was* a crook. Say what one will about Richard Nixon, but there was no curiously acquired radio or television station in his financial portfolio. There were in Lyndon Johnson's, though, as well as much else besides: Lyndon Johnson, who brought political deceit to a level of brazenness that makes Nixon's own tortured struggles with the truth seem like the utmost candor. But people intuitively realized this about Johnson—part of his genius as a legislator had been to play off of people's distrust of him, to use it to enhance his power.

John Kennedy may have been even worse, insofar as many believe the crookedness he countenanced in 1960 stole an election. Yet one would never hear a Kennedy say, "I'm not a crook." There were so many reasons for Nixon to resent the Kennedys—their wealth, their status, their social ease, their press coverage (that in particular)—but the one that surely rankled most, that came to affect his own actions most, was that the Kennedys didn't play by the rules and—far, far worse—*they got away with it.* They stole elections. They were promiscuous. They wiretapped and used the IRS for political purposes and committed outright crimes ("Nobody Drowned at Watergate," as bumper stickers so bluntly put it). As the sons of a rich man—an extremely crooked rich man—Jack and Bobby and Teddy were raised to believe in their droit du seigneur: that Kennedys' flouting the rules was not just allowed but almost *expected.* Breaking the rules was a way of demonstrating their inherent superiority (what Nixon did by earning a large salary they did by not having to earn a salary). "They thought because of who they were that they could get away with anything," Nixon was still complaining as late as 1992.[29] No such dispensation was granted Richard Nixon. Play as many holes as he might at Baltusrol, own as many vacation homes in as many states rich in electoral votes as he could, JFK's famous putdown of him still remained: "No class." Class was something he might never acquire, not even when he was the most powerful man in the world—no, not then especially— and he was burningly aware of that fact. The good boy who not only fails to receive favor for following the straight and narrow, but who sees others allowed to do wrong and then lauded for it: it's a situation to try the patience of a saint; and, unlike his mother, Richard Nixon was no saint.

Neither was he a movie star, and even more often remarked upon than his own lack of movie-star glamour has been the Kennedys' abundant possession of same. It is here, in the matter of culpability, that the stardom deficit is most telling. Yes, the Kennedys had good looks and sex appeal and carried themselves like athletes—just like matinee idols up on the screen—and Richard Nixon did not. More than all that, though, they possessed a kind of existential immunity: they could do whatever they wanted and (so utterly, so aboundingly, unlike Nixon) never have to pay for their actions. And therein lies the fundamental characteristic of Hollywood stardom: a complicity between audience and star that excuses anything he or she might do. James Bond has a license to kill—movie stars, or Kennedys, have a license for license. Given such a circumstance, *of course* the man upon the screen can fuck every pretty girl, murder every villain, spend every penny—even dress to the nines and never feel in the least bit silly (JFK decreed morning wear for his inauguration). Any crime can be committed, any action carried out when there's only a two-hour statute of limitations. The appeal of the movies at their most visceral is not about size or simulation or even the effect of light dispelling darkness. No, it is about the abolition of consequences. Stardom is its own dispensation, one shared not even by the world's most powerful man. "When the president does it," Nixon told David Frost, "that means that it is not illegal." The fact that there he sat, disgraced and so in need of cash as to be reduced to a grilling by the likes of David Frost, gives some small sense of just how unrealistic that view actually was.

It was all the more galling because, if only in his own eyes, Nixon always observed the proprieties—always "lived," in the words of Ralph de Toledano, the biographer who knew him the longest, "by the storybook precepts."[30] Gazing into the mirror, a Kennedy or Johnson might not only recognize his buccaneer side but also sneak the occasional prideful look. Nixon would simply fail to see it. Yes, he was known as "Tricky Dick," a name he'd earned barely four years into his political career and that trailed him the rest of his life, an ever-present general accusation, as unanswerable as it was damning. But so far as *he* was concerned, it was as undeserved as it was distasteful. That it had stayed affixed to him so many years was a fluke of history, a token of how much (not to mention how unfairly) his enemies hated him, the lowest sort of partisanship.

A legacy of the 1950 Senate campaign, the epithet originated in the Democratic primary. The nickname is generally credited to Helen Gahagan Douglas. In fact, it originated with Douglas's opponent, Manchester Boddy, the maverick publisher of the *Los Angeles Herald-Express*. "Look at Tricky Dick" declared a full-page Boddy ad attacking Nixon's efforts among Democrats to conceal his party affiliation.[31] Whatever support the ad gained Boddy was far from enough—he lost to Douglas by more than 350,000 votes—but it clearly succeeded in saddling Nixon with a new nickname. Speaking at a Douglas rally in San Francisco that fall, U.S. Representative John F. Shelley used the name against Nixon, then Douglas herself took it up.

Insulting names emerge in the heat of political battle. The troubling thing was how the nickname took on a life of its own after his landslide victory in November. While its longevity owed something to the near-rhyme it contained (for all Joseph McCarthy's mendacity, no one ever thought to call him "Tricky Joe"), it owed far more to Nixon's own ongoing behavior. As even his supporters finally had to concede, Richard Nixon and the truth were only intermittently on speaking terms. Johnny Carson was simply acknowledging what everyone already thought when he joked on the *Tonight Show*, "Whenever anyone in the White House tells a lie, Nixon gets a royalty."[32] Barry Goldwater put it even more bluntly,

"He was the most dishonest individual I ever met in my life,"[33] and that opinion was not unique to him. Yet in that dishonesty one can discern, however paradoxically, the curiously arrayed rectitudinousness of Richard Nixon.

He would have argued, for one thing, that in breaking the rules he was simply following the rules. As he told Leonard Garment on Election Night in 1966, "No man can hope to be a successful candidate and political leader unless he understands how to lie."[34] And within this general condition, Nixon regarded himself as a special case. Early on during the 1968 campaign, he told his aide John Sears, "John, you've got to understand one thing. . . . I can say things that if someone else said them, they would be lies, but when I say them, nobody believes them, anyway."[35] It was another, less august, version of "if the president does it, it's legal."

Even more than the degree of untruth Nixon demonstrated, it was *how* he demonstrated it that earned him this reputation. The more Nixon lied, the more strenuous he became, as if dissembling were a kind of athletic contest, another way to prove, as he had on the practice field at Whittier, that he could take the punishment, that he was tough. The more transparent the falsehood, the more diligently Nixon applied himself to putting it over. Not for Nixon the easy laugh, the ingratiating shrug or knowing wink (Richard Nixon . . . *winking?*). The well-told lie is a social lubricant, a demonstration of a man's ability to weave together the flaws of human nature with the flow of everyday speech, and the more seamlessly the better. With Nixon, the seams always showed; worse, the stitching rose up from the fabric, nubby and nicked with wear. His highly moral upbringing could not prevent his failing to tell the truth, but it could at least prevent his failing to tell the truth persuasively. Even when he behaved like Frank, Hannah was still in control. Her influence saw to it that Richard Nixon, even more than the truth itself, was his dishonesty's own worst enemy.

Thanks to Hannah, rectitude mattered to him. It got to the heart of who he was, how he was raised, how he justified his actions. Even more, he wanted a reputation for rectitude. He wasn't the law-and-order candidate just out of expediency. It was what he believed—how he saw himself—as well as simply being good politics. He was brought up to follow the rules and, more important, believe in the rules. "Mother, I would like to become a lawyer," he announced one day during the Teapot Dome scandal, "an honest lawyer who can't be bought by crooks."[36] Classmates couldn't understand it when, after failing to be hired by any of the eminent New York law firms he interviewed with during his final year at

Duke, he applied to become an FBI special agent. The third man in his class at Duke, someone who'd gone for interviews at Sullivan and Cromwell, at Donovan, Leisure—a mere G-man! What's surprising is that he let ambition (an early hint of his future taste for better things?) keep him from applying to the bureau first. An FBI post was not only consistent with how he pictured himself—upright, vigorous, using the law in the cause of good—but to a small-town boy during the late '30s, with J. Edgar Hoover's crime-buster reputation at its height, the bureau was far more glamorous than any white-shoe law firm.

Glamour is a complicated thing, but equally complicated is its absence. Nixon, who so famously lacked it, realized this. That he always observed the letter of the law so stridently—that he made a fetish, in de Toledano's nice phrase, of "pre-emptive virtue"[37]—was at least in part a response to that lack. It was a function of self-interest as much as self-image: no one with his lowly background, awkward manner, and (above all) ignoble looks could expect to get away with anything quite the way such starry malefactors as the Kennedys could. All he had to do was consider the fate of Lyndon Johnson—and Johnson at least cut an impressive figure, as Nixon most surely did not. Image in Washington is as much destiny as it is in Hollywood. Nixon had reason to know this better than any other leader of his time. Sam Rayburn, who spent nearly half a century as a congressman, differed from many of his colleagues only in degree of feeling when he declared Nixon had "the meanest face I've ever seen in the House."[38] Helen Gahagan Douglas remembered the description slightly differently: Nixon had "the most devious face" of anyone Rayburn had ever served with in Congress.[39] Either way, it was no superlative to cherish. Worse, a physiognomic distaste for Nixon extended far beyond Capitol Hill. When Walter Cronkite asked him in 1960 about many voters' indefinable feeling of unease about his presidential candidacy—"I don't know what it is, but I just don't like the man"—it was his looks that a perplexed Nixon cited in explanation (his perplexity owing not to the question but rather its inevitability). "When people take pictures of you or when you appear on television, you may not make the impression that they like. . . . I can shave within thirty seconds before I go on television and still have a beard," he lamented.[40] And it was true: the five o'clock shadow was bad enough, but along with the prim mouth and beetling brow, his face cried out to be distrusted. Precisely because he seemed so much to be a man on the make, Nixon had to play the part of straight arrow to the hilt. Someone who looked as suspicious as Nixon did had no choice but to go out of his way to emphasize good behavior as much as Nixon did.

This was his Boy Scout side, an aspect of his character no less sincere for its unrivaled capacity to infuriate his enemies. More important, it gained him many more admirers who took him at his word and valued a political leader so ardent in standing up for virtue. "From the start of my political career," he writes in *RN*, "I had tried to be scrupulously careful in the handling of public money. I grew up in a home where politics was frequently discussed, and where the greatest contempt was reserved for politicians on the take. If anything, I have always gone far beyond most people in government to document and account for public money, whether campaign or government funds."[41] It was, for example, the meticulousness—and frugality—of his congressional expense account that first made Rose Mary Woods, who went on to become practically a member of the Nixon family, want to be his secretary.[42] One can detect pride as well as humiliation in Nixon's detailing of his finances in the Checkers speech. In choosing what he would say, he made sure to play to what he considered one of his great strengths.

Nixon's punctilio served a double purpose: playing the choirboy allowed him to play the tough guy, too. (Nixon's opponents had acknowledged as much, however inadvertently, with the nickname they'd tried to saddle him with before "Tricky Dick": "Dick Tracy.")[43] If no one—in his eyes, anyway—could justifiably question what Nixon did, then neither could anyone question how he went about doing it. Eisenhower told Nixon that what had most impressed him about his role in the Hiss affair was that, even more than getting Hiss, Nixon had gotten Hiss "fairly"— and compared with standard HUAC operating procedure, he *had* observed the niceties while still getting his man. But the clearest instance of his fondness for marrying protocol to prosecution was Nixon's scoring of the Truman administration during his time in the Senate. If his dealings with Hiss let Nixon enact the G-man role he'd aspired to barely a decade before (has any other future president been photographed holding up a magnifying glass to microfilm?), then his hounding of Truman was Nixon's chance to play Mr. District Attorney. The closest Nixon had ever come was prosecuting the occasional drunk-and-disorderly as deputy city attorney for Whittier and La Habra. As a senator, though, Nixon got to rail against "five-percenters" and "mink coats" (there was a reason Nixon made such a fuss in the Checkers speech about Pat's outerwear). He got to sound like a crime buster—like a Thomas E. Dewey, one of his great patrons, the man who more than any other was responsible for putting him on the ticket with Eisenhower, who had earned his national reputation prosecuting racketeers; or an Earl Warren, whose lifelong enmity

Nixon earned in 1952, and who also got his political start as a crusading district attorney, in Oakland. For that matter, so had another Nixon nemesis: Pat Brown entered politics as a DA, across the bay in San Francisco. Dewey and Warren composed the GOP ticket in 1948. Clearly, prosecuting attorney was an attractive role for an ambitious politician, and Nixon played his version of it for all the role was worth.

Hiss and anti-communism earned Nixon a national reputation, but Harry Truman and "anti-corruptionism" enhanced and extended that reputation. It was his attacks on Truman that kept Nixon from seeming like a political Johnny One-Note, that contributed to a stature denied someone otherwise dismissible, in Adlai Stevenson's pungent gibe, as "Joe McCarthy in a white collar." As a hostile biographer was forced to concede in 1960: "In the climate of mink coats, deep freezes, and big and little scandals that pervaded the closing months of the Truman administration, he emerged as a champion of integrity in public life, a reputation that had no little bearing on his nomination for the vice-presidency."[44] Nixon knew a good thing when he saw one, and just as attacking Truman had helped put him in the vice presidency, so did he later hope it might help gain him the White House. "I can only say," he declared in a very obvious dig at Truman during the third debate with John F. Kennedy, "that I'm very proud that President Eisenhower restored dignity and decency and, frankly, good language to the conduct of the Presidency." Alas, that "good language" comment did not go unremarked when "expletive deleted" entered the vernacular.

It was only fitting that Nixon, having used Truman's reputation to advance his own, should then return the favor, his misdeeds being the single greatest factor (other than the thirty-third president himself) in the great revival of Truman's reputation, as Truman went from the least popular president of modern times to enjoying a rise in public esteem that has lasted to the present day. The combination of Watergate and the 1974 publication of *Plain Speaking*, Merle Miller's compilation of his bracingly candid interviews with Truman, brought home with stunning effect the contrast between the incumbent and his embattled predecessor. In a context of "at that point in time" and "to the best of my recollection," the title of Miller's immense best-seller provided an all-too-eloquent contrast between the two men and their dissimilar relationships to the truth.

Despite the air of corruption that surrounded the final two years of his administration, Truman's renown for personal probity has come to be unmatched among American presidents. The man who used his own stamps whenever sending personal correspondence from the White

House may have been the product of the Pendergast machine in Kansas City and too often lax in assessing the scruples of associates, but he is revered as a pillar of honesty. Nixon, who gained elective office untainted by machine politics and, as we have seen, rose high on the wings of his own repeatedly asserted rectitude, ended up an unindicted co-conspirator, reduced to publicly denying his crookedness, the sole chief executive forced from office. The irony is breathtaking. The Truman years had a litany of political disrepute ("natural royal pastel mink," "influence ped-dlers," "the mess in Washington") unsurpassed until the astonishingly rich lexicon of Watergate. Yet none of it stuck to Truman—certainly not the way everything, seemingly, stuck to Nixon.

Two days before he resigned, Nixon joked to Senator Hugh Scott, "Now that old Truman is gone, I won't have anybody to pal around with."[45] Even by Nixon standards, the humor was forced. Truman's de-testation of Nixon was no secret—though public awareness of just how ve-hement awaited publication of *Plain Speaking*. "Nixon is a shifty-eyed, goddamn liar," Truman told Miller; "all the time I've been in politics there's only two people I hate, and he's one."[46] Yet Nixon had tried to make amends—the tough guy taking a backseat to the choirboy, the sales-man refusing to take no for an answer—and soon after entering the White House, he paid a visit to the former president at the Truman Li-brary. Unfortunately, Nixon merely managed to underscore the sourness of their relations. He made a show of performing "The Missouri Waltz" on the piano as a tribute to his old adversary, oblivious to the fact that Truman loathed the song. The gaffe was compounded, or mitigated, by the fact that Truman, then eighty-four, was so hard of hearing he had to have the tune identified for him.

The Independence visit was a curiously muffled end to such a volatile history, disappointing enough to make one wonder what an encounter might have been like with the bark off, with a Truman in his feisty prime and a Nixon not aspiring to world-historical importance. Only a novelist or playwright might do such a clash justice, and in fact the closest ap-proximation we have comes in a drama written by a novelist-playwright, *The Best Man*, by Gore Vidal. The play was a great success on Broadway in 1960 and four years later was made into a film, directed by Franklin J. Schaffner. Schaffner won an Academy Award for his direction of the title most famously associated with Nixon's moviegoing, *Patton*. An even stronger Nixonian connection for the film comes courtesy of Vidal, who also did the screen adaptation. He has long and lavishly proclaimed a negative affinity between himself and Nixon, going so far as to cobble together a play, *An Evening with Richard Nixon* (1972), largely consisting of quotations from its subject. It is *The Best Man*, though, that gives the more interesting theatrical view of Vidal's nemesis.

The clash between Vidal's "Nixon" and "Truman" springs from their being two-thirds of the none-too-holy political trinity whose interplay provides *The Best Man* with its plot. The trio consists of the very Trumanesque Art Hockstader, a peppery and unpretentious former chief executive, and the two presidential contenders seeking his endorsement during their party's national convention. Joe Cantwell—a U.S. senator who is ruthless in action, dauntless in aim, and darkish in appearance—is the alarmingly Nixonian opponent to William Russell, who served as Hockstader's secretary of state and bears a more than passing resemblance to Adlai Stevenson.

Nixon never had to deal with Truman in his own party, of course, let alone turn to him as supplicant. But Cantwell's demeanor toward Hockstader—priggish, impatient, obtuse—convincingly suggests how it likely would have been: less a case of worlds colliding than of worlds repelling. Ideally, neither man would have anything to do with the other. But political practicalities dictate otherwise. Indeed, Hockstader has decided to support Cantwell (the name does lay it on a bit thick), endorsing him solely because he thinks Cantwell has what it takes to win and Russell does not. More than that, Hockstader recognizes in Cantwell a fellow political animal. Murray Kempton's great and mournful benison for the soul of Joe McCarthy—"a little of what is bad in myself was a great deal of what was bad in him"[47]—expresses this aspect of Hockstader's view of the younger man. Yet when Cantwell confides his intention to smear Russell, he decides to withhold his endorsement. Not for any moral reasons: it's the stupidity of the act that offends Hockstader. Vileness he can accept, but not stupidity.

Showing such "cynicism" on the part of the great still seemed daring in 1964, and *The Best Man* prides itself on presenting politics red in tooth and claw. Its knowing air can become rather thick with self-congratulation, though; and for all that it strives for an in-the-know verismilitude, *The Best Man* is not particularly convincing as a behind-the-scenes view of what really goes on behind closed doors. As JFK said to Vidal after reading the play, "You know, in a campaign we don't have all that much time to talk about the meaning of it all."[48] Unfortunate timing further hampered the movie. Between the play's Broadway run and its filming, Theodore H. White published *The Making of the President, 1960*. Americans' understanding of the nuts and bolts of presidential politics would never be the same, and White's book demonstrated how vastly more complex—and entertaining—the real process is than what Vidal purports to show. Worse, the film's shortcomings as reportage are mirrored by its limitations as art. The whole thing is far too tidily constructed, and Vidal's schematic arrangements leave no room for any real moral or emotional depth. The play, though not the movie, does offer one weirdly prescient instance of life imitating life, when Cantwell tells Russell that, in return for his support, he "can go as our first Ambassador to Red China."[49]

The interest the movie repays, as well as the not inconsiderable pleasure it affords, centers on its stars. Returning to the screen after a seventeen-year absence, Lee Tracy brings as much savor and glee to the role of Hockstader as Hockstader brings to the game of politics. That he lost the Best Supporting Actor Oscar to Peter Ustinov (for *Topkapi*) is one of the sadder examples of the Academy's hopeless weakness for posh accents. Tracy had been Hockstader in the Broadway production. Playing across from him as Russell was Melvyn Douglas. Douglas knew something about being on the receiving end of a Nixonian smear campaign: his wife was Helen Gahagan Douglas. It's hard to imagine a more suitable choice to play the rival of the Nixon-like Cantwell—except, of course, for the actor who plays Russell's onscreen incarnation, Henry Fonda.

A leading Hollywood liberal, Fonda had enthusiastically supported JFK in 1960. Beyond that, though, with his pained, painstakingly maintained nobility, Henry Fonda is the screen's pluperfect anti-Nixon: idealism incarnate, a figure almost ethereal in his honorableness. "I had to win," Nixon told an aide to U.S. Representative Jerry Voorhis a few months after defeating him in 1946. "That's the thing you don't understand. The important thing is to win."[50] What makes Fonda the supreme liberal icon of the screen isn't the fineness of his intelligence, the finickiness of his bearing, or even the unique ineffability of that faraway gaze—as near as we shall ever come, surely, to beholding Emerson's transparent eyeball on the hoof. No, it's that he's happiest, or at least most gratified, when his cause is lost. Nothing could be less Nixonian.

Throughout his career, Fonda is the perfect unsullied idealist—right down to the almost angelic angularity of his physique: too elegant to seem gawky or unnatural, too pared away to appear altogether of this world. Where his friends James Stewart and John Wayne are, respectively, the classic American innocent and the archetypal American man of action, Fonda is the American visionary personified (the American visionary purified): a little abstract, more than a little bloodless, but able to give decency and reflection an almost ravishing attractiveness. From *Young Mr. Lincoln* (1939) to Tom Joad in *The Grapes of Wrath* (1940) to Gil Carter in *The Ox-Bow Incident* (1943) to Wyatt Earp in *My Darling Clementine* (1946) to *Mister Roberts* and the unconvinced juror in *Twelve Angry Men* (1957), Fonda can be seen as an almost metaphysical epitome of the anti-Nixon: light against dark, scruple against grasp, secular grace against secular sin. (The contrast extends even unto the next generation: Jane and Peter as against Tricia and Julie.)

Fonda's dissenting juror in *Twelve Angry Men*—almost too perfectly attired in his white suit, an editorial writer's revenge on all those cowboys in their white hats—might be seen as the high-water mark of bien-pensant fifties liberalism: a character so easy in his confidence, so inevitable in the success of his case that the viewer hardly notices it's a case utterly patent and self-regarding in its fundamental contrivance. It was only meet and proper that, jury duty done, Fonda should move on and enter politics— if he hadn't existed, the Hollywood chapter of the League of Women Voters would have had to invent him—rising from Cabinet nominee in *Advise and Consent* (1962) to Cabinet office in *The Best Man* to the Oval Office itself in *Fail-Safe* (1964). In *The Candidate* there's a nice, and uncharacteristically subtle, joke about Hollywood's having elevated Fonda to the role of supreme civic icon. Political consultant Peter Boyle, looking for some private place to confer with his candidate, Robert Redford, has barged into the cockpit of the plane they're flying in. The pilot tells them to get out. Boyle reminds him that it's no less a figure than the Democratic nominee for senator from California he wants to eject. "I don't care if it's Henry Fonda!" the disgusted pilot counters.

Who better, then, to be entrusted with the future of mankind, thanks to the president's responsibility for the United States' nuclear arsenal, as he is in *Fail-Safe?* So that it should be *Henry Fonda* who actually drops the bomb is the ultimate Hollywood political joke. In its dark way, this is far funnier (conceptually, anyway) than Peter Sellers's overtly comic handling of a similar presidential dilemma in *Dr. Strangelove* (1964). Even the shock of seeing Fonda in *Once Upon a Time in the West* (1968)—as "the meanest man you ever saw in a spaghetti western,"[51] as the actor once happily described his character, a villain so vile he kills a man simply because he doesn't like his suspenders!—somehow pales by comparison. Sergio Leone's most celebrated bit of casting was to make Clint Eastwood the Man with No Name (Nixon was a big Clint fan), but his use of Fonda is every bit as inspired—and far more daring. Yet casting Mr. Roberts as a murderer, wonderful though it may be in the garishness of its perversity, is as nothing compared with making him the agent, however conscience stricken, of every Ban the Bomb picketer's worst nightmare.

Of course, Fonda might have played Cantwell: that would have been *truly* perverse. The actual casting is almost as disconcerting: Cantwell is played by Cliff Robertson, who in *PT 109* (1963) was none other than JFK (imagine the one-man show Robertson might have done of the 1960 debates). His Cantwell is all blinkered energy and heedless drive, his career predicated on no principle beyond self-advancement. It's a representative embodiment of the standard hostile view of the pre-presidential Nixon, and one indicator of Vidal's disdain for the character is how fundamentally uninteresting he makes him. Robertson is reduced to standing around looking simultaneously aggressive and uncomprehending. He also gets to use an electric razor in midafternoon, thus signaling even the dimmest viewer as to the identity of the five o'clock–shadowed original Vidal modeled him on. If that wasn't enough of a giveaway, Russell expresses his disgust when he chances upon a television screen showing Cantwell's face by saying, "I wouldn't buy a used car from that man." Clearly, Nixon's the one.

By 1964 the question "Would you buy a used car from this man?" had long been a byword among Nixon haters. It was such a commonplace that Dick Gregory was getting laughs four years later by suggesting that Hubert Humphrey looked like someone who'd buy a used car from Nixon—and George Wallace looked like someone who'd steal it.[52] "The phrase was one of the first used to derogate Richard Nixon in his California career," notes *Safire's New Political Dictionary*,[53] and the words soon took on a larger, more generic meaning as the classic putdown of a politician, a not-so-subtle calling into question of his veracity. That Nixon should have been the one to inspire it, and in California, is altogether fitting. He was the first national political figure associated with *Southern* California. Hiram Johnson (Theodore Roosevelt's running mate on the Bull Moose ticket in 1912), Herbert Hoover, Warren, all had come from the northern part of the state—the *normal* part of the state, the part least different from the rest of the country. Nixon's reputation drew on the reputation of where he came from—and, inevitably, he was perceived as being a man on the make from a region on the make.

As we have seen, the art of the deal was a Southern California specialty. And by the time Nixon was rising to national prominence, the late 1940s and early '50s, the ubiquity of the region's automobile culture was not going unremarked. California's first low-access highway, the Pasadena

Freeway, opened in 1940. The word "smog," a Pittsburgh coinage, made its debut in the *Los Angeles Times* on September 18, 1944.[54] The initial generation of car customizers had begun souping up woodies and Model A's. And owners of used-car lots were becoming minor celebrities with their late-night ads on local television, their manic pitches earning them a place in the well-populated pantheon of Southern California weirdness. Who knows: if Walter Neff had stayed on the (relatively) straight and narrow, he might have switched businesses after the war and become Cal Worthington without the dog and cowboy hat. How hard is it to imagine a saturnine face—if not MacMurray's, then Nixon's—squinting in bright sun beneath a string of fluttering plastic pennants, vexed at the question of how far back he can turn some trade-in's odometer without having prospective buyers notice?

Our folklore abounds in larcenous regional stereotypes (Yankee peddlers, Mississippi riverboat gamblers, Oklahoma Sooners); only Southern California's dates from later than its region's frontier period. Not until the Los Angeles basin was already heavily populated did its association begin in the national psyche with grifters, hustlers, used-car salesmen. There, and there alone, outlawry was a consequence of civilization rather than a prelude to it. If for that reason only, Los Angeles deserves pride of place over Chicago, Miami, and even New York as our cultural capital of crime. Chicago owes its notoriety to one man really, A. Capone, and the gangland struggles he spawned. Miami's ill repute is of recent origin, a product of the cocaine wars of the 1980s. New York's claim is generic: for in what remains the essentially Jeffersonian imagination of America, the city is the unredeemable sump of immorality. As the biggest of American big cities, New York is automatically the great bad place—the great *worst* place. But that is guilt by accumulation: the more people, the more criminality. The thing about teeming masses—and what Jefferson most feared about cities—is just that: they *teem*. They're faceless characterless, a threat by dint of sheer numbers: not who they are but how many. Southern California, where people could spread out even as they aggregated, is a far more logical setting for crime in fiction and lore than any other great city.

It is because Los Angeles is the *least* urban of cities that, in the popular imagination, it best lends itself to illegal activity. Crime becomes individuated there as in no other urban setting. Writers realized this long ago, and where else in America can one find such a gathering of detective heroes as Raymond Chandler's Philip Marlowe, Ross Macdonald's Lew Archer, Robert Towne's Jake Gittes, Walter Moseley's Easy Rawlins . . . all the way down to the mundane, just-the-facts-ma'am drudgery of *Dragnet*'s Joe Friday. First, that portentously ominous music, then Jack Webb's monotone announces, "The city is Los Angeles . . ." Exactly.

What other place could produce a sensibility as morally void as James Ellroy's—or inspire a title as swaggeringly matter-of-fact as *L.A. Confidential* (1997)? Inimical to truth as well as consequences, Los Angeles and its surroundings have long seemed to operate under a general moral anesthetic. The region's famed lack of permanence, its openness to change, has appeared to express itself in a more generalized shiftiness, a propensity for the fake and ephemeral. Hemmed in by desert and ocean, Southern California is a self-contained entity (so long as the water it cozened away from other, less arid localities keeps flowing in), morally blank, and ethically uninterested. There is something suspect about L.A., the suspicion being that the place nurtures an inner nullity to balance such an abundance of happy externalities. There is nothing *earned* about its blessings. The weather is too nice, the living too easy: all that sunshine somehow has an unsavoriness to it. True, Southern California's cloudlessness "is a sort of general disinfectant," as James M. Cain once observed; yet such a general and pervasive disinfectant must needs indicate the presence of a very large infection.[55]

There was nothing grand or imposing (indeed, there was something unmistakably sinister) about its glamour. Frank Lloyd Wright spoke for many when he lamented, "It is as if you tipped the United States up so all the commonplace people slid down into Southern California."[56] A name like "Tinseltown" does not flatter, after all; and during the years of Richard Nixon's early adulthood—even more then than now—the rest of the country saw Los Angeles as shoddy and on the make. The classic statement of this view came in 1939, with publication of *The Day of the Locust*, but in the '30s alone it can be found in sources as diverse as Edmund Wilson's *The American Jitters* (1932), Horace McCoy's *They Shoot Horses, Don't They?* (1935), J. B. Priestley's *Midnight on the Desert* (1937), and Aldous Huxley's *After Many a Summer Dies the Swan* (1939). Los Angeles was a city whose most famous industry retailed falsity under the guise of recreation; one of whose most famous citizens, Aimee Semple McPherson, retailed falsity under the guise of redemption. (Though Nixon's family, as we have seen, rarely went to the movies when he was growing up, he noted in his memoirs that they "often" made the drive to Los Angeles to hear McPherson.)[57]

Fairly or not, some of this sense of the bogus inevitably rubbed off on Nixon. Being from Los Angeles County—"our own county,"[58] as he and

Pat called it when declining an invitation from the Eisenhowers to spend Election Night in 1952 in Washington—was a political plus for Nixon, but a moral minus. None of the dolce or éclat of Southern California attached itself to him, as it so manifestly did to Ronald Reagan. Instead, it was the region's reputation for phoniness and avarice that helped define him: that overriding sense the rest of the country had then, as now, that its earthquake-prone terrain is not, perhaps, the only shifty thing about the Los Angeles basin. This is where Richard Nixon sprang from—Southern California, with its inexplicable, inexpungeable creepiness: the dark underside of all that endless sun, the way Lotusland can breed such noxious fumes—and no matter how many other places he lived over the nearly half century between 1946 and his death, Nixon would never quite shed the connection between himself and his native region. It helped promote him to national office; far more subtly, it helped prepare him for national obloquy.

All the attention Los Angeles gets, Reyner Banham once complained, is "like the attention that Sodom and Gomorrah have received, primarily a reflection of other people's bad consciences."[59] Banham, who did so much to make affection for the Southern California megalopolis intellectually respectable, came, of course, from somewhere else—London, a distant and foggy somewhere else. So far as those who have always known it are concerned, the matter-of-fact miraculousness of L.A. obscures how magnificent it can be (how dreadful, too), its amazingness lost in a haze of ozone-filtered sunshine. The outsider, though, the outsider cannot help but recognize the miracle spread before him. Not the least of the reasons that nothing has ever evoked Los Angeles more compellingly than *Double Indemnity* is that Cain (from Maryland), Wilder (from Vienna), and Wilder's co-scenarist, Raymond Chandler (from London), were outsiders and possessed of an appreciation of the region—one touched with loathing as well as wonder—forever denied a native Californian like, say, Richard Nixon.

Look closely, and one finds in Wilder's film a sort of unannounced poem to Southern California. As Richard Schickel has noted: "Few movies of any era have more deliciously proved . . . that landscape is character. You could charge L.A. as a co-conspirator in the crime this movie relates."[60] The script is a veritable gazetteer of Southern California, with references to Glendale, Westwood, Santa Monica, Hollywood, and Long Beach. In the novella, Cain calls the firm Neff works for "General Fidelity," and the joke is pretty obvious; Wilder and Chandler trade jape for geography, making it the "Pacific All-Risk Insurance Company." The opening shot reveals an automobile speeding past a sign bearing the words "Los Angeles Railway Company" and then the "Go" and "Stop" of an old-fashioned traffic light—a nice joke on the centrality of Southern California's automotive culture as well as an acknowledgment of how important the region's inter-urban rail system was. Trains and automobiles are crucial to the plot. It's on a Palo Alto–bound train that Phyllis's husband has his deadly "accident," and the metaphor of "Taking the trolley to the end of the line" recurs several times at the movie's climax. Walter commits the murder in the car of Phyllis's husband, and it's Walter's coupe that provides him with his seemingly ironclad alibi.

Neff's car also takes him to a drive-in restaurant, one of a number of Southern California institutions scattered throughout the film. Such local landmarks as the University of Southern California and the Hollywood Bowl figure in the movie (Cain mentions neither). The script offers its own Los Angeles street directory. The Dietrichsons live, felicitously enough, off of Los Feliz. Another character lives on La Brea Avenue. The Pacific's headquarters are on Olive Street. Walter takes Phyllis's stepdaughter to "a Mexican restaurant on Olvera Street" (the senior partner and his wife took Nixon to an Olvera Street restaurant in early 1938 to celebrate his joining Wingert & Bewley).[61] Visiting Walter's apartment for the first time, Phyllis (a native Angeleno) hears him describe getting his meals at a drugstore and is moved to state the fundamental fact of Southern California life—at once lure and indictment—"Sounds wonderful: just strangers beside you." It's not so much the emptiness of the life there: it's that the emptiness has an aura. Who knows, if the drugstore is Schwab's, the stranger may be a talent scout and only a solitary meal (or two) might stand between you and stardom.

The evocation of the region includes less obvious references and allusions. Walter and Phyllis hold two crucial rendezvous at a supermarket—such establishments were as yet a novelty in much of the rest of the country. The Spanish revival architecture of the Dietrichsons' house and the stuccoed blandness of Neff's apartment would look out of place anywhere else. So, too, would the sense of choking fecundity—"How could I know that murder can sometimes smell like honeysuckle?" Neff later wonders—and of brilliant sunshine simultaneously cherished and evaded. We first meet Phyllis coming in from sunbathing, barely covered with a towel. Yet that same light, indoors, becomes threatening, as an array of blinds and lattices creates a tracery of shadows that looks like nothing so much as prison bars. To heighten this effect, and make it literally palpable, Wilder's cinematographer, John Seitz, put finely ground aluminum filings in the air when shooting the interior of the Dietrichson house, to give it a dusty, laden atmosphere.

Appearances matter in *Double Indemnity*, but so do words. The perfection of the title—so direct and literal, yet at the same time darkly poetic, with those plosively alliterative *d*'s mimicked by the *b* and *t*—announces at the outset the film's appreciation for verbal fineness. It continues with the leading characters' surnames, which Wilder and Chandler took the trouble to improve from those Cain gave them—and they are an improvement—from "Huff" to "Neff," as we have seen, and from "Nirdlinger"* to "Dietrichson." This verbal care is most apparent in the dialogue, very little of which remains from Cain. "Nothing could be more natural and easy and to the point on paper," Chandler wrote to Cain of his use of dialogue in the novella, "and yet it doesn't quite play."[62] In the movie, there's nothing natural or easy about the dialogue—but it certainly does play—and Chandler can be heard in almost every line. The incessant insinuation and straining for offhandedness, the overripeness of imagery and self-consciousness of language (which wonderfully suits such scheming characters): *Double Indemnity* might have lifted its dialogue straight from one of Chandler's novels. In fact, no small part of what makes Walter Neff so arresting a character is that while he looks and acts like just another horny hustler in a cheap suit, if you close your eyes he sounds like no one so much as his moral antithesis, Philip Marlowe. Chandler once wrote to a reader inquiring about Marlowe's background that he had worked as an insurance investigator before moving to Los Angeles. Even without that knowledge, there can be no doubt Marlowe would have fit right in to *Double Indemnity*.

Sherlock Holmes excepted, no detective has been so variously impersonated on the screen—actors playing Marlowe include Humphrey Bogart, George and Robert Montgomery, Dick Powell, James Garner, Elliott Gould, Robert Mitchum, and James Caan—or so celebrated by Hollywood. How could it be otherwise, for Marlowe is the *ur*-L.A. dick, both the template from which the conception of all other Los Angeles private eyes sprang and the standard by which they are measured. Where Richard Nixon is the great and terrible real-life embodiment of the region's notoriously halfhearted struggle between right and wrong, Mar-

---

*The name of the department store in the Coen brothers' noir send-up, *The Man Who Wasn't There* (2001), is "Nirdlinger's." What other filmmakers have ever been so relentless in their knowingness?

lowe is the supreme fictional example. There's nothing halfhearted about *his* struggle, though. That's one reason why when he's around, right always wins; the other is that he's fictitious. If Nixon is any indicator, not succumbing to wrong in Southern California is in real life rather a more difficult task.

It's this inherent unreality of Marlowe that helps make him so irresistible a character. Who could fail to respond to this seedy Southern California Übermensch—insolent, world-weary, immured in his own moral superiority—a Nietzschean knight, of sorts, made uneasy by how at home he feels in a city beyond good and evil. Nothing stands between him and his code. Other than his pipe, a chessboard, and the bottle, there are no solaces in his life except for the code of right and wrong he abides by. As we have seen, the city where he lives is oblivious to the existence of any such code, so the extent to which his life lacks ligatures—no friends, no associates, no family, not even a secretary—comes as little surprise. Estranged in a very strange land, he is as alone as a cowboy riding the range or an angel on a terrestrial errand. "Don't look back, Henry," Nixon told Kissinger at the time of the Cambodian incursion. "Remember Lot's wife." Marlowe could have been the angel (*pace* Reyner Banham) who destroyed Sodom and Gomorrah. Instead, he's the angel who patrols them.

What makes so implausible a figure unforgettable (what makes our suspension of disbelief so willing) is Marlowe's milieu—or, rather, Chandler's rendering of it. He didn't so much capture a time and place as create them: Southern California during the years when every man wore a hat, few women went without a girdle, and people used a hard *g* when they pronounced the name of the city of the angels, a city whose inhabitants as yet remained apologetic that Los ANGLE-eez wasn't somewhere back East. "I was the first writer to write about Southern California at all realistically,"[63] Chandler liked to boast. In fact, it was Cain. Yet Cain, at his best, wrote a kind of small-bore Greek tragedy in which his characters were undone not by the gods but their own unrepressed urges. Chandler wrote Southern Californian tragedy. His fiction is unthinkable anywhere else, just as Southern California—or at least our understanding of it—is now unthinkable without his fiction. If only for that reason, his removal from our literature would diminish it as the disappearance of many a finer novelist would not. At his atmospheric best, Chandler is as unimprovable, as only-in-America, as seemingly effortless as DiMaggio rounding third or Jo Jones tattooing the hi-hat: contemporaries of Chandler who also demonstrated the glorious aesthetic result when American freedom is kept in absolute balance with American rigor. Chandler achieved something great and unique and lasting, but the achievement is ultimately extraliterary: an aftereffect of the writing rather than something intrinsic to it, an achievement owing more to sociology or history than to literature. In the end, it is as the basin's poet laureate/pissed-off castigator that Chandler endures. He celebrates Southern California, he hates it, he can't get away from it—and, certain protestations of his own to the contrary, he doesn't altogether *want* to get away from it.

This is the true, sustaining glory of the Marlowe books. The myth of Los Angeles and environs as an endless array of sunshine abundance, and sleaze—an immense orange grove of orgies—long ago became a commonplace. But Chandler, more than any other writer, made it so. He is the one who formed our vision of what he famously described as "California, the department-store state. The most of everything and the best of nothing." There's "Hollywood, that sinful city." There's the Sternwoods' Pasadena, suffocating and proper, in *The Big Sleep* (1939). There's "the best policed four square miles in California," Beverly Hills. Above all, there is, as he calls it in *The Little Sister* (1949), the "mail order city": Los Angeles minus Hollywood, its glamour subtracted, its allure reduced to the merely meteorological. This world is one that Marlowe passes through on his way to do battle with the Dr. Feelgoods and hired goons and crooked cops, a world he takes note of even as he knows he can never belong to it—would never *care* to belong to it—for it is so surpassingly unheroic, so glumly normal, with its "small exact houses squatting behind small exact lawns."

It is as a sort of spiritual geographer that Chandler secured himself a permanent place in our national imagination. And it is less by the mean streets down which Philip Marlowe goes than the meandering, middling, middle-class ones—streets that, as it happens, the young Richard Nixon aspired to; streets the older Richard Nixon, on his way to Key Biscayne and San Clemente, left behind; streets whose residents the candidate Richard Nixon depended on for votes—it is via these streets that Chandler entered American literature. "I drove east on Sunset," he has Marlowe tell us in *The Little Sister*, "but I didn't go home. At La Brea I turned north and swung over to Highland, out over Cahuenga Pass and down on to Ventura Boulevard, past Studio City and Sherman Oaks and Encino. . . . Fast boys in stripped-down Fords shot in and out of the traffic streams, missing fenders by a sixteenth of an inch, but somehow always missing them. Tired men in dusty coupes and sedans winced and tightened their grip on the wheel and ploughed on north and west towards home and dinner, an evening with the sports page, the blatting of radio, the whining of their spoiled children and the gabble of their silly wives." Just as easily, Marlowe could have gone south on Highland, then swung east on Wilshire and kept going: past downtown, through Boyle Heights and East Los Angeles, leaving the city behind, moving southeast now, into what was the Twelfth Congressional District, through Montebello, and on to Whittier, perhaps even as far as Yorba Linda—why stop?—driving toward a different, but no less depleting home.

In either direction, there was the same emptiness for Marlowe to imagine and inhabit. What Whitman is to amativeness, Chandler is to anomie. "The United States themselves are essentially the greatest poem," Whitman wrote—and California, Chandler could have added, is the greatest tragedy. To reach a continent's end and discover in overabundance not eventfulness and grandeur but dailiness and the mundane, that is the reality he has his detective find—a reality all Marlowe's derring-do and fixation on that code of rightful conduct allow him (usually) to ignore. Seen in that light, the oppressions a man as able as Marlowe willingly puts up with in his line of work—no, he embraces them—may not seem like such a bad bargain. A dusty office, the occasional blow to the head: it's a small price to pay for the preservation of one's illusions. It is no small thing what terror of the great silent majority and the lives of quiet desperation its members lead might bring a man to do.

Of course, appreciation of them can do even greater things—as Richard Nixon's career so phenomenally attests. But to raise that career from Kiwanis lunches to Capitol Hill, and to do it in less than a decade, that required the intervention of an enormous and unprecedented force, a force that carried in its wake Richard Nixon's career, which it helped transform every bit as much as it transformed the Los Angeles basin. The Second World War changed everything. It altered America's social and political landscape and, in doing so, made inevitable a man like Nixon: a man without qualities from this place without qualities. It made a man like Marlowe obsolete. It made a place like Southern California the future—and by 1945 the basin would be an arsenal of democracy, the nation's second-largest manufacturing city, with 780,000 more inhabitants than it had had six years earlier, immeasurably wealthier than at decade's start and poised to be vastly wealthier still by decade's end. If only Walter Neff had waited, had had some patience, he could have enjoyed his fair share of it (*more* than his fair share). Instead, he ended up facing a murder rap. Richard Nixon, though, waited and, with Southern California about to boom as never before, he bided his time, going off first to wartime Washington to serve in the Office of Price Administration and then, having joined the navy, to the South Pacific, little aware how far that boom and all it wrought would help take him. Yes, the war would change everything.

George C. Scott and Henry Fonda

PATTON / MISTER ROBERTS

■■■■■■■■■■■■■■■■■■■■■■■■■■■■■■■■

That's the one place where they say, "Yes sir," instead of "Yes, but . . ."
RICHARD NIXON, AFTER CALLING THE PENTAGON TO GIVE AN ORDER TO
CHAIRMAN OF THE JOINT CHIEFS OF STAFFS ADMIRAL THOMAS MOORER[1]

Who gives a damn how many generals and admirals there are anyway?
NIXON, TO WHITE HOUSE MILITARY OFFICE DIRECTOR BILL GULLEY[2]

Had Marlowe in fact driven east, he'd likely have returned by a
more northerly route, the sights being far easier on the eye in the
Twelfth District's tonier precincts: San Gabriel, San Marino, South
Pasadena. New money in Los Angeles—real estate money, show
business money, Jewish money—settled on the city's West Side:
Beverly Hills, Brentwood, Bel Air, Holmby Hills, Pacific Palisades.
Older money had its enclaves elsewhere, east of Los Angeles, ab-
juring Pacific light and ocean breeze for an inland preserve,
closer to the desert and that much farther from the great urban
unwashed. Here lay what Kevin Starr calls "the absolute center of
the Southern California establishment."[3]

It was Pasadena, with its Tournament of Roses and Greene & Greene houses, that became a cynosure for gracious living in the basin. It was in San Marino that Henry E. Huntington, heir to the Southern Pacific Railroad fortune, had his 207-acre estate and priceless collection of books and manuscripts, the Huntington Library. And it was in San Gabriel, next to San Marino and about ten miles north of Whittier, that George Smith Patton, the scion of a prominent Virginia military family, chose to make his home after marrying the daughter of Benjamin D. Wilson, the first elected mayor of Los Angeles and owner of some twenty thousand acres of prime Southland property.

Patton's eminence befit the dowry of such a wife. He served as district attorney of Los Angeles County, was co-guarantor of the bond that brought the Pacific Electric trolley line to Whittier in 1903, and won the Democratic nomination for U.S. senator in 1916. He lost in November to Hiram Johnson, yet even had he won, George Smith Patton would remain best known today for an earlier accomplishment: fathering the most colorful, and controversial, general in U.S. history. Patton fils would also prove to be one of Richard Nixon's heroes, an admiration famously attested to in the spring of 1970 by the president's multiple viewings of the film version of the general's life. If there is one fact people know about Richard Nixon and Hollywood, it's that he loved *Patton*. Even Chou En-lai was aware of Nixon's enthusiasm for the film, going so far as to obtain a print to look for insights into the presidential character.[4]

Yet the film's protagonist figured in Nixon's career long before 1970 —before Nixon even had a career, really—for he and Patton once might have become political rivals. In October 1945 a groundswell sprang up to get the general the Republican nomination for the Twelfth District congressional seat in 1946. "'Old Blood and Guts' against blue-blooded, wealthy, left-wing Rep. H. Jerry Voorhis," argued the *Los Angeles Times* was "a political ten-strike if it could be done." The next day Patton scotched all such hopes, announcing his intention to "keep completely out of politics."[5] There but for the general's distaste for the democratic process, the world might never have heard of a passed-over congressional candidate named Richard M. Nixon.

Nixon, who at the time of the Patton boomlet was a navy lieutenant commander stationed in Maryland, had already been contacted by a prominent local Republican about running for Voorhis's seat and expressed eagerness at the prospect. Some residual gratitude toward its subject might have added to his enthusiasm for *Patton*. Not that he needed much encouragement: the man himself fascinated Nixon. A martial hero who spoke his mind and acted accordingly—macho, swaggering, impulsive—Patton was a Nixonian beau ideal: an example to aspire to, even if not (alas) a model to live by.

There was one area where Nixon could fully identify with Patton. Old Blood and Guts had had more than his share of troubles with the press. It was columnist Drew Pearson's publicizing the two incidents where Patton had slapped soldiers suffering from battle fatigue in 1943 that had created an international scandal—and directly led to Omar Bradley, rather than Patton, being chosen to command U.S. forces in the Allied invasion of Normandy. It was press reports about various belittling and/or bellicose comments Patton made about the Soviet Union that got him into more hot water than any battlefield action ever did. It was a postwar interview wherein he compared membership in the Nazi Party to affiliation with the Republican or Democratic Party that moved Eisenhower to relieve him of command of the U.S. Third Army. No surprise, then, that Patton should feel the press was out to get him. On Memorial Day in 1945, he visited a military cemetery in Germany. Crowded by a group of reporters, Patton indicated the grave site where he had just placed a ceremonial bouquet and announced, "That man died so bastards like you can continue to breed!"[6] How could Nixon not thrill to such an example?

The president's chief of staff, H. R. Haldeman, records Nixon spending a Camp David weekend "engrossed" in a Patton biography in April 1969 and, a month later, quoting the general's views on leadership to White House staffers. Apparently, the words had little effect, for in November Nixon was subjecting subordinates to the same Patton aperçu that "there are more tired division commanders than there are tired divisions."[7]

When *Patton* was released three months later, Nixon wasted little time in having it screened. He saw it on April 4 at the White House with his wife, daughter Julie, and son-in-law, David Eisenhower. Three weeks later he again watched it at the White House, this time in the company of Attorney General John Mitchell, Bebe Rebozo, and an unmoved Henry Kissinger. ("Inspiring as the film no doubt was," he noted in his memoirs, "I managed to escape for an hour in the middle of it to plan for the next day's NSC meeting.")[8] Nixon's passion for *Patton* remained unabated— "It comes up in every conversation," Secretary of State William Rogers told Darryl F. Zanuck, the head of 20th Century–Fox, which had released the film—and he saw it for a third, and final time, at Key Biscayne, on June 12, joined by Haldeman and Robert Finch.[9]

"He inspired people, charged them up," Nixon had remarked to Haldeman on April 7 about Patton, urging the film on his chief of staff. As we shall see in chapter 7, the need for inspiration and charging up was much on Nixon's mind that month. Three weeks later he would announce the invasion of Cambodia, telling a nationwide television audience, "If, when the chips are down, the world's most powerful nation, the United States of America, acts like a pitiful, helpless giant, the forces of totalitarianism and anarchy will threaten free nations and free institutions throughout the world," thereby plunging his administration into the worst crisis of Nixon's first term.

Old Blood and Guts, in what he did as in what he said, was anything but pitiful or helpless. At a time when Nixon felt beleaguered as never before—when he felt, rightly or wrongly, that the prospect of military defeat in Indochina was a real possibility—George C. Scott's personification of Patton offered boundless reassurance and support. "Americans play to win all the time," Scott declares in the celebrated speech that opens the film. "That's why Americans have never lost, and will never lose, a war." Such words carried real weight with a man who'd announced to congressional Republicans less than two years before, "I will not be the first president of the United States to lose a war."[10] When Nixon had made that statement, it recalled Churchill (another Nixon hero) and his famous declaration about not having become prime minister so as to preside over the dissolution of the British empire. Now it seemed a foreshadowing of Scott's Patton. The martial tale was wagging the presidential dog.

One must needs emphasize Scott here rather than Patton proper because the actor's rendering of the general, that most outsized of military heroes, dwarfs even the original. Not only did the real Patton lack the advantage of being photographed in 70 mm; he did not cut quite so bravura a figure as Scott does. Patton's world-class cussing did not sound forth in the compelling tones of the actor's magnificently gargly bark. In fact, Patton possessed what Kay Summersby, Eisenhower's wartime driver (and putative mistress), termed "the world's most unfortunate voice, a high-pitched womanish squeak."[11] It was a voice befitting a man his friends invariably called "Georgie," a less-than-heroic appellation used in the film only by Eisenhower's irritable chief of staff, General Walter Bedell Smith (Edward Binns), whose employing the diminutive is meant to seem sarcastic rather than affectionate. Nor does Scott's character suffer from any humanizing domestic attachments. He is apart and solitary, unto a god—no wife or children to be seen, and hardly any friends— whereas the actual Patton was surprisingly uxorious, devoted to his two daughters and son, and so convivial a personality his name regularly graced prewar society pages.

One also emphasizes Scott because while the general's reputation would have managed well enough without reliance on the actor's talents, the same cannot be said of the film that so strikingly utilizes them. *Patton* without Scott is as unthinkable as Watergate without Nixon. He commands the film no less absolutely than Patton commanded his troops, and it's difficult to say where the general's vainglory ends—and the actor's begins. This is one of the most overwhelming performances (if also among the least subtle) in Hollywood history. When Scott refused the Best Actor Oscar for his performance, it could almost be seen as the final act *in* his performance: at once dismissive toward the Academy and deferential toward his craft, it was just the sort of gleefully superior gesture Patton delighted in.

The role was an actor's dream. Just as war, in Clausewitz's renowned formulation, is politics by other means, so was Old Blood and Guts' career often dramaturgy by other means. What press agent could have improved upon that nickname? What costumer could have bettered his carefully chosen getup? (Not that his famed ivory-handled revolver was meant to be fired in anger.) When Eisenhower spoke of 'George's flair for the dramatic," he knew only too well whereof he spoke, for his legendary subordinate was as much actor as general: a melding of the two, really, the classic miles gloriosus (in the film, we even get to see him riding a white horse).[12]

Patton underscores this point, memorably so, with Scott's opening monologue, the one great sequence in what otherwise is a surprisingly spiritless film. A tour de force for Scott, it's just as much a tour de force for Patton, with the actor playing the part of the general playing the part of . . . well, it's hard to say exactly, so sui generis is the self-assigned role: warrior demigod? embodiment of the martial id? spirit of the eternal masculine? A giant U.S. flag fills the screen, like Pop Art wallpaper. Voices and ambient noise suggest the presence of an unseen audience. It's not in the theater, though, for when a voice calls out "Ten-HUT," we hear the unseen audience snap to. Then from a set of hidden steps emerges Patton, who comes to attention and salutes as a bugle plays "Reveille." He stands before us, stark against the flag, like a dive bomber about to come out of the sun and scream down on its targets.

The camera can't get enough of this improbable figure in full lord-high-supremo toilette—knee-length boots, jodhpurs, an impossibly gleaming helmet—and in a series of close-ups, it lingers almost sensually over Patton's bedizenments: first his eye (more glittering than all the rest of his regalia combined), then his rings and riding crop, his medals and braid, sash and decorations, that pistol (it's monogrammed), finally the stars and army insignia on his helmet. For the next five minutes, often in long shot, Patton rants, raves, and rains verbal destruction down on his audience: the ultimate coach ("An army is a team," he announces) in history's most overblown pep talk. It's the speech's bloodthirstiness and blue language ("We're going to murder those lousy Hun bastards by the bushel") that got all the attention when the film was released, but it's that ever-present flag—the unblinking eye of a bloodshot God?—that dominates the proceedings, and what sets the tone is that fetishistic cataloguing of Patton's accoutrements. The sequence verges on camp, and Patton comes perilously close to seeming like a reverse drag queen, parodistically masculine rather than feminine (later in the film, we'll see his orderly dress him as painstakingly as if the general were a menswear mannequin).

This is star power at its most breathtaking, as well as its most preposterous, an apparently seamless joining of actor and part. Yet the film's producer, Frank McCarthy, had been trying to get a picture made about Patton since 1951, and long before Scott came along for his lead he'd considered Rod Steiger, Spencer Tracy, Burt Lancaster, Robert Mitchum, and Lee Marvin.[13] Scott's best-known previous role was as another military man, Buck Turgidson, the bomb-happy, gum-chewing air force general in *Dr. Strangelove*, and the distance between the two characters isn't all that great. A year after *Patton* was released, Scott was the second choice—after Olivier!—for the title role in *The Godfather*. Turgidson to Patton to Corleone: one contemplates the possibility of the same actor playing such a uniquely American trio with something approaching awe.

Besides the power of his performance and the relentlessness of the character he plays, Scott's dominance has an additional source: the way the production has been weighted in his favor. *Patton* employs the proverbial cast of thousands, but they're almost entirely nameless, faceless. Even when a character is someone the audience recognizes—Montgomery, say, or Rommel—he's played by a nonentity. Karl Malden, as Omar Bradley, is the only other well-known actor in the film. Yet as if to make amends for enjoying such a singular status, Malden plays Bradley as if he, too, were a nonentity, a spongy foil to Scott's galvanic Patton. People always seem to be coming to see Patton, instead of the other way around, as if *he* were the one in charge of the Allies in Europe; and Bradley can at times seem like Eisenhower's personal Western Union messenger rather than Patton's immediate superior.

Of course, that's the whole point of the movie: Patton has no real superior, at least not as a fighting man, and he's made to suffer for his superiority. The only peers he has are the Nazis (Germans are *real* fighting men as, apparently, Americans and Britons are not). Certainly, they're the only ones who appreciate his true worth. "Would they sacrifice their best commander because he slapped a soldier?" the Nazi General Jodl asks. His dismissive "Humph!" gives the serious military man's response.

Patton does get sacrificed, though; and whether it be on the altar of human decency and military discipline or, as the film wants us to think, public opinion and bureaucratic spinelessness is for all intents and purposes moot. What matters is that Patton's misunderstood, underutilized, an outcast. He is, in a word, a rebel. This was 1970, after all, and the movie's official title, *Patton: A Salute to a Rebel*, did its best to exploit the tenor of the times. "Patton was a rebel before it became fashionable," the film's publicity poster declared. "He rebelled against the Establishment—and its ideas of warfare." In his way, Patton hated authority as much as the longhairs did—more, actually, since those in charge stood in the way of *his* being final authority. Old Blood and Guts may enforce the rules for everyone else (when a doctor in a field hospital explains his failure to wear a helmet by noting it prevents him from wearing a stethoscope, Patton tells him to cut a pair of holes in it), but he glories in breaking many of them himself. His paeans to battle make warfare sound like a giant head trip, and his belief in reincarnation and indulgence in poetasting—not to mention his love of garish costume—further mark him as a sort of proto-freak, albeit one who prefers firepower to flower power.

"It's a far-out movie passing as square," Pauline Kael shrewdly observed in her *New Yorker* review, "and finally passing over."[14] *Patton* succeeded in having it both ways, earning "right on's" from student audiences as well as multiple viewings at the White House, and as proof of its nonsectarian appeal, there were eight Academy Awards (including Best Picture) and the fourth-biggest grosses of 1970. "I can't see the reason why such fine young men get killed," a mournful Scott proclaims at one point in the film—a nod to doves that is immediately followed by a concession to hawks: "There are so many battles yet to fight." With something for everyone in the audience, *Patton* was part of an even larger balancing act, belligerent yin to the irreverent yang of another wildly popular war picture also released that year by Fox, *M*A*S*H*. The irony is that Scott's Patton makes Elliott Gould's Trapper John and Donald Sutherland's Hawkeye seem models of restraint by comparison.

Richard Nixon may have had little patience for any interpretation of modern warfare as hallucinogen or the creative use of costume as communication skill, but he did see himself as a bold and decisive outsider who loathed red tape and would do whatever it took to get results, from pulling all-nighters at Duke to using the CIA to put off the FBI's investigation of the Watergate break-in. Nixon's Nixon and Scott's Patton were can-do guys in an increasingly can't-do world. Call that being a rebel, or call it being a one-term president ("I would rather be a one-term president," he declared in the "pitiful, helpless giant" speech, than "see this nation accept the first defeat in its proud 190-year history"): it amounted to the same thing, so far as Nixon was concerned. "They have their schedule," Patton remarks of the U.S. Senate to a shocked Bradley early on in the movie, "and I have mine." Still smarting from the Senate's rejection of another of his Supreme Court nominees on April 8, three days after he saw the movie for the first time, Nixon must have liked hearing that one again at subsequent viewings.

His liberal critics said Nixon fastened on *Patton* as a way to stiffen his resolve to invade Cambodia. Besides being an implicit insult to Nixon's manhood (some men have to get their courage from a bottle—he had to get his from . . . a movie?), that interpretation is as unnuanced as Scott's performance. Whatever Nixon's failings, no one could say that a man who had stood up to mob violence as he had in Caracas during his 1958 tour of South America (the fourth of his six crises) lacked physical courage. At the same time, even Nixon's most fervent admirers have to admit that, from his mania for football to his lionizing of Teddy Roosevelt, he kept revealing an unbecoming obsession with manliness.

"What starts the process, really," he told a former aide a few months after resigning the presidency, "are laughs and slights and snubs when you are a kid."[15] And what ends the process—what redeems it, what justifies the suffering and certifies the victory—is revenge, the ultimate macho vindication. Nixon, the man who forgot nothing, wanted to avenge everything: *he* would show *them* (a free-floating, ubiquitous "them": schoolyard bullies, the Kennedys, whomever). How else account for what Kissinger, with his usual admixture of acuity and condescension when describing Nixon, termed his patron's "Walter Mitty dream of toughness," "his cult of the tough guy"?[16] He'd make up for the college student not good enough for the football varsity, the young lawyer meek enough to offer to drive his future wife to dates with other men, the vice president so put upon he could take "satisfaction"—and then boast of it—in kicking a demonstrator who spat in his face.[17]

Not only could a tough guy avenge such slights: he could remain impervious to their hurt. That was the idea, anyway—hence the appeal of a swaggery pose and the consistent need for muscle-flexing rhetoric: to say was to do; to say was to *prove* (here we find Walter Mitty at his most wishful). Heated debate with Khrushchev (the fifth crisis) became "cold steel between us all afternoon," seven hours of "virtual hand-to-hand combat."[18] Nixon sounds like Scott in the movie yearning to have it out with Rommel: two men, two tanks, one outcome. It's easy to dismiss such inflated language as self-serving hyperbole: cold war stories told with an eye on the ballot box. Except it was more than that. The worship of toughness came to influence everything—to *infect* everything—from Nixon's assessment of leaders to his taste in organ chorales. "I can't see the Russian people respecting wimps like that," he said to an aide after meeting Russian foreign minister Andrei Kozyrev in 1992. Sitting next to Gary Hart at Jacob Javits's funeral, he made conversation by observing of the musical program, "Bach is much better than Brahms. Because Bach is *tougher* than Brahms."[19] It became a way of political life and, ultimately, recipe for disaster. "Play it tough," Nixon can be heard telling Haldeman on the "smoking gun" tape, the recording of the June 23, 1972, conversation that finally forced him to resign. "That's the way they play it and that's the way we are going to play it." He didn't need *Patton* to get up the nerve to invade Cambodia. He needed *Patton* so he could enjoy the company of a kindred spirit.

Patton's deepest appeal for Nixon had to do with fighting old battles rather than girding for new ones. It took Garry Wills to note what should have been apparent to anyone who stopped to think about why that particular movie should so exercise this particular president: "*Patton* was not about male aggression satisfied, but about the baffling of a good man's energies—and by Eisenhower! Nixon was not bracing himself with vicarious aggression, but with shared rejection."[20] To be sure, Eisenhower is never seen in the movie, but he looms over it, an invisible-man version of that screen-filling flag. He is a name to be invoked, incorporeal and omnipotent: what Eisenhower wants, Eisenhower gets. Usually, it's Patton's hide. The movie sees him as the most onerous affliction—the paper-pusher as tormentor—that its fighting-man hero must bear. The film loves to personalize Patton's Second World War, to reduce it to a series of personalized duels: Rommel vs. Patton, Montgomery vs. Patton, even Patton vs. Patton. What goes unsaid is that the biggest joust of all pits Eisenhower vs. Patton.

In real life, the two men had a long, and extremely complicated, relationship. They had become close friends shortly after the First World War when stationed at Camp Meade, Maryland. Twenty years later, when Patton was given command of one of the army's first two armored divisions,

"Georgie" wrote "Ike" to ask if he'd like to serve under him as either chief of staff or a regimental commander. The latter eagerly accepted, only to be prevented by the army's chief of staff, George C. Marshall, who had bigger things in store for him. Within eighteen months, Eisenhower outranked Patton, and the dynamic of their relationship would never be the same.

Patton would have had to be superhuman not to feel at least some resentment. Making it far worse was the fundamental difference in their outlook and experience. The very model of a modern military bureaucrat, Eisenhower never held a combat command; he was the ultimate staff officer, as much politician as soldier. Patton was death on organization and process, "the pure warrior, a magnificent anachronism," as Captain Steiger (Siegfried Rauch), the German officer assigned to compile a dossier on Patton, calls him in the movie. There wasn't a politic bone in Old Blood and Guts' body, a fact he knew and gloried in. "I have no political ambitions after the war," Scott's Patton announces, accurately reflecting his character's views . . . but not those of certain other generals? The dig at Eisenhower is left unstated. The real Patton made it explicit. Ike had the "style of an office seeker rather than that of a soldier," he noted in his diary shortly after D-day. "I try to arouse fighting emotion—he tries [to get] votes." That view of the supreme commander as supreme politician crystallized over the next eighteen months, and on his deathbed Patton was heard to say of his former friend, "I hope he makes a better President than he was a General."[21]

They represent the two polarities of the U.S. military tradition, which might alternately be expressed as Eisenhower/MacArthur or Bradley/Patton: Roundhead vs. Cavalier, paleface vs. redskin, sensible citizen-soldier vs. flamboyant professional warlord. A nation that has as one of its founding principles "no standing armies" while also owing its very existence (and its continent-spanning expansion) to the force of arms must needs have a highly conflicted view of its military. On the one hand, the public has always distrusted the armed forces—they're hierarchical, regimented, conformist—as something alien to democratic society. On the other hand, that very foreign quality has made the military seem exotic, impressive, thrilling even. In an Eisenhower or Bradley, the public liked to think it could see itself writ large and thus be reassured that the military was representative of the society as a whole. In a Patton or MacArthur, the public liked to think it could see itself written out of the picture and thus be reassured as to the military's essential anomalousness. "Don't see how a country can produce such men as Robert E. Lee, John J. Pershing,

Eisenhower and Bradley and at the same time produce Custers, Pattons and MacArthurs," Harry Truman once complained in his diary.[22] What he failed to realize was that such seeming irreconcilability made perfect sense. Its two warrior traditions allowed the United States to have things both ways: depending on the military even as it distrusted the military.

In the choosing up of sides over conduct of the American way of war, Nixon once again demonstrated how antipathetic he and Truman were, for he very much preferred what he once described to Kissinger and his deputy, Alexander Haig, as "the unconventional brilliance of Patton and MacArthur" to the more reassuring (and plodding) efforts of a Bradley or Pershing.[23] Abidingly Roundhead in personal style as well as political belief, Richard Nixon was nonetheless fervently Cavalier in armchair generalship. There were several reasons for such a seeming contradiction. The full-blown bellicosity of the Cavalier tradition had a forbidden-fruit attraction for a birthright member of the Society of Friends—especially one who, in his early political campaigns, gloried in the epithet "Fighting Quaker." Nixon also had a weakness for hero worship, and few figures in our history have played to such a weakness more shamelessly (or effectively) than Patton and MacArthur. More directly, as commander in chief, he had firsthand experience of just how maddeningly conventional can be the Pentagon (that citadel of by-the-book Roundheadedness). Above all, there were the myriad indignities Nixon had had to suffer at the hands of his foremost—and most reluctant—political patron, someone who had hamstrung Patton even as he would later denounce something he described as "the military-industrial complex": that great, grinning Roundhead, Dwight David Eisenhower.

Nixon's first sight of Eisenhower came during a Manhattan ticker-tape parade. It would prove prophetic: the lieutenant commander lost in the crowd; the five-star general acclaimed and distant. At a time when Eisenhower's estimation of him continued to have appreciable consequences, Nixon still couldn't keep himself from noting in *Six Crises* that during eight years of loyal service as vice president, "I remember him thanking me personally" all of three times.[24] It's hard to say which is a more telling commentary on their relationship: Ike's being so unforthcoming or Nixon's needing to call attention to it.

He got a taste of what the next eight years would hold when he visited with Eisenhower at a Colorado resort shortly after the 1952 Republican convention. Having put Nixon to work peeling potatoes, Ike then ordered his running mate to don fishing gear and join him in a trout stream. Nixon, who had never fished before and kept fouling his line, was made to look and feel like a fool. Nixon's was not to reason why, though, and Eisenhower's treatment of him that day was the first indication he would have of what was to be the fundamental dynamic between them: what he called Eisenhower's "great capacity for friendliness" notwithstanding, Ike "also had a quality of reserve which, at least subconsciously, tended to make a visitor feel like a junior officer coming in to see the commanding General."[25] Agreeable though it undoubtedly is to discover reservoirs of amiability in a world leader, no imaginable amount of friendliness can make a United States senator—let alone a vice president—enjoy being made to feel like a junior officer. Worse, Eisenhower not only had a knack for making Nixon look bad; he seemed to relish it.

The classic instance of this came just a few weeks after the fishing scene: the fund crisis. What everyone remembers about the crisis is its denouement, Nixon's Checkers speech. What tends to get overlooked are the circumstances necessitating the speech: the way Eisenhower had spent the better part of a week letting his running mate twist slowly, slowly, in the political wind. He would neither stand by Nixon nor come right out and replace him. Instead, he let various intermediaries intimate that it might well be for the best if Nixon decided to remove himself (the most egregious of these "helpful suggestions," a phone call from Governor Dewey urging Nixon to resign, came but an hour before he was to deliver his speech). At one point, Nixon became so frustrated with Eisenhower's aloofness that he lectured him, "There comes a time in matters like this when you've either got to shit or get off the pot." It did no good, and only the public's overwhelmingly favorable response to the speech forced Eisenhower's hand. He no longer had any choice: he had to support Nixon, whether he liked it or not.*

Their relationship never got over Checkers. How could Nixon ever trust the man who had hung him out to dry so publicly? Twenty years later the memory still rankled. "That's what Eisenhower—that's all he cared about. He only cared about—Christ, 'Be sure he was clean,'" Nixon complained to John Mitchell on March 22, 1973. Yet how could Eisenhower ever warm to someone who had come so perilously close to tarnishing the general's reputation? Worse, there were Nixon's twin acts of lèse-majesté: that scatological injunction (*no one* talked to General of the Armies Dwight D. Eisenhower that way, least of all an overeager junior senator), then the way Nixon had put Ike on the spot by urging in his

*Not that it was any consolation, but the fund crisis at least brought Nixon and Patton together, if only in Eisenhower's mind. Ike compared the Checkers affair to the slapping incidents, as each man "had made a mistake and been forgiven."

speech that all the other national candidates release their financial information, too. Nixon felt he'd been sold down the river, even as Eisenhower (who at the time he'd signed off on Nixon's vice-presidential nomination had thought his running mate several years older than his actual age of thirty-nine) felt he'd been sold a bill of goods.

Bill of goods or no, Eisenhower recognized a fait accompli when he saw one. The day after the speech, he summoned Nixon to join him in Wheeling, West Virginia, where the general was scheduled to give a campaign address, greeting his newly refurbished running mate with the enthusiastic declaration, "You're my boy." That's what Nixon was to remain for him: a boy, someone to patronize, put up with, assign chores to. (On three separate occasions, in 1958, 1964, and 1967—when Nixon was, respectively, forty-five, fifty-one, and fifty-four years old—Eisenhower told the same friend, "You know, Dick has matured.")[26] Little wonder Nixon broke down in tears at the sound of Eisenhower's words. Now that it was expedient to do so, the prodigal had been welcomed back to the bosom of his father.

The complexity of Patton and Eisenhower's relations was as nothing compared to those between Nixon and Eisenhower. It was Ike who'd brought him within reach of the presidency—and it was Ike who frequently appeared to be doing his best to remove it from reach, time and again making Nixon appear ridiculous, malicious, or both to the American people. Prior to becoming vice president, Nixon's image had been that of a vigorously take-charge leader: the political tyro who'd pummeled two nationally known opponents, first Voorhis and then, four years later, Douglas; the tough-minded anti-communist who'd gotten Alger Hiss; the sharp operator who at the 1952 convention had somehow managed to cozen the Warren forces, placate the Taft forces, and satisfy the Eisenhower forces, and all in such a way as to win himself a place on the national ticket. Yet this was the same man who, less than a decade later, had become such a figure of ridicule that *Esquire* could build its annual "Dubious Achievement Awards" around a photograph of him captioned, "Why is this man laughing?" The question became a national catchphrase, one more in the catalog of Nixon embarrassments. No publication would ever have thought to do such a thing until Ike got his hands on him, saddling Nixon with the faintly ludicrous image that would bedevil him to the end of his days.

Nixon was Ike's errand runner, his hatchet man, the butt of a seemingly inexhaustible stream of slights and snubs. It wasn't just that Eisenhower kept him at arm's length (that came with the territory as vice president), but that he seemed to take such satisfaction in doing it, and doing it so publicly. There was the unconscionable way he made Nixon stew over whether or not he'd remain on the ticket in 1956. Or his notorious answer during the 1960 campaign to a reporter's question about "what major decisions of your administration" his vice president had participated in: "If you give me a week, I might think of one." That response did Nixon real damage, and Eisenhower came to regret it—though his failure to watch the first Nixon-Kennedy debate indicates just how ambivalent he was toward Nixon's succeeding him.[27] And what might have been the worst damage he did Nixon was unconscious. Paul Nitze, who briefly served in Ike's State Department and played a key role on Nixon's SALT I negotiating team, declares in his memoirs that it was the example of Eisenhower's duplicity (as Nitze saw it) that paved the way for Nixon's fall during Watergate. "Considering himself to be generally more intelligent than Mr. Eisenhower, he reasoned that if Ike could reconcile two mutually inconsistent propositions, he could do so with three or four or even more."[28]

Eisenhower's personal treatment of Nixon was even worse—and quite purposeful. "I wouldn't have him on the place," Harold Macmillan remembered Eisenhower telling him of Nixon's bootless quest to spend a weekend at Camp David.[29] Or there was the campaign picnic at Eisenhower's Gettysburg farm in 1956 when the president turned to a companion and announced, "Did you hear that? Dick says he's never seen the inside of the house here!" It's not the lack of an invitation that's necessarily so striking; it's that Eisenhower neither saw anything unusual about it nor realized that it might be a sensitive matter for his vice president. Why would he want to have *Nixon* inside his home?[30] The president never invited the Nixons to his White House residence. Conversely, he and Mamie managed to avoid visiting chez Nixon until the end of 1958.

One can hardly imagine the delicacy, or duration, of the negotiations conducted before that event could take place. Each man needed the other—without Ike, Nixon was just a youngish former senator; without Nixon, Eisenhower was vulnerable to the GOP's right wing and unprotected on Capitol Hill—and that mutual need made their relationship all the more intricate, all the more perplexing. A sense of how lethally polite was the minuet the two men danced comes across in this passage from *Six Crises*: "He never ordered me to do something. He would wonder aloud if I might like to take over this or that project, always couching his recommendations in terms which would cause no embarrassment to either of us if I preferred to say no. There was, of course, never an occasion when

I did not willingly accept the assignments he suggested."[31] Rarely has trigger pulling so much resembled teeth pulling (after you had the gun, Alphonse; after you aim it, Gaston).

"He was not the kind of man who appreciated undue familiarity," Nixon would write of Eisenhower in his memoirs, putting the best face possible on Ike's keeping his distance.[32] Still, he nursed the memory of how he'd been treated, refusing to let the wounds heal. Almost a quarter century after Ike's death, Nixon continued to complain. "Eisenhower was bigger than life," he told an aide in 1991, which only made it all the more dismaying that "he could also be a pretty petty guy. He held grudges and was so protective of himself politically sometimes that he didn't stand up for the people who had served him loyally." He "tried to protect himself, but often at the expense of screwing those closest to him."[33] It doesn't require much imagination to figure out whom Nixon meant by "the people who had served him loyally" and "those closest to him."

Note, however, the refusal to unleash a full assault. Nixon concedes Eisenhower was "bigger than life" and was only "pretty" petty. Always there was a balance in Nixon's assessments, an attachment to both sides of his love-hate view of Ike. In *RN*, he writes that "the best description I can give of Dwight Eisenhower is that he had a warm smile and icy blue eyes."[34] In *Six Crises,* there is the rather astounding description of Ike as "a far more complex and devious man than most people realized, and in the best sense of those words."[35] The taking away (the nation's grandfatherly ex-president "devious"!) followed by the almost instantaneous giving back ("and in the best sense"): here we find epitomized Nixon's hopelessly tangled attitude toward Eisenhower, an attitude even more tangled than Eisenhower's toward him.

For while, yes, he used Nixon badly—far more humiliating than that, in fact, Ike used him badly so *casually*—he did keep him as a running mate in 1952 and 1956, support him for president in 1960 and 1968, and would like to have supported him in 1964 as a GOP unity candidate against Goldwater. He was on record as calling Nixon "the most valuable member of my team" and "one . . . of the great leaders of men"; and while a president is never under oath when offering public praise, it's also true that Milton Eisenhower, who was perhaps Ike's closest confidant (as well as someone not necessarily predisposed to admire Richard Nixon), declared that his brother's "confidence in Nixon was unquestioned."[36]

So Eisenhower did his own giving and taking away where the other man was concerned. In neither action, however, was it personal for Eisenhower, who never cared what Nixon felt about him. This simply made it all the harder for Nixon to take, since he clearly did care about Eisenhower's opinion. The man who had raised him up on high could, and did, bring him down as might no other. "It is not telling tales out of school," Ralph de Toledano wrote in 1968, that as a result of Eisenhower's consistently high-handed treatment, "Nixon would return from meetings of the National Security Council to his offices in the Senate Office Building as close to tears as any grown man can be."[37] There's only one source de Toledano could have had for such a personal description—and it's a sign of the degree of hurt that the source would be so forthcoming about his feelings. This was one area where even Nixon couldn't quite control his emotions, for Ike wasn't just the nation's father figure; he was Nixon's, too, and toward him Nixon exhibited a blend of almost filial devotion and near-parricidal bitterness.

On the one hand, he might speak of Eisenhower (privately, to be sure) as "a senile old bastard" after Ike endorsed Goldwater in 1964.[38] Or he might express his disdain (again, in private) by assigning Eisenhower to the same niche in a taxonomy of previous chief executives as so dim a predecessor as William McKinley.[39] Less overtly, yet this time quite publicly, Nixon could fail to include Eisenhower in his book *Leaders*; an omission underscored by the presence of a chapter on MacArthur (that weakness for Cavaliers again), whom Ike had served as an aide and come to detest.

Yet he could never bring himself to blast Eisenhower outright. Certainly, he could never disown him. The bond was too deep, the yearning for approval too strong. "And I say let's win this one for Ike," he declared in his acceptance speech at the 1968 convention. As was so often the case with Nixon's public utterances, he was being both self-serving and sincere—clutching at the coattails of the most popular living American, yet also humbling himself as he indulged in the political equivalent of ancestor worship. Nine months later news of Eisenhower's death moved Nixon to tears (the tears he'd felt welling up after those NSC meetings at long last emerging?), and that afternoon he wept openly in front of Haldeman, Rogers, Kissinger, and others in the Oval Office. "He was such a strong man," Nixon sobbed to Haldeman.[40] That was high praise, indeed, coming from such an aficionado of toughness, yet surpassing even that compliment was the act of shedding tears. So emotionally inhibited a man could offer no greater tribute. It's unthinkable that any other figure outside his family might have affected Nixon so.

Then again, at the end of Eisenhower's life, he and Nixon did become relatives, or at least their families were joined, in a dynastic union that finally made real the symbolic patrilineal association between them. When Britain's Prince Charles and Princess Anne visited Washington in 1970, press reports highlighted the amount of time Charles was scheduled to spend in Tricia Nixon's company, and even the prince found himself wondering whether the president might be hoping to effect a match.[41] What such speculation ignored was that a Nixon marrying into the House of Windsor was but a Graustarkian reverie as compared to the far sweeter reality of a Nixon having married into the House of Eisenhower. Yes, there was the opening to China, as well as détente with the Soviet Union, the Vietnamese peace accords, and the landslide victory in 1972, but at some wholly personal, wholly visceral level, wasn't Nixon's most gratifying triumph the marriage of his younger daughter to Dwight David Eisenhower II? This was the ultimate acceptance—or as close to it as Nixon was ever likely to get. He liked to say that "peacemaker" was the title he most wanted to earn as president. Yet being known as "General Eisenhower's grandson's father-in-law," as he was heard on occasion to introduce himself, could not have been far behind.[42] After Ike's death, this process of Nixon becoming an honorary Eisenhower took on a life of its own as Ike's widow, Mamie, became akin to a maiden aunt in the Nixon family, frequently dining at the White House and spending weekends at Camp David. If Nixon couldn't be an actual Eisenhower scion—and he made a point of naming Ike's real-life son, John Eisenhower, his ambassador to Belgium—he could at least make Mamie part of *his* family.

Nixon's ambivalence toward Eisenhower mirrored his feelings toward military leaders generally. Part of the reason he so admired Patton and MacArthur was their anomalousness. What Nixon considered the typical general to be like can be gathered from an observation recorded in his journal after meeting with Ike while on a European fact-finding mission in 1947: "Eisenhower of all the generals had the abilities of a military man with none of their stupidities."[43] Nixon prized the abilities of a military man, no question. He exalted the martial virtues—loyalty, courage, sacrifice—the Cavalier virtues. But Roundhead virtues—those most often characteristic of U.S. military leaders: deliberation, deference, thoroughness—amounted in his eyes to so many stupidities. Nixon revered what the military stood for and esteemed what it could do. Yet he scorned the way the military went about doing it.

There is no clearer demonstration of this than the stratospheric ascent of Alexander Meigs Haig Jr., the army colonel who used the access he had gained to Nixon through his service on the National Security Council to earn, in Roger Morris's acid formulation, "four stars in four years" ("promotions," Morris notes, "comparable only to Dwight Eisenhower's in the tumult of World War II").[44] Haig's progress concluded with a rush, as Nixon vaulted him over 240 senior officers and skipped the intervening rank of lieutenant general in promoting him from major general to full general in 1973. Yet even that elevation pales by comparison to what the president had wanted to do two years before during the disastrous South Vietnamese incursion into Laos. According to Haig, an enraged Nixon ordered him, "Go pack a bag. Then get on the first available plane and fly to Saigon. You're taking command." Even Haig, equally attentive to his master's wishes and his own advancement, was shocked by the prospect of a mere brigadier replacing a four-star general, Creighton Abrams. "Good God, Mr. President," he exclaimed, "you can't do that!"*

Nixon was ultimately dissuaded, but the impulse was telling. For all that he professed to honor the soldierly values—valor, duty, selflessness—he almost gleefully flouted the fundamental military virtue, respect for the chain of command. Elmo Zumwalt, chief of naval operations from 1970 to 1974, likened the treatment the Joint Chiefs of Staff received at their annual meetings with Nixon to that accorded "performing poodles or trained seals."[45] To be sure, the Joint Chiefs treated Nixon even more outrageously, going so far as to assign a navy yeoman working for the NSC to pilfer secret documents for them. Nixon's pronouncement on the incident in his memoirs—"spying on the White House for the Joint Chiefs is something that I would not particularly be surprised at, although I don't think it's a healthy practice"—is a model of bland understatement.[46] If such behavior didn't confirm his suspicions about the top brass, nothing could.

As a citizen-serviceman during the Second World War, Nixon had had ample opportunity to shed any schoolboy illusions about the infallibility of admirals and generals, and his experience with the military bureaucracy made him deeply suspicious of the officer class generally. Then as commander in chief during the Vietnam War, he had even more ample opportunity to gain a jaundiced view of the military hierarchy. A spying yeoman here or there was ultimately trivial compared with the far more vexing problem of simply fighting the war. The brass, Nixon came to feel, were as much politicians as soldiers. "One of the most frustrating prob-

---

*"I will not pretend I was not tempted," Haig admits in his memoirs. Characteristically eschewing false modesty, he adds, "I had no doubt I could do the job." Alexander M. Haig Jr., with Charles McCarry, *Inner Circles: How America Changed the World: A Memoir* (New York: Warner Books, 1992), p. 275.

lems I had to deal with in conducting the war," he wrote in his book *No More Vietnams*, was "the tendency of our armed forces to confuse *military* analysis with *political* analysis. . . . The fashionable idea that all military leaders are superhawks who will generally take bold and even rash action has no basis in fact. It has been my experience that professional military leaders are by training and instinct cautious and seldom advise bold action. The Pattons and LeMays are not the rule but the exceptions."[47] One can almost hear the sigh at the end of that last sentence. Nixon knew he was a better politician than anyone in the Pentagon, and he increasingly came to suspect he was a better military leader. During the 1972 North Vietnamese spring offensive, he complained in his diary, "I am so disgusted with the military's failing to come up with any idea, and failing to follow through."[48] It was a refrain he had sounded throughout his first term—the Pentagon's lack of daring and imagination, its negativism and standpat attitude—and it drove him to distraction.

Before taking office, Nixon had sworn that he would never get bogged down in micromanaging the war as Lyndon Johnson had. LBJ had ended up jabbing his finger at maps of North Vietnam, personally selecting bombing targets, a neophyte tactician in chief. Yet Nixon had also sworn not to get bogged down in the war, period, a pledge mocked by the four years he took to end U.S. involvement. By the time of the Christmas bombing of North Vietnam in 1972, he found himself recapitulating Johnson's experience, trying to be his own LeMay. On December 28, he congratulated himself in his diary for having "raised holy hell about the fact that they kept going over the same targets at the same time. . . . Finally, we got the military to change their minds."[49] The B-52s would go where *he* wanted them to. It seemed an endless struggle to Nixon, and endlessly frustrating: not so much the war in Vietnam as the war with his own military.

Further complicating his response to the Pentagon was Nixon's being, as he later described it, "Commander in Chief at what was perhaps the most troubled time in the history of our armed forces."[50] Nixon's aggressive response to this situation helped obscure his own generally critical views of the defense establishment, views he decisively acted upon. Nixon's rally-round-the-flag tributes to the armed forces in this "most troubled time" in their history cannot hide an inescapable conclusion concerning their degraded state in the first half of the 1970s. In the words of Stephen Ambrose, a leading military historian as well as Nixon's most comprehensive biographer, "It was his own fault."[51]

True, Nixon delighted in high-profile gestures—the military equivalent of flag lapel pins—meant to show how strongly he backed the armed forces: ordering that army Lieutenant William Calley be confined to quarters, rather than placed in a stockade, after receiving his life sentence for the My Lai massacre; hosting a dinner at the White House on May 29, 1973, for all 591 prisoners of war who had been held in North Vietnam and their families. At the same time, he further encouraged the military's exclusion from U.S. society by ending the draft in 1971 and instituting an all-volunteer military. The move was politically popular, but for years to come would lower the overall quality of service personnel. Far more significant, Nixon directly contributed to the U.S. armed forces' declining effectiveness by reducing defense spending in each of the six budgets he submitted to Congress. Even factoring in the substantial savings derived from the ongoing U.S. withdrawal from Indochina, these cuts verged on the drastic. Pentagon outlays (in constant 1981 dollars) bottomed out in fiscal year 1975, the last budgetary year Nixon was responsible for, at $133.8 billion—$2.8 billion less than they had been in 1960![52] Unwilling to put his money where his mouth was, Nixon wanted to have it both ways: to act tough, sound decisive, throw his weight around—and do it on the cheap. His ideal was a Hollywood version of the military, one where orders could be conveniently disobeyed, victory was assured, and box-office receipts always recovered costs.

This was a John Wayne vision of war: vivid, stirring, beguilingly fictive. Even more than Scott's ivory-handled rebel, the Duke was a Nixon idol—as his nickname indicates, an American Wellington, another blueblood of military prowess to join the line of Nixon's beloved Cavalier soldier-aristocrats—the ultimate movie he-man, sans peur et sans reproche, a figure (dare one say it?) to out-Patton *Patton*. In his celebrated 1971 essay, "The Political Theatre of John Wayne," Eric Bentley called the actor "the most important American of our time" because of his influence on—indeed, his providing a literal embodiment of—the United States' image of itself. Bentley did not mean this description as a compliment. Nor did he wish to flatter when he wrote that "if Wayne was the icon, Nixon has long been the iconographer." Yet it's hard to imagine a statement that could have gratified Nixon more—other than Bentley's concluding assertion: "If John Wayne is the artist a President like Nixon deserves, Nixon is the President a nation of John Waynes would deserve."[53]

Pleasing though Nixon might have found such a statement to be, it was nonetheless absurd: for how could there be a nation of John Waynes? There was only one John Wayne, and no one knew that better than

Nixon. The Duke was Nixon's favorite movie star—hands down (according to Kissinger, he was Brezhnev's favorite, too).[54] How could it have been otherwise? Nixon liked Westerns and action pictures and made no secret of favoring just the sort of manly, larger-than-life heroes—Pattons on the hoof?—Wayne specialized in. Nor did Wayne's super-patriot politics detract from his appeal. Not hardly: as Garry Wills has written, "Nixon had *policies*, but beneath those positions were the *values* Wayne exemplified."[55]

A month before the actor won the Best Acting Oscar for *True Grit* (1969), Nixon sent him a fan letter. "Dear Duke: I have been delighted to read the rave reviews. . . . I saw it in the W.H. with my family and for once we agree with the critics—you were great!"[56] After Wayne won, Nixon called to congratulate him. "The whole family watched the Awards and I just want to tell you I'm proud of you—on the screen and off."[57] In all, Nixon saw twenty-five Wayne movies during his presidency ranging from such classics as *Stagecoach* and *The Searchers* (1956) to the most incongruous feature title in Wayne's filmography, *The Conqueror* (1956), in which an understandably bewildered Duke plays Genghis Khan.

One of those twenty-five, *Chisum* (1970) got Nixon into even bigger trouble than *Patton* did. Three months after the Cambodian incursion, while speaking extemporaneously in Denver about criminal justice, Nixon chose to use this "very good Western" as an illustrative text. He had seen the film the previous weekend, he announced, and clearly it had made an impression on him with a message that he construed to be "there was a time when there was no law. But the law eventually came and the law was important from the standpoint of not only prosecuting the guilty, but also seeing that those who were guilty had a proper trial."[58]

Not only was turning to John Wayne for a jurisprudential role model somewhat unusual (even for Nixon), but to cite this particular film as any sort of legal exemplum makes as much sense as Wayne's casting in *The Conqueror*. His title character, a wealthy rancher in territorial New Mexico, takes the law into his own hands when a villainous local merchant (Forrest Tucker) tries to pull off a major land grab. "If he does it," an admiring federal magistrate says of Wayne as the star rides off at the head of a hastily gathered posse, "it'll be legal." It's not that the things Wayne does are themselves legal; it's that *Wayne's* doing them makes them so. *Chisum* is a movie of neither laws nor man, but of one particular man. "I'm not going to the sheriff, the governor, or the president of the United States," he tells Tucker. "I'm coming after *you*." Equal justice under Duke might serve as the film's motto, and it's a mark of just how smitten Nixon was with the Wayne persona that he could laud such a primitive conception of the law—let alone be willing to make himself appear so foolish by publicly saying so.

Nixon had never been one to disguise his enthusiasm for Wayne, or Wayne his for Nixon. "I want to thank you, Mr. President, not for any one thing, just for everything," the actor said before the assembled gathering at the White House gala on May 23, 1973, honoring the prisoners of war returned from North Vietnam.[59] The two men enjoyed a personal relationship, albeit more mutual admiration society than friendship. Its roots lay in the shared ardor of their anti-communism. Wayne had supported Nixon against Voorhis in 1946. Five years later Nixon repaid the favor, taking to the Senate floor to enter into the *Congressional Record* praise for Wayne's *Flying Leathernecks* ("an original story portraying the immortal achievements of our Marine Corps air arm").[60] Wayne sought Nixon's endorsement for his 1960 blockbuster, *The Alamo*, and scheduled its world premiere in San Antonio for the end of October, hoping that the film's patriotic message would assist Nixon's electoral chances. Wayne saw to it that advertisements for the film included the line, "There were no ghostwriters at the Alamo"—a none-too-subtle gibe at the authorship of *Profiles in Courage*.[61] As it happened, Nixon lost Texas—though that owed less to Wayne than to Lyndon Johnson's presence on the Democratic ticket.*

Wayne spoke at the 1968 and 1972 Republican National Conventions and recorded radio ads on Nixon's behalf. Once in office, the president was enraged to find that the Internal Revenue Service was auditing Wayne's tax returns.[62] Détente put their relationship to the test—Wayne wrote Nixon in October 1971 to criticize the China trip, which he characterized as "a real shocker." The president hastened to reassure him that "we have no intention of abandoning Taiwan," and the actor remained firmly in Nixon's camp.[63] Yet after initially dismissing Watergate as a frame-up by "those bastards!" in the press, Wayne became increasingly perplexed. He asked Nixon over dinner at San Clemente in January 1974 what was going on. The president assured him he was blameless. Eight months later, when the "smoking gun" tape was released, a shocked Wayne blurted out, "Damn. He lied to me."[64]

Nixon had lied to Wayne, yes, and to all Americans, but it's not too much to say that Wayne had himself lied to Nixon and the rest of Amer-

---

*Not that Wayne was much of a judge of the political impact of his work: eight years later he predicted in a *Variety* interview that his second directorial effort, *The Green Berets*, "will help re-elect LBJ."

ica—or, one might more accurately say, lived a lie. The super-hawk, super-patriot, super-soldier superstar had been thirty-four when the Japanese bombed Pearl Harbor, married, and as the father of four young children, exempt from the draft. Yet so were such other overage stars as Clark Gable, James Stewart, Robert Montgomery, and Henry Fonda. They all enlisted. Wayne did not. His great ongoing role as Hollywood's supreme military hero was just that: a role, something with as much basis in reality as Groucho's greasepaint mustache or Francis the Talking Mule's powers of speech. The irony is that while Richard Nixon may have wanted in his heart of hearts to be John Wayne, his own wartime service demonstrated far more heroism than anything the actor ever did.

To be sure, Nixon was no war hero as, say, John F. Kennedy or George H. W. Bush was. He never fired a shot in anger, and his war consisted almost entirely of simply getting by and doing what needed to be done: sweat and toil, with no blood and a minimum of tears. After receiving his commission in October 1942, Ensign Nixon spent an unhappy seven months at Ottumwa Naval Air Station in Iowa doing office work before being posted to the South Pacific Combat Air Transport Command. Over the course of the next thirteen months, he would do his own less exalted version of MacArthur's island-hopping, supervising the loading and unloading of transport planes on Espíritu Santu, New Caledonia, Guadalcanal, Vella Lavella, Bougainville, and Green Island. It was demanding work, but not dangerous. Though the Southwest Pacific was a combat area, the airstrips where Nixon was based tended to be on the fringes of battle. The occasional shelling and air raids he had to endure were more annoyance than hazard. "The only things that really bother me," he wrote his mother, "are lack of sleep and the centipedes."[65] Back in the States, he spent the rest of his navy service doing legal work in San Francisco and on the East Coast.

It wasn't for lack of trying that Nixon had such an uneventful war. He later recalled how he had "wanted to get where the action was" and "spent a lot of my time trying to get a battle-station assignment."[66] He listed "Ships and Stations" as his first choice when he got out of officer training school. At Ottumwa he applied for sea duty. Still, the most heroic thing about Nixon's military career was the simple fact of his having served. He didn't have to; like Wayne, he was exempt from the draft. As a Quaker, he could have easily obtained conscientious-objector status. Furthermore, he had been making a contribution to the war effort outside the service, having joined the Office of Price Administration as a lawyer in Washington in January 1942.

Even so, Nixon felt uncomfortable not serving in the military. The OPA's dirigiste activities left him uneasy (even if not so uneasy as to keep him twenty-nine years later from being the only peacetime president to impose war-and-price controls). He chafed at being a part of the bureaucracy and did not fit in with his mostly New Dealer colleagues. There were also future considerations to ponder. Nixon had come very close to running for a California state assembly seat in 1940, and it took no great insight to realize that a candidate who wasn't a veteran would be at a distinct disadvantage in postwar politics.

Running against Voorhis in 1946, Nixon made a point of calling attention to his military service. His stump speech featured a promise "to preserve our sacred heritage, in the name of my buddies and your loved ones, who died that these might endure."[67] Such talk underscored that Nixon hadn't been a stay-at-home or slacker. It also implicitly reminded voters of what Nixon's campaign literature made explicit: the incumbent had "stayed safely behind the front in Washington" while his opponent, "a clean, forthright young American . . . fought in defense of his country in the stinking mud and jungles of the Solomons."[68] Not wanting to miss any opportunity to drive home this point, Nixon had originally intended to campaign in his old uniform, until it was pointed out to him that there were many more former soldiers and sailors than former officers. As soon as he could, he switched to mufti, though initially he *needed* to campaign in uniform: Pat had given away all Nixon's old suits to a cousin while he was in the Pacific. (In 1960, up against an honest-to-goodness war hero, Nixon had to swallow a dose of his own medicine. A campaign poster announcing "I Served" showed him at attention in a dress-blue uniform, a far cry from its Kennedy counterpart, which depicted Nixon's opponent at the helm of PT-109, shirtless and smiling in sunglasses and cap.)[69]

Yet the overriding reason behind Nixon's enlistment transcended any workplace unhappiness or even political calculation. His country in peril, Richard Nixon answered its call. It was as clear-cut as that, a motivation common to millions of other Americans of his generation. In a way that seems barely credible today, patriotism was simply a given. Serving one's country was a duty to honor, not an issue to debate.

After 1945 the widespread affluence victory brought in its wake, followed by the social turmoil affluence brought in *its* wake, first segmented and then fractured the society in such a way that a roll-up-your-sleeves, get-the-job-done effort spanning the political spectrum and uniting all classes became no longer tenable. The sheer exhilaration of such an experience and its impact on an individual participant are hard to exaggerate, and Richard Nixon felt this no less than his comrades did. For all that was onerous about his war experience—"Life is first boredom, then fear," that mordant summation of human existence in Philip Larkin's poem "Dockery and Son," conveys the essence of Nixon's time overseas—the larger memory of it was something to cherish. The war came to have happy associations for him, and reminders of what that time had been like provided ways of escape. His favorite play was *South Pacific* (1949). Thirty-three of the films he watched while president were about the war or had a wartime setting. One of them was *Victory at Sea* (1952), which he saw the night after his landslide victory in 1972—the old navy man choosing to celebrate his greatest triumph with the famed documentary tribute to his branch of the service. The night after his victory in 1968, he was heard to play at a resoundingly jubilant volume the recording of Richard Rodgers's score.

Victory at Sea was among Nixon's favorite pieces of music, and it takes nothing away from Rodgers's compositional abilities to suggest that this partiality owed not a little to the sense of purpose and triumphant sacrifice the suite evoked. What had seemed matter-of-fact at the time eventually came to be understood as a defining moment in the lives of those who took part in the war. By joining the navy, Nixon joined something far more significant, more powerful even, than just the U.S. military. He gained his place in a generation that would dominate U.S. politics for more than three decades. Writing near the end of his life about his decision to enter politics, Nixon recollected that "what primarily motivated me was that I was part of the World War II generation." He was being somewhat disingenuous—but only somewhat. For along with ego and ambition and the simple lack of anything better to do (it's because he had grown tired of practicing law in Whittier that he'd gone to Washington to work for the OPA), Nixon couldn't help but partake of this generational dynamic. It was simply in the postwar air, inescapable and unprecedented, a salubrious fallout. That Nixon and his fellows should have "strong feelings about war and peace and the kind of nation we had been fighting for" was inevitable. Wasn't that why they had served? "We respected the leadership that had led us to victory in war, but we felt that the challenges of peace required new, younger leaders."[70] Tempered by their wartime experience, they were ready to take charge and eager to do so.

Truman and Eisenhower had belonged to the World War I generation, and the latter's landslide victories in 1952 and 1956 marked the farewell to power of the Second World War leadership class. In 1960 two men who had been junior navy officers in the Solomons contested the White House.

Had Nixon won, it would have marked a by-the-book transition from the generals and flag officers to their youthful subordinates: the next generation promoted. Instead, JFK jumped ranks. Either way, the torch had been passed. In every succeeding presidential election until 1992, the victor would be someone who had served during the war; and every remaining presidential election in the twentieth century would feature at least one candidate who'd been in uniform during the conflict. Not even the Civil War had created such a generational dominance of the electoral process. Bob Dole's defeat in 1996 truly marked the end of an era.

In his eulogy at Yorba Linda in 1994, Dole called the previous half century "the age of Nixon." That age encompassed the entire period of the World War II generation's grasp on power. Indeed, Nixon helped lead his age cohort to leadership as that generation's first representative to hold national office. He signally benefited from his generational membership; it had helped put him on the GOP ticket as chronological balance to Ike's senior statesman. More than that, though, Nixon took pride in being one of those who had fought in the war. He sought out his fellows and distrusted those without some military background. "Are you a veteran?" Haldeman asked William Safire before offering him a job at the White House. "The Boss has a thing about people who ducked the service."[71] Nor did someone have to be an associate for Nixon to wonder about whether he had served his country. "What is McG's record in combat?" Nixon asked in the margin of his May 7, 1971, news summary. In fact, George McGovern had a military record notably more impressive than Nixon's, having flown thirty-five combat missions as a B-24 pilot and won the Distinguished Flying Cross. In fairness, one should note that such inquiries weren't unique to Nixon. According to Ben Bradlee (another veteran of navy service in the Pacific), JFK, Nixon's great generational counterpart, also liked to dwell on "the war records of political opponents."[72]

The war didn't make Richard Nixon—the making of him would be his opportune proximity to the collision when the irresistible force of Whittaker Chambers met the immovable object of Alger Hiss; that, and the complaisant intervention of Dwight D. Eisenhower four years later—but his wartime experience saw to it that such fabulous opportunities would not be wasted on him. The death of Nixon's two brothers' had been the major formative experience of his youth, and the war was the major formative experience of his adulthood. From his faith in American invincibility to his distrust of the military brass, Nixon had his thinking profoundly shaped and colored by being part of the World War II generation. It took him to places he'd barely imagined existed—from Ottumwa to the Solomons—and introduced him to countless new people and experiences. The South Pacific was his Yale College, his Harvard.

"I grew up in the Navy," Nixon remarked in 1971.[73] That sounds like simply another example of his favorite retrospective device, exaggeration recollected in tranquillity; he was, after all, twenty-nine when he entered the service. Yet the Richard Nixon who received his discharge in January 1946 differed markedly from the man who entered naval officer candidate school at Quonset Point, Rhode Island, in August 1942. In the interim, he experienced loneliness and boredom and danger as never before. The result was a new Nixon, the first and most authentic in that long protean line. This was an appreciably happier Nixon, more reflective and less intense, one whose overseas letters betray a tenderness toward his wife and a more general openness toward experience not to be found anywhere else in the record of his life.

On a more mundane level, he companionably answered to the nickname "Nick" while learning how to curse and smoke cigars and, a talent proving otherwise elusive to him, to fit in and truly be one of the guys. The most obvious proof of this was the taste he developed for poker, especially five-card stud. Such was Nixon's proficiency that he managed to win upward of $10,000 by the time he returned stateside. How serious was he about poker? Invited to a small dinner in honor of Charles Lindbergh, then touring the area on an inspection trip, Nixon demurred in favor of a game scheduled for that night.[74]

Being eight thousand miles from home and facing the possibility of violent death brought a sense of perspective and proportion formerly lacking in so driven a personality. Nixon was discovering what did and did not matter to him. He was learning what internal resources he had to draw upon and, even more significant, that they were not found wanting. Most important of all, he was finding out how to be his own man—paradoxically enough, as part of a vast organization predicated on emphasizing the group at the expense of its members. Whether he liked it or not, Nixon's ingrained, otherwise inexpungeable sense of isolation went on hiatus for the duration. That was the redeeming side of the military's distrust of individualism and emphasis on uniformity: the cultivation of a sense of belonging and creation of camaraderie. As Ambrose notes, "He was, for the only time in his life, genuinely popular with those around him. In the Southwest Pacific, Nixon could relax, suppressing his ambitions rather than himself."[75] Taking part in something so much larger than himself encouraged Nixon *to be* larger than himself.

For better or worse, the vagaries of war denied Nixon the opportunity to test himself in combat, but his dedication to duty and seeing through whatever job needed doing was consistently exemplary. He thought nothing of pitching in to help the dozen enlisted men under his command in the exhausting labor of unloading the planes. On Bougainville and Green, he set up on his own initiative a canteen where weary fighter pilots and bomber crews could get beer and hamburgers while their aircraft refueled. The establishment was dubbed "Nick's Snack Shack," and its proprietor worked tirelessly to scrounge supplies for it. His devotion to his men and the flyers earned him their devotion. In the words of one navy comrade, "If you ever saw Henry Fonda in *Mister Roberts*, you have a pretty good idea what Nick was like."[76]

That is high praise, indeed, for in the popular imagination there is no more beloved Second World War figure than the eponymous hero of Thomas Heggen's novel, which Heggen and Joshua Logan adapted into a famously successful play that ran for 1,157 performances on Broadway. Just as Ernie Pyle became the war's archetypal journalist, and Bill Mauldin's Willie and Joe its archetypal enlisted men, Doug Roberts was its archetypal junior officer. No figure could differ more from Scott's Patton or any of Wayne's fighting men. Where they are the antithesis of the team-spirit ethos of the Allied war effort, Roberts supremely embodies it. His primary concern isn't destroying the enemy; it's protecting the sailors who serve under him. Nurturing and saintly, he never kills or even fires a weapon. In fact, the only fighting he does is with the petty-tyrant captain of the bilgy cargo ship on which he sails, the all too aptly named USS *Reluctant*. The vaguely superior honorific he bears is far more a function of merit than rank, for this Mr. Roberts is a democratic ideal—a seafaring, egalitarian Galahad—noble, yes, but in an utterly unassuming way: a model for the sort of man an officer corps drawn from a free land's citizenry should comprise.

He is, in other words, Henry Fonda. With the exception of Stanley Kowalski with Marlon Brando, no other serious role in postwar American theater is so indelibly associated with a single actor as is Roberts with Fonda. This owes something to longevity (Fonda spent four years playing Roberts on stage before portraying him in the 1955 film version) and something to shared experience (Fonda served as a junior navy officer in the Pacific). More than that, though, it had to do with the remarkable affinity between Roberts and the actor's persona. So deep was this affinity that Fonda could succeed at playing a character who was supposed to be twenty-six, even though he himself was forty-three when the play opened and fifty when it was filmed. Age was irrelevant. Roberts was Fonda reimagined, and Fonda, Roberts incarnate—for other than Hollywood's great idealist totem, who could have done justice to the great idealist totem of the World War II generation?

There is an odd triangulation here. If Nixon is so like Roberts, and Roberts so like Fonda, then Nixon has to be like Fonda. Yet how can this be? As we have seen, everything about Fonda's screen iconography conspires (a suitably Nixonian word) to make him movie master of all that is anti-Nixon. That very contradiction is precisely the point. It underscores the utter singularity of this period in Nixon's life. "Nick" Nixon stands at as distant a remove from "Tricky Dick" as, say, Tom Joad or Wyatt Earp does. What's implausible isn't that Mr. Roberts is another—and assuredly the most attractive—in our line of alternate Nixons. It's that the Richard Nixon who would hold such a dark place in the national psyche for almost half a century should be the same person as the idealistic junior officer manning the counter at Nick's Snack Shack.

Nixon had the movie screened at San Clemente on August 25, 1970. Regardless of whether he saw himself in Fonda's Roberts, he could not have helped but feel the familiarity of Roberts's wartime experience. That all *Mister Roberts*' best-remembered scenes are comic set pieces (the concocting of a quart of Scotch out of medicinal alcohol, Coca-Cola, and iodine; the spying on showering nurses; the Vesuvian cascade of suds from an exploded ship's laundry; Roberts's drunken defenestration of the captain's palm tree) cannot obscure that what it's really about is boredom and despair. According to no less an authority than Joshua Logan, who in addition to adapting the novel directed the Broadway production, *Mister Roberts*' "central theme" was "the sadness and dreariness and loneliness of war."[77] No previous work about the Second World War had shown such a willingness to confront—indeed, to single out and even ennoble—the primacy of boredom in the experience of nearly everyone who had served in the conflict.

Surely, it is this emphasis on the inherent tediousness of wartime life that, more than anything else, accounted for the phenomenal success of both play and movie. For in truth, *Mister Roberts* has not aged well. The movie especially is a lackluster enterprise, showing the effects of having had to satisfy the demands of three different directors (John Ford, Mervyn LeRoy, and, for just a few scenes, Logan). William Powell, in his last screen role, plays the ship's doctor with his usual peerless suavity. James Cagney manages to show the humanity behind the captain's odiousness. Jack Lemmon's Ensign Pulver made his reputation and won him a Best Supporting Actor Oscar. And Fonda is, well, Fonda—only more so. Yet even they can't disguise the essential mediocrity of their high-prestige vehicle. No, that audiences became so fiercely attached to *Mister Roberts* had less to do with art than it did with nostalgia.

"Nostalgia" isn't quite the right word, though, for that suggests a retrospective sunniness, a softening of hard memories. "Recognition" better describes the impact *Mister Roberts* had on those who saw it—or at least those of the World War II generation. Action is the irresistible lure attached to any work about war: action as spectacle and action as catharsis, yet also action as anomaly—for action is very nearly as uncommon in wartime as it is in peacetime. *Mister Roberts* managed to resist that lure and, by concentrating on dullness as the common denominator of military life, so made itself uncommon. Veterans seized upon it as *their* story—a revelation of wartime truth as they had experienced it—in a way they could not with other works about the war.

Doug Roberts is a shining knight of the navy, yes, but his rust-bucket Rosinante rides through an ocean of ennui. The essence of his heroism, like that of Nixon and so many of their fellows, was simply that he endured. Roberts, however, refuses to recognize this as a form of heroism. It never occurs to him that there might be anything heroic about the nature of his service: his de facto noncombatant status shames him. It's not that he's unwilling to fight—in fact, he's eager to—it's that he's unable to fight. Yossarian in Joseph Heller's *Catch-22* (1961) might be seen as a sort of Roberts in reverse: the former is as determined to evade combat as the latter is to seek it. In any character less supernally sane than Fonda's, one would see this determination as verging on madness. Instead, more than his kindness, more than his shrewdness, more than his nobility, this becomes Roberts's defining attribute: that he wants to see action and feels unfulfilled because he hasn't been in battle. This becomes, in fact, the ultimate proof of his selflessness; for having finally gotten his transfer, he loses his life in a kamikaze raid.

In failing to recognize that there can be any heroism in the proposition that they also serve who only stand and wait, Roberts finds himself in agreement with someone who would otherwise seem utterly inimical to him, Richard Nixon's less congruent Second World War soul mate, Georgie Patton. The sole demand both Patton and Roberts make of military service is the opportunity to fight. Patton's desire is born of sheer belligerence, Roberts's of a martial variant of civic virtue (or is it just that he'll do anything to escape the boredom of life aboard the *Reluctant?*), but it's the same end each man wants.

They share one other attribute. Both manage to be rebels even as they serve as authority figures: that is, they uphold the system *and*, as it suits them, work to subvert it. They follow orders; they give orders—yet Patton also bedevils Ike; Roberts also sabotages his skipper. Both flout regulations for what they consider a greater good—to fight the enemy more effectively, to protect the men under them—but they're still breaking the rules.

Here, and here alone, the feared Old Blood and Guts and the beloved Mr. Roberts might be seen to link arms, joining in the role of good soldier/sailor who doubles as bomb thrower (or palm-tree flinger). All they care about is fighting, and to do that they have few qualms about going their own way, no matter that the system they have sworn an oath to defend abhors its members acting on their own and categorically forbids any such action. It is a curious position—in effect, a structural contradiction—to be a pillar of a system one considers oneself above, but this position is what seals their connection to Nixon. For he, too, made a specialty of trying to have it both ways: the mouther of homiletic platitudes who delighted in fighting dirty; the law-and-order leader who condoned break-ins and ordered cover-ups; and, yes, the commander in chief who grew teary-eyed in the company of POWs even as he derided their superior officers.

In wartime, such behavior is dangerous as well as forbidden—but the history of warfare makes a certain allowance for such conduct so long as it demonstrably conduces to the hastening of victory. In peacetime, such behavior is simply known as hypocrisy and tends sooner or later to catch up with its practitioners—viz. Watergate. Nixon, as a sort of existential Clausewitzian, considered life to be war by other means and expected the wartime allowances to be made for him. They weren't. The real-life counterpart of Mr. Roberts, who in some driven part of his soul identified so with Patton, found himself unable to bring off their balancing act.

Still, it would take him nearly three decades before he had to confront his failure. Starting with 1946, things looked very rosy, indeed. Patton, warlord grandee and conqueror of nations, clearly belonged to the past. Mr. Roberts, sailor-citizen and carrier of a clipboard, belonged to the future, even if he never gets to see it. His real-life counterpart, though, the proprietor of Nick's Snack Shack, not only belonged to the future; he *was* the future. Eighteen months after V-J day, as Patton lay in a military cemetery in Luxembourg and Mr. Roberts in a watery grave off Okinawa, Mr. Nixon goes to Washington.

Charles Laughton, left; *Peter Lawford,* center right; *Walter Pidgeon,* right

ADVISE AND CONSENT

■ ■

We had been friends, as Senators are friends. RICHARD NIXON, ON HIS
RELATIONSHIP WITH JOHN F. KENNEDY[1]

You liked people, usually, or you weren't in this business.
ALLEN DRURY, *Advise and Consent*

Nixon later conceded that on first entering Congress he had the
"same lost feeling" he had had when he entered the military.[2]
That feeling didn't prevent his rising in barely seven years from
navy lieutenant commander to vice president of the United States.
Even so, such anxiety was understandable. Nixon was by no means
unworldly. He had read widely and intensively in college, spent
three years at a prestigious eastern law school, and during the war
crisscrossed the country before spending fourteen months stationed eight thousand miles from home. Nor was he a stranger to
Washington, having served his eight months at the OPA in 1942.

Yet that was a different Washington—or set of Washingtons—from the one he was about to enter. He'd known wartime Washington, official Washington, time-serving Washington, not congressional Washington. *That* Washington was a world apart and comprised a society as nuanced and stratified as any on the continent. It was precisely because Nixon had a sense of this that he felt lost. For he knew that going from Southern California to Capitol Hill was an immeasurable leap for a thirty-four-year-old small-town lawyer. In certain key respects, it was a distance he would never quite traverse, and the failure to do so would plague him the rest of his days.

At least the House of Representatives wasn't as daunting as the Senate. It was more energetic, more partisan, far less hidebound. More important, Nixon arrived under notably favorable circumstances. For one thing, he entered the House in the majority, a boon enjoyed by few Republicans in the latter two-thirds of the twentieth century. For another, Nixon got to Washington already bearing a reputation: he was seen as something of a giant killer, having defeated a nationally known Democratic incumbent, his upset victory written up in both *Newsweek* and *Time*. Above all, there were Nixon's own talents, which quickly won him praise from House Speaker Joseph Martin as "one of the ablest young men to come to Congress in many years."[3] With the Speaker's approval, Nixon was awarded seats on the Education and Labor committee—the body that would draft the most celebrated piece of legislation to come out of the Eightieth Congress, the Taft-Hartley Act—and HUAC, "a choice assignment in 1947," as Martin notes in his memoirs.[4]

Thanks to the Hiss case, the latter appointment would prove crucial in Nixon's rise. No one could have predicted that at the time, of course. A far greater mark of the high regard in which Nixon was held was his being chosen for the House Select Committee on Foreign Aid, popularly known as the Herter Committee, after Christian Herter, the Massachusetts Republican who served as chairman. The committee's nineteen members were to investigate conditions in Europe and so assess the feasibility of the proposed Marshall Plan. Realizing both the importance of that proposal and what little appeal it then held for the American public, the congressional leadership chose the committee's membership with care. Nixon was both its youngest member and the only one from the far West. Clearly, he was a man to be watched.

If ability were all that mattered in being a congressman, Nixon would have flourished on Capitol Hill. It wasn't, though, and he didn't—not altogether, anyway. Just as his association with Herter on the committee in-dicates the positive side of his early congressional experience, so did another encounter with Herter exemplify the negative. Asked by the patrician congressman to a black-tie dinner party, the Nixons misread the invitation. He arrived wearing his best blue suit and she, a new cocktail dress.[5] It was an embarrassing reminder that, as a member of the House, he belonged to a highly intricate society in which manner could count for as much as matter. In a way, having been elected to Congress meant being a candidate all over again: one had to court other representatives no less than one had previously courted voters, and issues could often take a backseat to personality in determining one's advancement. "Personality" was never a word Nixon was comfortable with. Here he labored under a severe disadvantage. He was not someone others naturally warmed to. A man driven to attempt—and achieve—so much, he nonetheless drew the line at conviviality and camaraderie; not only were they frivolous; they were also, as even he realized, not attainable for the likes of him. It was with equal parts regret and pride that he told Stewart Alsop in 1958: "It doesn't come natural to me to be a buddy-buddy boy."[6]

The term he chose suggests what scorn Nixon reserved for the type—and the implicit superiority of his own apartness—but that didn't mean he failed to recognize the handicap his lack of social ease posed to his continued rise. Nixon was too canny not to realize, and too ambitious not to act upon, the need for a certain amount of buddy-boying. The clearest instance is his helping to found the Chowder and Marching Society, "a friendly group of Capitol Hill jocks and imbibers," as a contemporary journalistic account put it.[7] The society's fifteen members, junior Republicans all and most of them World War II veterans, met every Wednesday over supper to share information and unwind. The group's self-consciously hail-fellow-well-met name summons up the image of a somewhat superannuated college social club or fraternity. That was only appropriate, for the society very much resembled a similar organization Nixon helped found as an undergraduate at Whittier: the Orthogonians, or square shooters, another hale-and-hearty band of institutional out-siders. Nixon had formed it in contradistinction to another group, the Franklins, which claimed the campus elite. "They were the haves and we were the have nots," he later explained.[8] The Chowder and Marching Society was the Orthogonians redux: if you're not sure how to join a club, form one of your own. Once again, it was Nixon the loner, aware of the requirement to be just one of the boys, but overdoing the bonhomie. In matters social, he invariably knew what he needed to do without ever quite figuring out how it's done. Socially, there was nothing *instinctive* about Nixon, and when in doubt he turned to what he was most comfortable with: football and Robert's Rules of Order.

The Chowder and Marching Society was founded with an eye toward attracting notice beyond Capitol Hill. (The group's emblem, a large lobster encircled by the group's name, appeared on the aprons members wore along with chefs' toques, and as William "Fishbait" Miller, the longtime House doorkeeper observed, "they made sure the emblem was big enough so it would photograph well.")[9] Nonetheless, the group's primary concern was with the House. It was a means to gain influence through pooled knowledge and to demonstrate to other representatives that the society's members were regular guys—sound and sociable and down-to-earth—the sort of fellows who tended to do well in the House. For the House was a chummy place, its chumminess dictated by sheer numbers. There were 435 representatives, a number too large to cohere, yet too small to atomize. A representative was one of many, but not too many. He had no choice but to make alliances, to *join*—conferences and caucuses and, yes, Chowder and Marching Societies—if he wanted to prosper within the larger body.

Even a Nixon, the last man anyone would think to call a joiner, had to acknowledge that fundamental principle of advancement in the House. Such a premium on sociability was one of the reasons he would move up to a Senate seat less than four years after entering Congress. Another would also be a function of the House's size: the anonymity it bred. "A man who cuts his way through to the top" of the House, a contemporary observer noted, "must reconcile himself to spending enormous devotion, enormous labor at the grinding routine of the place, and to a striking lack of either public awareness or public interest in his life and career."[10] "Grinding routine" Nixon could handle—it was, in fact, his natural element, the sky in which he soared, the sea in which he swam—but "lack of either public awareness or public interest" was another matter.

Compounding the problem was the Republicans' electoral humiliation in 1948. "Dewey's defeat and our loss of both houses of Congress turned me overnight into a junior member of the minority party," Nixon wrote in *RN*, "a 'comer' with no place to go. For the first time I began to consider the possibility of trying to move up on my own instead of patiently waiting for seniority or party preferment in the House of Representatives."[11] That "for the first time" merits a question mark; but, otherwise, yes, that accurately summarizes how he perceived his situation in the House—and how inimical that situation was to his own ambitions. Because of the Hiss case, Nixon had no need to worry about lack of public awareness or interest. What he had to worry about was lack of power; and where anonymity would have been bad enough, anonymity without power was intolerable.

The irony is that Nixon found himself even less suited to the Senate than he had been to the House—and that unsuitability helped bring him a heartbeat away from the presidency. House Speaker Sam Rayburn happily predicted Nixon would be "buried" in the Senate.[12] He knew that Nixon would not fit in there and he was right. Where the House was chummy, the Senate was clubby. That clubbiness threatened to make Nixon's legislative life miserable: where he could ape fellowship in the House, he could not manufacture acceptance in the Senate. What Rayburn failed to realize was that this would not impede—rather, it worked to accelerate—Nixon's rise to an even higher position. It made it that much easier for him during his first eighteen months as a senator to be constantly on the road—he averaged three fund-raisers a week in 1951[13] —waging what was, for all intents and purposes, a campaign to significantly increase his visibility within the party.

The Senate was no place for "a little man in a big hurry," as Robert Taft called Nixon shortly after the '52 convention, and his consciousness of that fact spurred him to hurry all the more. "Men who have reached national fame in less than two years in powerful non-Senatorial office," William S. White, the *New York Times*' congressional correspondent, wrote in 1956, "have found four years and more not to be long enough to feel free to speak up loudly in the Institution. All the newcomer needs, if he is able and strong, is the passage of time—but this he needs indispensably. . . ."[14] Time is the Senate's fuel: what it runs on, what propels it. But it is a peculiar form of propulsion, for the fuel has more of the properties of molasses than gasoline. The self-styled "world's greatest deliberative body," while not always great, is always deliberate. That was far from an appealing characteristic to the youngest senator in the Eighty-second Congress. Worse, there was nothing hungry about the Senate. Six-year terms and two-person delegations had an emollient effect that, after the anthill hurly-burly of the House, seemed deadening to Nixon. Bad as the House was, at least things *happened* there. The Senate, like Pope's wounded snake, drags its slow length along—and, unlike the snake, prides itself on so doing. If it had been a Senate committee that had heard Whittaker Chambers's allegations, Alger Hiss might have ended up secretary of state in the first Stevenson administration.

Everything about the Senate encouraged Nixon to be in a big hurry, yet the curious thing about all his hurrying elsewhere was that, in the end, it simply served to bring him back to the Senate chamber. He was no longer a senator, of course; he was instead presiding there as vice president. It brought him the worst of both worlds, going from Claghorn to Throttlebottom, as Nixon had to suffer continued exposure to (in fact, it was now an immersion in) the interminable niceties of being a senator but having now lost the power and influence that comes with being a senator. When Nixon writes in *Six Crises* about the famous "kitchen debate" that Khrushchev "was easy to handle compared with some of the Senate sessions over which I had presided!"[15] he wants us to think he's referring to the presumed Sturm und Drang of debating the Republic's future and forging its laws. The exclamation mark is nicely emphatic, making Nixon's efforts sound heroic, demanding. They were demanding, yes, but the demands were those of tedium and pomposity, not tumult and drama.

Twice he had an opportunity to display his disdain for Senate protocol, and neither time did he fail to take advantage of it, throwing the chamber into turmoil in both 1957 and 1959 by ruling in order an insurgent motion to make it easier to achieve cloture (the closing off of debate, which would have the effect of making it easier to cut off filibusters). These acts of institutional lèse-majesté infuriated traditionalists of both parties and they were very much Nixon's own doing. Nixon's rulings defied the Senate Republican leadership; and as Joseph Alsop reported in his syndicated column, the GOP leadership troika of William Knowland, Leverett Saltonstall, and Styles Bridges "came as close to blows" with Nixon over the cloture ruling "as men can without actually using their fists."[16]

Clearly, Nixon was no friend of Senate tradition, though the institution would have its revenge on him with his last act as its presiding officer. Presidential candidate Nixon had to suffer the supreme indignity of presiding over the official tabulation of his own defeat, the first man to have to do so since 1860. And eight years later, he might have gotten some sourly belated recompense, visiting the same fate on Hubert Humphrey, another senator turned vice president—except Humphrey managed not to be present for the tally. There was a certain justice in that, though, for Humphrey had fit in the Senate as Nixon never had.

Rayburn's adage "To get along, go along" was formulated with the House in mind. The Senate, however, was different. Getting along there was a given, what with that body's all-but-reflexive affability, its fondness for numbingly formulaic courtliness. Stodgy, stagy, self-congratulatory, the Senate doted on formality and procedure, and it was by a man's relations to procedural matters that one might best size him up. Clinton Anderson, a liberal Democrat from New Mexico who was very much a Senate insider during his four terms there, "couldn't believe it" when he heard Eisenhower had selected Nixon as his running mate, such were his "profound misgivings" about his Senate colleague. Yet when Vice President Nixon made his cloture rulings—it was Anderson who'd offered the motion Nixon ruled in order—it "demonstrated to me, whatever the criticism directed at him, that he was a fundamentally decent fellow."[17] This is the Senate attitude seen at its most maddeningly, finically senatorial: so long as someone's good on the rules, well then, it really doesn't matter what one thinks about the defects of his character or the distastefulness of his politics; he can't be all that bad.

This is the same attitude that had long ago so arranged affairs on the Senate floor that even the bitterest dispute could sound like the blandest of diplomatic communiqués. "Senators do not grow," Woodrow Wilson complained. "They swell." Nowhere do they distend more than in their language, and the body's love of verbal elaboration and ornate rhetoric can make floor debate seem like an exchange of toasts at a state dinner. Here one might well understand Nixon's unease in the Senate. Such carrying-on seems completely alien to him: not just unlike Nixon, but repugnant to him. "The esteemed gentleman from here," "the distinguished gentleman from there": try as it might, the mind's ear cannot summon up such phrases cloaked in Nixon's darkling baritone.

During his time on Capitol Hill, there was a single great exception to this rule of baroquely civilized behavior, one that illustrates just how deeply the Senate valued the appearance of comity. It wasn't Joe McCarthy's lying that led his fellow senators to censure him; it was his lying in such a harsh and unseemly fashion. The resolution condemning him states that McCarthy's "conduct"—such a prim, elbows-off-the-table word—was "unbecoming . . . contrary to senatorial traditions, and tends to bring the Senate into disrepute. . . ." Yet even McCarthy wasn't completely indifferent to the tug of institutional civility. The resolution originated with Ralph Flanders. After the Vermont Republican filed it, McCarthy greeted him with a cheery "Hi, Ralph," put an arm around Flanders, and gave him a smile.[18] Partly, that was just McCarthy's standard bravado, yet it also owed something to the inherent clubbability of the Senate. Early in the next session of Congress, Flanders was seated in the Senate dining room next to an empty chair. He looked up to see

McCarthy seeking a place to sit and beckoned him over. The two men soon fell to examining Flanders's new briefcase. "From that time on," Flanders approvingly notes in his memoirs, "our personal relations were friendly."[19] It's the characteristic senatorial note: "personal relations" rather than friendship, "friendly" rather than intimate or close. As Tessio says at the end of *The Godfather* after his conspiring to kill Michael Corleone has been discovered, "Tell Michael it was only business. I always liked him."

Getting along was always business in the Senate and, as such, one could simply take it for granted. No body that sustains a custom so refractory as the filibuster might ever be seen as encouraging the act of going along, however. The analogy to diplomacy is again useful: each senator was like a sovereign principality, a power unto himself, separate but maddeningly equal, only slightly affected by party discipline, and immune to any greater sense of unity beyond the purely institutional ("filibuster," appropriately enough, derives from the Spanish *filibustero*, for "freebooter"). Nixon's comment about Kennedy is wonderfully telling in this regard—telling not just about his relationship with his great rival but about senatorial dealings generally. "We had been friends, as Senators are friends"? Implicit in that statement is the truth that senators are hardly ever friends, or at least not as the rest of us understand the word. Colleagues, to be sure, or allies, supporters, even confidants—but friends? As a senator who served on Capitol Hill during Nixon's vice presidency put it when asked to describe relations with his fellow legislators: "It is rather like the friendships that might develop within a band of outlaws."[20]

Seen in that light, the Senate's placing such stock in social punctilio makes absolute sense. When an institution lacks the substance of goodwill, its best recourse is to the forms of goodwill. A constituent once asked U.S. Senator Prescott Bush (the father of one president and grandfather of another) about the Senate's reputation as "the most exclusive club in the world." "Well, that could possibly be said," he replied. "We all call each other by our first names. We treat each other with scrupulous courtesy. We and our wives occasionally get together socially. But if one of our members stubs his toe, we EAT him."[21] No member of an outlaw band could have put it better.

The sense of community to be found in the House, the sense that informed such enterprises as the Chowder and Marching Society, has no counterpart in the Senate. Senators consider themselves above such things as wearing lobster emblems on their aprons—and that's assuming they'd deign to wear aprons. They are above the sense of mutual fellowship indulging in such behavior suggests. Uneasily joined together in a matrix of tradition and status, senators share a role but rarely much else. What's unusual in the Senate isn't its members going their separate ways; it's when they don't go their separate ways. Illustrating that point is a footnote to the 1972 presidential campaign that, for all Nixon was astounded by its ultimate consequences, could have come as little surprise to him. When George McGovern selected Thomas Eagleton to be his running mate, the two had met only twice[22]—once in the Senate steam room and once at a dinner gathering—and this despite the fact that they were of the same wing of the same party, both from the Midwest, and had served together for nearly three and a half years! They had been friends, presumably, as senators are friends.

In the Senate, as in outlaw bands (or, for that matter, any organization where no objective hierarchy obtains), one's equal is one's potential rival. The nature of the rivalry extends from floor debate to office space to— and here the Senate truly lacks any equivalent body—the White House. It is in the last-named area that the pressures generated by the Senate's being a breeding ground of rivalry are most acute. There are three levels of federal elective office. The ratio between the second and third, of senators to representatives, is one to nearly four and a half. The ratio between the first and second, of presidents to senators, in Richard's Nixon time on Capitol Hill, was one to ninety-six. The effects such a radical increase in disproportion must have on senators are easily imagined, and the dictum of Hugo Black, who spent two terms as senator from Alabama before gaining his seat on the Supreme Court, is as pertinent today as it was six decades ago: "You shouldn't be elected to the Senate unless you want to be President."[23]

One might think such a rivalrous environment ideally suited to someone so intrinsically a free agent as Nixon was—rivals can be friends, as senators are friends?—yet while the Senate may not be about friendship or even necessarily alliance, neither is it about isolation. Its preferred view of itself is as "the world's most exclusive club," a phrase that suggests many aspects of the institution, not least of all its sense of shared membership. As Nixon explained to Jack Paar during a *Tonight Show* appearance in 1960: "We're members of what we call 'the Club.' Anybody who has ever been a member of the Senate is a member of a club."[24] One detects a degree of strain in that repetition of the first-person plural, a suspiciously emphatic declaration of insiderdom. Fortunately, for Nixon, "anybody" is an all-inclusive term. As in any club, however, there are members—and there are members—and Nixon's membership was, at best, ex officio. Even his admirers admitted as much. Starting with that 1946 feature about his defeat of Voorhis, the Luce publications had been among Nixon's most ardent supporters. Not surprisingly, then, a 1953 *Life* cover story strove to be as upbeat as possible, noting that as a senator Nixon had been "well liked, respected, marked as a man of the future"; nonetheless, the article conceded, "he was never 'one of the group.'"[25]

No, Nixon was never a member in the way such contemporaries as, say, Lyndon Johnson, or Richard Russell, or even George Smathers was. They belonged, as he most surely did not. Murray Kempton describes a Capitol Hill encounter between Nixon and Johnson in the summer of 1960. "Well, Dick, you boys gonna 'nigger' it at your convention this year?" A blushing Nixon replied, "We will certainly try, Lyndon."[26] It's as if the two speakers hailed from different planets: Johnson, the born politician—vulgar, arrogant, in charge—demonstrates his utter mastery of the language of power and shows that it is his native tongue; while Nixon, prissy and proper, sounds like a civics teacher auditing an etiquette class. A man comfortable with being with other men does not talk that way, and Nixon's words have no more relation to the language of power—the incongruity, the sheer obtuseness, of that forlornly affirmative "certainly"!—than they do to Esperanto.

For all that the enforced sociability that went with being a member of Congress made Nixon's time as a legislator such an anomaly in his career, his years on Capitol Hill were utterly of a piece with the rest of his adult life, so much of which had as its defining characteristic the fact of not belonging. What made him so anomalous as a politician generally—the forced-march effortfulness of his attempts at extroversion, his clear distaste for the company of other people—made him particularly anomalous as a senator. Barry Goldwater, who got to know Nixon when he was vice president, recalls him as being "outwardly friendly but inwardly remote" and notes his "reputation of being a loner—not something normally said about a politician."[27]

Indeed, this least clubbable of men was, not surprisingly, the least poll-like of men. Watching him campaign in Wisconsin in 1968, Garry Wills observed that Nixon "has the effrontery, for which he may never be forgiven, of carrying out before the public an embarrassingly private set of eyes, eyes unable to rest vacuously on the pomp of Fond du Lac's Lincoln Day bunting."[28] How much greater the effrontery to have those eyes squirming around a Senate chamber full of backslapping, glad-handing men, men whose power is most deeply acknowledged by the frank openness of the gaze they rest upon one another? Nixon's furtive look—a shrink of recognition—implicitly indicted the whole system of elaborate collegiality by which the Senate operates. Even worse, it communicated some sense of the isolation his abhorrence of the buddy-buddy-boy routine imposed upon him. Having only superiors and inferiors, a man without peers inhabits the cell of his own sui generis state.

He was that rarest of political animals: a legislator without cronies (a magazine article described Nixon in 1952 as "almost hermitlike in his associations with others . . . a man who hasn't a single crony in the Senate or House").[29] Nixon shied away from intimacy with anyone, even his family; nor did he have a knack for any of the habits or gestures that draw others into social association with oneself. Even when he did make an effort at conviviality, it tended to backfire. As vice president, he occasionally took part in a regular Wednesday poker game that drew on a group of seventy-five or so present and former members of Congress. Tip O'Neill, a junior congressman then and a regular at the table, recalled how whatever social good Nixon's appearances might have done him was negated when he would "take advantage of the fact that he was the highest-ranking person at the game" and ask "other players how many cards they had drawn."[30] Nixon similarly wore out his welcome in the Senate dining room, where, according to Louis Hurst, who ran the facility for many years, he had a reputation for never picking up a tab. "The check was too heavy for him to lift," his fellow senators liked to say.[31]

The wonder isn't that he lacked cronies, but that there was anyone even close. Smathers, the likeliest candidate, was elected to the House and Senate in the same years Nixon was. The Florida Democrat had won by red-baiting with such skill in the Democratic Senate primary that Nixon "carefully studied" his campaign and "adapted what he could" for his race against Helen Gahagan Douglas.[32] Nor was that all Nixon got from the Floridian: it was Smathers who introduced him to Bebe Rebozo, who would later become his best friend, during a Florida vacation the two senators took together in 1952. Astonishingly, Smathers was the same man whose love of the high life was such that it elicited the envy of no less a connoisseur than JFK, himself a friend of Smathers's. Yet the sybaritic Floridian, who claimed he had befriended his priggish California colleague because he looked so uncomfortable at a congressional stag party,[33] was more of a Nixon intimate than any other senator, even if the only real bond they shared was a love of Florida sunshine. (It was from Smathers in 1968 that Nixon bought the first of the five houses that would form his Key Biscayne compound.) How close Smathers felt toward Nixon can be inferred from his later calling Nixon "the most calculating man I ever knew."[34] Shortly after the election in 1952, Smathers and J. William Fulbright announced they would introduce legislation requiring that in the event of a chief executive's death, the vice president would remain president only until the next congressional election. The sponsors specifically stated that their bill wasn't aimed at Nixon, but the fact of the president-elect's advanced age, the vice president–elect's relative youth, and the timing of the senators' announcement made their denial somewhat suspect.[35] (Smathers and Nixon had been friends, presumably, as senators are friends.)

Clearly, the benefits of senatorial collegiality extended only so far, at least where Nixon was concerned. Ever alert to slights, Nixon did not let such behavior go unremarked. It was just one more reminder that, for him, the Senate was a means to an end. Even more than the ninety-five other members, Nixon understood what Hugo Black had been driving at. It is this, more than anything else, perhaps, that made Nixon so uncomfortable as a senator—what traveler with a pressing destination ever feels comfortable at a mere way station, however grand, however imposing?— and this is what made him so atypical. For all that every senator may think about the White House, hardly any let such thoughts define and determine their time on Capitol Hill. As William S. White once wrote, "The Senate type is, speaking broadly, a man for whom the Institution is a career in itself, a life in itself and an end in itself. This Senate type is not always free of Presidential ambition. . . . But the important fact is that when the Senate type thinks of the Presidency he thinks of it as only *another* and not as really a *higher* ambition. . . ."[36] For Nixon, by this time, it was the *only* ambition. The idea of being satisfied with staying in the Senate was as inconceivable as staying in the House had been.

In the months before the 1952 Republican convention, Nixon sought to put the Senate behind him, actively (if covertly) pursuing the vice presidency. Once the nomination was offered to him, the only thing that might have prevented his accepting it was Pat Nixon's opposition. To persuade her, he called in Murray Chotiner, his political *éminence noire.* Chotiner could argue with Pat and articulate what Nixon thought, as Nixon himself could not—not without revealing to her the fact that he had long ago decided to accept. The speaker was Chotiner, but the opinions expressed were very much Nixon's own. "Dick, you're a junior senator from California," Chotiner declared, "and you will always be a junior senator from California. Bill Knowland is young and he's healthy, and unless something should happen to him, you will always be second man in

California. The junior senator from California doesn't amount to anything. There comes a time when you have to go up or out."[37]

Two things stand out in Chotiner's advice: disdain for the Senate ("The junior senator from California doesn't amount to anything") and a skewed sense of duration ("a time when you have to go up or out"). Nixon, remember, had been in the Senate a little more than a year and a half. Johnson, his successor as vice president and a man who differed from Nixon little if at all in degree of ambition, served in the Senate twelve years before seeking higher office. Alben Barkley, Nixon's immediate predecessor as vice president, served as a senator twenty-two years before he went "up or out." Both men were consummately of the Senate, as Nixon most assuredly was not. Little as that body impressed Chotiner (a senator from the nation's second most populous state "doesn't amount to anything"), it's fair to say that it ranked even lower in the estimation of his boss. One gets a sense of how highly Nixon regarded those in the Senate from a diary entry made almost twenty years after Chotiner's harangue, wherein he describes Soviet president Nikolai Podgorny as being "like a Midwestern Senator";[38] it's hard to say which party comes off worse in the comparison. Senators, midwestern and otherwise, did not much impress Richard Nixon.

Nixon accepted the nomination because it put him so much closer to the White House. Yet it had the additional virtue of getting him out of the Senate. It's not that Nixon was, per se, unpopular on Capitol Hill and that's why he felt so uncomfortable there. It was more his unsuitability, a fact he was too astute not to recognize. Give and take, dicker and debate, that was not Nixon's style—well, debating was, but the sort of gassy, free-form bombinating the Senate specialized in wasn't debate; it was speech-making. Cut and thrust, logic and fact, those Nixon flourished on; and those were not the order of the day on the Senate floor. He didn't fit in and didn't really want to. So he managed as well as he could, but as soon as he was able to he moved on. He never looked back. Regrets Richard Nixon would have, but abandoning Capitol Hill was never one of them.

Neither Nixon's predecessor in the White House nor his successor could say the same. Johnson, universally deemed the greatest majority leader in Senate history, would have been a happier man, we now know, and surely have a far less ambiguous reputation, if he had stayed in the Senate. Gerald Ford never sought the presidency; his great dream was the House Speakership. Of course, Johnson and Ford were creatures of Capitol Hill as Nixon never was. They belonged to that society. They flourished in that society. They *required* that society, as Richard Nixon did not. It wasn't just that the president or vice president has more power than a senator, let alone more prestige, that so attracted Nixon. It was that, in the president's case, he gets to operate alone—and in the vice president's, he serves in the shadow of only one other man rather than ninety-five.

Alger Hiss, who had occasion to give much thought to what drove Richard Nixon, hit upon something central to his adversary's career when he characterized him as "just a solo operator making his way in the world."[39] Nixon was a Melvillean *isolato*, a man almost oceanically alone throughout his life's journey. This makes him utterly singular in our politics. Gatsbys and Snopeses our public realm has abounded in, Babbitts and Tom Sawyers even more so, but nary an Ahab or Ishmael. What is even more singular, though, is that Nixon's success consistently drew on that sense of isolation. Chained to no faction, he could—and did—make expediency into a personal dogma. The one great cause identified with him, anti-communism, soon came to be such a universally accepted tenet of our politics that his association with it would allow Nixon leeway to do almost anything he wanted so far as the other side of the Iron Curtain was concerned. Détente is, however, only the most striking example of how Nixon thrived on his deracination and solitariness. The invasion of Cambodia, the imposition of wage and price controls, the ending of the war in Indochina, the resupply of Israel during the Yom Kippur War: all these and more Nixon accomplished by essentially acting on his own. FDR had his Brains Trust; JFK, his Irish Mafia; Reagan, his California Kitchen Cabinet; Clinton, his Friends of Bill. No one has ever spoken of "Friends of Dick." Rather, Nixon prided himself on needing no such group. Instead, he relied on his two right-hand men, H. R. Haldeman and Henry Kissinger. The former specialized in keeping the number of people Nixon saw to an absolute minimum, the latter in doing everything possible to immobilize the State Department so as to preserve U.S. foreign policy as the personal fiefdom of Nixon and himself. This captain preferred to pilot his *Pequod* with a skeleton crew.

Never happier than when alone, Nixon also never performed better than when alone or, the next best thing, in a small group. This pattern extended even to the most public of political arts, oratory: all his best speeches came before television cameras rather than live audiences. Performance was hardly ever the problem; people almost always were. Ensembles were alien to his sensibility. If this was true even during his time as president (his abhorrence of Cabinet meetings verged on the comic), then it was surpassingly so during his stay on Capitol Hill. A president is to a great extent expected to be alone: only one person at a time can hold "the world's loneliest office." Not so with senators and congressmen, who are plural by definition. The mystery isn't Nixon's spending so short a time in Congress; it's his having managed to stay there as long as he did.

Richard Nixon had painfully few of the attributes we associate with movie stardom: not charm, not grace, not glamour, not assurance . . . the list goes on. Yet in his leeriness of the group, his constant seeking after singularity, he possessed one of the signal qualities of Hollywood stardom. Stardom is about isolation—and specifically movie stardom, for even alone in the spotlight a performer on stage shares space with the audience, *responds* to the audience. But the movie star, singled out in the close-up, the grace-bestowing predicate in the grammar of film, is supremely alone. So, too, with Nixon, and it is his inherent aloneness, a quality unmatched by any other twentieth-century chief executive, that helps enable us to speak of this peculiarly unstellar man as the "movie-star president." In this one respect, and this respect only, he behaved every inch like one of Hollywood's exalted: no ensembles for him. In almost any other case one might cite, ensembles are an inescapable element of political stardom. Not so with Nixon, who always behaved as if his most fervent belief was that he who travels alone travels farthest—all the way to the White House, in fact.

One of the reasons Hollywood has never been comfortable with political movies has been its own profound distaste for ensemble. Norman Mailer was on to something in naming his novel about the motion-picture industry *The Deer Park* (1955), after Louis XV's private pleasure preserve, for the fundamental onscreen social structure apes that of the ancien régime: a starry first estate of cinematic royals and aristocrats, a smallish second estate of established supporting actors, and a teeming third estate of extras and bit players. The second estate, a clerisy of superior virtue and not-so-grand airs, is the estate best suited to ensemble. It is also, for that matter, the one best suited to politics, as anyone with any knowledge of the internal workings of the Vatican knows. "Leave government to clerks and desks," Emerson once wrote. Stars get in the way of getting things done. No studio chief could have put it better.

There are, of course, other, more concrete reasons for Hollywood's avoiding politics as a subject. It has always worried about offending those in power. Even something as essentially innocuous as *Mr Smith Goes to Washington*, the greatest of all American political movies, inspired such anxiety among the moguls that they tried to have it suppressed. A fear greater even than giving offense has been failing to make a profit, and that, too, has affected political movies, what with foreign markets' presumed uninterest in films about U.S. politics. Another way of making that point is to note the general absence in politics of American movies' two favorite commodities, violence and sex. For that reason, perhaps, political movies have tended not to be box office at home, either. As the founding editor of *People* magazine liked to say about cover subjects: "Young is better than old, pretty is better than ugly, television is better than music, music is better than movies, movies are better than sports, anything is better than politics." The last clause of that sentence is as much of a Hollywood mantra as the first two are.[40]

Nonetheless, there are also reasons why Hollywood should find political subjects appealing. For all that politics may lack sex and violence—or, one should say, ostensibly lack them—conflict is a given. Thanks to Washington's stage-set predilection for monuments and marble, solid visuals are a given, too—a locational advantage even nonpolitical movies have taken advantage of. Recall the lip-smacking demolition of the White House in *Independence Day* (1996). The strongest argument for the lure of political movies is based on kinship. "Politicians and movie stars spring from the same DNA," according to Jack Valenti. "Both hope for applause, read from a script and hope to persuade audiences."[41]

That kinship also creates difficulties, and they may have a great deal to do with the problematic nature of the political movie genre. Understandably enough, Hollywood projects its own standards onto politics and so, inevitably, equates leadership with stardom: selling tickets is equivalent to getting votes, glamour the same thing as electability. There is a good deal of truth to that equation, the career of John F. Kennedy being the foremost example. Lest we forget, though, Ronald Reagan was a much bigger star in politics than he ever was in show business. The abiding mystery of democracy is the balance between how simple and precise it is in theory and how complex and enigmatic in execution. For once, Hollywood prefers the theory to the practice, going with the clear-cut rather than the unfathomable. Individuals who would never make it past the first casting call—bald, overweight, wheelchair-bound, elderly (and not just merely elderly: wrinkled!)—win resounding electoral victories. Worse, good looks can actually be held against candidates as a sign of shallowness or insincerity.

From Hollywood's standpoint, it makes no sense, but there it is; and so, the mystery of political leadership being even greater than the mystery of stardom, the movies are left to fall back on what they know best: matinee-idol looks and sex appeal. Alas, just because an actor is attractive on the screen does not automatically mean he's attractive to voters. The insuperable problem with *The Candidate* is that Robert Redford's title character is such a stiff: male-model handsome, yes, but utterly implausible as a vote getter. Richard Nixon's saturnine looks did not keep him from winning six out of eight elections and, in the last of them, taking the third-largest percentage of the popular vote in our history. It's only fitting, perhaps, that the sole actor to win an Academy Award for a performance as a U.S. politician, Broderick Crawford for his Willie Stark in *All the King's Men* (1949), should have been so unprepossessing in appearance.

The great stumbling block for political movies is audience familiarity. These films take place in a realm of society that moviegoers are already acquainted with. Backroom deals we are not privy to, but speeches, rallies, demonstrations, these we all have seen or participated in. Part of the love of Hollywood for spectacle and the exotic is due to the simple fact that it's a lot easier to have an audience suspend its disbelief when what it's seeing has nothing to do with its own experience. *Seven Days in May* (1964), one of the best American political films—not least of all because it's ultimately more about suspense than politics—has a scene where the president is told the full name of his chairman of the Joint Chiefs of Staff. True, we in the audience would otherwise have no idea who "General James Mattoon Scott" is, but that's not the point; the *president* would know. The requirements of exposition always take precedence over the requirements of verisimilitude, and nowhere does that have more injurious consequences to a movie than when politics is the subject.

What political movies there have been have tended to be about campaigns—all the razzle-dazzle and son et lumière, the power deferring to the glory—with soundtracks that are full of fife and drum or, alternatively, effulgently Coplandesque. Externalities have always been what the movies do best, and externalities are the least of politics—or, rather, the least of democratic politics. The movies have effectively left untouched the *process* of politics—the way it relies on nuance and protocol and etiquette: its foundation in acceptable deceits, shifting traditions, and endless talk. What is most characteristic about politics—certainly what is most efficacious, and, ultimately, what is most interesting—is the working out of it: not what gets done, or even why, but how. Hollywood has never cared for process, and the political film has suffered accordingly. It's somehow appropriate, then, that this disdain of process becomes outright detestation in the genre's masterpiece, *Mr. Smith Goes to Washington*. In that sense, the political movie might almost be seen as subversive in the context of American film, for Hollywood defines itself by action. American politics, predicated on checks and balances, defines itself by inaction—and in no precinct of American politics is this truer than in the Senate.

Mr. Smith hinges on that tension between stasis and action; not surprisingly, everything in the movie favors the latter—even the filibuster conducted by James Stewart's title character, for all that it is meant to block a piece of legislation, is a form of action, at least so far as the camera is concerned. Among the factors that make Otto Preminger's 1962 film version of Allen Drury's novel *Advise and Consent* (1959) striking is its willingness to find process so interesting and stasis so dynamic. If *Mr. Smith* is the greatest of American political movies, then *Advise and Consent* is the densest, the most fully devoted to the form, the most eagerly canonical. It embraces politics with a thoroughness and enthusiasm beyond that of any other Hollywood production, going so far as even to abandon the conventions of the star system. Like the Senate, *Advise and Consent* is about a single class of peers rather than a hierarchy of individuals. It is ensemble with a vengeance. Its top-billed star—Henry Fonda—is onscreen for only twenty-nine minutes, barely a fifth of the film's 142-minute running time. The movie's true star is the Senate itself.

It's long been a truism of American cinema that action is character. *Advise and Consent* may be the only film Hollywood has ever produced in which it could be said that process is character. The system, much more than those who people it, is what interests Preminger. Indeed, *Advise and Consent* comes as the middle title in a quintet of films that, for all their grounding in standard Hollywood melodrama, can also be seen as examinations of contemporary social systems. The best of these films, *Anatomy of a Murder* (1959), looks at the courts. *Exodus* (1960) is a case study in modern nationalism. *The Cardinal* (1963) examines religion and the Catholic Church, and *In Harm's Way* (1965), the military. *Advise and Consent* is the most explicitly focused of these films, the least distracted from the central task of systemic presentation. Each of the others is a star vehicle; and whether it be James Stewart's lawyer, Paul Newman's freedom fighter, Tom Tryon's priest, or John Wayne's navy officer, its leading man defines each film. All *Advise and Consent* needs is the system.

Preminger's film comes by this reverence for the system naturally. The novel on which it is based has as a co-dedicatee "The Senate of the United States" and its members, "without whose existence, example and eccentricities this book could have been neither conceived nor written." It's a wholly accurate statement, for *Advise and Consent* is besotted with the Senate, not just beholden to it for subject matter and setting, but committed to it as an ideal of conduct and exemplar of community.

The novel comprises four sections, each focusing on a different senator. It begins with the majority leader, Bob Munson (in the film, expertly played by Walter Pidgeon), who's charged with the unenviable task of shepherding through the Senate the highly controversial nomination of Robert Leffingwell (Fonda) as secretary of state. Leffingwell, a left-leaning senior bureaucrat, once offended Senator Seabright "Seab" Cooley (Charles Laughton, in his last role), a South Carolina Bourbon given to white suits and homiletic oratory. Cooley, the second section's protagonist, vows to defeat Leffingwell. In an effort to expedite the nomination, it's rather implausibly shunted to a subcommittee of the Senate Foreign Relations Committee chaired by Brigham Anderson (Don Murray), an upright young Mormon from Utah. It turns out that Anderson has a skeleton in his closet—a wartime same-sex fling—that comes to the attention of Senator Fred Van Ackerman (George Grizzard), who is even more obsessively committed to Leffingwell's confirmation than Cooley is to his defeat. Anderson refuses to buckle and, preferring death to so sordid a dishonor, kills himself. The fourth section, in which the confirmation vote takes place, focuses on Senator Orrin Knox (Edward Andrews), who becomes a leader in the eventually successful fight against Leffingwell.

All this, and much else besides, gets played out over the densely printed course of the novel's 616 pages; and even by the not-so-exacting standards of best-sellerdom, *Advise and Consent* is a ponderously bad novel. Even so, it became a publishing sensation and stayed on the *New York Times* best-seller list for 102 weeks. Drury received letters of praise from forty senators, including Goldwater, Everett Dirksen, and Mike Mansfield. JFK was reading *Advise and Consent* in June 1959, and Jackie gave it a try, too, though a dozen years later she admitted to Nixon that she never managed to finish it.[42]

Drury had spent fifteen years covering Washington for the United Press, the *Washington Evening Star*, and the *New York Times* before turning to fiction, and his first novel is nothing if not well informed. The core of the novel's appeal is the impression it gives of relating the way things "really" are in the Senate. This is an impression the movie wants to give, too, as memorably expressed by its Saul Bass logo—a stylized rendering of the Capitol dome opening up to reveal the title lurking beneath. The meaning is clear: we're getting what's been previously hidden and kept under wraps, the inside story. The very first sentence of the novel hints at what the reader is in for, announcing that Munson awoke that morning at precisely 7:31. Some authors strive to be up to the minute. Drury is down to the minute.

Preminger does his best to retain Drury's veneration for the Senate. In some ways, he improves upon it, for what Drury keeps telling us, Preminger far more persuasively *shows* us. These are giants striding the Capitol's corridors, larger-than-life figures—they're movie stars, aren't they?—and the sleek self-satisfaction of power is everywhere to be seen. Presumably that would have looked damning if the movie had been made even a few years later, but in 1962 it's meant to seem reassuring. The system is never called into question. Rather, we're to cherish it—and on the basis of what we're shown, why shouldn't we? The one truly odious senator, Grizzard's Van Ackerman, is explicitly singled out as unsenatorial and ends up a pariah. In the context of *Advise and Consent*, no greater punishment can be imagined for a man than, having been admitted to this Olympus of governance, he should find himself ostracized within it. "Brig knows how to be a senator," we are assured—unlike Van Ackerman, who bridles at the contrast. What motivates Van Ackerman to blackmail his colleague is as much jealousy at Anderson's status as dedication to Leffingwell's nomination.

Van Ackerman's the classic bad apple, except that not even an apple this bad can spoil such an upstanding bunch. True, there's Anderson's brief straying from the sexual straight and narrow—but it's made explicit that that was an aberration brought on by the rigors of wartime and his being so "lonely" overseas—and it's an action for which he is more than suitably ashamed. There's an elderly senator who snoozes at his desk, and another who overindulges his fondness for the fair sex. And that's about the extent of awfulness on display. Or at least of legislative awfulness—executive awfulness, with a president and several presidential appointees who lie with abandon, is another matter. The flaw of the occasional individual senator merely casts into greater relief the unimpeachability of the institution itself, and the flaws of other elected officials underscore that it's not government per se that *Advise and Consent* lionizes but rather that uniquely noble and august body, the United States Senate.

What's so peculiar about this Senate is that it's self-enclosed and self-contained, a kind of political terrarium. It's a Burkean body, one in which neither electoral politics nor public opinion merits mention, as if it were vulgar for a senator to concern himself with such things. This is one political movie without marching bands or bunting, and the senators onscreen are as unconscious of the voters they serve as they are of the moviegoers over whom their Panavision images loom. For that matter, the media are as extraneous to the senatorial process as the voters are. They don't even qualify as Greek chorus, their standard, all-else-failing function in a political movie on those rare occasions when a reporter or editor doesn't have a top-billed role. The concept of "back home"—with all that it implies of roots elsewhere, concerns elsewhere, another *reality* elsewhere—does not exist for the senators of *Advise and Consent*, which any real-life senator would envy beyond words. These men may reside elsewhere (Anderson in an Ozzie-and-Harriet split-level, Munson in a hotel suite), but they *live* beneath the Capitol dome. It's where they're most at home, a great good place that provides emotional sustenance, comradely warmth, and familial attachment.

To be sure, it's a curious kind of home and lopsided sort of family (women never advise but are always expected to consent). Made at the heresy-free high noon of U.S. power, *Advise and Consent* unwittingly captures a triumphalist, father-knows-best world in which automobiles are big, budget deficits small, and Vietnam likelier to be referred to as French Indochina. Television is the merest presence. Authority, even when explicitly duplicitous, goes unquestioned. And homosexuals are, literally, thrust into the gutter. When Brig Anderson confronts his ex-lover in a gay bar in Greenwich Village, the senator rejects a plea for understanding by sending him flying off the sidewalk. Most telling of all is the near-complete absence of women. There are only two female senators, and they are clearly peripheral to the workings of power. Women are peripheral generally. "Since when have I become the little woman who's supposed to sit at home and know nothing?" Anderson's wife asks him. "Since always, actually" is the message the movie sends. Females hardly ever appear on the screen, and they're almost invariably wife, mistress, or secretary.

That is one thing, at least, *Advise and Consent* has in common with other political movies. Just as politics used to be an almost exclusively masculine preserve, so, too, with political movies. There are wives, of course, who tend to be either adoring helpmeets or selfish obstacles, and female reporters, from Jean Arthur in *Mr. Smith Goes to Washington* to Julie Christie in *Power* (1986). Otherwise, the exceptions are painfully rare. A female in a political film is generally either a figure of fun, such as Ann Sothern's chatterbox national committeewoman in *The Best Man*, or menacing. *The Contender* (2000) is all about the uproar when it's learned that a female vice-presidential nominee (played by Joan Allen) once had a vigorous sex life. The uproar is meant to be an indictment of the hypocritical morality of politics. Yet there's a prurience at work that owes far more to Hollywood than Washington.

It's a cardinal axiom of studio moviemaking: Aberration onscreen always arouses distrust, and nothing is more aberrational to Hollywood than a forceful woman involved in politics. Angela Lansbury demonstrates this memorably in not one but two roles: as the newspaper publisher/kingmaker in *State of the Union*; and, in one of the most chilling performances in all of American film, as the title character's mother in *The Manchurian Candidate* (1962). Easily the strongest figure in either film, Lansbury is a dynamo of will and ambition, a fact each movie can square with her sex only by portraying her as an utter monster.

Strong women in political films have been unusual. Sympathetic, or at least three-dimensional, politicians have been even more so. It is a mark of Hollywood's discomfort with politics that on those rare occasions the movies have grappled with public life, the focus has almost always been on a citizen-politician rather than a professional: James Stewart's Jeff Smith, Brian Donlevy's title character in *The Great McGinty* (1940), Gary Cooper's title character in *Meet John Doe* (1941), Spencer Tracy's Grant Matthews in *State of the Union*, Robert Redford's Bill McKay in *The Candidate*, Eddie Murphy's con man/congressman in *The Distinguished Gentleman* (1992), Tim Robbins's *Bob Roberts* (1992), Kevin Kline's impostor president in *Dave* (1993). The movies have almost always portrayed the professional politician as either buffoon or bounder—more often the latter. And even when the politician proves to be neither fool nor felon, he (the pronoun is inescapable) generally requires the intervention of some private citizen to redeem him. Examples range from Donlevy's McGinty with wife Muriel Angelus to Tracy's Matthews with wife Katharine Hepburn to Michael Douglas's title character with girlfriend Annette Bening in *The American President* (1995). Of course, in *Wag the Dog* (1997), Dustin Hoffman's private citizen isn't female and what's redeemed are the president's poll ratings rather than his morals, but the point is the same. It's a sad state of affairs when a Hollywood producer is seen as morally no worse—maybe even better—than the president of the United States.

The inevitable corollary to this suspicion of the professional politician is the fostering of a febrile faux-populism that borders on civic nihilism. As political reporter Van Johnson says to Tracy of the latter's nascent candidacy in *State of the Union*, "Mr. Matthews, you have just created the ideal political platform: drown the politicians!" Certainly, that has long been the movies' ideal political platform. It rests on a fundamental dichotomy, that between upright citizen and crooked politician. As Tracy expresses it, "The world needs honest men today more than it needs presidents." A modern-day Diogenes couldn't have put it better—or more simplistically. Almost three decades later, *The Parallax View* opens with television reporter Paula Prentiss broadcasting the arrival of a presidential hopeful at Seattle's Space Needle. Senator Charles Carroll, she informs her viewers, is "so independent that some say they don't know what party he belongs to." It comes as no surprise that such a nonpartisan marvel is about to be assassinated. Hollywood's political calculus being what it is, there's no way the political system would let him survive.

Such a blend of knowingness and naïveté is alluring in the extreme, or at least it is until one realizes to what extent cynicism informs both. If the type of man the world needs more than presidents is an honest one, then neither presidents nor most men must be honest. Under such circumstances, democracy is worse than a joke; it's a danger. Willie Stark—or, for that matter, unindicted co-conspirators in the White House—should be the norm. "Jack, there's something on everybody," Crawford's Stark tells John Ireland's Jack Burden, in *All the King's Men*. "Man is conceived in sin and born in corruption." This is the only possible conclusion to be drawn from the assumptions about human nature that inform most political movies. Yet instead of condemning the system, most films offer weirdly layered celebrations of it, in which the innocence of our past (the Founding Fathers and the Constitution) is threatened by the corruption of the present, only to be rescued by the presumed innocence of the future (the outsider-candidate hero). The box-office virtues of such a schema are readily apparent: the way in which it ensures conflict, equates a specific individual with right while identifying wrong with a general abstraction, and honors the system in principle even as it vilifies it in practice. Less obvious, but far more vexing, is the schema's fundamental drawback: sheer illogic. If all politicians are bad, and they are elected by the people, mustn't there be something fundamentally amiss with the people, the system, or both?

This explicitly scornful view of politicians—and implicitly scornful view of the electorate—achieves a kind of apotheosis in *Power*, the story of an almost comically omnipotent political consultant (Richard Gere). His candidate-clients are presented as nothing more than a higher form of software, almost as afterthoughts in the real electoral process in which voters are as much controlled by media-savvy insiders as the politicians are. The movie ends with a montage of our new political leadership class—main frames, television monitors, VCRs, computer printers, mixing boards—and the sight of all this hardware is accompanied, in case anyone failed to get the message, by a rousing rendition of "The Stars and Stripes Forever." At least it isn't "Hail to the Chief." Even such leftish efforts as *The Candidate* and *Bob Roberts* (the latter especially) hold the electorate in contempt and portray the people as being so many manipulable boobs. If the viewer can see through these men so easily, why can't the voter? It's anti-democracy in action. Clearly, we, the audience, are superior to them, the electorate. Yet one man's electorate is another's audience, and it's almost as if Hollywood is transferring to the political realm its own attitude toward the populace: We provide and profit; you accept and pay.

Among the things that make *Advise and Consent* so singular among political movies is just this: the way it concentrates on and, indeed, celebrates the professional politician. By contrast, the one nonpolitician who figures prominently in the film, Fonda's Leffingwell, not only prevaricates but is secretly an ideologue, and the one thing Hollywood is uneasier with in a movie than politics is ideology. No ideology taints any of the senators, of course, other than Van Ackerman, for they are the highest form of politician.

Advise and Consent, above all, demonstrates the depth of its commitment to professional politicians as a class by consciously violating one of the cardinal rules of Hollywood storytelling: it takes for its hero a resoundingly unheroic character—and "takes" is the right word. Drury's hero is Orrin Knox, a giant of the Senate and long a national figure, whereas Preminger and his screenwriter, Wendell Mayes, relegate him to the film's fringes. Instead, they pick the vice president, Harley Hudson, a man who for much of the movie easily lives up—or down—to his blithely innocuous name.

Hudson is an afterthought, an appendage, a friend of a friend of a friend. As winningly played by Lew Ayres, there's something feckless and wan about this vice president. He exhibits Dr. Kildare's best bedside manner—Hudson's the one character to recognize Brig Anderson's torment and reach out to help—but this physician has a practice without any patients. Ignored by a president whom he must uncomplainingly support, patronized by the senators he must tediously preside over, Hudson is such supernumerary political cargo that after a speech in New York, he flies back unaccompanied on a commercial flight. "I'm not included in very much either," he assures a disaffected senator, and his consistent exclusion verges on a running joke. This remains the case even when rumors about the president's health become widespread—so widespread, in fact, they reach even Harley. He remains the forgotten man of the Senate—forgotten, that is, until the rumors prove to be well founded and he becomes president. It's just one more vindication of the system, since all along we've been shown what a fine and decent man Harley Hudson really is: as worthy of the office of president as the office of vice president was unworthy of him.

Vice presidents do not tend to be movie-hero material. Rare as political films have been, notable vice presidents are even rarer. "Your Superfluous Highness" Benjamin Franklin proposed calling holders of the office. John Adams, the first vice president, lamented that his position was "the most insignificant office that ever the invention of man contrived or his imagination conceived." For the next 160 years, it remained little more than a means to balance political tickets and, on too-frequent occasions, elevate nonentities to the White House.

This was the office to which Richard Nixon ascended—if that is the verb—in 1953. Murray Chotiner had to make such a forceful argument to Pat Nixon in favor of taking the vice-presidential nomination not just because of her strong dislike of politics, but also because of the office's history of being little more than an exalted joke. Previously, vice presidents had been expected to be neither seen nor heard—except, perhaps, at election time. It was Nixon more than any other person who helped change that. He logged nearly 160,000 miles in overseas travel on diplomatic missions to some fifty-eight countries. His trips to Asia in 1953, the Hungarian border after the 1956 revolution, South America in 1958, and Moscow in 1959 drew worldwide attention. By the time he left the vice presidency, Nixon had become an international figure second only to Eisenhower among U.S. officeholders. No one could ever again take the vice presidency so lightly or dismiss its holder so readily. Part of the reason Dan Quayle inspired such mockery three decades later was that so much more had come to be expected of a vice president.

A good deal of that rise in expectations could, of course, simply be attributed to altered circumstances. As the United States' role in the world changed radically with the onset of the cold war, so did the expectations for both its leader and the man next in line to succeed him. Yet that change didn't prevent Truman's vice president, Barkley, an able politician who had led his party in the Senate for more than a decade, from being seen as anything other than an amiable placeholder whose sole legacy in the office was the term "veep." It was Nixon, through his own diligence and ability as well as circumstances, who elevated the office. As even Tip O'Neill had to concede, "No man was ever better prepared for the presidency."[43] Because he took the office so seriously, the nation finally began to. "Richard Nixon," Tom Wicker argues, "essentially . . . created the modern vice presidency."[44]

That creation was born of an actuarial imperative. Three times Nixon had to fill in for Eisenhower: during the latter's heart attack in 1955, his ileitis operation in 1956, and his stroke in 1957. With each succeeding health crisis, Nixon's relative youth and vigor took on greater importance as a (necessary) complement to Eisenhower's advanced age and relative frailty. A frustrated Adlai Stevenson, unable to attack Eisenhower directly, spent much of the 1956 presidential campaign calling attention to Nixon's proximity to the Oval Office.

Politics was the other great factor in making Nixon a new kind of vice president. Because of politics, Eisenhower needed Nixon almost as much as Nixon needed Eisenhower. A superb natural politician, Ike nonetheless eschewed the hurly-burly of Washington politics—and shrewdly so, for his seeming detachment from political infighting further enhanced his elder-statesman image. Hence the need for Nixon, not only as the administration's chief political advocate—or "hatchet man," as his detractors saw it—but also, more significantly, as Eisenhower's eyes and ears on Capitol Hill. Other than testifying before the occasional congressional committee, Eisenhower possessed no legislative background. "I was never trained in politics," he said to Theodore H. White in 1964; "I came in laterally, at the top."[45] Nor did most of his Cabinet have political training; of its ten original members, only three had held any sort of elective office.[46] Even if Nixon hadn't been the supremely political animal he was, he would still have had to serve as the administration's Capitol Hill consigliere solely on the basis of his legislative experience. Eisenhower, who generally had little to do with his vice president, saw Nixon at least three times a week when Congress was in session. He was, in effect, Eisenhower's G-2. It's an indication not just of the distance Ike kept between them but also of where his importance was perceived to lie that, of the trio of offices Nixon maintained, none was in the White House or Executive Office Building. All were on Capitol Hill. That's where Eisenhower wanted Nixon: far away from him and close to Congress.

During his first two years as vice president, Nixon had an additional reason for staying near the Senate chamber. The Senate was divided between forty-eight Republicans, forty-seven Democrats, and one independent (Oregon's Wayne Morse), thus increasing the likelihood that Nixon would have to cast tie-breaking votes, in his constitutionally mandated role as president of the Senate. Not that Nixon did much actual presiding over the chamber. He spent less than a tenth of his time doing so, preferring instead to spend most of his hours in the Capitol at his private office hard by the Senate floor, from which location he was readily available should the need arise to break a tie. Otherwise, his standard routine was to call the body to order, listen to the opening invocation and

Majority Leader's announcements, then hand the gavel over to a junior senator.[47] An obvious exception were occasions of major political import, such as the final debate on McCarthy's censure in 1954.

How to deal with McCarthy was the Eisenhower administration's foremost dilemma during its first two years. That Nixon should have chief responsibility for handling the senator was just one more indication of his importance to the administration. "With his own creditable record in ferreting out Communist conspirators," Sherman Adams, Ike's chief of staff, wrote in his memoirs, "it was to be expected that Nixon should have taken a personal interest in McCarthy's investigations. Indeed, he tried as best he could to keep the Senator within bounds."[48] As Nixon was to Congress in general, so was he to McCarthy in particular: Eisenhower's chief emissary and explicator.

That "creditable record" was owing to the Hiss case, of course, which had given Nixon unassailable anti-communist credentials. Too unassailable, perhaps: Stevenson, one will recall, mocked the vice president as "McCarthy in a white collar," while Sam Rayburn liked to tell friends, "Nixon is the next thing to McCarthy."[49] At least such characterizations made it all the easier for Nixon to act as a brake on McCarthy's more outrageous actions. So, too, did their generally amiable relations—"friendship," in the great senatorial tradition, would be too strong a word—and Nixon held to the view that for all McCarthy might be "irresponsibly impulsive," he was nonetheless "personally likable."[50] At Nixon's suggestion, they vacationed together at Key Biscayne in 1953—George Smathers's hospitality had won another convert to Florida sunshine—and McCarthy invited Vice President Nixon and Pat to his wedding, as did another senator, John F. Kennedy. It was, however, only McCarthy's that the Nixons (escorting Alice Roosevelt Longworth, no less) managed to fit into their schedule. The vice president was the most prominent attendee there, as he was four years later at McCarthy's funeral.

Whether it be intervening in a fistfight between McCarthy and Drew Pearson ("If I hadn't pulled McCarthy away, he might have killed Pearson," Nixon told Ralph de Toledano)[51] or getting the senator to tone down his attacks on Eisenhower's nomination of Charles E. Bohlen as ambassador to the Soviet Union, Nixon was more successful than anyone else in tempering, if not controlling, McCarthy's behavior. It wasn't enough, though, as he learned when he tried to head off the Army-McCarthy imbroglio, which ultimately led to McCarthy's censure. "Once again I seemed to be the only person with enough credibility in both camps to suggest a compromise," he would later write.[52]

One can all but hear the exasperation in that "Once again." What matters isn't Nixon's inability to broker a deal, but that he alone could plausibly attempt to do so. No one else had the ties to both camps he did, but that also meant he was suspect in both camps. Eisenhower's dependence on Nixon to help him negotiate the intricacies of Capitol Hill didn't prevent him from keeping his vice president at arm's length. And, if anything, Nixon's anti-communist allies in the Senate held him in even lower regard. Months before the censure, McCarthy had already taken to referring to the "constant yack-yacking" of "that prick Nixon."[53] More significant was the strained state of Nixon's relations with William Knowland, California's senior senator, who had held the upper hand over his junior colleague when Nixon was in the Senate. Knowland detested Nixon for what he perceived to be his betrayal of their fellow Californian Earl Warren at the 1952 Republican convention. More to the point, Knowland regarded Nixon as his leading rival for the GOP presidential nomination in either 1956 (should Eisenhower not seek reelection) or 1960. Unfortunately for Nixon, it was Knowland who succeeded Taft as Senate Republican leader in 1953. Unlike McCarthy, the Californian was no lone wolf. The most influential and prominent Republican senator was not someone a vice president wanted to have against him, yet William Knowland was no friend—even in the sense that senators are friends—of Richard Nixon.

McCarthy and Knowland had specific personal reasons for distrusting Nixon, reasons that superseded even stronger ideological ones for supporting him. If presumptive allies felt leery of him, what must senators without any predisposition toward him have felt? Nixon's being Eisenhower's chief conduit to Capitol Hill spoke more to the White House's lack of political experience than it did to Nixon's "popularity" in Congress. As we have seen, Nixon never really fit into the Senate, and his ascent to the vice presidency did nothing to change that. If anything, it worsened things. His elevation inspired jealousy (and in some cases, such as Clinton Anderson's, incomprehension) even as it weakened his membership in the club—which had always been, at best, exiguous.

Now doubly an outsider, Nixon further suffered by comparison with his predecessor. As a longtime Capitol Hill staffer put it, Nixon "was never received at the Senate with the universal benevolence accorded to Alben Barkley."[54] Barkley served twenty-three years in the Senate and, more important, was clearly a man of the Senate. After leaving the vice presidency, Barkley ran again for the Senate (successfully) at the age of seventy-six. Nixon, the younger man by three decades, never even considered trying to return to the Senate after leaving the vice presidency. Hubert Humphrey went back, too, and without hesitation. For that matter, Barkley's predecessor, Harry Truman, always said he was far happier as a senator than as president.

Truman, Barkley, Humphrey: all found the Senate to be a convivial, congenial environment—and this was as true when each was vice president as when a senator. It's impossible to imagine any one of them displaying anything like the uncomfortableness that Hugh Sidey, a Washington correspondent for *Time* during the '50s, recalls Nixon exhibiting whenever on Capitol Hill: "Of course he had to sit up in front of the Senate, but when he was off duty you would see that hunched figure trying to skulk off down the back ways."[55]

Nixon didn't see it that way, of course. "I was a man of the Congress," he declares in his memoirs, "and I was proud of the fact."[56] The statement has a nice ring to it, noble even—certainly politic—like a bit of campaign oratory. "Man of the Congress" just doesn't square, though, with what we know about Nixon, his time on Capitol Hill, or his attitude toward the Senate and House. Men of the Congress do not hunch their way down its more obscure corridors—let alone men of the Congress who are second in line to the presidency. Men of the Congress stride and strut and *belong* there, and that Nixon never did. To be fair, he never really wanted to. How could he have? What comes across as his fundamental attitude toward the legislative branch is a mild, ongoing disgust: disgust for all its thick encrustation of custom, for its unwieldiness and obduracy, its utter reliance on something so baffling and undependable as personal relations. "Congress," in Jimmy Breslin's evocative formulation, "is afternoon baseball."[57] A day at the ballpark is a lovely way to spend three hours. It is, however, no way to make history, no way to change the world: a way, perhaps, for an ambitious man to matter—but not to *really* matter. Nixon, more than any other man of his time, wanted to really matter.

Nixon was almost always most revealing about himself when he's supposed to be discussing something else. For example, he was ostensibly talking about the art of compromise and how one gets things done in Congress when he told Stewart Alsop in 1958, "You get here and you've got to learn how to operate—the boring and frustrating committee system and so on,"[58] but what he was really expressing was how he really felt about Congress as an institution: that it was "boring" and "frustrating" and, most damning of all, that I-can't-be-bothered "so on." Congress was a place awash in "so on's": not a place for vision, certainly not a place for decisiveness and action.

It's telling that only one of the *Six Crises*, the Hiss case, has to do with Congress—this despite the fact that at the time of the book's publication in 1962, Nixon had spent all his public life either in Congress or presiding over its upper chamber. For that matter, in Nixon's telling, much of that episode occurs away from Capitol Hill: in New York, on Chambers's Maryland farm, even at sea, where Nixon first learned of the existence of the Pumpkin Papers. The Hiss chapter is additionally anomalous in that it deals with Congress in its least typical mode, the investigative. Focusing on that aspect would prove prophetic, for it was just that congressional prerogative that would come back to haunt Nixon a quarter century later with Watergate. It's one more sign of how foreign Congress was to him that he would later fail to anticipate anything of the sort happening. "I don't see how the Senate can destroy us," he'd scoffed when a resolution creating the Senate Select Committee on Presidential Campaign Activities had been passed (unanimously, in fact).[59]

Lyndon Johnson "never understood the difference between the Hill and the White House," one of his aides complained to Theodore H. White in 1968.[60] Nixon understood the difference only too well—he cherished it, he nurtured it, and had begun to do so long before he moved up Pennsylvania Avenue. Where Johnson tried to collapse the difference between the two, Nixon did his best to heighten it. Sometimes this could assume a comic aspect, as at Tricia Nixon's wedding: invitees included not a single member of Congress, even with a guest list otherwise large enough to include Red Skelton, Art Linkletter, and Ralph Nader.* More often, though, the divide was a matter of deadly seriousness. The notorious siege mentality of the Nixon White House is most often seen in terms of the counterculture or the press or the Eastern liberal establishment. Yet the administration's sense of fear and loathing extended to Congress, too. That Nixon was the first president since Zachary Taylor to be elected without a majority in either house simply made it that much easier for him to write off the legislative branch, to see it as (at best) an obstacle, and (at worst) something alien, worthy only of suspicion or scorn.

"Deep down in his heart," one of Gerald Ford's closest aides felt, "Nixon had a classic case of contempt of Congress." That aide, Robert Hartmann, attributed Nixon's contempt to his being "a solo player; he didn't understand the power of the Congress—this kind of bonding of the patriarchs."[61] Implicit in Hartmann's assessment is the belief that his

*Nader was a guest on the groom's side, Edward Cox having worked for him as a summer intern.

own boss did have such an understanding, and there's no better proof of that than on the night Nixon announced Ford's nomination as vice president. The announcement came before an East Room gathering composed largely of congressmen and it brought a round of cheers from the audience. "They like you," Nixon whispered to Ford. The obvious corollary went unspoken: they didn't like *him*.[62]

Well, truth be told, they'd never much liked him. Nixon had been right to feel lost when he first got to Congress, yet that feeling had less to do with inexperience than aptitude. He had an aptitude for politics, to be sure, one that would prove legendary. It was an aptitude for legislating that he lacked. Soon enough, Nixon learned the ropes on Capitol Hill— in fact, sooner than most. What he never learned was how to enter into the rhythms and routine of Congress, how to flourish in the society it comprised, how to enjoy its (for lack of a better term) way of life. And the more powerful he became, the more uncomfortable he felt about it. By the time he entered the White House, the self-styled man of the Congress wanted to have as little to do with the Congress as possible. (The most thankless job in the Nixon administration wasn't White House press spokesman but chief congressional liaison.)

It could even be argued that Nixon felt more comfortable with reporters than he did with congressmen. As Stephen Ambrose has noted, "Nixon probably had more friends in the press corps than among the politicians" when he was a senator. If anything, that was truer during his time as vice president and after.[63] Not that Nixon was any great friend of the press—far, far from it. For all that he might have felt uneasy with members of Congress, he didn't *hate* them—and he hated the press. Nixon did, however, respect what reporters could do for him. Certain journalists had, in fact, done a very great deal for him, as he knew perfectly well. There was also a question of affinity. Members of the press were more interested in results than process. Attuned to the effects of words and (some of them, at least) the power of ideas, they tended to be quick and sharp and in the know, qualities Nixon prized in himself as well as in others, qualities rarer than one might like to think among congressmen. True, it was a curious sort of relationship that existed between Nixon and his friends in the press—more symbiosis, really, than friendship. They were, let us say, friends as journalists and politicians are friends. That may not be friendship as the term is generally understood. But it would be hard to dispute that the way in which Nixon and the press were friends was richer, more complex, and certainly more varied than the way in which senators are friends.

Burt Lancaster and Tony Curtis

SWEET SMELL OF SUCCESS

■ ■

But unlike some people, I've never canceled a subscription to a paper and also I never will. RICHARD NIXON, AT HIS "LAST" PRESS CONFERENCE, NOVEMBER 6, 1962

Let's go to El Morocco and have some spaghetti! NIXON, TO AIDES EAGER TO CEL-EBRATE THE REPUBLICAN OFF-YEAR COMEBACK HE HAD HELPED MASTERMIND, NOVEMBER 3, 1966[1]

Kyle Palmer was dying; there was little doubt about that. Within seven months, he'd be dead from leukemia. Palmer's condition did simplify things for Richard Nixon, however. After consider-able struggle, he had finally decided on September 26, 1961, to run for governor of California. He had had many misgivings about entering the race, misgivings that would prove well-founded. But now that the decision had been made, there were political niceties to be observed. Close friends and generous sup-porters needed to be notified before Nixon made his decision public—and as one who had come within a hundred thousand votes of the presidency, he had acquired many close friends and many generous supporters. Yet when Nixon realized that his "must" list would easily exceed a hundred people—a hundred who needed to be called or sent handwritten notes within a day—he chose to limit himself to just two, a pair of men even the thinnest-skinned among the spurned must grant pride of place to. Indeed, who might not concede primacy to Richard Nixon's political father and political godfather, Dwight D. Eisenhower and Kyle Palmer.[2]

Eisenhower, of course, needs no introduction. Kyle Palmer's contributions were well known, too, among the political cognoscenti who made up Nixon's list. For without Kyle Palmer, Richard Nixon almost certainly would not have achieved a position that allowed him to join Ike on the ticket. So in placing the call to Palmer, there was not only the sentimental gesture of honoring a dying friend; there was a kind of filial devotion and the acknowledgment of his own past in equating a *Los Angeles Times* political editor with the former president of the United States. Indeed, the call symbolized the complexity of Nixon's tangled relationship with the press, of how much he gained by it as well as lost. Then, too, there was his future to consider: for unlike the former president, the former political editor might very well help get Nixon elected governor of California—or so the former vice president assumed, an assumption that would help doom his campaign and have near-fatal consequences for his political career.

Nixon's opposite in nearly every way, Palmer was short, sunny, a bon vivant—by all accounts a most agreeable companion, a man who married several times and lunched regularly at the best table at Perino's, on Wilshire Boulevard. (It was to Perino's that Nixon went for a small celebratory dinner after the nationally televised address announcing he would visit China.) Palmer's tastes were those of an eighteenth-century epicure, and his writing style—ponderously ornate, weirdly refined—was that of a thoroughly minor eighteenth-century man of letters. It is harder to assign a century to his politics, other than to say it most definitely was not the twentieth. Born in Tennessee in 1892, he hated labor unions and believed uncompromisingly in the racial order he had grown up with. After *Brown v. Board of Education*, he could be overheard berating his old friend and protégé Earl Warren about the ruling as they ate at Perino's. The chief justice of the United States, who was also the most popular vote getter in California history as its three-term governor, took no offense at this public dressing-down. It did not pay a politician—no matter how exalted his office or secure his position—to anger Kyle Palmer.[3]

"Genial and puckish" was how a colleague once described him.[4] The geniality was hard to see if you were a Democrat. For three decades, he was the éminence grise of the California GOP. "One cannot overstate Kyle Palmer's influence," recalled Robert Finch.[5] He was the party's Mr. Inside and Mr. Outside rolled into one: actively brokering deals and controlling political contributions while influencing public opinion through his widely read *Times* column and unquestioned control of the paper's political coverage. Not for nothing was he known as "Mr. Republican" and "the Little Governor." In a state notoriously fluid in its politics, Kyle Palmer and his influence seemed as solid as the Sierra Nevada.

No one believed in Palmer's influence more than Nixon did, for no one had benefited more from it. He had Palmer's imprimatur when he sought the Republican nomination to run against Jerry Voorhis in 1946—and, with it, the support of the *Times*. Three years later, as Nixon began to contemplate a campaign for the Senate, it was Palmer who first encouraged him. In 1958 it was Palmer who engineered "the great switcheroo" whereby Governor Goodwin Knight ran for Senator William Knowland's seat after Knowland had announced he was running for governor. This ensured Nixon would remain first among equals in California's GOP leadership troika and remain the front runner for the 1960 presidential nomination.

In his history of the *Los Angeles Times*, Marshall Berges goes so far as to say, "Nixon had been invented by the paper."[6] He exaggerates, but not by much. The dominant voice in California politics, and the supreme voice in Southern California politics, the *Times* at midcentury was as Republican a big-city paper as there was beyond the circulation area of the *Chicago Tribune*, and its political reporting clearly reflected this. It wasn't just that Nixon and his fellow Republicans got good press from the *Times*, which they certainly did. It was also that their opponents effectively got no press—right down to having a hard time getting their campaign schedules printed. Nixon, who had gone from congressional aspirant to vice president in less than seven years, was the most extreme example of the power of the paper's backing. No other institution could as justly echo Eisenhower's declaration to Nixon: "You're my boy!"

Such a degree of support carried a very real danger with it, however. Seeing that "the *Los Angeles Times* was Nixon's patron," Theodore H. White writes, Nixon inevitably "expected that other publishing enterprises would treat him with similarly unbalanced kindness."[7] Kyle Palmer had set an unrealistic standard at the very beginning of Nixon's political career, creating a template in his mind for how the press ought to treat him.

During Nixon's vice presidency, the *Times* began to change, but he was three thousand miles away and had other, more pressing concerns than the political realignment of his favorite paper. With his return from Washington in 1961, the *Times*' evolution became rather more relevant. The most obvious manifestation of the new *Times* was that Palmer was no longer political editor. Small matter: the candidate assumed he could still depend on the paper; and if for some reason he couldn't, he knew whom to turn to, to square things. So when the paper's coverage took a new nonpartisan direction he had not anticipated—even the column inches devoted to Nixon's opponent, the incumbent, Pat Brown, were measured against the number devoted to Nixon—he began calling Palmer to complain. It did no good. The *Times* not only had a new political editor but a new editor and publisher, too, each committed to building the paper's reputation for objective reporting. Win or lose, Nixon was going to have to do it without the *Times*.

His charged history with the paper lay behind his "last" press conference the morning after Brown's victory. Nixon went on for fifteen tortured minutes about why he'd lost; and even if his manner bespoke a man in a haze, his syntax remained crisp and his sentences all too parsable. The speech comprised a defense of his campaign organization, several jabs at Brown, the question of his own future ("You won't have Nixon to kick around any more"), but kept returning to the question of campaign coverage. The speech's real message centered on the *Times* and, as Nixon saw it, how the *Times* had turned on him. More broadly, this was Nixon's response to all the abuse he'd had to suffer (in his eyes, uniquely suffer) from the press over the years: the *New York Post*'s wildly overplaying the fund story, which led to the Checkers speech; the Herblock cartoons in the *Washington Post* that showed him ill-shaven and emerging from a sewer; the favoritism so many campaign reporters had demonstrated toward John F. Kennedy in 1960; and now the *Times*' betrayal. All the resentment and distrust finally, all too publicly, boiled over, but in that Heepish, verbally-veiled-yet-emotionally-transparent way of his that only made things worse. Every punch followed by a pat on the back, each snarl balanced (or so Nixon always seemed to suppose) by a novocaine grin: it made him appear phony as well as mean.

Overall, though, Nixon was right: the press did largely loathe him, and his political fortunes suffered for it. Yet this was only half the story. He'd had other benefactors in the press besides Palmer and the *Times*. He even had much in common with the journalists who covered him—a love of politics, an appreciation for the word, a fondness for the intensely masculine locker-room milieu of a campaign—and Nixon did not fail to recognize that common ground. As he told Jules Witcover in 1966, "I like the press guys, because I'm basically like them."[8]

It was a puzzle, actually. Tactically, Nixon understood the press so well—far better than the lion's share of his peers—which made all the more mystifying his larger incomprehension. And this pattern would hold true throughout his career. The politician who made the press's enmity a point of personal pride also spent his entire professional life seeking out reporters, flattering them, trying to use them. Recall Stephen Ambrose's remark about the California senator having more friends among reporters than politicians. The man who saw himself as the press's favorite whipping boy would remark how, given the chance to live his life over, he'd like to be a sportswriter. The president who unleashed the White House Plumbers was himself a champion leaker. Like every politician, he had a symbiotic relationship with the press—it was just that, in his case, the relationship was so much more extreme, and extreme for both parties.

In his book *The Nixon Memo*, Marvin Kalb captures the ambiguity that informed the thirty-seventh president's relations with the press. "Nixon never liked reporters. He always felt the need to control, manage, taunt, tease, threaten, attack, and criticize the press. He often applied a surgeon's skill to the manipulation of newspaper publishers and television correspondents. At other times, he was about as delicate as an 800-pound gorilla. Yet, in an odd way, he respected the journalists' position in society, even if he did not fully understand it, and he recognized their importance to the political process and their value to him."[9]

How could he not? Nixon had surely been too inexperienced to altogether grasp what was going on with Palmer and the *Times* in 1946, how phenomenally lucky he had been to be anointed. Two years later, with the Hiss case, he knew better. Looking back in 1952, Nixon wrote Bert Andrews, the *New York Herald Tribune*'s Washington bureau chief, that "the whole course of the investigation was determined" by the visit Andrews had paid with Nixon to Whittaker Chambers's Maryland farm in 1948. Andrews had won a Pulitzer Prize that spring for a 4,600-word investigative piece on a disloyalty witch hunt in the State Department. Nixon, thus thinking him predisposed to favor Hiss over Chambers (and perfectly aware that the *Herald Tribune* was the leading organ of Eastern establishment Republicanism), sought out Andrews as his press connection. If Nixon could convince *him*, the battle would be all but won. After three hours of interviewing Chambers, Andrews told Nixon he now believed the charges against Hiss. Indeed, he went on to become an unofficial, and vitally important, adviser to Nixon. It was Andrews who suggested the House Committee on Un-American Activities subpoena Chambers, which produced the famed Pumpkin Papers. In 1950 Nixon wrote to Helen Reid, the *Herald Tribune*'s owner, "Had it not been for Bert Andrew's [*sic*] work, the Hiss case might never have been broken at all." Andrews was not unwilling to repay the favor, once telling his *Herald Tribune* colleague Robert J. Donovan that "he intended to make Dick Nixon President someday."[10]

Nixon knew quite well that the relationship between press and politician is mutually advantageous, necessarily so—and as inescapable as that between addict and dealer. "Reporters are not the only con artists," Nixon once acknowledged. "Public officials devote enormous energy to trying to rig the news to be reported their way. When two savvy insiders, reporter and official, are in the ring together, each trying to bamboozle the other, neither should complain."[11] Nixon's great mistake with the press lay in not following his own advice. He kept complaining right to the end, or even beyond the end: not missing the opportunity in his last book, *Beyond Peace*, to direct a posthumous shiv at reportorial ribs. "A bygone era's ink-stained wretches, as depicted in the classic film *The Front Page*—amiable, scandal-mongering slobs sitting around the courthouse pressroom playing cards and waiting for the next hanging—have become our era's self-certified saviors of the republic."[12]

The reference to *The Front Page* (1931) may seem like an afterthought, but it is by no means gratuitous. Part of Nixon's problem with the press was that by the time he began to joust with it, it had acquired an enviable image, thanks to Hollywood. As we have seen, politicians generally fare badly on the screen; for every Jefferson Smith there are several Willie Starks. Not so with journalists: the balance tilts very heavily in their favor. And as Nixon spent some four decades forced to observe, the odds are against you when your opponent has a halo, worn at however rakish an angle.

In fact, it is very much owing to Hollywood that journalism came to attain its inky glamour. For all Carlyle's talk a century and a half ago of a "stupendous Fourth Estate," with "wide world-embracing influences," members of the press—if not the press itself—had a mostly unsavory reputation prior to the 1930s. Throughout the nineteenth century and well into this one, reporters either had no real public image or, to the extent they did, they were seen as dubious figures: snoops, sensationalists, or both. One need only recall such specimens as the expressively named

George Flack in Henry James's *The Reverberator* (1888) or Matthias Pardon in *The Bostonians* (1886): "the most brilliant young interviewer on the Boston press," Pardon "might flatter himself that he had contributed in his measure, and on behalf of a vigilant public opinion, the pride of a democratic State, to the great end of preventing the American citizen from attempting clandestine journeys."[13] James didn't direct such sarcasm at the war correspondence of his friend Stephen Crane. But someone like Crane, or the even more celebrated Richard Harding Davis, was hardly a typical figure. Even the most famous acknowledgment of the journalist as hero from the early years of this century—Theodore Roosevelt's "Men with the muckrake are often indispensable to the well being of society, but only if they know when to stop raking the muck"—is as much reproach as accolade. No, the great mass of reporters plugged away at their task with little public recognition. The *Oxford English Dictionary* doesn't record the first appearance of the word "by-line" until 1926.

The movies helped change all that, transforming the basic disreputability of journalists into a glamorous badge of honor. As Frank Craven announces to Miriam Hopkins in *Barbary Coast* (1935), "Newspapermen are either idealists or drunkards." In the moral calculus of post-Prohibition, mid-Depression America, that was an all but unbeatable perlay, something that screenplay's authors, two veterans of Chicago's newspaper wars, were perfectly aware of. Those gentlemen were, of course, Ben Hecht and Charles MacArthur. It was their play *The Front Page* (1928) that began the mythologizing, but it was the coming of talkies that secured newspapermen their starry new niche in American culture.

For starters, many screenwriters were themselves former journalists. What better preparation for cranking out screenplays than a profession that called for highly verbal men (and the overwhelming majority of screenwriters in the '30s were male) used to meeting frequent deadlines and producing generous amounts of copy? Journalism's most valued practitioner in those days of multiple editions and intensely competitive papers was "the rewrite man"; any profession that so honored such a position couldn't help but serve as excellent preparation for the vagaries of "authorship" as understood in Hollywood. Journalists were also savvy and unpretentious and, best of all, they wrote the way people who bought movie tickets actually talked. Snappy patter and snapped brims: No Theater Guild gush for the likes of Hecht (perhaps the greatest of all Hollywood screenwriters), MacArthur, Herman J. Mankiewicz (who won an Oscar with Orson Welles for the screenplay to *Citizen Kane,* 1941), Samson Raphaelson (a former *New York Times* reporter who became Ernst Lubitsch's favorite scenarist), Jo Swerling, or Robert Riskin (Frank Capra's favorite scenarist). "MILLIONS ARE TO BE GRABBED OUT HERE AND YOUR ONLY COMPETITION IS IDIOTS," Mankiewicz announced to Hecht in a now-famous telegram. "DON'T LET THIS GET AROUND." He did, though, and the movies were never quite the same thereafter.

As Pauline Kael has argued, "In the silents, the heroes were often simpletons. In the talkies, the heroes were to be the men who weren't fooled, who were smart and learned their way around. The new heroes of the screen were created in the image of their authors: they were fast-talking newspaper reporters."[14] Sure, why not put themselves in the spotlight: let *this* get around. Structurally, it made excellent sense. Journalists are an ideal audience surrogate, professional observers whose job it is to be in the know and plant themselves in the middle of the action: taking it all in. And if the budget didn't allow for action sequences, very well, a reporter hero still fit the bill: leave the news hawk or hen on the quasi–stage set of a city room or pressroom surrounded by a ready-made ensemble, the supporting cast of fellow reporters and editors. A newspaper setting was colorful and gabby, close enough to audiences' experience to let them have some identification with it (everyone read the paper, right?) but without being so familiar as to become passé. Finally, there was, as these newsroom refugees might have put it during a story conference, the personal angle to consider: celebrating the profession they'd left behind let them indirectly salute themselves ("Ah, see what bravos we once were") while disdaining their current occupation ("Reporters, now *those* are people to conjure with—unlike our current poor, corrupted incarnation, as *screenwriters*").

The result was a flood of pictures with newsroom settings and/or journalists playing prominent parts: *Platinum Blonde* and the first of several movie versions of *The Front Page* (1931); *Doctor X* (1932); *It Happened One Night* and *Hi, Nellie!* (1934); *Libeled Lady, Theodora Goes Wild,* and *Mr. Deeds Goes to Town* (1936); *Love Is News* (1937); *Mr. Smith Goes to Washington; Foreign Correspondent, His Girl Friday,* and *The Philadelphia Story* (1940); *Penny Serenade, Meet John Doe,* and, of course, the greatest newspaper movie of them all, *Citizen Kane.* This is only a sampling. There were even historical dramas featuring journalists, such as *Stanley and Livingstone* (1939) and *A Dispatch from Reuters* (1940). Some of these films are now classics, others forgotten. Some, such as *It Happened One Night,* have only a passing connection with journalism—Clark Gable works as a reporter, though we barely see him at his trade. But a press card was a real asset for someone onscreen during Hollywood's Golden Age. Knowing a character was a journalist was enough to reassure an audience about his or her bona fides.

Journalism became a part of movie shorthand. Just as having John Wayne in a cast connoted an action picture, so did newspaper characters communicate the likelihood of cinematic snap, crackle, and pop. "A newspaper picture meant a contemporary picture in an American setting," Kael has noted of the period, "usually a melodrama with crime and political corruption and suspense and comedy and romance."[15]

Indeed, these movies were defining a certain type of uniquely American style. Journalist heroes and heroines were not complete originals, to be sure. They talked back to authority, just as Huck Finn had. They were hard-boiled, like Hemingway characters (Hemingway, of course, had started out as a journalist). They drank too much, like holdovers from the Jazz Age. But in how they concocted the cocktail of their screen selves— with wit and dash and savvy and an absolute horror of pretense—they were something fresh and innovative. They were not alone in being a new American archetype launched before a broad audience at the movies. But unlike cowboys, they belonged to the present. Unlike screwball-comedy sophisticates, they remained, for all their urbanity, regular Joes. Unlike mobsters, they stayed on the right side of the law (while still suggesting some of the colorfulness of outlawry). Hard to fool and easy to love, they were up-to-the-minute American heroes. Thanks to motion pictures, newspapering had not only entered the mainstream; it was now part of the American grain.

To be sure, there have been exceptions to Hollywood's fondness for the news business. From *Five Star Final* (1931) and *Nothing Sacred* (1937) to *Absence of Malice* (1981) and *Shattered Glass* (2003), journalists have worn black hats. But these films are anomalies in what has almost exclusively been one long love affair between city room and soundstage. That television news has so often fared badly at the hands of Hollywood—think of *Network* (1976) or *Mad City* (1997)—simply underscores the point. The problem with TV news is its being such a different animal from print. Even something as scabrous as Billy Wilder's *Ace in the Hole* (1951), featuring Kirk Douglas as a wildly remorseless reporter desperate for a big story, indicts an individual and his audience rather than the profession he belongs to.

The same cannot be said about a movie released six years later, a film that remains unrivaled as a portrait of journalistic megalomania and malice—its very title a boastful condemnation—*Sweet Smell of Success* (1957). It is the movie Richard Nixon might have made had Richard Nixon been a movie director: the movie that aims to show what journalism is *really* like. Douglas's ruthless reporter in *Ace in the Hole* behaves despicably, but he doesn't lecture U.S. senators (shades of Kyle Palmer) or lay claim to a readership of 60 million, as does *New York Globe* columnist J.J. Hunsecker, the film's key villain. The film's view of the profession—at once contemptuous and fascinated, breathless and knowing—is one that Nixon all too visibly shared. This is a newspaper movie recognizably in the tradition even as it creates its own genre: newspaper noir. There is enough cracking wise and tough talk here to fill an entire Sunday paper— just as in any other newspaper movie. There is, however, nothing heroic or winning about any of it—unless one considers self-aggrandizement heroic or unscrupulousness winning. Savvy has turned into a shortcut to self-loathing, hard-boiled a synonym for heartless. The profession as presented here is unremittingly corrupt, duplicitous, evil: a sordid means to a hateful end. This is one movie about journalism Nixon might have enthusiastically endorsed—and whose world he would have found beguilingly recognizable.

The very obvious model for Hunsecker is Walter Winchell. During the late '20s and '30s, Winchell was every bit as new and phenomenal a presence on the American scene as Hollywood's reporter heroes—indeed, each helped shape the other—and he would retain a hold on the public imagination into the 1960s. For as long as there had been journalists, there had been gossip columnists—that's what James's George Flack had been—but they were *society* columnists, genteel individuals gingerly reporting the doings of swells and aristos for (relatively) genteel audiences. They were like footmen at the ball: as dressed up as the people they wrote about, distinguishable from them only in having to work while those around them were at play. Winchell changed all that. The coming of mass communication after the First World War—tabloid newspapers, glossy magazines, 78-rpm recordings, commercial radio, the talkies—meant both a new audience for writers of gossip and a whole new set of subjects for them to write about: individuals who belonged to professions that either hadn't existed before (radio and movie stars, for example) or hadn't been publicized to nearly the extent they were now. (Al Capone may not have been any more vicious than previous gangsters, but his name was vastly better known.)

These structural changes in American society underlay the coming of celebrity culture, a culture that had for its tribune the new-style gossip columnist. Such writers were very much the product of social forces— and Winchell had all sorts of competition—but it's hard to imagine another individual better suited for the job of revolutionizing gossip. Fast, tough, ruthless—extraordinarily good at what he did—Winchell wrote like the vaudeville hoofer he'd once been: a song-and-dance man of newsprint, coining new phrases ("whoopee," "phffft," "Reno-vate") the way he'd once tried out new steps. The landscape for both the production and dissemination of gossip had changed, and it was Winchell who supremely succeeded at exploiting that change, who uniquely shaped it. At the height of his popularity, two out of three adult Americans either read his column or listened to his radio broadcasts. Part reporter, part commentator, part wit—and all drive—Walter Winchell (such a preposterous-perfect name: at once stagy and unprepossessing) was the god of gossip.

In 1947 Alistair Cooke watched Winchell deliver his weekly radio broadcast and was astonished. "He was the promise of American freedom and uninhibited bounce; he was Americanism symbolized in a nose-thumbing at the portentousness of the great . . . ; he was the defender of the American faith."[16] A *conscious* defender of the American faith, Cooke might have added. Politics was very much a part of his columnizing; indeed, that was another element that set Winchell apart from his predecessors. He realized early on that the premier marquee name in the United States throughout most of the '30s and '40s belonged to Franklin Delano Roosevelt. Celebrity was simply about fame—not wealth or birth or talent (though as it happened, FDR possessed all three)—and a public official could be just as exciting a public figure as a starlet or socialite. Indeed, the runner-up in Winchell's pantheon was J. Edgar Hoover, the bureaucrat as crime-buster superstar. (It was around this time, remember, that Richard Nixon, just finishing law school, sought to join the FBI.)

After FDR's death, Winchell just as quickly grasped the fact that America's most-hated villain was a generic heavy known as the "Red." Winchell's rabid anti-communism was shared by such competitors on the East Coast as the Hearst newspapers' Jack O'Brian and the *Daily News*' Ed Sullivan (the same Ed Sullivan whose variety show on CBS would be a Sunday-night institution for nearly two decades) and on the West Coast by Louella Parsons and Hedda Hopper. Acting out of conviction as well as calculation, the gossip columnists of the late '40s and '50s recognized the intersection of anti-communism and entertainment and strove to publicize the connection—more, they defined it. Anti-communism had simply become part of the popular culture, like blue notes in music or the Method in acting. It was Red-baiting that would make Joe McCarthy (or, for that matter, Nixon) a star. Good copy is good copy, and these columnists were as likely to lard their offerings with political digs as celebrity tidbits.

Now that Winchell was a committed anti-communist—even more than as a devout New Dealer—"Americanism" was something he took very seriously. Jackson Lears is not altogether fair when he dismisses Winchell as "a Vegas patriot."[17] Yes, his high-profile patriotism was show biz—but it was *sincere* show biz. One can chart Winchell's political trajectory through his attitude toward Nixon. In 1952, still proclaiming himself an "FDR Rooter," Winchell lambasted the vice-presidential candidate at the time of the fund crisis. "Senator Nixon should get off the ticket. The nation, which completely trusts the heart of the General, shudders to think that ONLY that heartbeat may separate Nixon from the Presidency. . . . Nixon's explanation may or may not be sufficient for a U.S. Senator. It certainly is not enough for a possible future President of the United States." (The political self-importance of that declaration—Winchell seeing himself kingmaker—is, as we shall see, worthy of J.J. Hunsecker.) Yet eight years later, Winchell happily invited Nixon to be a guest for the debut of his new television series.[18] It was a sensible transaction: Nixon made Winchell classier; Winchell made Nixon sexier; and, together, each made the other more famous.

Winchell's ubiquity was a mark of his unparalleled success. Besides print, radio, and television, he also turned up in the movies. He played himself in two 1937 films for 20th Century–Fox, *Wake Up and Live* and *Love and Hisses*, but his most notable movie "appearances" took place with Winchell nowhere to be seen—and everywhere to be felt. *Sweet Smell of Success* is the foremost example, but a quarter century before its release Winchell provided the model for the at-any-cost columnist heroes of *Love Is a Racket* (1932), *Okay, America* (1932), *Clear All Wires!* (1933), *I'll Tell the World* (1934), and what may be the most frenetic of all the early newspaper movies, *Blessed Event*.

A 1932 Warner Bros. comedy based on a minor Broadway hit, *Blessed Event* was unabashedly inspired by Winchell, right down to the title, perhaps his most enduring coinage, indicating a baby's birth. The Winchellesque columnist is played by Lee Tracy (the original Hildy Johnson in *The Front Page*), and his Alvin Roberts is even more of a star turn than his Art Hockstader in *The Best Man*. True, Tracy is too puckery, too ardently *goyisch*, to be much of a Winchell—worse, he's an out-and-out mama's boy, right down to sharing his spacious digs with a doting parent—but he certainly possesses the roundhouse flair and manic stop-the-presses energy of the great man himself. Alvin's having the time of his life, and America loves him for it.

Watching Alvin, we don't see Winchell—but we begin to understand him. Alvin writes a column called "Spilling the Dirt" and greets all and sundry with the question "What do you know that I don't?" He is a young man carbuncular thrilled to have worked his way up from ad taker to reputation breaker: indeed, he's so taken with his success that it's awfully hard for a viewer not to be, too. Even when he double-crosses a pregnant showgirl by announcing her condition on the air, Alvin still doesn't really lose our affection. The showgirl accuses him of being "a 24-carat, 100 percent rat," and who are we to disagree? Yet for all that Alvin is a heel, he's a thoroughly engaging one. There's something winningly larky about his attitude, and it sets the tone for everyone else on camera. "Have you ever heard of the power of the press?" he declares at one point, trying to intimidate Allen Jenkins's Mob enforcer. "What is it," Jenkins replies, "a movie?"

Citing no less an authority than Oscar Wilde, Winchell liked to say that journalism "is 'organized gossip,' which is where I came in."[19] Such utter lack of illusion is what is most appealing about both him and Alvin. Certainly, it is what is most appealing about *Sweet Smell of Success.* If anything, the movie romanticizes its lack of illusions (which, of course, places it very much in the standard newspaper movie genre). It opens with a bang: papers coming off presses, delivery trucks roaring out from loading docks, stacks of first editions tossed out to newsstands, and all the while Elmer Bernstein's faux-jazz score pounds away. The sides of the trucks bear ads for "The Eyes of Broadway," the remotely Orwellian name of Hunsecker's column. The current column, however, does not include the item a press agent named Sidney Falco has guaranteed a client would appear there. One look at the paper, and Falco (played by Tony Curtis) tosses it into a trash can. Abrupt, dismissive, *done,* it is a gloriously expressive gesture—and one that accurately represents how much the movie values journalism.

Sidney works out of a combination office/apartment off Times Square. The sign taped to his door says "SIDNEY FALCO, PUBLICITY." Everything is on the cheap for him, except his ambitions, and J.J. (Burt Lancaster) is "the golden ladder to the places I want to get": an all-powerful opinion-maker whom even Winchell might have had to defer to at the height of his popularity. Sidney has somehow gotten himself onto the columnist's blacklist. The only way to reenter J.J.'s good graces is to do a bit of domestic dirty work: end the romance between J.J.'s sister and a young jazz musician.* To accomplish this, Sidney spends the course of the movie performing a tour de force of odiousness: toadying to J.J., prostituting an old girlfriend (Barbara Nichols), trying to blackmail another columnist, very publicly smearing the musician, and generally bearing out J.J.'s assertion that Sidney is "a man who lives in moral twilight."

He is so visibly on the make, he seems almost laughable—which is fine with him, since while you're laughing he can more easily lift your wallet. *Saturday Review*, that bastion of fifties bien-pensant muddle, lamented the failure of the film to portray "a poverty-haunted childhood that might explain Curtis's unscrupulous drive."[20] The point, of course, is that the source of Sidney's ruthless ambition doesn't matter. It's simply there, like mud at the bottom of a geyser. "From now on, the best of everything is good enough for me!" he proclaims to his secretary. It's as much blueprint as boast.

Sidney is the latest in our series of alternate Nixons—and perhaps the most spiritually congruent. He is a New York Nixon—his unction more ethnic, his ambition smaller bore and more naked—but recognizably Nixonian, nonetheless. They both so transparently want success. Crucially, it is success for its own sake. For both men, aspiration is their true ideology. Sidney is curiously sexless. Material things (if his clothing or office/apartment is any indication) would appear to mean little to him. Making it, in and of itself, is what matters, what motivates him: strive to survive, use or lose. "It's a man's nature to go out and hustle and get what he wants," Sidney says in his own defense. They're words that might have appeared in a first draft of *Six Crises*. The mileage might differ, but the distance one must travel to get from Yorba Linda to the Oval Office is not so much more than that between an outer borough and J.J. Hunsecker's regular table at El Morocco or Toots Shor's.

Unethical and grotesque though he may be, Sidney isn't truly amoral. This is one of the movie's flaws (like Sidney, it ultimately lacks the courage of its own lack of convictions), but it adds to the Nixon resemblance. Both men know qualms, if not remorse. Their squeamishness in the end betrays them. Both pride themselves on their ruthlessness, even as their scrupling at it seals their fate (Nixon refuses to burn the tapes; Sidney finally rejects J.J., thus setting up his beating at the hands of a pair of corrupt cops). Sidney is Nixonian not least of all in believing that candor, as Philip Kemp acutely puts it, "is a form of contempt."[21] The truth shall make you free? Don't get your hopes up, pal: only if you're a chump,

*The musician, a guitarist, is a member of the Chico Hamilton Quintet. The quintet's pianist, Fred Katz, bears a somewhat alarming resemblance to Henry Kissinger.

it will. The truth shall make you the owner of a bridge to Brooklyn—or a defeated candidate. "It's a dirty job, but I pay him clean money," a client of Sidney's complains.

Sweet Smell of Success bears such a nakedly Nixonian title, unleashing the poetry of his id without the prose of his superego. As that little boy lay in bed hearing the distant whistle of the Santa Fe locomotives and dreaming of far away, it wasn't steam or coal smoke he was smelling. The title is perfect, at once too much and just right (just like the movie). The aptness goes deeper than the merely titular, however. Nixon is some weird union of Sidney and J.J.: the oozing avidity of the one, the dark implacability of the other. Sidney is a soul mate, but J.J. resonates on Nixonian frequencies, too.

If only all journalists could have been like Hunsecker—a man Nixon could understand, could do business with, could (dare one say it?) relate to—all his media problems would have been solved. "He's told *princes* where to go and what to do!" Sidney marvels to Susie Hunsecker, trying to argue her brother's case. How can an ambitious man not respond to someone like that? It's a fact to stir the envy of even a vice president of the United States, let alone one so overflowing with resentment of his betters.

To Sidney's corrupt moth, J.J. is a very dark flame. "Your friend Hunsecker," another columnist says to Sidney. "Tell him for me he's a disgrace to his profession." Who are we to disagree? Other than that glimpse of his image on the placard alongside the delivery truck and the sight of his face atop the column just before Sidney deposits it in the trash can, J.J. remains unseen until well after the movie has started. We are meant to conceive of him as this awful, awesome, even awe-inspiring figure: the man to whom the mighty truckle, hoping "to see their names in my column all over the world," as he later boasts. No one needs to tell J.J. how powerful he is; no one needs to tell him anything, in fact. "Why is it everything you say sounds like a threat?" a U.S. senator asks him. It's a rhetorical question.

If anything, the movie goes slightly haywire in its portrayal of J.J.'s megalomania. It makes Andy Griffith's power-mad "Lonesome" Rhodes in *A Face in the Crowd*—Elia Kazan's film, also released in 1957, to which *Sweet Smell of Success* bears many striking similarities—seem timid by comparison. When Steve, the jazz musician, finally stands up to J.J.—"To me, Mr. Hunsecker, you're a national disgrace"—the latter sees the act not just as a personal affront but as something treasonous, un-American (that most loaded of postwar modifiers). "Don't you see?" he rages to Susie.*

*Susie wears a mink coat her brother has given her. When she finally rejects him, she does so by leaving it behind and walking away in a good (Republican?) cloth coat.

"That boy today wiped his feet on the choice and the predilection of 60 million men and women in the greatest country in the world. . . . It wasn't me he criticized. It was my readers." And Susie's presence reminds us of something even more sinister: the nature of Hunsecker's beyond-fraternal feelings.

Trying to express his disdain for Sidney, J.J. instead indicts himself. "It's a publicity man's nature to be a liar," he sneers. But it's a columnist's nature to make use of publicity men. This is the dark underbelly of Hollywood's romance with newspapering: its consistent inability, or unwillingness, to see how deeply mendacity can inform journalism. Even Charles Foster Kane, the grandest newspaper villain in movie history (perhaps the grandest villain in movie history, period) is overwhelming in his charisma. Welles's charm as Kane is invincible, and his character's corruption begins in an idealism we can't help but admire and, later, keep in the back of our minds. He really did mean well, at least for a while.

There is, however, nothing attractive or well intentioned about Lancaster's Hunsecker. The wizard of an obsidian Oz, he is the chilliest of monsters in this most heat-seeking of professions; gossip items, in his hand, turn into so many icicles aimed at vital organs. The glasses he wears tell us everything we need to know about J.J. Those glasses—surely, Ezra Taft Benson's was the only other nose whose bridge might have borne the burden of their full fifties ugliness—create an emotional moat. It was the inspired idea of the film's cinematographer, James Wong Howe, that Lancaster wear them, thus making him seem not only evil but inhuman. "Throughout the entire film," the movie's director, Alexander Mackendrick, later recalled, "a light moved with Burt, just in front of him, often with Jimmy holding it himself, to produce this strange mask of a face": visual opacity as evocation of moral obtuseness.[22] Again and again, we see Lancaster, the most physical star since Errol Flynn, seated, standing still, or otherwise immobilized. No motion, no emotion: his Hunsecker is the most marmoreal gossipmonger imaginable.

Or, rather, *not* imaginable. Gossip, by its very nature, uniquely combines the ephemeral and the carnal: inside knowledge and outré urges. Hearing the bark of Winchell's voice or reading the rat-tat-tat of his prose, one could not help but sense behind it a human presence. Lancaster is too smooth, too assured, too . . . disembodied. The actor's marvelous physique notwithstanding, his Hunsecker is effectively incorporeal: a creature defined by others' genuflections and his own preposterously repellent pair of spectacles. "The Eyes of Broadway," that's who J.J.

is, as well as the column he writes; and the eyes are lidless, faceless, flesh-less. Mackendrick had wanted to cast Hume Cronyn as Hunsecker—a shrewd choice: a small-boned, ferrety man who, himself uncaged, can now rejoice in caging others. There was also talk about casting Welles in the role, and one salutes the rightness of that instinct. This would have been Welles just before *Touch of Evil* (1958), his shamed, shocking bulk able to embody gargoyle menace and mandarin disdain as Lancaster—prettier, prouder, prissier—never could, even if he'd dared.

Small matter, *Sweet Smell of Success* is Tony Curtis's picture. He is its lizard king, basking in a sun of his own imagining, the master of all he purveys. The pouty lips, the long lashes, the liquid eyes, they belong to Bernie Schwartz from the Bronx, and here he makes up for a decade of empty, nothing parts by summoning an intensity that remains transfixing almost half a century after the film's release. Has a cheapjack hustler ever been played with such authority? Has a matinee idol ever been so willing to besmirch his image? As David Thomson has written, Curtis's Falco is "one of the first portrayals of unprincipled American ambition and of the collapsible personality that goes with it. It was man on all fours some years before America really noticed the posture."[23] (That last statement is not quite accurate. America first noticed it, and applauded, five years before *Sweet Smell*'s release, during the Checkers speech.) No, the screen goes dead during those rare moments Curtis absents himself from it. He owns the movie the way a pimp owns his stable: through preen and prance and a constant threat of violation. Our hearts are supposed to be with Sally, Sidney's frumpily decent secretary, with Susie and her beau—the good people, the honorable people—but everything in the movie points us to Sidney. He stands solitary and smirking at the movie's magnetic north: drawing us to him, arctic in his irresistibility.

In fact, what is best and truest about the movie is how it flirts with what is vile and *almost* embraces it. If *Sweet Smell of Success* had been made ten years later, it would have celebrated the vile, wallowed in it; but ten years later, *Sweet Smell of Success* wouldn't have been made; it would have been—at best—a period piece, a period piece about a period no one cared about anymore (try to tie-dye a sharkskin suit). It would have had to have been set in L.A., J.J. would have been a recording executive, and Sidney . . . Sidney would have been his boss, with both of them licking the Bea-tle boots of Steve, who'd have given up jazz to join the Byrds.

By no means is *Sweet Smell of Success* a great movie—it's too baroque, too conscious of its own perversity—but it has undeniably great things in it. And even the not-so-great things—from Barbara Nichols's *echt* sluttiness to Susan Harrison's somnambulism as Susie (if J.J.'s obsessed with *her*, he's even stranger than we thought)—possess a weird relentlessness and lodge themselves in a viewer's consciousness. In fact, the most singular thing about the movie, its dialogue, is emblematic of the film as a whole, being simultaneously dreadful and inspired. The characters' speech can be vivid, pithy, ornate, garish, overripe . . . or all of the above. This is a movie in which even cops sound affected. "Come back, Sidney," a policeman says to Falco. "I want to chastise you." Its tough/tender poetry of the streets frequently veers into realms not previously known to human speech ("What am I, a tangerine that peels in a minute?" Nichols asks), yet that very implausibility sometimes produces an inexplicable aptness, as when J.J. says, "Sidney, conjugate me a verb," a grammatical request that comes across with an insinuation that makes sex seem impoverished by comparison.

The basis of *Sweet Smell of Success* was a "novelette" by Ernest Lehman that appeared in *Cosmopolitan* in 1950 entitled "Tell Me About It Tomorrow" (not wanting the word "smell" to appear in large type in his pages, the editor decreed the name change). The final script was a collaboration between Lehman and Clifford Odets. While it's now largely impossible to assign credit for who contributed what to the final version, the dialogue's pistony vigor and shameless overreach are distinctly Odetsian. For that matter, Odets seems distinctly Odetsian: after enjoying dizzying success with the Group Theatre in 1935 with *Waiting for Lefty* and *Awake and Sing*, he went to Hollywood in 1936 and descended into hack work. He then spent the better part of two decades in a largely fruitless effort to regain his early promise. He's best remembered not for his writing but for testifying as a friendly witness before HUAC in 1952. It's worth noting, then, that one thing certain about the script is that its references to anti-communist hysteria came from Lehman. Indeed, with its elements of paranoia, conspiracy, whisper campaign, and sudden destruction, the movie clearly has the Red Scare for a subtext.

Years later Mackendrick recalled Odets saying to him, "If you're worried that my dialogue is overblown, too flowery and purple-passagey—well, *don't* worry, because the scenes are well-constructed. Play it fast, and don't pay attention to the words—just play the action, and it'll work."[24] Listening to the movie's lyrical-louche argot, one can see—or rather hear—how shrewdly self-aware Odets was.

Credit must go to Mackendrick, too, of course, for having the sense to follow such advice. Best known for directing such Ealing Studios comedies as *Tight Little Island* (1949), *The Man in the White Suit* (1951), and *The*

Ladykillers (1955), he would appear an odd choice for *Sweet Smell*—just one more surprising ingredient in a stew of seeming irreconcilables. Yet Mackendrick's very anomalousness contributes to making the movie such a striking piece of work. There was nothing about this world for him to take for granted, to allow for any going through the motions. What might look tired or clichéd to American eyes looked fresh and provocative to him. Conversely, there was nothing so utterly foreign here as to mystify or delude him. Mackendrick had gone east before coming west. Raised in Scotland, he'd been born in Boston. America was not home, but neither was it a soundstage fantasy. No one might ever mistake him for a *Cahiers*-schooled Frenchman aching to romanticize urban America. For all that Mackendrick gives us an outsider's nose-against-the-glass view of New York, the glass never clouds over. Of course, James Wong Howe had not a little to do with that. What Atget and Brassaï did for Paris earlier in the century, what Berenice Abbott did for New York twenty years before the film was made, Howe does for it in the '50s. "I never want to lose that city" of skyscrapers, he later told an interviewer, explaining his reliance on low angles, his filming of master shots with a telephoto lens and close-ups with a wide-angle lens, both of which reversed standard procedure. "I would lose the city by shooting down at the pavement. What the hell is a piece of pavement? You see, that's what the story is—it's about the city—so you have to make them remember that."[25] The resultant compositions have the crisp particularity of the finest photography, images that can stand on their own, frame by frame. These are moving *pictures*, Winchell as reimagined by Weegee. Just as important, they have the uncanny rightness of dreams: vivid nightmares filled with narrow-lapeled trolls. And Howe's interiors are every bit the equal of his exteriors. The venues these characters patronize are *night*clubs, vessels of darkness, black-box reliquaries. Indeed, to attain the effect he wanted, Howe oiled the walls for a look of glistening sleaze.

The look with which he captures the city is poised between romantic evocation and realist precision. Previous movies shot on location in New York and focusing on its gritty underside, *The Lost Weekend* (1945), say, or *Pickup on South Street* (1953), seem superficial, stagy, or both compared with Howe's nocturne-nacreous Times Square and environs. This is both New York as it was and as it wants to be seen: a heartless yet beckoning world, both alluring and grotesque, defined by a chiaroscuro of hard-edged light and insidious shadow that Howe suffuses with a ravishing, ravaged glow. "I love this dirty town," Hunsecker tells Sidney as they walk down a nighttime street. So long as we can see the city with Howe's assistance, that statement makes absolute sense. Lancaster gets top billing, Curtis walks away with the picture, but Howe is the one who monumentalizes *Sweet Smell of Success*, whose work constitutes its greatest achievement.

Notably sensual, Howe's cinematography extends the understated yet palpable eroticism that suffuses *Sweet Smell of Success*. What is remarkable for the period is how almost every manifestation of that eroticism is aberrant: from Sidney's pandering to J.J.'s unnatural attachment to Susie to the subtly homoerotic bond between him and Sidney. Despite Curtis's matinee-idol looks—a cop describes him perfectly as "the boy with the ice-cream face"—he remains weirdly neuter. But his bond to J.J. gives off a peculiarly charged vibration, as of a catamite with his master. Everything in the movie indicates that Sidney would stop at *nothing* to get ahead, and it more than hints at the oddity of J.J.'s desires. "I'd hate to take a bite out of you," he sneers at Sidney, at one point. "You're a cookie full of arsenic." It's a line that carries more taint than simply that of bad writing.

Quite overt, of course, is J.J.'s hunger for his sister. The incestuous nature of his love recalls that of Paul Muni's Tony Camonte in Howard Hawks's *Scarface* (1932). "I've got an idea that the Borgia family is living in Chicago today," Hawks told his screenwriter, Ben Hecht, in describing his conception for the film.[26] Watching Lancaster and Curtis, the sense we get is of so many refugees from Caligula's Rome now relocated to New York. There is a certain logic to that association, for Sidney and J.J.'s New York—even more than it is decadent—is central, monumental, *imperial*. Columnists like J.J. no longer exist. They were emblems of a time when New York really was the center of the American world—the place where everyone who mattered went, and which everyone who wanted to matter dreamed of—"the city of ambition," as Stieglitz called his famous photograph of the lower Manhattan skyline. The interstate highway system remained as yet incomplete; all roads still led to Gotham.

No movie has so captured—no, so assumed—this centrality of New York. Every frame emphatically declares the axiomatic truth that *no place else really matters*. True, *Sweet Smell* was made after the city began to slip; but the film remains oblivious to the possibility of slippage. Indeed, the two great forces that altered midcentury America are barely visible. In only one scene do we see evidence of television (J.J., like Winchell, has his own show). And race is even less present (not only is the jazz musician white—he's played by Martin Milner). But it's precisely this late-in-the-day quality that adds to the movie's peculiar kick. The city remains imperial—it's just that the empire has entered its Byzantine phase. The dialogue is the least of the things that are overripe in *Sweet Smell of Success*.

One of the movie's subtler touches is locating J.J.'s apartment in the Brill Building, the headquarters of Tin Pan Alley, source of so many anthems echoing through the kingdom of night. At one point J.J. looks out from his balcony, and it's like Ming the Merciless surveying his domain: fabulous and electric and, yes, a little bit terrifying. These are the sensations of living in New York, that top-heavy monument to the overwhelming. Even more than as an indictment of a certain type of journalism, *Sweet Smell of Success* stands as a rhapsody to New York. David Denby is right to call it the best of all New York movies, with its "ironically loving view of a city devoted to money, power, and sex,"[27] for that is indeed how New Yorkers see their city, how they justify its oppressiveness and learn not just to endure but embrace its outrages. About to begin his rounds, J.J. stops to ask a policeman in a patrol car the status of a crime victim who's been in the news. "She died twenty minutes ago," the cop informs him. "Well, that's show business," he shrugs. In this version of New York, even corpses do shtick.

This Manhattan is the ultimate stage set, stunning in its facture as in its facticity, and all these people are playing self-assigned roles (the more interesting ones *know* that that's what they're doing). Jumping into a cab, Sidney announces with utter matter-of-factness the three syllables of his destination: "21." That's all: no address, no further designation, certainly no emotion: "twen-tee won." Charlus telling his coachman to take him to the Guermantes' couldn't have spoken more mechanically.

A gaudy, pulsing, contrived world, this New York is most itself after dark ("the city that never sleeps," as the song has it), and almost all of *Sweet Smell* takes place under artificial light: New York as Nighttown. In fact, it's the daytime scenes that seem unreal; artificial light is this city's most natural illumination. Only Venice surpasses New York as a monument to urban artifice; and what a lagoon is for the one, information is for the other: the medium on which the city floats. J.J. and Sidney could not thrive anywhere else—could not survive anywhere else—nor, ultimately, could Richard Nixon. He, too, came to cherish his table at 21— during the '80s he liked to lunch there—and, more generally, to recognize the usefulness of Manhattan's theatrical properties. For it was here he came—no, had to come—to stage his two comebacks, to enact the role of "new Nixon" and then that of elder statesman. Just as J.J. and Sidney could not be the people they were anywhere else, so Nixon needed to come here to be recognized as Nixon.

For nearly as long as there has been a United States, New York City has drawn not just the tired, hungry, and poor of other lands, but also the rising, ruthless, and driven of America: those who are hungry in a different way. Richard Nixon was one of them. Even as an impoverished law student at Duke, he managed to scrape up the money for a pair of visits to "that cold and expensive city"[28] (note the two qualities that stood out in the memory of the poor boy from sunny California). His first time in New York, he went to the Metropolitan Opera; "gazed up at the skyscrapers so long he got a crick in his neck"; saw several plays on Broadway, including (yes) *The Front Page*; and got a bargain price ($10) on a pilfered fox fur piece from a Saks errand boy, which Hannah Nixon later received as a Christmas present.[29] Already, the big city had lessons to teach.

The next visit saw his first abortive assault on the city. Hoping a white-shoe law firm would hire him, he interviewed with John Foster Dulles and "Wild Bill" Donovan, senior partners at great downtown firms with "plush, polished mahogany and leather reception rooms," as he recalled them half a century later.[30] Clearly, the memory of such luxury—such New York luxury—did not fade. Then in 1945 he and Pat briefly lived on West Ninety-third Street in a $90-a-month sublet, and he had his pocket picked during the V-J celebration in Times Square. Rube! It would not happen again.

Following the example of his onetime sponsor Thomas E. Dewey, Nixon responded to crushing political defeat by becoming a Wall Street lawyer. Yet unlike Dewey, one of the great figures of imperial New York and himself another hardworking boy who had come to the big city from the provinces, Nixon did so not to remove himself from the pursuit of electoral office but rather to reposition himself to pursue it more successfully.

Even more than now, New York was the media nexus: the place people went to be seen, heard, *regarded*. In moving from California, Nixon was abandoning his base, yes; he was also burnishing his image, altering it, and lifting it to a higher plane. In Washington, he had had his duties as legislator and vice president to attend to: being a candidate was a function of what he did, not who he was. Back in California, there remained too many other demands on him: titular party head is a thankless role, all the more thankless as a titular party head and two-time loser. In New York, all that changed. He could hire himself out to a prestigious law firm; and though he did work at the job, and work hard, his legal duties never took priority. Being a candidate—or, rather, reaching the position to be a candidate again—that came first. Before he could become president, he had, in a sense, to conquer New York, to reestablish his credentials, to forge a peaceful coexistence with the Eastern establishment he so despised and that so despised him. He went to Fifth Avenue Presbyterian Church on Sundays or to Marble Collegiate to hear Norman Vincent Peale preach. He sent his daughters to Chapin and saw them presented at the International Debutante Ball. He could write influential articles for *Foreign Affairs*, be seen in the right places by the right people, auditioning for the part of world leader. (Even more than being president, Nixon, perhaps uniquely among those who have aspired to the White House, wanted to be a world leader.) What better preparation for such a role than residence in the capital of the world?

The city appealed to him at a visceral level, as well. When this most achingly competitive of men returned to New York in 1963, he chose to live in the same building as Nelson Rockefeller. Beating a man at his own game is one thing; doing so on his own court is that much better. "New York is the fast track," he'd habitually say in explanation of his two moves there. The phrase would sound just as characteristic coming from Sidney Falco. Nixon's twelve-room apartment on Fifth Avenue and, later, after he came back in 1980, his town house on East Sixty-fifth Street were continents away from Sidney's Times Square, but it was the same bitch-goddess croon both men heard emanating from Manhattan. Where else could a Sidney get to know a J.J.? Where else could a Richard Nixon (buying a pineapple, no less) run into an Andy Warhol?[31]

"New York is very cold and very ruthless and very exciting, and, therefore, an interesting place to live," Nixon told the *New York Times Magazine* two years after he had moved there. "It has many great disadvantages but also many advantages. The main thing, it is a place where you can't slow down—a fast track. Any person tends to vegetate unless he is moving on a fast track. New York is a very challenging place to live. You have to bone up to keep alive in the competition there."[32] The "fast track," Darwin for experts, New York as daily matter of life-and-death Sidney couldn't have put it any better. The chill gleam of Howe's black-and-white cinematography is something Nixon would have recognized as emblematic of his new home—no, more than that: as one of its attractions.

New York was a way to get somewhere else: to the White House, the first time; to respectability, the second. You don't make many demands of a place you don't consider home, nor does it make many of you. Like Sidney and J.J., Nixon needed New York for acceleration. Unlike them, he did not need it for definition. Rootlessness had long been central to who he was; in moving to New York, he didn't so much acknowledge that fact as exploit it.

The anonymity of the city held a powerful appeal to such a man. He was "a stranger in a town of strangers," recalled Theodore H. White, who occasionally saw him socially during those years, and "Nixon in New York was a more attractive personality than he had ever been."[33] It was that classic American formula: a poor country boy, in going to the big city, becomes doubly blessed, enriching himself by shedding his past as well as securing his future.

Like Hildy Johnson, say, or Charles Foster Kane, Richard Nixon got to display talents in the big city he might not even have known he possessed had he stayed in his hometown. And for all the allure of what the big city had to offer—a regular table at 21, one's name in boldface in "The Eyes of Broadway"—that might not be as much of an inducement to relocate there as escape was. No need to see Pat Brown's name in print every day, to suffer further displays of the local paper's unfairly "balanced" coverage, to endure reminders from hometown benefactors of all he owed them. In New York, that was all behind him. Who knows? Maybe he felt he could actually forge a better, happier association with the press now that he was in Manhattan and he didn't have to see the *Los Angeles Times* every morning and be reminded in finger-smudging black-and-white of his love-hate relationship with the media.

Of course, Nixon hadn't had to cross a continent to cease seeing the *Times*. He hadn't spoken the truth when he said at his press conference the morning after losing to Brown that he'd never canceled a subscription to a paper; he'd twice canceled home delivery of the *Washington Post*.[34] That statement had simply been a not-so-subtle jab at JFK, who earlier that year, in a fit of pique, had briefly terminated the White House's twenty-four *New York Herald Tribune* subscriptions. But Nixon had also said he never would cancel. It was a pledge that did not keep him from terminating his *Times* home delivery a few days later,[35] thus ensuring himself a whiff, however faint, however papery, of the sweet smell of revenge.

TWO RODE TOGETHER

■ ■

The political leaders with whom we are familiar generally aspire to be superstars rather than heroes. The distinction is crucial. Superstars strive for approbation; heroes walk alone. HENRY KISSINGER[1]

We've gone through all this . . . like two men in a foxhole. KISSINGER, IN 1972, ON HIS SERVICE AS RICHARD NIXON'S NATIONAL SECURITY ADVISER[2]

Even more than Richard Nixon, Henry Kissinger knew the lure of New York. It was to New York that his family came after fleeing Europe in 1938. Seventeen years later, as a Harvard professor, he arrived at the Council on Foreign Relations, its stately quarters lying six miles south and several worlds distant from Washington Heights, where the Kissingers had found a home in the New World. There on the corner of Park and Sixty-eighth he made his first crucial contacts with the foreign policy elite, serving as staff director for a council study group whose findings resulted in his first book, *Nuclear Weapons and Foreign Policy*. A year after that, he

Richard Widmark and James Stewart

shifted over to 30 Rockefeller Plaza as director of a Rockefeller Brothers Fund Special Study Project—and in so doing gained further entrée into the world of power and privilege, attaching himself to Nelson Rockefeller, his first and most congenial political mentor. Most important of all, it was in New York that he had his first three meetings with Richard Nixon, the man who enabled him to achieve such extraordinary power and fame.

They initially met at a cocktail party—Manhattan conviviality at its most efficient—on December 10, 1967, at Clare Boothe Luce's apartment, eighteen blocks up Fifth Avenue from the Nixons'. "I knew that if Henry spent an hour talking with Nixon," Luce later explained, "the two men would get along famously." As it happened, they spent only five minutes together during which they made awkward small talk. Most of that five minutes was devoted to Nixon praising *Nuclear Weapons and Foreign Policy*. It was a somewhat strained conversational gambit, as Kissinger had since published three titles and had substantially changed his views. Even so, he allowed afterward as to how he found Nixon "more thoughtful" than he'd expected.[3]

The next two meetings also took place on Fifth Avenue, at the Pierre Hotel (Kissinger's New York, like Nixon's, had come to include only the best addresses), and these encounters proved rather more momentous than their first. The Pierre was Nixon's transition headquarters, and the president-elect had brought Kissinger there on November 25, 1968, to size him up for one of his administration's most important posts, national security adviser. The two men spent three hours discussing U.S. foreign policy and the nuts and bolts of how best to conduct it. Nixon became so caught up in their conversation that he forgot to mention the job. It was two days later, at the second meeting, that the actual offer was made. Kissinger took another two days to accept, but the delay was only for appearance's sake. There was little doubt how much he wanted the job.

In retrospect, the pairing seems inevitable: no twentieth-century president and adviser are as closely linked in the public imagination as Nixon and Kissinger. Yet at the time, it appeared anything but inevitable. In his memoirs Kissinger recalls that, as recently as eight weeks before Nixon's inauguration, the idea he might be asked to join the administration seemed "preposterous."[4] Even allowing for Kissingerian self-inflation, there is considerable truth to that statement. A subsequent book, *The Necessity for Choice*, had flayed Eisenhower's foreign policy. He had voted for Kennedy in 1960, then worked for his administration (unhappily, as it turned out) as a foreign policy consultant. During the fall of 1968, Kissinger had maintained contact with the Humphrey campaign. Humphrey later said that, had he won the election he, too, would have chosen Kissinger for national security adviser. Earlier in the year he had been heard to pronounce Nixon "unfit" to serve as president.

That remark could be attributed to the heat of battle, perhaps, as Kissinger had been serving as Rockefeller's chief foreign policy adviser, but the Rockefeller association was a problem in itself. Why would Nixon choose someone who for more than a decade had worked closely with his chief Republican rival? Nor was Kissinger's allegiance to Rockefeller merely mercenary. His attachment to his patron was such that throughout his time in office it was to the Rockefeller estate at Pocantico Hills that he entrusted his personal papers for safekeeping. It's only appropriate that Kissinger should receive his summons to the November 25 meeting at the Pierre while lunching with Rockefeller. Quite uncharacteristically, Kissinger would remain loyal to Rockefeller right up to his patron's death—and even beyond. *White House Years*, the first volume of his memoirs, bears the dedication "To the memory of Nelson Aldrich Rockefeller."

Why, then, did Nixon choose him? "I had a strong intuition about Henry Kissinger," he would write in *RN*, admitting the "uncharacteristically impulsive way" he had made Kissinger his choice.[5] He makes it sound like kismet—and, surely, there was a bit of that—yet even before their meeting took place the Harvard professor had emerged as the leading candidate for the job. Kissinger was by no means an unknown quantity. Since 1957, when *Nuclear Weapons and Foreign Policy* had spent fourteen weeks on the best-seller list, he had been one of America's most prominent policy intellectuals and his brilliance was widely recognized. The fact that he had surreptitiously passed on information to the Nixon campaign during the fall of 1968 concerning the Paris peace talks and Johnson's bombing halt did not hurt his cause, nor did his complete agreement with Nixon that foreign policy should emanate from the White House. That he could already offer particulars on how the National Security Council might go about achieving that goal clinched it.

"The combination was unlikely," Nixon conceded, "the grocer's son from Whittier and the refugee from Hitler's Germany, the politician and the academic. But our differences helped make the partnership work."[6] It wasn't the differences that did it, though, so much as the similarities. One of the more singular peculiarities of Nixon's career was its tendency to breed doppelgängers: Nixonian doubles, equals and opposites whose reputations would become intertwined with his as they simultaneously recapitulated and negated aspects of his personality. While any political leader tends to become paired in the public mind with his leading opponents, Nixon took that phenomenon several steps further. Between his spending five decades in the public eye and (even more decisive) his uniquely charged valence, he demonstrated this binary condition of public life to an unprecedented degree. Again and again, we find such figures shadowing him: Nixon and Voorhis, Nixon and Hiss, Nixon and Rockefeller, Nixon and Kennedy, Nixon and Kennedy's ghost. He even came to be seen as his own duality, as an ever-shifting series of new Nixons did battle with the old, right down to the antinomy's final, cruelest variant, the one that dogged him to the end of his days: Nixon the

Elder Statesman vs. Nixon the Unindicted Co-conspirator. Perhaps the most complicated of all these relationships, more complicated even than Nixon *malgré lui,* was Nixon and Kissinger.

Not the least of the reasons that theirs was the most complicated of all these relationships was its being the only one in which Nixon's double was a colleague as well as a competitor. Kissinger was *right there* as none of the others had been, and for someone like Nixon that posed unique problems. This most desperately private of public men was comfortable, truly comfortable, only when by himself. In his own eyes, he was his only peer; everyone else stood either above him or beneath: someone to cultivate . . . or scorn (his favorites were the ones who started out as one and ended up the other). Chief among the many rationales he had for pursuing the presidency so relentlessly was that the office certified him as *everyone's* superior.

That superiority extended to Kissinger, too, of course; yet here, as in so many other ways, the doctor was different. Between Nixon's rank and Kissinger's brains, a kind of truce could obtain—if not true equality, then clear duality—which let them treat each other as intellectual peers: a matched pair of tough-minded visionaries, dreamers who got things *done.* They both looked at the same things, pondered the same questions, saw them the same way. Someone like Bebe Rebozo was an inferior (that was part of his appeal), someone who would listen and not talk back. Someone like John Connally—so strong and decisive—was, at least in Nixon's eyes, his better. Henry, though, inhabited the same mental landscape— the worldscape, if you will—that he did. Again and again, journalistic accounts from the early days of the first Nixon administration describe William Rogers, Nixon's secretary of state, as one of the president's oldest and closest friends. That was true, yet the idea of Nixon discussing foreign policy with him daily for hours on end is unthinkable, a fact borne out by Nixon's shockingly dismissive treatment of Rogers. Instead, he turned to Kissinger, doing so with an almost greedy delight. So long as he was there, Nixon could feel alone without feeling isolated. "After all," as Kissinger bragged to his first biographers, Marvin and Bernard Kalb, "I was one of the few people he could talk to that he could consider an equal in knowledge."[7]

Small matter that Kissinger was Jewish and talked funny and came from Harvard. Harvard might even be seen as part of his appeal—a bit of one-upmanship directed at the New Frontier—and, in fact, Nixon also boasted a Harvard man for his chief domestic policy adviser, Daniel Patrick Moynihan, the one member of the administration whose intellect rivaled Kissinger's. But Moynihan, for whatever reasons (the Kennedys, that Irish twinkle, the bottle), was always a trifle suspect. Kissinger, though, Kissinger had nothing of the leprechaun or liberal about him.* What made *him* suspect was also what made him strong—what made him some-one Nixon could fully respect and relate to—for Kissinger realized the importance of deceit, of its grim, urgent inescapability. Not a pretty thing, no, but necessary. As a word, *Realpolitik* sounded so much more ex-alted when Henry uttered it, so much more authentic (and his accent was the least of it). Henry knew about playing the game, as they all probably did back at Harvard; but unlike the rest of them, he had the guts, the *strength* to practice it, to do what needed to be done—and this was the hardest part, not to look back. When all hell broke loose after Cambodia, Nixon said to him, "Henry, remember Lot's wife. Never turn back. Don't waste time rehashing things we can't do anything about."[8] Kissinger un-derstood.

Both given to secretiveness and suspicion, they shared a mania for the conspiratorial. It may well be that that predilection was what most united them. (Shrink from others as he will, a conspiratorial loner still requires another person to conspire with.) That they abhorred transparency helped them do great things—the opening to China being the supreme example. It also led them to do silly, even counterproductive things—al-most till the end, Kissinger's clandestine negotiations with the North Vietnamese differed from the official negotiations only in proving even more futile. Finally, it brought them to do things that were explicitly de-structive—both literally, as in the secret bombing of Cambodia and the destabilizing of Salvador Allende in Chile, and figuratively, as in their ob-session with leaks and the use of wiretapping. An argument can even be made that Kissinger was the more "Nixonian" of the two, the more thor-ough—the more enthusiastic—representative of the age of surveillance. The difference is *he* got away with it: got away with his having aides listen in on his telephone calls and his seeing to it that his personal files (the ones sent off to Pocantico Hills) included transcripts of all his phone con-versations with the president. The great risk that arises when conspirato-rial individuals join forces is that one may come to conspire against the other. Haldeman once told White House Domestic Council head John Ehrlichman that Nixon's chief reason for installing the White House tap-ing system was "in order to demonstrate that the foreign-policy initiatives

*He did, however, have a good deal of the competitor. Asked about having Moynihan in the administration, he urged Nixon not to. "Moynihan will only go off and write a nasty book about you." Rarely has psychological projection received a clearer demonstration.

of his Presidency were in fact his own, not Henry's."[9] Kissinger wasn't just more Nixonian than Nixon: he managed, disastrously, to make Nixon more Nixonian, too. It was a case of foreign policy à deux.

The differences between them were obvious—and, just as obviously, immense—but what mattered were the even more considerable ways in which they were alike. Haldeman, for one, who spent more time with Nixon than anyone else during his first term and was the one presidential aide whose authority even Kissinger had to defer to, felt that the two men's personalities were "astonishingly" similar.[10] Uneasy egotists, saturnine gamblers, the two of them were ruthless and driven (one of Kissinger's greater achievements was managing to disguise the extent to which he was even more ruthless and driven than Nixon was), a pair of suspicious and insecure loners. Kissinger's wit and cosmopolitan air helped mask his insecurities and anxiousness, but in his own way he could be as uncomfortable with others as Nixon was. "I'd never seen fingernails bitten so close to the quick," Ehrlichman said of Kissinger.[11]

The two of them, so phlegmatic in manner, so stodgy in appearance, shared a hopeless weakness for staginess. How could it have been otherwise, with the love each had for subterfuge, improvisation, coups de théâtre? At the moment of their greatest triumph, when it became apparent that their overtures to China had succeeded, the two of them summoned up all the giddy melodrama they could muster. "This is the most important communication that has come to an American President since the end of World War II," a breathless Kissinger told Nixon upon receipt of the Chinese invitation for his secret visit in 1971. Not to be outdone, Nixon replied, "Henry, I know that, like me, you never have anything to drink after dinner, and it is very late, but I think this is one of those occasions when we should make an exception," and he broke open a bottle of "very old Courvoisier."[12] When two men who excel at existential stagecraft collaborate at such a level, astonishing creations can result—whether they be petty tirades or arms treaties, bureaucratic bloodlettings or superpower summits.

Even their differences, as Nixon contended, played to their mutual advantage. Far from being the least among the many reasons for the success of their relationship was the way each man let the other live vicariously: Kissinger had impeccable intellectual credentials, an Ivy League background, excellent press, a reputation for sexiness and panache. "For Nixon this was a great thing," Morton Halperin, one of Kissinger's closest aides and later a bitter enemy, told Seymour Hersh. "He was sitting with this distinguished Harvard professor, talking about the future of the world."[13] For Kissinger, it was even greater: *he* was sitting with the president of the United States and helping *determine* the future of the world.

Incongruous as Kissinger may seem when juxtaposed with Nixon, the two together seem even more out of place when juxtaposed with previous mandarins of U.S. foreign policy—a fact crucial to the success of their association. It says something about both men's relationship to the Eastern establishment that Nixon should have seen Kissinger as being a part of it. To be sure, both knew their way around its precincts—their articles published in *Foreign Affairs*, their opinions sought and valued, their phone calls quickly returned—but neither truly belonged to the club. Each was ineluctably an outsider. This was famously the case with Nixon, but so, too, with Kissinger. (The great difference between them was that Kissinger thrived on being an outsider; he made it seem like a preference; Nixon did not.) As Tom Wicker has pointed out, he was as much of a self-made man as Nixon was (or even more: Nixon never had to take out citizenship papers).[14] Tenure at Harvard does not a member of the establishment make. If anything, Harvard helped mask Kissinger's outsider status. In the words of Roger Morris, who served under him on the National Security Council and later became one of his most insightful critics as well as Nixon's most exhaustive biographer, Kissinger was "a house academic in a club dominated by the lawyers and business men who had held high office in Washington for years." "He was an adornment," said one of his policy academic peers, "more hired hand than member."[15]

For almost as long as there had been a United States, the conduct of its foreign policy had been an all but private preserve. If the Anglican Church is the Conservative Party at prayer, then the State Department was the Eastern establishment in command. The occasional appointment of a William Jennings Bryan or Cordell Hull as secretary of state merely underscored the preponderance of investment bankers, scions of old money, and foundation heads as the architects of U.S. foreign policy. A list of leading U.S. diplomats during the first two-thirds of the twentieth century—John Hay, Elihu Root, Charles Evan Hughes, Henry Stimson, Sumner Welles, Dean Acheson, John Foster Dulles, Christian Herter, the Bundy brothers—might double as a volume of the *Social Register*. And when a leader of the foreign policy establishment was not a member of the elite by birth, he would more often than not be an example of that establishment's ability—its genius, really—to absorb new blood and age it. John J. McCloy, Dean Rusk, and George Ball may have started out as poor, or relatively poor, provincials—as, respectively, the son of a Pennsylvania Dutch hairdresser, a boy from rural Georgia, and a product of deepest, darkest Des Moines—but in time McCloy would become chairman of Chase Manhattan Bank; Rusk, president of the Rockefeller Foundation; and Ball, a senior partner at Lehman Brothers: each a high priest of the foreign policy clerisy.

Kissinger and Nixon changed that. The evolution of the foreign policy establishment from a body largely comprising patricians and amateurs to one of academics and bureaucrats had already begun, but the Nixon years saw it come to fruition. Surely, part of the enormous attraction foreign affairs held for Nixon was that it let him beat the white-shoe boys at their own game. As for Kissinger, even with his chair at Harvard, past service with the Council on Foreign Relations, and association with Rockefeller, he never truly assimilated, never acquired the correct style. Rusk may not have ventured from the South until he was twenty-two, but it didn't take him long to remove all but the merest trace of his Cherokee County drawl. Kissinger, who fled Germany at fifteen, always retained that thick Teutonic accent. (His brother Walter, only a year younger, spoke unaccented English. "I am the Kissinger who listens," he liked to say.) Coincidence or no, Rusk joined the club; Kissinger did not.

It rankled. When three NSC staffers resigned in protest over the Cambodian invasion, Kissinger dismissed their act as "the cowardice of the Eastern establishment."[16] In that charge, one can hear the echo of years of hurt pride and a painstakingly maintained amour propre. Kissinger knew he was smarter than "they" were, that he could do greater things and dominate diplomacy as their entire class did not and could not. Yet they were the ones who acted as if they were his moral superiors. Confronted with the rejection of his policies, he condemned it as a latter-day trahison des clercs. After all, if the Eastern establishment were cowards, didn't that lionize—even ennoble—his own outsider status?

As if to underscore the way in which his coming to power marked a clear departure (and equally clear advance?) in the conduct of U.S. foreign policy, Kissinger notes in the first few pages of *White House Years* how McGeorge Bundy "tended to treat me with the combination of politeness and subconscious condescension that upper-class Bostonians reserve for people of, by New England standards, exotic backgrounds and excessively intense personal style."[17] What an artful and revealing statement this is: shaped to deflate Bundy ("by New England standards"!) and elevate himself ("excessively intense personal style" sounds so much grander, laudable even, than "ambitious" or "opportunistic"). By the time he wrote those words, the tables had been turned. Bundy had been

Kissinger's benefactor both as Harvard dean, having seen to his getting tenure, and then again as Kennedy's national security adviser, securing him his consultancy. More, it was Bundy who was the internationally known figure at the end of 1968. A decade later Bundy was still doing intellectual penance for his part in furthering U.S. involvement in Vietnam and had become a figure of the past, powerless to help (or harm) his one-time subordinate, who now owned one of the world's most celebrated names. How better to even the score than to recall someone who ought to have known better being so foolish as to have treated *Henry Kissinger*— who would soon be receiving an approval rating of 85 percent in a Harris survey, the highest recorded figure for any government official in the poll's history; who would be voted "greatest person in the world today" by no less a body than the contestants in the Miss Universe Pageant—with mere "politeness" and "subconscious condescension"?

He had resented such treatment then and, despite doing his best to seem above such trivial considerations, continued to resent it later. That was another bond between him and Nixon, for Nixon knew what such treatment could be like—he had experienced far worse than Kissinger ever would—and resentment was one thing Nixon understood all too well. How ironic, then, that the way Bundy treated Kissinger was but a more circumspect version of how Kissinger treated Nixon. While he had had to reevaluate that "unfit to be president" statement—clearly, Nixon was neither oaf nor Neanderthal—it remained a defining element in Kissinger's view of the man he had agreed to serve. "The capacity to admire others is not my most fully developed trait," he allows in *White House Years*, and no one suffered more for it than Nixon.[18] The ceaseless flattery he lavished upon the president did not prevent Kissinger from denigrating him behind his back as "that madman" and "our drunken friend" or telling NSC staffers who prepared materials for Nixon, "Don't ever write anything more complicated than a *Reader's Digest* article."[19] Kissinger had his cake and spat it out, too. As Moynihan observes of Kissinger in his book *A Dangerous Place* (the title refers to the United Nations but could just as well describe the Nixon White House): "It was his obsession that no one ever should appear closer to the president than he, while neither should anyone be seen to hold this president in greater contempt."[20]

When it suited him (at a Georgetown dinner party, say, or when lunching with a liberal columnist), Kissinger might indicate to outsiders this contempt for Nixon; and there was the celebrated incident in Ottawa in 1975 when he was heard to remark, over a microphone he didn't know was open, that Nixon "was a very odd man . . . a very unpleasant man . . . an artificial man." Yet it was left to Kissinger's memoirs to reveal the extent of his weary, wary scorn for the man who had brought him to the mountaintop.

Midway through *White House Years*, the author humbly records that "one of the rewards of my public life has been that in a moment, however brief in the pitiless measurement of history, I could work with a great man across the barriers of ideology in the endless struggle of statesmen to rescue some permanence from the tenuousness of human foresight."[21] Alas, it's Chou En-lai who's the lauded colleague, not Nixon. The tone for *his* treatment is set no later than the book's second paragraph when, in describing Nixon's first inaugural, Kissinger pauses to comment on a deficiency in the new president's wardrobe, "his pant legs [were] as always a trifle short."[22] It is hard to say which is more patronizing, that "as always" or the "trifle." Here we find epitomized the subtle belittling and *almost* overt contempt that over the course of nearly three thousand pages (the first two volumes in toto and a fair portion of the third) will characterize his treatment "of the not inconsiderable man who was to shape the destiny of our country for a turbulent five and a half years."[23]

Dealing with that destiny-shaping man, Kissinger presents himself as a sort of Germanic Jeeves, unflappable and long suffering, who again and again saves the day for his maladroit employer, a malevolent, egregiously Middle American Bertie Wooster. Kissinger's general air of exasperation is unmistakable—and frequently quite amusing—as he speaks of such afflictions he must labor under as "Nixon's psychological peculiarities,"[24] his "Walter Mitty" personality, and having to confront "yet one more from my chief's inexhaustible store of surprises."[25] Not that Kissinger could have expected better from "this withdrawn and elusive man" who showed the scars of having been "a poor, somewhat resentful young man from a little town in California" and then, having been elected to the nation's highest office, "desperately wanted to be told how well he had done."[26]

Even when giving Nixon credit, as he frequently must (the administration's diplomatic successes require acknowledgment since they're Kissinger's, too), he does so in a style of encomium that can best be described as obsequious disdain. What is likely the most striking example of this damning with rote praise comes not in the memoirs but rather in the eulogy Kissinger delivered at Nixon's funeral (Rockefeller wasn't the only patron toward whom he maintained a consistent attitude even unto the grave). The tribute concludes, "It was a privilege to have been allowed to help him."[27] The penultimate syllable does its work almost imperceptibly, but there it is, unmistakable in its variation from the verb customarily employed in such a context: "help," not "serve." It is subordinates who serve; it is equals who help (so can betters).

Kissinger's most damaging treatment of Nixon doesn't appear in his memoirs. Rather, it *is* his memoirs. *White House Years* (a title that all but intimates it was Kissinger, not Nixon, who was actually president) and *Years of Upheaval* are very good books that aspire to the condition of literature, and at times manage to attain it, as *RN* (let alone any of Nixon's later books) never even approaches. Nixon, who took such pride in authorship and labored over it so, making it the prime engine of his rehabilitation, never got the hang of writing. The thudding on-go of his style makes all of his books heavy going, each one an earnest gumbo of lawyer's brief and homiletic tract, after-dinner speech and op-ed piece. Even *In the Arena*, the most readerly of his books (because the most varied), is, at best, stiff and leaden. Compared with Nixon's books, Kissinger's memoirs seem a marvel of suppleness, concision, and pacing—and this despite their stupefying length. (Kissinger requires more than two and a half times the number of pages Nixon does to cover the same period of time—in fact, a considerably smaller amount, since Nixon devotes more than a third of his eleven hundred pages to the years before he became president—and this ratio conveys an inescapable corollary concerning the two men's relative importance.) And being the better writer conduces to more than just Kissinger's vanity. The better the prose, the more likely it can be to persuade. Perhaps Nixon had a presentiment about this. When Kissinger reassured him two nights before his resignation that historians would treat him better than his contemporaries had, Nixon kept repeating, "It depends on who writes the history, Henry."

Nixon, of course, tried to put his own interpretation on their relationship. His more elevated position as a former president, along with his more exposed position as a former president forced to resign from office, ensured he wrote in a more guarded fashion than his onetime aide did. A comparatively rare instance of his treating Kissinger with a spitefulness as explicit as Kissinger's comes in his book *Leaders*. Perhaps with the Chou tribute in mind, Nixon notes that Kissinger's high regard for the late Chinese premier was all the more impressive insofar as his former aide "is seldom that lavish in his praise of people who are out of earshot."[28] More generally, one has to read between the lines or look to Nixon's intimates to find out how he actually felt about Kissinger. When Julie Nixon Eisenhower writes that her mother "had no illusions that the Nixon-Kissinger relationship was anything more than a marriage of convenience," this can surely be considered ex cathedra.[29] So, too, with the description offered by Jonathan Aitken, Nixon's most sympathetic latter-day biographer, of Kissinger as "an intellectual valet of prodigious industry": *this* is the view Nixon wished to see propagated.[30]

Unfortunately, it is a truth universally acknowledged that no man is a hero to his valet, intellectual or otherwise, and Kissinger's prodigious industry has seen to it that the Aitken/Nixon line is a distinctly minority opinion. Back when he was president, Nixon could joke to Mao about Kissinger's "girls," to Golda Meir about his accent, and to Brezhnev about not plying him with vodka. Nixon used Kissinger as an uncomfortable comic foil then—and that is how Kissinger has come to use Nixon since.

Nixon's jokes served a dual purpose: to help keep Kissinger in his place and to provide an outlet for the president's growing resentment of his national security adviser, resentment inspired by everything from the duplicities he practiced to the excellent press he received. The two men had never had an easy relationship. Of course, Nixon never had an easy relationship with anybody. But even by his standards, the degree of distrust and jealousy between them was striking. Even as familiarity had increased the grudging respect they had felt for one another at the administration's outset, it had also placed increasing strains on a relationship that was, as Kissinger diplomatically puts it in *White House Years*, "close on substance, aloof personally."[31] That statement makes all the more ironic the fact that it was substance that came to be the greatest cause of friction in the relationship. It wasn't so much any differences over administration foreign policy as the assigning of relative credit for its successes. The pivotal event was Nixon's greatest triumph, the opening to China. Once the president revealed Kissinger's secret trip to Beijing in 1971, "it [became] possible for Nixon's critics to diminish his achievements by exalting my own. And while I did not consciously encourage the process, there was no consistent record of my resisting it, either."[32]

If Kissinger was ungracious and two-faced, Nixon was petty and vindictive. Jokes were the least of his behind-the-scenes efforts to cut his national security adviser down to size. In the speech he gave on January 25, 1972, revealing Kissinger's series of secret peace talks with the North Vietnamese, he emended William Safire's draft so that every use of the phrase "I asked Dr. Kissinger" became "I directed Dr. Kissinger."[33] Four weeks later, when Air Force One landed in Beijing, Nixon saw to it that Kissinger was kept quite literally in his place as "a burly aide blocked the aisle" to ensure the publicity-loving national security adviser did not emerge from the aircraft while his boss was greeting Chou.[34] Nine months later Nixon emphasized during a Camp David monologue, as recorded by Ehrlichman in his notes of the meeting, that the "President's genius needs to be recognized, vis-à-vis HAK."[35] That no such recognition ensued only made things worse. *Time*'s naming Nixon and Kissinger 1972's Men of the Year in an unprecedented joint selection left the president "close to white-lipped in anger," Haldeman records; and when Kissinger won the 1973 Nobel Peace Prize with Le Duc Tho, an envious Nixon felt the award "should have gone to himself."[36]

Nixon's ire at Kissinger even extended to the one arena where the president might have been expected to view his aide's accomplishments with no competitiveness whatsoever: Kissinger's carefully cultivated—and almost entirely illusory—image as a self-described "secret swinger." Not the least of Kissinger's many accomplishments is his managing to make a tubby, owlish-looking intellectual's newfound penchant for being seen with famous and beautiful women work somehow to enhance his image rather than be considered a symptom of incipient male menopause. Nixon saw what was really going on. During a staff meeting in early 1971, the president complained to Haldeman that because of Kissinger's "insistence on flitting around with movie stars," he was "making a fool of himself. Grown men know better. Henry has got to stop this. Do something. Do something."[37] One can only speculate as to the look on Haldeman's face as Nixon repeated the injunction, but the chief of staff did what he could, decreeing that at state dinners "Henry should not always be put next to the most glamorous woman present."[38] But it was too little, too late; he had already become the world's unlikeliest sex symbol.

It wasn't that Kissinger was himself sexy, of course. He derived his sexiness from the company he kept. He delighted in being photographed with the likes of Elizabeth Taylor, Liza Minnelli, and Raquel Welch and proclaimed that meeting Lana Turner was "one of the great moments of my life."[39] More celebrated still were his "dates"* with such other screen actresses as Samantha Eggar, Shirley MacLaine, Marlo Thomas, Liv Ullmann, Candice Bergen, and Jill St. John. (Kissinger's most frequent Hollywood companion, St. John actually found herself being introduced to

*The consistently chaste nature of these encounters made them more celebrity summit meetings than romantic trysts. In the stylish formulation of Walter Isaacson, his most authoritative biographer, Kissinger practiced "lascivious celibacy."

Brezhnev at San Clemente in 1973.) Both Ullmann and Bergen have described the experience of having Kissinger for an escort.

For "my good friend the talented and beautiful Norwegian actress Liv Ullmann," as Kissinger calls her in *Years of Upheaval*, it was her first blind date. So flustered was she when she learned of his interest, she "forgot to ask when he'd fetch me."[40] A few months later, Ullmann inadvertently got her revenge when she telephoned from Oslo just as Nixon was about to begin a televised press conference with the announcement of a major appointment. The impending nominee took the call as Nixon was about to speak; "by the time I hung up the phone I had missed hearing myself named as the next Secretary of State."[41]

As for Bergen, she had already rejected several overtures when she finally agreed to go out with Kissinger. She notes her escort "had two ball-point pens clipped to his jacket pocket and seemed at once a little uneasy and solidly self-assured." He showed up late and in the company of two Secret Service agents; they would remain present for the remainder of the evening. The musical soundtrack for his arrival couldn't have been improved upon: blasting from the poolside speakers was Bob Dylan's "Ballad of a Thin Man," that ultimate counterculture putdown of squares who just don't get it. "The night belonged to Kissinger," Bergen writes. "Spinning stories, weaving tales of his [first China] trip, adroitly answering careful questions, he was clearly a man at home in his glory, confidently commanding center stage." Bergen, a committed if unemphatic liberal (she had Abbie Hoffman as a houseguest at the time), did her best to debate Kissinger on foreign policy. "He was predictably patient and polite, adept with this raving dove in the back seat," Bergen concedes. "He even gave me the sense of shared secrets—probably the same set he gave every antiwar actress. . . ."[42]

Kissinger's backseat adeptness was solely verbal. Consorting with the stars was what mattered to him; anything beyond that was unnecessary so far as he was concerned, even undesirable (it was cachet he wanted, not scandal). These actresses attracted him less as objects of desire than validations of his own glamour. Here again we see how he and Nixon were at once similar and different. They both loved the movies, yet where Nixon loved them because he identified with the characters up there on the screen—he wanted to be Patton, not George C. Scott—Kissinger loved them because he identified with the stars, not the characters. Unlike Nixon, Kissinger had star power himself; not for nothing did his friend Robert Evans, the head of production at Paramount, call him "Cary

Grant with a German accent."[43] Nixon tapped into the movies as fantasy, Kissinger as fantasy lifestyle.*

"One day I hope I, too, can get a tan," he said at a Hollywood dinner in his honor and got a big laugh.[44] Insofar as "a tan" might be seen as metaphor for movie-land citizenship, it was also true. When *Gandhi* (1982) won the Best Picture Oscar, a wag attributed its victory to the title character's possessing the three attributes most prized in Hollywood: the Mahatma was "thin, moral, and tan." That's what Henry Kissinger, among many other things, wanted to be (two out of three, anyway). He fit right in. The actresses were good for his ego, as well as his image, but the more significant, if less well publicized, aspect of his relationship with Hollywood was his associating with the likes of Gregory Peck and Kirk Douglas (the latter threw a dinner party at his home in honor of Kissinger after the announcement of his secret mission to China), and such entertainment executives as Hal Wallis, Taft Schreiber, and Lew Wasserman. In *Years of Renewal,* the third volume of his memoirs, Kissinger interrupts his account of the fall of Saigon to record "a genuine act of grace, and I have never forgotten it": an uplifting telephone call from Wasserman. The momentous message offered by the Hollywood elder statesman was ". . . there are a lot of your friends out here who are thinking about you."[45] There certainly were, and not just then.

Above all, there was Evans, who came to consider Kissinger one of his closest friends—and set him up on many of those celebrated dates. Apparently, the national security adviser considered himself in the studio executive's debt. When Marlon Brando backed out at the last minute from appearing at the world premiere of *The Godfather,* Evans importuned Kissinger to fly up to New York. He agreed, this despite the premiere's taking place at the height of the North Vietnamese spring offensive of 1972, not to mention the fact he had a seven-thirty meeting the next morning with the Joint Chiefs of Staff about mining Haiphong harbor, then was scheduled to depart for Moscow.[46] (If he'd waited nine days, he could have watched *The Godfather* with Nixon, when the president had it screened at Camp David.) Later, when Evans's marriage to the actress Ali MacGraw broke up, Kissinger offered his services as intermediary. "If I can negotiate with the North Vietnamese," he told his friend, "I think I can smooth the way with Ali."[47] He had more success with Le Duc Tho.

*It's only just, then, poetically if not historically, that when the cable network TNT did a movie adaptation of Isaacson's biography in 1995, it was called *Kissinger and Nixon*—rather than the other way around.

Kissinger's Hollywood connection finally did get him in trouble, but not in any way Nixon could have anticipated. The scandal was intellectual in nature rather than libidinal, and the woman involved wasn't an actress but a journalist, Oriana Fallaci. The occasion was the notorious interview she conducted with him in November 1972; more specifically, it was his reply to her asking, "How do you explain the incredible movie-star status you enjoy?" In answering the question, Kissinger happily accepted its flattering premise and proceeded to make himself, however briefly, an international laughingstock.

Perhaps he sensed what thin ice he was on, for at first he tried to parry Fallaci's question. Yes, he had such a theory, Kissinger admitted, though it was quite different from others' theories—attributing his success to his intelligence, for example—but he refused to tell her and instead asked Fallaci what her own opinion might be. She had none, she conceded, though she wondered if the sheer magnitude of his success—China being the prime example—didn't lie at the heart of it. That was true, Kissinger agreed, but it was of incidental importance, and with that he could contain himself no longer. He would now be press agent as well as star.

"The main point arises from the fact that I've always acted alone. Americans like that immensely. Americans like the cowboy who leads the wagon train by riding ahead alone on his horse, the cowboy who rides all alone into the town, the village, with his horse and nothing else. Maybe even without a pistol, since he doesn't shoot. He acts, that's all, by being in the right place at the right time. In short, a Western."*

Though Kissinger didn't know it, the noose was already around his neck (presumably, he had never seen *The Ox-Bow Incident*). Now there was no stopping him. "All he needs is to be alone, to show others that he rides into the town and does everything by himself. This amazing, romantic character suits me precisely because to be alone has always been part of my style or, if you like, my technique. Together with independence. Oh, that's very important, in me and for me."[48]

Kissinger called the interview "without doubt the single most disastrous conversation I ever had with any member of the press." For Nixon, the interview's publication in late November 1972 could hardly have come at a worse time, detracting from his landslide reelection victory and

---

*At this point, Fallaci interrupts, trying to get Kissinger to clarify his statement. He sees himself, then, "as a kind of Henry Fonda, unarmed and ready to fight with his fists for honest ideals." Not John Wayne or James Stewart or Gary Cooper, more celebrated Western heroes, but Fonda—whose figure we encounter now dogging not just Nixon but even Nixon's chief associate.

adding to the ignominy of the collapse of the Vietnamese peace agreement. With frosty understatement, Nixon characterized his aide's performance as "debilitating to a negotiator."[49] What makes Kissinger's indiscretion so ironic is that, foolish as he was to have confided in Fallaci as he did, what he told her was quite simply wrong.

First off, while the Kissinger persona did possess a motion-picture pedigree (of sorts), and it did contribute to his powerful hold on the public imagination, it had nothing to do with Westerns. America had already been prepared for Kissinger, or a Kissinger type, by Walter Matthau's Walter Groeteschele, a chillingly emotionless analyst of nuclear destruction, in *Fail-Safe*, and most especially by Peter Sellers's title character in *Dr. Strangelove*. Sellers's post-Nazi policy adviser had been inspired by NASA's Wernher von Braun, with elements of Herman Kahn, the author of *On Thermonuclear War*, and Edward Teller, the physicist father of the hydrogen bomb. More distantly, Strangelove evokes Fritz Lang's Dr. Mabuse and, at that much further a remove, Mary Shelley's archetypal mad scientist, Victor Frankenstein. There might even have been the faintest touch of Kissinger himself. *Nuclear Weapons and Foreign Policy*, which takes what even at the time seemed an alarmingly complaisant view of the use of tactical nuclear weapons, had put him in the public eye in 1957 as a best-seller and selection by the Book-of-the-Month Club.

Neither Groeteschele nor Strangelove was a pure leap of the imagination on the part of Eugene Burdick and Harvey Wheeler or Peter George, the respective authors of the novels on which *Fail-Safe* and *Dr. Strangelove* were based. Rather, they were inspired by an utterly new type of figure, a type that would attain its highest form (and greatest influence) in the person of Henry Kissinger. For out of the cold war confluence of émigré thinkers, defense intellectuals, academic consultants, systems analysts, and RAND researchers, there had emerged an apocalyptic high priesthood handsomely supported by Pentagon funding and disturbingly fluent in an abstruse nuclear gnosticism: the lethal calculus of kill rates, throw weights, and megatonnage. What the Hessians had been for the British during the Revolution, these foreign mercenaries of the mind were for America during the cold war. Thrilling, alarming, not a little mysterious, the labors of such men (they were invariably male) owed as much to morality as science, theology as government. What the arrogance of Promethean urges had been to an earlier age, the madness of calibrating nuclear destruction was now. But where Frankenstein's ambition to create life had been heroic as well as horrifying, Strangelove's technocratic dream of fine-tuning the details of mass death was simply horrifying.

It's no surprise that so arresting a type found its way to the screen. Such a character, though (to state the obvious), remains at the opposite extreme from the classic cowboy hero: contemplative not active, reflective not impulsive, verbose not laconic, Old World not New. He is a character to recoil from—bloodless, unnatural, and (quite literally) foreign. Inspiring not fear and loathing, as the classic villain does, he instead induces anxiety and bewilderment. Above all, he is that most perplexing of types to the American mind—as well as the utter antithesis of the cowboy—the intellectual. Yet however paradoxically, these very attributes also ensure he is a figure to respect, even look up to, because of his expertise, authoritativeness, and the unmistakable air of cultural superiority imparted by his European background.

Numbering among Henry Kissinger's greater achievements was his almost always being able to emphasize the positive associations of his Strangelovean background while managing to suppress or, failing that, make light of its darker connotations. White House staffers, according to Jeb Magruder, referred to Kissinger's "Dr. Strangelove" accent, while Nixon and Haldeman actively feared the possibility of voters' making such a connection. To ensure that didn't happen, they prevented him from appearing on broadcast media until the last year of Nixon's first term. Incredible though it now seems, the press conference at which he stated "peace is at hand," which took place when he had been national security adviser for nearly four years, was just his second appearance on national television. "The White House public relations people," Kissinger writes with more than a touch of sarcasm, "were convinced that my accent might disturb Middle America."[50]

Once the public did at long last become familiar with Kissinger, it embraced him with such enthusiasm that the stereotype of the émigré cold warrior soon became as much a part of governmental folklore as the irrelevant vice president and, yes, patrician diplomat. Certainly, Jimmy Carter wasted no time in making sure that in Zbigniew Brzezinski (a bitter Kissinger rival) he had one for his own administration. By dint of his foreign birth, the émigré policy adviser was disallowed from the presidency. In practical terms, the nature of his background also essentially excluded him from the pursuit of any elective office. Rather than being detrimental, this was another aspect of the appeal such a figure held. It left him free to focus on higher concerns, lending him an aura of objectivity and (relative) detachment. He was, then, the very type of the adviser, the éminence grise (an appropriately Old World term): an individual whose importance wholly derived from that of another.

Kissinger knew this perfectly well—"I have a constituency of one man," he would remind his aides—but that didn't mean he liked to dwell on it.[51] What made the cowboy image so seductive for him was the way it seemed to mask this inescapable, intolerable fact of his situation. Unfortunately for Kissinger, rather than being the cowboy star in a close-up he boasted of to Fallaci, he was the ultimate sidekick in a two-shot: Tonto to Nixon's Loneliest of Rangers.

Here was Kissinger's other mistake: the cowboy isn't a *lone* hero—hardly ever, anyway—and this has been true throughout the Western's history. From the outlaw gang in *The Great Train Robbery* (1903) to the rather different outlaw gang in *The Wild Bunch* (1969), from John Wayne with Montgomery Clift in the greatest of all Westerns, *Red River* (1948), to Wayne with his motley jailhouse ensemble in *Rio Bravo* (1959) to Wayne with Kim Darby and Glen Campbell in *True Grit*, the Western has predicated itself on team play, affiliation, *joining*. That's how the West was won, with a group effort, and even Gary Cooper's famously isolated sheriff in *High Noon* (1952) requires the intervention of his young bride, Grace Kelly, to survive.

There are two great exceptions to this rule, and their anomalousness simply reinforces the larger point: Alan Ladd's title character in *Shane* (1953) is transparently an anachronism—those Daniel Boone buckskins!—whose solitary departure at the film's end underlines his deviation from the norm; and Clint Eastwood's Man with No Name in Sergio Leone's spaghetti Western trilogy. Eastwood's character is a quite conscious reductio ad absurdum of the Western hero—and, equally pertinent as a gloss on the Kissingerian misreading, very much a European view of the Western. Even so, it is only in the first film, *A Fistful of Dollars* (1964), that he operates alone. He joins forces with Lee Van Cleef in *For a Few Dollars More* (1965) and, rather more problematically, with Eli Wallach in *The Good, the Bad, and the Ugly* (1967).

Kissinger's remark to Fallaci reveals his cultural obtuseness as much as his egotism. He might have turned to Nixon for guidance, for Nixon knew his Westerns. He saw fifty-six of them while president, and any number of those titles demonstrate the genre's abhorrence of individualism. The defining element of these films—from the initially treacherous and ultimately comradely relationship between Randolph Scott and Joel McCrea in *Ride the High Country* (1962) to the fraternity of technique that unites Lee Marvin, Robert Ryan, Burt Lancaster, and Woody Strode in *The Professionals* (1966)—is cooperation and alliance.

It's only appropriate that the foremost exponent of the Western's communitarian ethic should also be the genre's universally acknowledged master. For John Ford, the heroic is inherently plural. The band, the team, the troop, the unit, the settlement, even just the friendship: in such human comminglings resides all virtue, through them all good gets done. There is the disparate group of passengers who end up becoming a kind of family in *Stagecoach* (1939); or the outlaw trio (Wayne, Pedro Armendariz, and Harry Carey Jr.) in *Three Godfathers* (1948); or Travis and Sandy (Ben Johnson and Carey), the dual heroes of *Wagon Master* (1950), and the group of Mormon pioneers whose wagon train they agree to lead; or the pursued tribe in *Cheyenne Autumn* (1964). Even *The Searchers* (1956), the darkest of all Ford's films, Western or otherwise, is about reuniting—however violently, at whatever cost—the last remaining members of a shattered family. Its protagonist, John Wayne's Ethan Edwards, is the most alienated and murderously individualistic of all Ford's heroes—perhaps the most murderously individualistic in any Western. Yet even he cannot go it alone. During the seven years he spends seeking his abducted niece (Natalie Wood), his stepnephew (Jeffrey Hunter) never leaves his side. Edwards doesn't want his company but accepts it, for that is simply how things are in a Ford Western.

Perhaps the clearest expression of Ford's reverence for the social fabric of the frontier comes in *My Darling Clementine*—not when Wyatt Earp (Henry Fonda) teams up with his brothers and Doc Holliday (Victor Mature) to confront the Clantons at the O.K. Corral, but rather on the cloudless Sunday morning when he shyly attends a church-raising dance. The image of the good men and women of Tombstone executing an intricate yet carefree choreography on a newly lain floor, its lovingly joined planks open to the desert sky, epitomizes the Fordian vision of human society civilizing the emptiness of the West. The only solitary figures here are villains—or corpses.

In that respect, the West is merely the most exposed arena for Ford to stage his recurring dialectic between the individual (bad) and the community (good). Whether it be for the residents of the migrant camps in *The Grapes of Wrath*, the ship's crew in *The Long Voyage Home* (1940), the Welsh mining family in *How Green Was My Valley* (1941), or the inhabitants of the Irish village in *The Quiet Man* (1952), the great good place requires but one essential condition for its greatness, its goodness: the presence of interdependent others. Conversely, the most tragic figures in

Ford's work are invariably outcasts, regardless of whether it is they who reject society (Ethan Edwards, Tom Joad) or who are themselves rejected (the Cheyenne, Victor McLaglen's Gypo Nolan in *The Informer* [1935]). Attribute it as one may—a Catholic upbringing's emphasis on universal oneness? a self-conscious patriot's overfond embrace of e pluribus unum? an unhappy husband and father's idealizing imaginary alternatives to his own troubled domestic life?—Ford's fervent allegiance to a more taciturn version of Whitman's adhesiveness is the sole constant in a wildly uneven career that spanned half a century, nearly 150 films, and multiple genres.

The church excepted, the nation-state is the highest form of social integration. The displays of patriotic emotion in Ford's pictures may verge on the jingoistic—and they more than verge on the simplistic—but they also directly follow from this most consistent of Fordian themes: "us" vs. "I" as well as "us" vs. "them." "What are you aiming at," PT-boat commander Robert Montgomery asks Wayne, his hot-headed subordinate, in *They Were Expendable* (1945), "building a reputation or playing for the team?" The man on his own, the individual, is nothing without the larger group to belong to and a greater loyalty to follow. Ford's fondness for military organizations owes as much to his recognizing the premium the military places on working together for the common good as it does to any warlike tendencies on his part. It also brings us full circle, back to the Western, for the most exalted social entity in the Fordian canon, the Seventh Cavalry, combines this ethic of the soldier with the closely related ethic of the cowboy. In *Fort Apache* (1948), *She Wore a Yellow Ribbon* (1949), and *Rio Grande* (1950), Ford shows a West that is at the furthest remove from anything like the heroic singular limned by Kissinger. The regiment comes before all—before love (in *She Wore a Yellow Ribbon*), before family (in *Rio Grande*), even before life itself (in *Fort Apache*)—and the regiment's troopers, not to mention the settlers they protect as well as the nation as a whole, are the better for it. The one character in the cavalry trilogy who fails to recognize both the primacy and the efficacy of the group is Lieutenant Colonel Owen Thursday (Fonda), who commands the regiment in *Fort Apache*. He is also the most complex villain in all of Ford's oeuvre: brave, dedicated, intelligent, but also not a little Kissingerian (as we might say)—smitten with the Old World, disdainful, egotistical, self-regardingly set apart, too in love with glory for his own good. A Patton who fails to get away with his vainglory, he leads the Seventh Cavalry into a disastrous Custer-like defeat, and it is left to Wayne's Captain Kirby York, who *does* understand the limitations of the individual vis-à-vis the strengths of the regiment, to stave off annihilation.

Nixon, who surely failed to note any Patton parallels, saw *Fort Apache* at the White House on July 24, 1972. The twenty-fourth was a Monday, thus making the Ford film a special treat: a weeknight movie. Of course, any time Nixon saw a Ford picture qualified as an occasion, since he was the president's favorite filmmaker. Twelve days before seeing *Fort Apache*, he'd sent Ford a note acknowledging a telegram praising the president's performance at a recent news conference. At the bottom the president added a postscript in his own hand: "John Wayne was in to see me a few days ago. I asked him who was the best all time Director. He replied instantly. 'John Ford.' I agree!"[52] There was nothing phony about that exclamation mark. Nine months later Nixon told a Hollywood gathering, "I think I've seen virtually all of the one-hundred-forty movies" made by Ford. It was classic Nixon hyperbole—so eager to please, so eager to impress, so undiscriminating in exaggeration, so transparent in falsity—but he did see twenty Ford films while he was president, more than twice the number he saw by any other director.

That Richard Nixon—wearer of flag pins and celebrant of the Western—should have for his favorite film director John Ford makes perfect sense. "Too many of his characters," as Andrew Sarris gingerly puts it in *The American Cinema*, "wear uniforms without tortuous reasoning why."[53] "Tortuous reasoning why" was *not* what Richard Nixon watched movies for. And the more Ford went out of fashion—the more a taste for his films became a political as well as an artistic statement—the more pleasure Nixon could, and did, take in the director's work.

There was a deeper appeal, though, one that transcended ideology, that went beyond art. Who's to say how much Nixon's love of Ford's films had to do with this implicit sense of *belonging* that they present? Nixon, Safire writes, "saw his character the way he would like himself to be: the John Ford hero."[54] This element of identification is striking for, as we have seen, what is most characteristic of Ford's work, what is most *Fordian* about it, is his films' condemnation of apartness and isolation. Nixon was too smart (too aware of his vulnerability to ridicule) ever to imagine himself atop a horse or riding to the rescue; rather, it was this idea of being one of the boys, of being accepted, that held such a deep appeal for him. Yes, courage and heroism and patriotism, these were virtues Nixon eagerly responded to—*Patton* being only the most celebrated cinematic example—but they could be found in many places. What helped make

Ford's work so meaningful to him was that his films were about those qualities in the context of *connection*. "John Ford is one of my heroes in every sense of the word," Nixon wrote to one of the filmmaker's biographers, Joseph McBride, in 1988. "John Ford was to motion pictures what Tolstoy was to literature."[55]

Ford reciprocated Nixon's admiration. During the 1930s the director had liked to boast of his socialist leanings and had been a leading Hollywood supporter of the Spanish Republic. In 1950, at the height of the Red Scare, he had single-handedly quelled a McCarthyite effort to force a loyalty oath on the board of the Directors Guild and throw out its liberal leadership. Yet he voted for Nixon in 1968 and 1972; and after her husband's death, Ford's widow hung by her bed a photograph of Ford and herself posing with Nixon.[56]

The photo had been taken when Ford was presented the American Film Institute's first Life Achievement Award. Nixon's participation in the evening was both a coup for the institute and a mark of the president's special regard for the recipient. "Oh, it was fine. A great occasion," Ford told the director Lindsay Anderson four months after the event (and just six weeks before his death). "The President made a speech. Of course, he didn't know much about it, but he did it very well. I was touched."[57] The ceremony was the crowning moment in Ford's life, honoring him as patriot and military man as well as filmmaker. In addition to the Life Achievement Award, he received from Nixon the nation's highest civilian honor, the Presidential Medal of Freedom and (what meant the most to Ford) an unofficial promotion to the rank of admiral in the naval reserves.

In its own way, the AFI dinner provided Richard Nixon with one of the great moments of his life, too. At the end of the evening, Ford spoke only briefly. Rather than discuss his film career, Ford preferred to dwell on the recent return of the POWs from North Vietnam. He admitted that their arrival had moved him to tears. "Then," he added, "I reached for my rosary and said a few decades of the beads, and I uttered a short fervent prayer, not an original prayer, but one spoken in millions of American homes today. It is a simple prayer, simply 'God bless Richard Nixon.'"[58] ("It really stuck it to the anti-Nixon types in the film crowd," a pleased Haldeman noted in his diary.)[59]

"God bless Richard Nixon." How that must have thrilled and moved Nixon: to hear John Ford—*John Ford*—say such a thing, and to say it in front of Duke Wayne, Jimmy Stewart, Chuck Heston. Kissinger could date every starlet in creation and knock back diet colas at the Polo Lounge with any studio executive willing to put them on his tab. But this, this was acceptance by Hollywood at a level of magnitude surpassing anything Kissinger had even dreamed of: the movies' grand master, the century's greatest American mythmaker, supplicating the Deity on Nixon's behalf.

Small wonder that at San Clemente the next evening he should choose to celebrate by screening a Ford movie. Unfortunately, *Two Rode Together* is far from being the director's best ("The worst piece of crap I've done in twenty years," he told Anderson), even if Jean-Luc Godard did name it the best film of 1961.[50] The plot concerns an ill-suited duo (Stewart and Richard Widmark) attempting to retrieve a group of Indian captives. As Philip French has pointed out, this is simply *The Searchers* by other means—and far lesser means, at that. Drab and sour, it's the first Western Ford had done since his silent-movie days with no exteriors shot in Monument Valley. It feels unmoored and distracted; only a single shot, an elegiac yet gloriously vivid tableau of Stewart arriving back with one of the captives (Linda Cristal), the two of them outlined against a glowing twilight sky, seems unmistakably Fordian. Indeed, the best thing in the movie, a long single take where Stewart and Widmark chivvy one another as they wash up along a riverbank, feels so loose and fresh it seems to have wandered in from a Howard Hawks picture. Yet even here, in so atypical a work, we observe the essential Fordian dynamic, the film's title pledging allegiance to the principle of shared effort in succinct refutation of the Kissinger thesis.

The title's three words had an additional resonance, albeit one surely lost on Nixon. They described the fundamental dynamic that had defined foreign policy during his administration. The two who rode together were, of course, the president and his national security adviser, and only the addition of a fourth word, "roughshod," might have improved the title's accuracy. Nor was the use of the past tense incorrect. Nixon saw *Two Rode Together* nine days after Judge Sirica had sentenced the Watergate defendants and, far more significant, revealed the contents of James McCord's letter charging political pressure, perjury, and secret offers of clemency in return for silence. The cover-up had begun to spin out of control. Before the month was out, Nixon would be accepting the resignations of Haldeman and Ehrlichman and confessing that he yearned for death ("when I went to bed . . . I had hoped, and almost prayed, that I wouldn't wake up"). "It's all over, Ron, do you know that?" Nixon said to his uncomprehending press secretary, Ron Ziegler, the day of the resignations. He meant his presidency, but he could just as well have been describing his partnership with Kissinger. As the latter writes in the second volume of his memoirs, "One of the more cruel torments of Nixon's Watergate purgatory was my emergence as the preeminent figure in foreign policy."[61] The absence of gloating is as surprising as it is commendable.

The balance between them had begun to shift with the announcement of Kissinger's secret mission to China in 1971. By the time of his "peace is at hand" pronouncement, the national security adviser's popularity almost made it seem as if the president was little more than an appendage to the conduct of U.S. foreign policy. The failure of the peace talks, the Fallaci interview, and Nixon's consciously distancing himself from Kissinger briefly righted the balance, so much so that Kissinger had decided to leave the administration some time later in 1973. But Watergate made Kissinger not just useful to Nixon, but indispensable. The *New York Times* called him "president for foreign affairs," and with Nixon beginning to appear on magazine covers in a convict's stripes, *Newsweek*'s cover featured Kissinger in a Superman suit.[62] The adviser was now for all intents and purposes the senior partner, a shift tacitly acknowledged in August when Nixon grudgingly named him to the nation's highest appointive office, secretary of state (that sanctum sanctorum of the foreign policy establishment, the seventh floor at Foggy Bottom, now his).

Of course, by then the great deeds had been done: the opening to China, détente with the Soviet Union, SALT, the Vietnamese peace accords. The diplomatic landmarks of the remainder of Nixon's administration, and those of the Ford years as well, were all either reactions to events arising elsewhere, such as the Yom Kippur War, the oil embargo, shuttle diplomacy; or direct results of the accomplishments—and failures—of the first four years: another Soviet summit, the fall of Indochina, the Helsinki Accords. Two no longer rode together—Nixon had fallen off his horse—but it hardly mattered by then. How telling that Kissinger, the most self-justifyingly exhaustive of modern memoirists, should have waited almost a quarter of a century before writing about his two and a half years of service as secretary of state under Gerald Ford, as if implicitly acknowledging that all that had *really* mattered was his time with Nixon.

Each made the other's success possible; each made the other a greater, more intriguing figure. Even as Nixon's decline worked to increase Kissinger's power—and his departure increased it immeasurably, as a president who was an admitted neophyte in foreign policy had to give free rein to his secretary of state—Nixon's fall nonetheless managed to diminish Kissinger, too. Proximity to Nixon, the ultimate flak catcher, had made Kissinger seem more temperate, more enlightened, less opportunistic. It had also given him, in a term popularized a dozen years later in the Iran-Contra scandal, "plausible deniability": all the mistakes were Nixon's, all the successes his own. That changed with Kissinger now so clearly in charge.

Watergate, in an odd way, helped undo *him*, too. In the course of inventing détente and perfecting superpower summitry, Nixon and Kissinger had invented and perfected a model of diplomatic synergy, the whole of their efforts markedly greater than the sum of their respective contributions. Nixon aide Charles Colson, one of the president's few partisans in his rivalry with Kissinger, described them as "dependent on one another like two tightrope walkers."[63] What's so extraordinary about their relationship was that they didn't just walk on the rope together; they had erected it, too. With one of them gone, more than just their balance went awry; so did the rope.

Even in the Fallaci interview, Kissinger had conceded the necessity of Nixon's presence for his own success ("the cowboy who rides all alone into the town" has to have someone provide him with a horse). And it wasn't just that his master was the president, but that his master who was president was this *particular* president. "I'm not at all sure that I would have been able to do with another president what I've done with him. Such a special relationship, I mean the relationship there is between me and the president, always depends on the style of the two men. . . . [W]hat I've done has been possible because he made it possible for me."[64] Such words could be dismissed as so much boilerplate (the first rule of bureaucratic candor: always praise your boss before praising yourself), but even in private Kissinger would at times evince a sense of dual destiny, as when he said of Vietnam to Safire, "Because the two of us are here, the President and myself, we have a chance of *winning* this thing." Of course, the idea of their dual destiny worked both ways, for as Safire quickly adds after recounting Kissinger's remark, 'In Henry's mind, 'only Nixon could have' was absolutely true, once modified to 'only Nixon and Kissinger could have.'"[65]

Nixon knew this as well as Kissinger did, understood how intricate and indissoluble (how vexing, too) was the bond that joined them. The clearest proof of this realization came during Nixon's darkest hour at the very nadir of his presidency. For on the night before he announced his resignation, whom did he summon but Kissinger to join him in that remarkable scene of soul baring and prayer? For better or worse, this has become the most famous moment of the final days, as well as one of the most famous of Nixon's life, a more definitive tableau of his leaving office than even the final V-for-Valhalla wave from the helicopter about to spirit him away from the South Lawn. Protocol dictated that it be Kissinger, as secretary of state, to whom Nixon addressed his official letter of resignation. But that was pro forma—it could as easily have been Rogers (a nice bit of just desserts) or the man initially slated to succeed Rogers, Kenneth Rush. It was Wednesday night's meeting that truly announced—emotionally, psychically, poetically even—Nixon's surrender of his office. "For some reason the agony and the loss of what was about to happen became most acute for me during that conversation," Nixon later recalled. "I found myself more emotional than I had been at any time since the decision had been set in motion."[66]

Kissinger may have been, as he himself delicately put it, "the one associate about whom [Nixon] was the most ambivalent."[67] And ever since his becoming secretary of state, they had grown even further apart as Kissinger consciously distanced himself in hopes of keeping his own reputation unbesmirched ("I cannot let my policies or myself be dragged down with that man," he'd complained to his aides two months before the resignation).[68] Nor was Kissinger known for any particular capacity for sympathy or talent for benediction. Yet it being Kissinger Nixon should turn to at this climactic moment was as it had to be, as if in strict observance of some Aristotelian dramatic unity.

Early in the spring of 1969, more than five years before the final scene in the Lincoln Sitting Room, at a time when such a moment would have seemed fantastical beyond words, Nixon had met with Kissinger in another encounter that also expressed this sense of their dual destiny—in this case, just as it was beginning to emerge, with Kissinger's name as yet barely known to the public and Nixon's presidency still replete with freshness and promise. The president had given in to Kissinger's urgings to make what would prove to be his sole appearance before the National Security Council staff. It was meant to boost their morale, to indicate how important they were in the president's scheme of things. As such, the appearance was a nod to Kissinger, with the president's devoting his precious time to a meeting with (relatively) unimportant staffers meant to demonstrate the value he placed on his chief foreign policy adviser.

It turned into something even more than that, though. Roger Morris recalls how Nixon concluded the meeting with eight simple words spoken to Kissinger concerning the succubus that, having haunted the nation for much of the decade, would nearly destroy the administration and bedevil it into its second term: "And you and I will end the war."[69] There it was, with breathtaking matter-of-factness, a statement that would take nearly four more years to fulfill, and then not at all in a way Nixon or Kissinger had envisioned. But even at that early juncture, confronted with the central dilemma of his presidency, Nixon acknowledged this duality: that it was two of them together—neither president nor (most assuredly) national security adviser alone—on a ride that would eventually take them to Beijing and Moscow, Paris and Saigon, and many more places besides.

Some of those places they themselves never actually went to, of course; only their power did. Perhaps the most notable such destination was Cambodia. Certainly it would prove the most disastrous, unleashing a frenzy on U.S. campuses and (less directly but incalculably worse) contributing to the triumph of the Khmer Rouge. There the Old Testament lesson Nixon drew for Kissinger shouldn't have concerned Lot's wife and the temptation to look back but rather Nebuchadnezzar and the tendency of rulers to become temporarily deranged.

Walter Huston

AMERICAN MADNESS

■ ■

That Lincoln Memorial. Gee whiz! Mr. Lincoln, there he is: He's just looking right straight at you as you come up those steps—just sitting there like he was waiting for somebody to come along. JAMES STEWART, AS JEFFERSON SMITH, *Mr. Smith Goes to Washington*

President Nixon got loose once, too. H. R. HALDEMAN, ON NIXON'S VISIT TO THE LINCOLN MEMORIAL EARLY ON THE MORNING OF MAY 9, 1970[1]

H. R. Haldeman concluded his diary entry for April 29, 1970, with ominous terseness: "Will be a tough couple of days."[2] He was anticipating what effect the next day's announcement of the U.S.–South Vietnamese invasion of Cambodia would have. Yet even Haldeman, with his mania for damage control and staying ahead of events, could not have imagined what the next week and a half would hold in store, how it would rock the administration and the nation like no comparable period during the five and a half years Nixon was in the White House.

Only the Saturday Night Massacre, and the subsequent outrage over the firing of Watergate Special Prosecutor Archibald Cox and resignations of Attorney General Elliot Richardson and Deputy Attorney General William Ruckelshaus, surpassed the invasion of Cambodia in terms of sheer intensity of public reaction. Cambodia and the events that followed in its wake divided the country to an extent unprecedented even for the deeply polarized days of the Nixon presidency. Those who supported the move saw it as necessary and overdue to protect the lives of U.S. fighting men. Those opposed saw it as a cynical and disastrous betrayal of every promise to end U.S. involvement in Southeast Asia. Between the two camps lay no common ground, and the clash between them would see such vituperation, such protest, even such bloodshed, that it produced an increasingly strong sense that the entire nation had lost control—and that loss extended all the way to the Oval Office. Ten days after Haldeman wrote his diary entry, the madness culminated in what William Safire has called "the strangest, most impulsive, and perhaps most revealing night of Nixon's Presidency."[3]

So strange were the events of May 8–9, 1970, they seemed like something out of a movie—a specific movie at that: Nixon's predawn visit to the Lincoln Memorial to commune with the spirit of his greatest predecessor was straight out of Frank Capra's *Mr. Smith Goes to Washington.* That celebrated paean to American democracy has two classic scenes: the title character's heroic Senate filibuster, and what leads to the filibuster— what overcomes Jefferson Smith's dejection and gives him the courage to persevere—his visit to the Lincoln Memorial the night before. "I remember that movie well," Nixon told Stewart Alsop in 1958.[4] Twelve years later he was reenacting it. A Hollywood classic, *Mr. Smith* is at once rapturous in its celebration of the democratic verities Nixon professed and very nearly deranged in its detestation of the political realities he so skillfully practiced. It is in its own way as confused as Nixon himself was that early morning in May.

No filmmaker could have imagined such a scene: the leader of the Free World abandoning his trappings of power to draw inspiration from Honest Abe; then, like a latter-day Hārūn ar-Rashīd, moving unannounced among the people to hear their plaints in a time of trouble. The idea of such a visit was absurd, incredible—and, because it really did happen, more than a little unnerving. For days the country had seemed on the verge of cracking up. Now the president, "having reached a point of exhaustion that caused his advisers deep concern,"[5] in the carefully chosen words of Henry Kissinger, appeared to be cracking up, too.

Considered in the context of the previous ten days, such bizarreness had its own crazed logic. Haldeman had realized the attack on North Vietnam's Cambodian sanctuaries was certain to be controversial. Even within the administration, the proposal had proven fiercely divisive, with both Secretary of State Rogers and Secretary of Defense Laird opposing it, and four members of Kissinger's staff preparing to resign in protest. But even such remarkable internal dissension could not have suggested the nationwide firestorm the decision would trigger.

For much of the fury, Nixon had himself to blame. The day after making the Cambodian announcement, he had visited the Pentagon. Leaving the building, he made some offhand remarks about student protesters. "You see these bums, you know, blowing up the campuses. Listen, the boys that are on the college campuses today are the luckiest people in the world, going to the greatest universities, and here they are burning up the books, storming around." Though Nixon had directed his comments at students who engaged in violent protest, his remarks were taken by many to have been aimed at all student protesters. Certainly, that was how his words were interpreted on many college campuses, where they set off a burst of more, and even more heated, demonstrations.

One of them took place three days later, on May 4, in Ohio. National Guardsmen shot and killed four students and wounded eleven others, and the words "Kent State" became a battle cry, an accusation, a national wound. "My child was not a bum," the father of one of the dead students told the press; and many Americans, recalling Nixon's Pentagon remarks, held him responsible.

"Those few days after Kent State were among the darkest of my presidency," Nixon later recalled. "The daily news reports conveyed a sense of turmoil bordering on insurrection."[6] With a national day of protest called for that Saturday, May 9, campuses exploded: 448 colleges and universities went on strike, commencements were canceled, and 100,000 demonstrators streamed into Washington, many of them camping on the Ellipse within sight of the White House. National Guardsmen were sent to campuses in sixteen states. A national coordinating office for striking students was set up at Brandeis University. The Nixon family itself was affected: the president had already decided it would be prudent for him and Mrs. Nixon not to attend either Julie's upcoming graduation from Smith or David Eisenhower's from Amherst.

The turmoil did not issue solely from the antiwar movement. When Mayor John Lindsay ordered the American flag at New York City Hall flown at half-staff, three hundred construction workers responded on

May 7 by attacking a group of student protesters and raising the flag. The next day Charles Colson invited leaders of the construction workers union to meet with an appreciative president. Headlined "CRISIS OF LEADERSHIP," the *New York Times'* lead editorial that Sunday feared that "the nation has lost its sense of direction."[7]

Part of Nixon's rationale for going into Cambodia had been his unwillingness to see the United States rendered "a pitiful, helpless giant." Was that fate now his? Two days after the shootings, he bowed to public opinion and met with a delegation of six Kent State students. The same day the text of a letter from Secretary of the Interior Walter Hickel urging Nixon not to ignore the students' message was released. Both Rogers and Laird had already leaked to the press their opposition to the Cambodian incursion. Now not even Nixon's own Cabinet could be relied upon for support. Nixon was like a prisoner. The day after the shootings, he canceled all trips for the rest of the week; and, as a defensive measure, fifty-nine city buses ringed the White House. Leaving the office late Friday night, Haldeman complained about being "jammed in by the troop trucks unloading the Third Army into the EOB. A very strange feeling as the White House and DC batten down for another siege."[8]

Nixon had been under enormous pressure for almost two months, dating back to mid-March when the overthrow of Prince Sihanouk had precipitated the administration's internal debate over Cambodia. Such pressure made all the more impressive his handling of a nationally televised news conference Friday night. Some attempt had to be made to calm the nation, and it was decided (not without some misgivings) that a question-and-answer session with the press would be the easiest—and safest—way to get results. Nixon spoke of the demonstrators in conciliatory terms and announced that U.S. troops would be out of Cambodia by the end of June. It was a reassuring performance. Perhaps the worst was over.

Nixon admits in his memoirs that after the broadcast he "was agitated and uneasy as the events of the last few weeks raced through my mind."[9] There ensued a night of restless phone calling—a night that was, in some respects, even odder than the Lincoln Memorial visit that followed. Between 9:23 P.M. and 3:50 A.M., Nixon made fifty phone calls. Among those he telephoned were Kissinger (eight times), Haldeman (seven times), Nelson Rockefeller and Thomas E. Dewey, Hickel, Rogers, Laird, Bebe Rebozo, religious leaders (Billy Graham and Norman Vincent Peale), journalists (Nancy Dickerson and Helen Thomas), and even Paul Keyes, the man who arranged Nixon's celebrated four-word appearance—"Sock it to *me?*!"—on *Rowan & Martin's Laugh-In* in 1968. Safire, whom Nixon called at 11 P.M., describes him as being "in an odd mood . . . keyed up and relaxed at the same time, too exhausted to sleep, rambling in his remarks, and prone to take you into his confidence."[10]

He slept less than two hours and a little before 4 A.M. went into the Lincoln Sitting Room and began to play a recording of Rachmaninoff's Second Piano Concerto. Hearing the music, Nixon's valet, Manolo Sanchez, entered and asked if the president would like some tea or coffee. Nixon had been staring out the window at the Ellipse, the park between the White House grounds and Constitution Avenue, facing the Washington Monument. Ignoring the question, he said that he felt Washington's most beautiful sight was the Lincoln Memorial at night. Sanchez replied that he'd never seen it. "Let's go look at it now," Nixon said.

It's hard to imagine a more telling indication of how wound up Nixon had been than this least spontaneous of men proposing such an impulsive act. After days of confinement, the president would step out and, just like any other early-bird tourist hoping to beat the crowds, pay a visit to the most popular monument in the nation's capital. This was no photo opportunity, no carefully prepared bit of grandstanding: there would be no press, no retinue—just Nixon, Sanchez, and a scrambling Secret Service contingent "petrified with apprehension" (as Nixon later described it).[11]

Egil "Bud" Krogh, an aide to Ehrlichman, was in charge of security that night. (He's best known today for having headed the secret White House Plumbers Unit.) No one was in a better position to appreciate the surreal quality of the scene as Secret Service communications crackled with word that "Searchlight" (Nixon's code name) "is on the lawn," then "Searchlight has asked for a car," and finally that the car was going to the Lincoln Memorial. "I think he's taken off," a stunned Krogh telephoned an equally stunned Ehrlichman.

After the brief drive from the White House, Nixon and Sanchez walked up the steps to the building's rotunda. They admired Daniel Chester French's great seated figure of Lincoln, and the president read to his valet some of his favorite passages from the inscriptions carved on the walls. A small group of student protesters joined them. Nixon shook hands and tried to enter into a dialogue. "I know that probably most of you think I'm an SOB," Nixon later recollected saying to them, "but I want you to know that I understand just how you feel."[12]

Krogh looked on in amazement as the president and the students, their numbers slowly growing, talked for the next hour. "It was very quiet, even hushed, and the President was speaking in a very low, conversational tone to the students, really in with them, not out in front talking to them," Krogh later wrote. "I turned and looked out from the Memorial and saw that the Washington Monument was picking up a soft shade of pink. There was a haziness about the morning, and the profound quiet of the Lincoln Memorial blended beautifully with the changing morning colors."[13] Hollywood could not have improved on the scenario: democracy at its purest—and also its most terrifying—the leader among his people, ruler and ruled meeting one on one, immediate and unmediated, agreeing to disagree by the dawn's early light. "It was a moving feeling being there," Krogh wrote in his memo, "and I know the kids felt it, as I did."[14]

It was among the most startling moments of Nixon's so often startling career. Yet unlike the rest—the Checkers speech, the riot in Caracas, the kitchen debate, the debates with Kennedy, the 1962 exit speech, the visits to China and the Soviet Union, his resignation—it occurred away from the cameras. Nixon's entry into public life almost exactly coincided with the arrival of television in the national consciousness, and starting with the Hiss hearings (the first congressional hearings to be nationally televised), nearly all his career took place in the public eye. That very "publicness" makes the Lincoln Memorial visit all the more striking, certainly all the more intimate, and somehow all the more precious. Like an event preserved only in a family photo album, its visual record consists solely of snapshots—one of them taken at Nixon's own suggestion when, seeing "a bearded fellow from Detroit" readying his camera, he wondered if the young man might want to pose with the president. He did, and Nixon had Dr. Walter Tkach, the White House physician, take the photo (the presidential party had steadily increased during the eighty minutes since Nixon had left the White House). "He seemed to be quite delighted," Nixon recalled—"it was, in fact, the broadest smile that I saw on the entire visit."[15]

Krogh and the Secret Service were by now nearly frantic; the potential for violence in a Washington filled with demonstrators and armed troops was terrifying. At any moment an incident involving the president could occur. Nixon, however, oblivious to any threat, was savoring his freedom. "Have you ever visited the Capitol?" he asked Sanchez, and again they were off. Finding the Senate chamber locked, they sought out a custodian who let them into the House chamber. Nixon sat at his old House desk and had Sanchez deliver a speech from the Speaker's chair. Three black cleaning women approached the president; one of them, Carrie

Moore, had a Bible. Nixon inscribed it, telling Moore his mother had been a saint. "You be a saint, too," he urged.[16]

Outside the Capitol, the party was joined by a dumbfounded trio of Haldeman, Ron Ziegler, and appointments secretary Dwight Chapin. They accompanied Nixon to the Mayflower Hotel, where, having breakfasted on corned beef hash, he required strenuous persuading from Haldeman to keep from returning to the White House on foot. Haldeman's summary of the morning's events was as succinct as it was indisputable: "Very weird."[17] The whole episode, from departing the White House to finishing the hash, took less than three hours. Eliding travel time, it could have easily fit the length of a feature film.

Nixon realized something singular had happened (he took the time a few days later to dictate an eight-page memorandum describing the events) and also understood how inherently stagy the whole thing had been (it was he, after all, who had urged Sanchez to give that speech from the Speaker's chair). Such an awareness in no way detracts from the sincerity of his actions that day or the real sense of civics-lesson awe surrounding them. But the events of the morning of May 9 remind us once again just how much Nixon the politician subsumed and drew upon certain other Nixons: the college thespian, the dedicated moviegoer, the producer of his own world-historical scenario. "Nixon is a dramatist," his aide Leonard Garment often said, a description that, however surprising on the surface, can be seen on reflection to be as fair a summary as any of the career of a man who spent more than forty years presenting, as Garment pungently put it, "public theater without Joseph Papp."[18] Nixon's instinct for theatricality should never be underestimated, least of all when he was at his most unguarded. The Lincoln Memorial morning may be seen as the supreme example of this, surpassing even those two other great public instances of Nixonian self-revelation the 1962 concession speech and the 1974 farewell address to his White House staff when he repeated those words to Carrie Moore about his mother being a saint. (Richard Nixon wouldn't have been Richard Nixon if he'd been able to be *that* unguarded before a set of television cameras.)

Like the movies, this book predicates itself on shadowy emanations, emanations that—after enough darkened hours sitting before a lit screen, hours grounded in a requisite willingness to believe—can be regarded as something far more substantial: an index of our hopes and fears and national character rendered through the collision of the glamorous fiction of Hollywood and the glum, grinding fact of Richard Nixon. As Oliver Stone found out, the movies can hardly do justice to Nixon, for nothing they can show can provide weirder or more compelling images than did the man's own overwhelming actuality. But Nixon—self-scenarist supreme—can do justice to the movies, as the Lincoln Memorial incident so breathtakingly demonstrated. (Give Stone his due: he had sense enough to include the visit in his movie.) On that Saturday morning, the collision between meta-movies and meta-Nixon became congruence.

Walking up those marble steps, he was following in the footsteps of James Stewart; three decades after the fact, he was playing—no, *being*— a real-life Jefferson Smith, at once grander and paltrier than the original. Indeed, Nixon's visit almost eerily illustrates one of Hollywood's enduring contributions to our national psyche, the "Capraesque." That word's most superficial meaning is plain enough: "of or pertaining to the films of Frank Capra." Yet what it connotes goes far beyond that, reaching very deep (for better, for worse) into what it means to be American: a kind of self-awareness—self-congratulation, really—that prides itself on being absolute innocence.

There's a moment early on in *The American President* that nicely demonstrates the concept's peculiar ability to cloak contrivance in naïveté. Annette Bening pauses outside the White House prior to paying her first visit to the West Wing. Urged along by her more jaundiced companion, she declares, "I'm trying to savor the Capraesque quality." There's no irony intended; she really means it, or at least the screenwriter does. In a movie, how else would a high-powered political professional articulate what she feels before entering a national shrine than by evoking a moviemaker who made movies about high-minded political amateurs who feel humility before entering national shrines? The Capraesque is a civic aesthetic that sees itself as comprising equal parts idealism, humility, and virtue, whereas in fact it consists of nothing so much as an excess of deference, or perhaps envy, in the presence of power. In its unmatched effectiveness, as in its eagerly oblivious hypocrisy, it's a perfect patriotic expression of our national mania for having it both ways. As John Cassavetes, a much different sort of director, once said, "Maybe there really wasn't an America, maybe it was only Frank Capra."[19]

Like Nixon, Capra was born poor, grew up in Southern California, and was a lifelong Republican. Unlike Nixon, he was an immigrant and, his immigrant strivings having taken him so dazzlingly far but no further, he finally let his rage boil through the homiletic pieties he had spent decades professing. The seething resentments, cheerful boasting, frequent self-abasement (and myriad duplicities) that *RN* hints at but almost never expresses outright find their uninhibited, fully expressed counterpart in Capra's own autobiography, *The Name Above the Title* (1971). In that book's pages, Capra again and again sounds the way Nixon might have sounded if Nixon had ever allowed himself to sound like Nixon. *The Name Above the Title* is, in fact, a work remarkable for its blend of emotional nakedness, artful self-aggrandizement, and treacly sentiment. From the fury of its opening ("I hated being poor. . . . I wanted out") to the reflexive uplift of its close ("So hang in there! If doors opened for me, they can open for anyone"), the ego on display may be Capra's but the id might just as well be Nixon's. One man wanted an Oscar as desperately—as transparently—as the other wanted the White House. If only Nixon had ever managed to come right out and declare, as Capra does, "I had reached a lifetime goal: Making something out of nothing; a nobody became Mr. Somebody—and I made the world like it," it might have done his spirit almost as much good as beating Jack Kennedy would have. Instead, he preferred to proclaim his mother's saintliness—something Capra did, too: "Mama gave out light and warmth, but consumed herself in the process. . . . Her seed, and the seed of millions like her, created the American dream."[20]

Attribute it, then, to filial piety, but after coming to America, from Sicily, at age five, Capra spent much of the rest of his life making the American dream his own—or, more accurately, making *his* dream America's own. After starting out as a gag writer on silent comedies for Hal Roach and Mack Sennett, he went on to win three Academy Awards for Best Director between 1935 and 1939, becoming Hollywood's most acclaimed filmmaker of the 1930s. A case can be made that during the eleven years between the release of *It Happened One Night* (1934), for four decades the only film ever to win all five major Academy Awards, and the end of the Second World War, he was the most effectual filmmaker in the world. For in addition to being the Hollywood establishment's most honored director during the Depression, he served as America's chief film propagandist during the war, directing the highly influential Why We Fight series. Those films, he boasted in *The Name Above the Title*, "not only stated but, in many instances, actually created . . . policy. . . . Yes, I will say it. I was the first 'Voice of America.'"[21]

The War Department knew perfectly well what it was doing in handing him such a responsibility, for Capra had long since demonstrated his talent for blending entertainment and indoctrination. The army was recognizing Capra's status as "Voice of America," not bestowing it. Such films as *Mr. Deeds Goes to Town, You Can't Take It with You* (1938), *Mr. Smith*, and *Meet John Doe* had perfected a formula informed by an unabashed, perfervid patriotism. That formula, with its mix of vague populism, calculated mawkishness, and yammery idealism, was grounded in a sort of Norman Rockwell radicalism that called attention to its supposed controversialism even as it proclaimed the blandest of civic bromides. "I protest against the state of civilization," the title character declares in *Meet John Doe*, the most overtly ideological of these films (as well as the most politically confused and febrile). "The little people have always counted," he adds. "Because, in the long run, the character of a country is the sum total of its little people." Herman Mankiewicz bestowed upon his initial treatment of the script that would become *Citizen Kane* a one-word title: "American." In its inoffensiveness, as in its opacity and allure, it might have served even more aptly as a catch-all title for Capra's political films.

Yet for all their limitations, these movies reached something deep in America's conception of itself, mirroring that conception even as they simultaneously shaped and distorted it. Capra's abilities went into sharp decline after *It's a Wonderful Life* (1946), his postwar "comeback" film, which was a relative failure at the time but went on to become his best-known and best-loved work. After a brief efflorescence in the early '70s, his reputation resumed its steady fall. When he died, in 1991, Capra seemed to belong to a barely remembered, prelapsarian world. But that is precisely the point. The very alienness of these films—their seeming to emerge from a distant past, with their heart-on-sleeve idealism and endless capacity for belief—underlines the way in which they have become part of our collective national unconscious. Capra long ago entered the American bloodstream, *Mr. Smith* above all. "When it's my turn to speak," an idealistic young Senate candidate says before a televised debate in Sidney Lumet's *Power*, "maybe we should just turn down the lights and run *Mr. Smith Goes to Washington*." "Put on your Jimmy Stewart clothes," John Dean's lawyer told him when the decision had been made that he'd testify before the Ervin Committee. "You're going to the Senate!"[22] Even people who have never seen any of Capra's films are aware of them—and think, usually incorrectly, that they "know" them. Those films may be as barely comprehensible as the words in a rote recitation of the Pledge of Allegiance. But like the pledge, they are something we all share and that help define us as Americans.

Capra's films are full of moments—many appalling, some magnificent—that recall (or, more accurately, foreshadow) the scenes on display during the morning of May 9. A string of lump-in-your-throat, patriotic epiphanies—the visit to the memorial, the meeting with the students, the sky's roseate glow, the play-acting in the House chamber, the Bible-bearing cleaning woman . . . and if only Nixon *had* walked back to the White House after breakfast—it all out-Capra'd Capra, except that these scenes actually happened, and to no less a personage than the president himself.

That such relentlessly Capraesque scenes should have taken place in real life is little more astonishing than that the president they should have befallen was . . . *Nixon*? No, no, as Jack Warner might have said, "Jimmy Stewart for Mr. Smith, *Ronnie Reagan* for Mr. Smith as president!" For Ronald Reagan was the true political child of Frank Capra, the purest hybrid of Hollywood and Washington, of make-believe and pledging allegiance, the clearest proof imaginable of Capra's curious inescapability in American culture.

It was a line lifted from Capra's *State of the Union* ("I paid for that microphone, Mr. Breen!") that helped Reagan win the 1980 New Hampshire primary. It was *Mr. Deeds Goes to Town* that Reagan cited a year later in a speech to the National Alliance of Business defending his economic policies. The affinity went far beyond quotation, however. Like Reagan's politics, Capra's films enthusiastically (*and* sincerely) blend sentimentality, idealism, and manipulativeness. Both men shared, and derived so much of their popularity from, an unwavering commitment to a belief in the principle of my country right or unreal—or, as one might say, unreal *as* right—a relentless idealizing of America that is all the more potent for being narrowly grounded in fact. With both men, what's there is basically true—it's just that so much more gets left out! "It isn't that he tells us more than other people do of what we wish were true about America: it's that he tells us, finally, that the truth doesn't matter compared to the wishing." James Harvey makes that observation of Capra in his magisterial study *Romantic Comedy in Hollywood,* but it applies equally well to Reagan.[23] The very unreality of each man's vision of America laid the foundation for his success. A fairy tale as screwball comedy, a fairy tale as history in the making: either way, it's a pretty irresistible package.

"The Man in the Street" was how Capra initially described the figure he championed in his movies,[24] a figure that evolved in his major films into a type as indelible—and as calculated—as Chaplin's Little Tramp. "The essential American soul is hard, isolate, stoic, and a killer," D. H. Lawrence famously argued of James Fenimore Cooper in *Studies in Classic American Literature.* "It has never yet melted." Not in Capra's films it hasn't—for in every respect, the Capra hero is the antithesis of Lawrence's description. Easygoing, convivial, sentimental, gentle, he is just as much of an American archetype as Cooper's. But unlike Natty Bumppo, Jeff Smith and the rest don't *appear* to be anachronistic or fantasy figures. They are as average and accessible—as imitable?—as the fellow next door; and there is an inexorable, if patronizing, logic to the hero of *Meet John Doe* bearing the name he does.

The noble common man as exemplified by Longfellow Deeds, Grandpa Vanderhof (in *You Can't Take It with You*), Jefferson Smith, John Doe, and George Bailey (in *It's a Wonderful Life*) represents everything that is good about America: honesty, simplicity, decency, idealism—and winning. Indeed, for all that he celebrates the common man and his uncommon goodness, Capra loves him only to the extent he comes out on top. George Bailey, the protagonist of Capra's own favorite among his films, would be that much richer and more rewarding a character if in fact he wasn't redeemed at its end—as would John Doe if he had carried out his suicide attempt; as would Mr. Deeds if the judge had found him insane; as would Grandpa Vanderhof if he'd had to tangle with a malefactor of great wealth who, unlike Edward Arnold, did *not* have a weakness for harmonica duets; as would, not least of all, the hero of *Mr. Smith Goes to Washington* if his filibuster had failed, as by every reasonable measure it should have.

Of course, then none of them would have been a Capra hero. Capra considers losing to be neither romantic nor redemptive. It is, in fact, in his social calculus quite suspect, subversive even. It raises too many doubts, recalls too many unpleasant realities. Losing calls into question the very validity of the American dream. What's the value of there *being* an American dream if all good Americans aren't also winners. In these movies, the successful pursuit of happiness is what winning—which is to say, being American—is all about.

Capra demonstrates how shrewd he can be by defining success not just in terms of wealth or station, but also love and esteem. (It doesn't have to be lonely at the top so long as you bring your friends along.) The man who gets the girl and has the admiration of his peers is more successful than the plutocrat—wouldn't *you* rather be Jimmy Stewart than Edward Arnold?—and sometimes, if you're lucky enough (and this is one of the things that can make Capra so pernicious), you can get the girl, have the respect of others, *and* be filthy rich, like Deeds, or Grant Matthews in *State of the Union*, the film marking the transition between Capra's major period and his swift decline. Even more than ideology, it is the sense Ronald Reagan communicated of effortless, nearly uninterrupted success, of being an always smiling public man, that makes him seem like the crowning figure in the line that runs from Deeds to Matthews. The irony is that Reagan never played a Capra hero. To be sure, he wasn't under contract to Columbia, the studio for whom Capra made most of his major films. But then neither were the classic Capra leading men, James Stewart (who played Bailey as well as Smith) and Gary Cooper (who played Deeds and Doe). The real problem for Reagan was that he wasn't a luminous enough presence on the screen to qualify as a Capra hero. He had to become president for that to happen. Cinematically, he wasn't enough of a winner.

In image as in entelechy, Richard Nixon was no Reagan—let alone a Stewart or Cooper. He would, in fact, seem the very antithesis of a Capra hero: clammy and grasping; complex and opaque; a loner and schemer, forever making deals, with a roving eye for the main chance (no bashful dreamer he). Yet seen in a different light, Nixon was a Capra hero par excellence. He *was* shy, after all, albeit the shyness that helped make Jimmy Stewart so appealing made Nixon seem uneasy and aloof. He was also upright, hardworking, an unembarrassed patriot; a poor boy whose dazzling rise showed how America rewarded talent and effort. The tens of thousands of letters and telegrams pouring in after the Checkers speech were like something out of Capra—the people showing their support for one of their own, thus overwhelming the big wheels and money men who wanted to call the shots—and the similarity was noted at the time. Indeed, the climactic scene of *State of the Union* actually prefigures the Checkers speech, with Grant Matthews (Spencer Tracy) throwing open his private life in a televised campaign speech—with this crucial difference: using his family rescues the candidate from himself by ending his political career rather than saving it.

The Checkers parallel illustrates the problem, though: Nixon always went too far. Where Matthews's revelations are made to look ennobling, Nixon's seemed demeaning. So solemn, yet so ridiculous, in nearly everything he did: incongruity clung to Nixon, a perpetual "Kick Me" affixed to the seat of his pants. (It was an incongruity Capra indirectly exploited. In 1961 the producers of his last film ran an ad in the *Los Angeles Times* with the following copy: "When Richard Nixon Laughs, Everybody in Los Angeles Laughs! Lucky Him! He's just seen Frank Capra's newest picture—and the screen's biggest laugh-getter—*Pocketful of Miracles!*")[25]

That incongruity underlies what made Nixon most foreign to the Capra archetype: he was a loser—or rather, for all that his electoral record indicated otherwise (seven victories out of nine campaigns, four out of five successful national campaigns, the latter tally matched only by

Franklin Roosevelt), he had the *air* of a loser. Even worse, he made *America* seem like a loser. Nixon's criminality called into question our national goodness. The one consolation Watergate offered, its showing that in the end the system worked, was meaningless in Capra terms. For as we shall see when we look more closely at *Mr. Smith*, system and process are anathema to his films. They hunger for a government of men, not laws, and place all their faith in "the people," not the system. Yet who was it who had brought this man to power? The people, of course, and, in his most recent election, with one of the greatest landslides in U.S. history.

Bad enough that Nixon looked so bad—he made everyone else look bad, too. Watergate forced us to confront our limitations as a people— to suggest, even if only implicitly, that Americans were losers, too. Capra's villains, unlike his heroes, are never of the people (let alone by the people or for the people); they are clearly demarcated from the people, being richer, meaner, baser. They pose no threat to the audience's self-regard. Yet Nixon was of the people. Like Conrad's Lord Jim, he was, as Tom Wicker notes, "one of us." Other presidents have broken laws, behaved badly, yet none had it blow up in his face the way Nixon did. JFK managed to maintain the illusion: *he* got away with it. A true Capra hero doesn't ever cut corners. Well, Grandpa Vanderhof does cheat on his income tax, but "cheating" is not how it's described in *You Can't Take It with You*. Even if it were, though, in the end it's only the camera, the all-omniscient camera, that knows for sure whether someone isn't cutting corners or simply managing to conceal the fact (in cinematic terms, what we don't see, what we are not told, for all intents and purposes never happened). Nixon's ultimate odiousness, seen in a Capraesque context, lay not in his own crimes but rather in revealing the crimes of the system. Nixon robbed the presidency of its fig leaf; he denied believers (assuming they wanted to retain some connection to reality) their ability to believe. To be sure, if Nixon hadn't committed his crimes, or if he'd gotten away with them, then that would be a different story—but for the first condition to apply, Nixon would have had to be someone other than Nixon; for the second, he'd have had to be Michael Corleone.

After Watergate, Jefferson Smith—with his unbounded faith that the shining marble exteriors of Washington contained shining marble interiors—ceases to look like a hero. Instead, he stands revealed as a dangerously deluded simpleton. Twenty years after Watergate, Hollywood did a remake of *Mr. Smith*. Played by Eddie Murphy, its hero found himself reduced from senator to representative and—more to the point— had as his prior occupation not Scout leader but con man. Yet beneath the veneer of cynicism, *The Distinguished Gentleman* retains the original's inspirationalism (even Capra never stooped, as the remake does, to using as a plot device a child in remission from cancer). Not surprisingly, it failed at the box office: too much of the basic premise remained intact, and too much had changed in the world for that premise still to ring true.

The most political of Hollywood filmmakers, Capra embraces the American attachment to success (to the ideology of success) and dogmatizes it. Capra takes what Greil Marcus has termed the studios' "opulent American mastery . . . the winner-take-all fantasies that have kept the world lined up outside the theaters that show American movies ever since the movies began"[26] and presents them as being morally strenuous and politically engaged. He makes success seem as much a part of American democracy as disagreement is—except, of course, in a Capra film only the malcontent, corrupt, or otherwise suspect ever disagree with the un-wavering unanimity of "the people." Depicting politics as something bland, consensual, and, ultimately, subservient to the status quo, Capra effectively defined its use in the Hollywood film.

Capra's movies offer myth at the expense of praxis, national self-congratulation masquerading as self-examination. It's worth recalling that Capra, who as the title of his autobiography reminds us was the first director to get top billing, had the clout to impose something other than happy endings on his films. He never exercised it—even in a movie like *Meet John Doe*, where, as he himself admits, the tacked-on happy ending effectively subverts everything that preceded it (worse, it doesn't even work dramatically, as simple stagecraft). Nothing so upholds the status quo as Hollywood's favorite narrative recourse: the happy ending. It also perfectly suits what has historically been Hollywood's ruling dogma—a dogma of left as well as right—the politics of sentiment. Capra, in effect, codifies that dogma. He calls attention to it, "politicizes" it, and so makes it seem more impressive than it actually is, like a set of considered ideas instead of just a general inclination to please. Yet as Graham Greene, a Capra enthusiast, pointed out as early as 1938, "It is useless trying to analyse the idea behind the Capra films: there *is* no idea you'd notice, only a sense of dissatisfaction, an urge to escape. . . ."[27]

The contrast with the most political filmmaker in nineties Hollywood is instructive. Where Capra braids together success and sentiment, Oliver Stone sneers at success and replaces sentiment with sensationalism (both substitute for actual thought). What's dismaying is how little anything had changed. Ideas are alien to both men. If anything, placing one's faith in what a martyred JFK might have done had he lived or assigning the blame for America's decline on a Texas cabal is even more irrational than Capra's gee-whiz populism. Either way, melodrama does the work of argument, Stone's reflexive nay-saying all but mirroring Capra's equally reflexive yea-saying.

At least so indeterminate a conception as "the people" doesn't readily lend itself to refutation (or, for that matter, proof), whereas Stone has to jettison a rather considerable amount of historical ballast to keep his paranoid conspiracies afloat. The irony is that, in the end, Stone is as much a dreamer of patriotic dreams as Capra is—no, more so, for Capra doesn't have to disguise that fact behind pretensions to being anything else. "The people are right," Capra said in 1940, "people are good, never bad."[28] Fifty years later Donald Sutherland tells Kevin Costner in *JFK* (1991), "Remember, fundamentally, people are suckers for the truth. And the truth is on your side, bubba" (the condescension and multiple mendacities of those two sentences really do take one's breath away). "The people" are also a hopeless abstraction, and as such open to almost any reading, as likely to comprise millions of Edward Arnolds as millions of Jimmy Stewarts (no, likelier). Someone else could just as easily describe them as "the great silent majority of Americans," and someone else did. Whose truth were *they* "suckers" for?

Capra came to realize that being seen as a "political" director eventually hurt his reputation (as it had once elevated it), reducing him to the status of genre filmmaker—and a genre so limited as to include himself as sole practitioner. His contemporary Preston Sturges, who mocks Capra by name in *Sullivan's Travels* (1941), had none of Capra's prestige at the time they were both active in Hollywood; he was a director of mere comedies. Much of Capra's tragedy as a filmmaker was not just how hard he strove to put his early comic work behind him, but how well he succeeded. Yet Sturges's reputation has come to surpass Capra's—at least in part because his work isn't weighed down, as Capra's is, by any burden of topicality or political relevance. As Joel McCrea's director-hero learns in *Sullivan's Travels* after he sets out to emulate Capra and make a movie to be called *Brother, Where Art Thou?* (yes, the Coens know their Sturges), nothing is more profound or socially useful—or, by implication, artistically richer—than simply making people laugh.

"If you're a real artist, forget the politics," Capra told a Directors Guild seminar in 1981. "Forget all politics. Because if you politicize yourself, what you do is cut yourself in half."[29] Forty years earlier, though, he had felt quite differently, recognizing the powerful, if oblique, connection between entertaining moviegoers and controlling an electorate. "I never cease to thrill at an audience seeing a picture," Capra told an interviewer. "For two hours you've got 'em. Hitler can't keep 'em that long. You eventually reach even more people than Roosevelt does on the radio."[30] There is shrewdness in that statement, as well as delusions of grandeur. During the decade in which he flourished, Capra came as close to having it both ways—as civic conscience *and* artistic master—as has any filmmaker since Eisenstein. For the remaining half century of his life, Capra increasingly came to suffer for his simultaneous pursuit of both callings.

Yet Capra's very grandiosity of ambition helped secure his place as one of the three totemically *American* directors, men whose films continue to affect this country's conception of itself and our ongoing construction of a national mythology. The great silent directors are too far removed in time—*The Birth of a Nation* now seems artistically primitive to us, not to mention morally objectionable—and directors of a more recent vintage have had their influence dissipated in the visual inundation of television and a century's worth of celluloid. Capra, though, along with Howard Hawks and Nixon's beloved John Ford, created a body of work that has helped define America as well as American film. All three men had careers that began in the Silent Era and continued into the 1960s, and all three reached their artistic peak in the years between 1935 and 1950. During those crucial years leading to midcentury, a template was formed for our cultural standards and assumptions, a template formed when the movies were *the* visual medium, and these men were its American masters.*

Each man had his own emphasis: Capra, American in dream and aspiration; Hawks, in tempo and attitude; Ford, in space and locale. With all three at or near their peak then, the films they released in 1939 illustrate how they differ. Capra had *Mr. Smith.* Hawks had *Only Angels Have Wings*; and even with an Andean setting and Cary Grant as leading man, its tale of brave, bravura men flying the mail heedless of danger is as exhilaratingly American as a cross between the Pony Express and *Winner Take Nothing.* Ford released *Stagecoach* (which began his sacralization of Monument Valley), as well as *Young Mr. Lincoln* and *Drums Along the Mohawk.* As such films attest, Capra's Americanness is about believing, Hawks's about doing, and Ford's about remembering (Ford's Irishness is about nostalgizing). Hawks's treatment of what it means to be American always remains elliptical and unstated—the Hawksian code of profes-

*Orson Welles, a special case, was supranational. Illusion, not America, was his homeland.

sionalism would scorn anything so amateurish as an outright declaration of principles—and Ford oscillates between the explicit and implicit. Only Capra is unrelievedly insistent. Indeed, he grounds his political films in a very public worrying over what it means to be American. He tells us outright what Hawks (always) and Ford (usually) prefer just to show.

In his foreword to *The Name Above the Title*, Ford calls Capra "a great American . . . an inspiration to those who believe in the American Dream."[31] Himself a master mythologist, Ford was, if anything, an even more passionate celebrant of America than Capra was. Yet he restricted his mythologizing to the past—or Ireland. When he did address ideology, in *The Grapes of Wrath*, he made a film so politically unobjectionable—and artistically wan—as to earn him the 1940 Academy Award for Best Director. (Hawks had the good sense to avoid declaiming American creeds altogether—perhaps not the least of the reasons why his reputation has fared so much better than Ford's or Capra's.)

Surely the most notable tribute Capra ever received in this regard—as well as the most bizarre—came from the Nazis, who screened *Mr. Deeds* for German army officers to give them a sense of what the United States was really like![32] A more typical one came from Justice William O. Douglas (himself a highly conscious embracer of American myth), when he hailed Capra as "the Carl Sandburg of Hollywood who reminded all America of the faces of America we love and cherish."[33] The comparison to Sandburg is at once damning and apt—and not at all as complimentary as Douglas intended.

Douglas's view gets at the salient aspect of Capra's work—its adulation of all things American. But it also does that work a disservice, for when Capra abandons relentless uplift and forgets about fetishizing the Founding Fathers, his treatment of American politics can attain a frightening intensity. That intensity can spring from as small a detail as Edward Arnold's FDR-like pince-nez in the role of millionaire D. B. Norton, who in his sinister pursuit of the White House bankrolls the title character in *Meet John Doe*. Or there is the long shot of the D. B. Norton Motor Corps, a paramilitary motorcycle unit, conducting precision drill. In neither literature nor film will one find a more plausible (or tersely expressive) image of what an incipient American fascism might look like. The uniformed troopers on their roaring machines are at once precursors of Cocteau's angels of death in *Orphée* (1949) and throwbacks to the U.S. Calvary thundering to the rescue in countless Westerns. Visually, they are thrillingly kinetic—ideologically, terrifyingly blank.

Politically, *Meet John Doe* is a mess. Its opening announces a conscious engagement with the jabber and tumult of modern America, the credits rolling over a montage of factory workers, miners, farm laborers, soldiers, even a maternity ward. Yet over and against this ostensible commitment to confronting contemporary realities, there's blather of a high order, as when Spring Byington, playing the mother of Barbara Stanwyck, the newspaper columnist who ghostwrites the title character's speeches, explains to her daughter, "Darling, there are so many complaining political speakers. People are tired of hearing nothing but doom and despair on the radio. If you're going to have to say anything why don't you let him say something simple and real, something with hope in it." The sad thing is, not only does she really mean it, so does Capra.

Just as the story grounds good intentions in deceit (and vice versa), so does the film as a whole hopelessly confuse acuity and naïveté. After Stanwyck has been laid off, she writes as her last column a fictional account of an unemployed man so distressed by the state of society that he announces he will kill himself. The column makes such an impression that Stanwyck's editor rehires her, and they seek a man to assume the role of Doe. Their choice: a minor league pitcher reduced to hobodom by a bum arm. "He's perfect!" exclaims Stanwyck. "A baseball player—what could be more American?" No one, except a baseball player who's Gary Cooper. His John Doe is a bewildered, down-at-the-heels Longfellow Deeds, one who experiences growing dismay as he uses first the newspaper then radio to go from local craze to national sensation. Capra's media savvy is the best thing in the movie and an example of real prescience (the only thing that sells better than guilelessness is mass-marketed guilelessness). It's at this point, with his face on the cover of *Time*, that Doe decides to admit his fraud—and Norton (literally) pulls the plug on him. A chastened Doe disappears into the night, only to try to attempt suicide (as the original column said he would) by leaping from City Hall on Christmas Eve. Stanwyck, who has fallen in love with him, prevails upon Cooper not to jump. She's joined by several John Doe Club members who, after turning on him when Norton did, have decided he's not so bad after all. End of picture—except that Norton is still just as rich and malevolent, and no one can say that another movement, with a figurehead who's either more knavish or less intractable, might not gain him the White House after all.

In Capra's defense, he and his scenarist, Robert Riskin, were painfully aware of how muddled their film was—they shot no fewer than five different endings. But at a deeper level, *Meet John Doe* is utterly consistent in what it fundamentally assumes: the system is bad but the people are good. When the mayor of a small town asks to join the local John Doe Club, he's turned down. "I'm sorry, Mayor, but we voted that no politicians could join," he's told. "Just the John Does of the neighborhood, because you know how politicians are." Yes, in a Capra film everyone does—even the politicians themselves. Yet the resulting contradiction—if the people are so good, how come the system is so bad?—never gets addressed. The movie's last line is a ringing declaration—"There you are, Norton: the people, try to lick that!"—which is true enough, abstractions can't be licked, but neither can they be counted on. The people are fickle enough to believe utterly in John Doe, then reject him just as utterly within seconds. Capra fervently professes his faith in democracy—yet what he shows implies democracy's effective bankruptcy. As John Mitchell, Nixon's first attorney general, said upon taking over the Justice Department, "Watch what we do, instead of what we say."

It is Capra's masterpiece, *Mr. Smith Goes to Washington*, that provides the supreme example of this predilection for professing one thing even as he demonstrates his belief in the opposite. An idealistic young man—a Scout leader, no less—is appointed to fill out the term of a U.S. senator who has died in office. The impetus for the appointment doesn't come from a good government group but rather the statewide political machine. The boyish innocent is perfect for its purposes: the governor, a machine lackey, looks good for choosing someone apolitical; and the machine gets "an honorary stooge" who will let its graft-ridden appropriation for a dam sail through Congress unnoticed. And when Smith arrives in Washington, he has eyes on other things, going straight from Union Station to a tour bus to get a look at all the monuments and memorials. To give him something to do, Senator Joseph Paine (Claude Rains), his senior colleague (and secretly beholden to the machine), urges him to draw up a bill of his own. That bill is a proposal for a national boys' camp—coincidentally sited just where the dam is supposed to go. The senator tries to deter Smith, first using persuasion, then threats, and finally charging him with ownership of the land on which the camp is to be built. With the aid of a legislative assistant (Jean Arthur), Smith takes to the Senate floor to filibuster the approval of his ouster by the Committee on Elections and Privileges and in so doing simultaneously retrieve his honor and reveal the machine's chicanery.

Mr. Smith is easily the most "Sandburgian," as Justice Douglas might have put it, of Capra's films: the most emphatically—and self-consciously

—"American." The film's touchstone is Lincoln, whom Sandburg had celebrated in his six-volume biography more famously than anyone since Whitman. Capra went so far as to say that the film's "ringing statement of America's democratic ideals" has its "soul . . . anchored in Lincoln."[34] As it happened, 1939 saw Lincoln much in evidence on the screen. It was as if a nation still mired in economic depression and now fearing global war were seeking reassurance from the man who had guided the Union through its greatest historical crisis. Henry Fonda (who else?) played the Rail-splitter as an understated romantic in *Young Mr. Lincoln*; neither lengthened chin nor thickened nose could make even the most myopic viewer mistake those beautiful, dreamy eyes as belonging to anyone other than Fonda. Raymond Massey, in the performance of his career, presented a more authentic, if less affecting figure—rawboned, not a little awkward, the homeliness of the actor's flat Canadian inflections working to evoke the nineteenth-century frontier—in John Cromwell's *Abe Lincoln in Illinois*, based on Robert E. Sherwood's Pulitzer Prize–winning play.

Onscreen, Hollywood's favorite president has most often been represented symbolically, through his memorial. The building brooks few rivals as a sacred place in our secular landscape. Yet such events as Marian Anderson's 1939 concert after the Daughters of the American Revolution barred her from Constitution Hall (the site later that year of the world premiere of *Mr. Smith*) and Martin Luther King Jr.'s "I have a dream" speech in 1963 have helped ensure it remains alive in meaning and human implication—unlike, say, the Washington Monument or Jefferson Memorial. The movies have not hesitated to exploit the Lincoln Memorial's unique blend of marmoreal splendor and emotional expressiveness. Jimmy Stewart's three pilgrimages to the memorial in *Mr. Smith* (only two of which we see) are merely the most celebrated example. Others include Michael Rennie's suavely bien-pensant alien, Klaatu, paying an admiring visit in Robert Wise's *The Day the Earth Stood Still* (1951); Robert Walker's title character expiring on the memorial's steps in Leo McCarey's furiously anti-communist *My Son John* (1952); Tom Hanks silently addressing the antiwar rally in *Forrest Gump* (1994); and, most egregiously, its providing a meeting place in *JFK* for Costner's Jim Garrison and Sutherland's "X."

Nixon shared the movies' partiality to both Lincoln and the memorial. Remember that what triggered his early morning visit there was his remark that the memorial at night was Washington's most beautiful sight. On both sides of his family, the young Richard Nixon found himself steeped in Lincoln. One can hardly exaggerate the extent to which the sixteenth president—his memory, his image, his example—suffused mid-western Republicanism in the later decades of the nineteenth century and early decades of the twentieth. For a man like Frank Nixon, "a hard-line Ohio Republican," as his son later described him,[35] Lincoln was the supreme figure: father of the GOP, sacred martyr for the Union, the embodiment of wisdom, goodness, and humility. If anything, Nixon's maternal grandmother held him in even higher regard. "She virtually worshipped Lincoln," Nixon told his first biographer, Bela Kornitzer.[36] Nixon was Alma Milhous's favorite and he noted on numerous occasions how strongly she had influenced him. When he turned thirteen, she gave him a framed picture of Lincoln inscribed with lines from Longfellow's "Psalm of Life": "Lives of great men all remind us / We can make our lives sublime, / And departing, leave behind us / Footprints on the sands of time." Young Nixon hung the picture over his bed and slept beneath it until he left home to go to law school. "To this day," he wrote some forty years later, "it is one of my fondest possessions."[37]

It was inevitable that Nixon should inherit his elders' passion for the man. As a young person, he had learned by heart Lincoln's great speeches and read Nicolay and Hay's ten-volume biography (he even memorized passages from it). As an undergraduate, he studied Lincoln with Paul Smith, the Whittier professor who had the greatest influence on him. After moving to New York in the 1960s, he found the time to read Sandburg's biography in its entirety.

His fascination with Lincoln deepened and developed into outright identification after Nixon entered politics. He went out of his way to quote Lincoln in the Checkers speech—"God must have loved the common people since he made so many of them"—calling up Smith to check the citation. (As it turned out, Nixon got it wrong: "common-*looking*" was what Lincoln actually said.) Eight years later, accepting the Republican nomination for president in Chicago, he drew an explicit parallel between himself and the man who had received the same honor one hundred years before in the same city. After finally gaining the White House in 1968, Nixon would reforge that parallel again and again in private conversation. Looking at Lincoln, he saw another homely, embattled, bitterly traduced leader who had triumphed over humble beginnings—another uncommon common man—priding himself on doing the right rather than the popular thing as he tried to end a divisive war. Jonathan Aitken has noted that "Nixon's feelings for his great predecessor bordered on the mystical." His favorite room in the White House was the

Lincoln Sitting Room, and the Lincoln Bedroom had a special hold on him. "On special occasions," he told Aitken, he would enter the room "and have a moment of silent prayer because I sort of gathered strength just from being in this room where Lincoln had been."[38]

There is grim irony, then, in the fact that it was Nixon's Southern strategy that would undo the Republicans' moral ties to Lincoln, that would capture the Old Confederacy for the Grand Old Party and make the latter into an entity almost unrecognizable from the organization it had been for a century before. In doing so, Nixon was disavowing a part of his own history as well as his party's. During the '50s he had had cordial relations with Martin Luther King Jr. (Nixon "would call me frequently about things, getting, seeking my advice," King told an interviewer in 1964)[39] and served as the closest thing the Eisenhower administration had to an ambassador to the civil rights community. In 1960 he had seen to the inclusion of a pro–civil rights plank in the Republican platform. But he was too much of a political realist not to recognize the opportunities presented by the Democrats' association with the civil rights movement. Nixon was no racist, but he was—ever and always, and never more so than in his handling of the South—a political realist.

Of course, the same can be said of Lincoln, though one would never know it from *Mr. Smith*, whose Lincoln epitomizes the idealist. It was "with his ideals" that Lincoln "saved the Union," Capra says. "Our Jefferson Smith would be a young Abe Lincoln, tailored to the rail-splitter's simplicity, compassion, ideals, humor, and unswerving moral courage under pressure."[40] Nowhere does Capra mention Lincoln's ruthlessness, his ambition, his pragmatism—all crucial elements in his success and, far more important, in his bringing to a successful conclusion the Civil War. It is not that Lincoln lacked any of the qualities Capra attributes to him. It's just that he grievously limits the man—and diminishes his achievement—by leaving out these others.

Needless to say, Nixon took a far more nuanced view of his hero. When Chou En-lai observed to him that Lincoln had "finally prevailed because he had the people on his side," Nixon recorded the remark in his diary and added a revealing gloss. "While it is true that Lincoln is one of the few great figures in history, he was a total pragmatist."[41] Clearly, Nixon scorns any Capraesque view of Lincoln as pure idealist. Yet at the same time, he suggests a curious paradox. He implies that to be a world-historical figure one generally *needs* to be an idealist (otherwise why bother with the qualifier "While it is true"). Nonetheless, when he speaks of that other "total pragmatist," Lincoln, the self-identification is patent.

Nixon felt an affinity with the total pragmatists—and a comparable distaste for the total idealists. His political career had begun with the defeat of a Mr. Smith, Jerry Voorhis. Nixon, in fact, told Stewart Alsop that Voorhis was the model for Jefferson Smith. Nixon was wrong about that, as Capra told the Nixon biographer Fawn Brodie, but it certainly had a nice ring to it. It also was plausible, for Voorhis was as pure an idealist as American two-party politics has known. Paul Douglas, who got along well enough with the Cook County machine to win election three times as a Democratic senator from Illinois, could recall seeing "the eyes of hardened politicians moisten at the mention of [Voorhis's] name, and I believe he is truly one of the saints of the earth."[42] Nixon's own description of him is not dissimilar from Douglas's—and also thoroughly dismissive. "Voorhis was a Don Quixote, an idealist . . . who never accomplished anything much" ("Don Quixote Smith," his legislative assistant calls Jefferson Smith in the movie).[43] This is the bottom-line Nixonian judgment against idealists, all the dreamers and utopians and show horses, who get glowing press notices even as they never accomplish anything much. For the real problem with Quixotes isn't that the dragons they tilt at are actually windmills—it's that they fail to bring down the windmills.

Even so, Nixon the idealist was as much a part of his political character as Nixon the opportunist—his Hannah side constantly doing battle with his Frank side (it was Frank who finally, disastrously, won out)—and this uneasy, self-opposed coexistence contributes much to the man's endless fascination. Whenever his pietistic side peeked out, as it frequently did, his partisans clung to it as representing his truest self—even as his detractors fastened upon it as demonstrating his basic hypocrisy. Both were wrong, for both were attempting to deny him his essential complexity as thoroughly as Capra denied Lincoln's. Nixon was sincere in what he believed, secure in what he believed; it's just that he believed in so many things (and, far worse, *presented* those beliefs so insecurely).

Nixon owed his political career to his being seen as something of a Quixote in 1946, tilting at a well-known incumbent. Selecting an idealist was the pragmatic thing to do for the Republican leadership in California's Twelfth Congressional District. Nixon, who "except for a couple of speeches for Wendell Willkie before small audiences in 1940 . . . had no experience whatsoever in partisan politics,"[44] was formally pure as Voorhis was not: the citizen up against the politician, the amateur vs. the professional. "When I first ran in 1946 I was a bit naive about public service," he recalled twelve years later, "a kind of dragon slayer, I suppose." "A *Mr. Smith Goes to Washington* sort of thing?" his interviewer asked.[45]

Nixon readily agreed, for he partly saw himself as a Mr. Smith, the citizen-leader, the upright loner, beholden to no machine or interests, the honest outsider: a civics lesson made flesh. Part of him despised the Mr. Smiths: the idealists who accomplished nothing even as their posturing and gullibility got all the editorial writers' approval. Still, he couldn't be too hard on the Mr. Smiths: they'd done too well by him for that. Just as he owed his start to his having been a Mr. Smith, so did he owe much of his later success to nearly all of his opponents belonging to that breed. Kennedy and Pat Brown (no Jeff Smiths they) were the only political foes who beat him. It was the prairie Quixotes—Voorhis (born in Wisconsin), Hubert Humphrey, George McGovern—he'd feasted on. McGovern could even be said to have closed the circle: Nixon supposed that Voorhis had provided a model for Smith—and it was Smith who had provided a model for McGovern. "The Capra film *Mr. Smith Goes to Washington* definitely helped to awaken my early interest in our national government," he acknowledged in 1974.[46]

In that case, the joke was on McGovern. For instead of being the hymn to representative government that he presumes—and that Capra proclaims it to be—*Mr. Smith* reveals itself on closer examination to be a Dies Irae of democracy, and the film's bland, blind celebration of boyish innocence and airless principle stands as an absolute indictment (however unintentional) of "the people." For the political process that the film so deeply abhors is in point of fact how the people make their will manifest. Certainly, it's not through the Boy Scout anarchy of purity and abstraction that Smith embodies and the film upholds as exemplary. That model is as frightening in implication as it is unworkable in practice—as unrealistic a formula (and, to be sure, as superficially appealing) as boy meets girl/boy loses girl/boy gets girl. Capra refuses to acknowledge that sincerity is a means, not an end: Strom Thurmond attacking civil rights in his record-setting filibuster of 1957, was every bit as sincere as Smith—and, who can say, every bit as impressive. No, Jeff Smith is an infant Willie Stark, and his vision of how Washington should work is as democratic as a newborn's reflexive wail. It's just that Jimmy Stewart is so much more likable than Broderick Crawford. How could he not win our vote?

The irony, of course, is that he doesn't win *anyone's* vote. Jeff Smith is the least democratic senator possible, for no one elected him. It's not the people who put him into office; it's the system (worse, it's the system in an explicitly corrupt incarnation). When Smith does directly confront the workings of the system, at his hearing before the Senate committee weighing his culpability, he can't face it—he rushes from the room (the truth shall make you flee?). What finally rescues him has nothing to do with the people—or the system of government that represents them. It's a complete deus ex machina, a pistol shot just outside the Senate chamber, as a remorseful Paine attempts suicide. Regardless of how reverent, it's a peculiar vision of democracy that requires unelected legislators and the discharge of firearms for its functioning.

The neatness of artifice that gives Capra his ending—don't *all* villains suffer from stricken consciences just before the closing credits?—infects his view of how politics operates. Orderliness constitutes the highest good for Capra; that's why Smith likes those monuments so much: they're literally set in stone. It's not corruption he most truly detests: it's the complexity (the messiness) of process. For Capra, there is only monumental past and glowing future; the present is simply a sordid political miasma. Nor is this detestation born of ignorance. Jean Arthur has as her best scene a soup-to-nuts explanation of how legislation goes from initial proposal to final passage. No, the mechanics are understood perfectly well—and made to look all the more distasteful by being so clearly presented. Hollywood's historic attraction to heightened states of experience—its disregard for the mundane and day-to-day—takes political form in *Mr. Smith*. The film abhors (worse, it simply fails to acknowledge) the vast, soupy middle where things actually get done, where nearly all of life is conducted. In *Mr. Smith*'s moral taxonomy, there are cynics (bad guys); there are idealists (good guys); and there are cynics who are really idealists (Arthur and, in the end, Rains). Everyone in between gets banished—this despite the fact that it is, of course, in the in-between where democracy is most deeply rooted, where it best flourishes, where it is most (yes) democratic.

It's a little-boy vision of politics—and as the film constantly reminds us, that's what Jeff Smith is, a boy. Surely, no other work better demonstrates the truth realized by John Updike's Colonel Ellellou in *The Coup* "that, in America, a man is a failed boy." Stewart may have been thirty-one when the film was made, and Smith has to be at least thirty (the constitutional minimum for service in the Senate), yet one would never know it from the way he behaves. He still lives with his mother, and any male old enough to shave he calls "sir." In fact, the movie makes a fetish of boyishness. It's the Boy Rangers that Smith led before his appointment. It's with the governor's young sons that the idea of Smith's appointment originates. "Oh, he's a boy?" their father gibes when Smith's name is mentioned. It's his sponsorship of a national boys' camp that gets Smith in trouble. His most fervent admirers in Washington are the Senate pages—

who in the film are several years younger than actual pages are. Even the newspapermen, who play the role of the people's aundiced tribunes, are called "press boys."

In his filibuster, Smith best expresses the movie's callow moral calculus: "It's a funny thing about men, you know. They all start life as boys. I wouldn't be a bit surprised if some of these senators weren't boys once." Wordsworth couldn't have put it better, except that no children (ipso facto good) could be fathers to such men (ipso facto bad)—for goodness doesn't degrade in Capra's universe, it's inert and stays ever aloft, like one of the noble gases.

Fortunately for Capra, to play this preposterous man-child he has Jimmy Stewart. As only the greatest stars can do, Stewart squares the circle, making sense of nonsense and creating his own reality as Jefferson Smith. Far more than just the title character, he's the movie. He had appeared as the male romantic lead in Capra's previous film, *You Can't Take It with You*, with Arthur. This time around she gets top billing (was it based on the alphabet—or her being a Columbia contract player and Stewart's being on loan from MGM?), yet it is Stewart who holds the movie together, who makes it into something truly enduring. He takes an egregiously implausible character and manages to make him, through sheer force of sincerity, one of the landmark figures of American film, part of our common culture. Anyone other than Jimmy Stewart as Jeff Smith and the whole movie would come apart like a collection of campaign promises. Stewart's performance defined his screen persona; it was *Mr. Smith* that made Jimmy Stewart *Jimmy Stewart*. That persona is crucial to the film's success. Stewart's aw-shucks ineffability and convincingly artless artistry mask not just the unreality but also the dangerousness of what the movie propounds.

It takes a performance of Stewart's magnitude to keep Claude Rains from walking away with the picture. Where Stewart is the personification of boyish idealism, he is the embodiment of suavely knowing pragmatism. Rains's silver-haired gravity presents the very picture of the statesman-legislator—even as his deference to the political machine and willingness to destroy Smith demonstrate a lethal understanding of how much give the give-and-take of politics can demand. This is a man who knows all too well where the middle ground lies, and how many bodies are buried beneath it. The plot decisively hinges on his suffering for that knowledge; and Paine's surname is not just that of a great Revolutionary patriot but also a letter away from being a synonym for "hurt." Precisely because he manages to mingle so thoroughly the high-minded and base, he is the most compelling figure in the movie—a villain as rich in conception as Smith, the film's hero, is impoverished.

Not surprisingly, official Washington sided with Paine rather than Smith. Members of Congress didn't see *Mr. Smith* as a paean to the American way. Instead, they considered it a smear on their country and themselves (if not necessarily in that order). Capra even says in *The Name Above the Title* that Joseph P. Kennedy, at the time U.S. ambassador to Great Britain, cabled Harry Cohn, the head of Columbia, to urge the suppression of *Mr. Smith*, claiming that the movie's foreign distribution would damage democracy in Europe and aid the Axis cause. Capra gave Cohn an indignant, and wordy, dressing-down for going so far as to entertain such a proposal. "Oh, great! Speeches he gives me," Cohn muttered when Capra finally finished—thus inspiring another lengthier oration.[47]

Nothing came of Kennedy's suggestion (Joseph McBride wonders if Capra, who voted against the ambassador's son in the 1960 presidential election, didn't invent the incident), but the exchange it occasioned is sadly telling. It epitomizes the weird duality that came to inform Capra's work: an increasingly uneven battle between the bracingly hectic and the predictably hortatory. He had come to believe his own press, and to dire effect: what should have been Capra's line—demotic, punchy, nuts-to-you—instead went to Cohn.

Before he began reaching for higher meaning, before he became imprisoned by his ardor for prestige, Capra had made films that were fresh and flip and fast on their feet. He had started out, after all, as nothing more exalted than a gagman on Our Gang shorts. Flashes of this earlier stripped-down Capra can still be seen in *Mr. Smith*. But it's his early sound pictures that show Capra at his hardest driving and most flavorfully idiomatic. Such films as *Ladies of Leisure* (1930) and *Platinum Blonde* (1931) move with a headlong velocity that captures the pulsing newness, the sense of both discovery and dislocation, to be found in America in the years following the Crash. The movies were still new, and so were many of the subjects Capra was filming: *Submarine* (1928), *Flight* (1929), *Dirigible* (1931), *The Miracle Woman* (a thinly veiled treatment of Aimee Semple McPherson; 1931), *The Bitter Tea of General Yen* (the Chinese civil war; 1933), *Lady for a Day* (the Depression and gangsters; 1933). Even the classic romance of *It Happened One Night* (1934) offers a glimpse of the very height of up-to-the-minute mobility, an autogiro.

Perhaps the most characteristic title of all Capra's films belongs to this period: *American Madness* (1932). Certainly, it is the most resonant. Like

Mr. Smith or *Meet John Doe*, *American Madness* offers a sense of vibrant topicality—which, like them also, it proceeds to undercut with an implausibly plot-saving recourse to sentimentality. A robbery leads to a bank run; only the intervention of Walter Huston's gum-chewing bank president saves the day. He's a prototype of the classic Capra hero (his criterion for lending is character rather than collateral), but that didn't keep the movie from failing at the box office. It simply hit too close to home for audiences in 1932: the wishfulness of its happy ending could not compensate for the familiarity of its painful subject.

The true star of the film isn't Huston, but the bank's vault—a massive nickel-and-chrome wonder, lovingly photographed and worshipfully attended. In its modern, finely machined way, it's as much of a monument to the American system as the Lincoln Memorial is, as much a repository of hopes and fears and dreams. Its door opens and closes with the force of destiny, and every time it's on camera, Capra accords it the center-stage showstopper attention it cries out for. The vault is both part of the (literal) foundation of the bank, buried deep within the ground, and the abyss over which the institution trembles. Its solidity contrasts with the insubstantiality of the phone calls that spread the rumors setting off the run. Capra's rapid cross-cutting and pioneering use of overlapping dialogue are scarily effective—the panicked account holders' fury in the lobby looks ahead to the rainy mob in *Meet John Doe*—and "American madness" is an all too apt description for what we see on the screen. Here is a depiction of what public opinion can do far more potent—as well as far more realistic—than any to be found in Capra's later, better-known work. The film's emphasis is on Huston's populist lending policies and how they prevent the bank's failing, but what is unforgettable about *American Madness* is the all-too-believable tableau it presents of a society out of control. Cut away all the patriotic rhetoric and picnic-in-July sentiment and this is what is most truly—and lastingly—American about Capra's work: its evocation of American madness.

"He had a way of combining beauty, warmth, imminent disaster, and heart," noted Sam Peckinpah of Capra's essential formula.[48] "Imminent disaster" is exactly right: for what's ultimately most striking about Capra's films is their sense of being constantly on the brink, their imagination of catastrophe. Sentiment, patriotism, and rhetoric about the little man are what we commonly associate with Capra. But what is unique to his films, what remains most startling about them so many decades after they were made, is the sense they convey of looming destruction.

The films' underlying hysteria is the dark concomitant of their strenuous inspirationalism. Capra, a master of what François Truffaut called "the art of involving his characters in profoundly desperate situations,"[49] can communicate a kind of urgency unlike that of any other director: a hurtling of emotion, frantic and arresting, that redeems his work again and again. If his sentiments are hopelessly romantic and Victorian, his tempo is all modern and twentieth century. This weird disparity between belief and expression accounts for Capra's singular blend of power and woolliness. Behind all the patriotic pageantry and oppressive sentimentality lie a stunning ominousness and indeterminate fury. There are demons at work in Capra, demons whose presence his willed sunniness cannot altogether obscure. A death sets in motion *Deeds, Smith, The Miracle Woman*, and *State of the Union*. Suicides or attempted suicides occur in *Ladies of Leisure, The Miracle Woman, The Bitter Tea of General Yen, Smith, Doe, It's a Wonderful Life*, and *State of the Union*. Somehow Capra manages to sneak a suicide (albeit committed offscreen) into the muscular winsomeness of *You Can't Take It with You*, although nothing of the sort occurs in Kaufman and Hart's Pulitzer Prize–winning play. The sweet-tempered "pixillation" of *Deeds* harbors within it the despairing rage of the dispossessed farmer who tries to kill the title character. The crowd scenes at the beginning of *Lost Horizon* (1937), the Shanghai street scenes in *General Yen*, the tabernacle conflagration in *The Miracle Woman*: all bespeak a vision born of emotional extremis and spiritual duress.

It's a vision that Richard Nixon, of all people, could fully appreciate. It was something he and Capra shared: one man sought a life, the other an art, that could be all predicate. Just as Capra's films are at their most memorable when disaster threatens, so did Nixon see life as being most transcendent in the midst of crisis. This conviction had a number of sources—Nixon's concerns about demonstrating his manliness, a desire for self-aggrandizement, the simple recognition that his saturnine temper required large doses of external stimulation—yet, in the end, where such compulsive personal brinksmanship came from mattered less than where it took him. His quest for power wasn't born solely of ambition, but also of survival. The one time after the Second World War he was outside of politics and away from the pressure of public life, the period from 1963 to 1967, he writes, "I never found it fulfilling. . . . [I]f all I had was my legal work, I would be mentally dead in two years and physically dead in four."[50] He thrived on crisis; he needed crisis, seeking it out and constantly declaring his special affinity for it. It was almost a mania of Nixon's, extending to what a sympathetic associate once called his "lapel-grabbing insistence to all who will listen that he is cool in a crisis."[51] What "vim and vigor" had been in Kennedy's lexicon—a kind of potted autobiography and handy PR tool—"crisis" was in Nixon's. *Six Crises* he called his first book, telling its readers that "those who have known great crisis—its challenge and tension, its victory and defeat—can never become adjusted to a more leisurely and orderly pace. They have drunk too deeply of the stuff which really makes life exciting and worth living to be satisfied with the froth."[52] "Frothy" Richard Nixon was not.

Exhaustion constantly threatens such leaders, such artists, as both Nixon and Capra came to learn. Even an aficionado of crisis like Nixon could not survive the many unremitting months of Watergate. And the American madness that fueled what is best in Capra's films eventually overwhelmed him, too. Capra, in a way, had it worse than Nixon did, for the director had to contend with not just the darker but also the better angels of our nature. It was as if Capra found himself overwhelmed on both sides: the gravid sentiment of "Capracorn" smothering his art even as that art's sense of imminent disaster finally consumed itself. One need only look to Capra's own favorite among his films to see this happening. Equal parts fairy tale and nightmare, *It's a Wonderful Life* is the hopelessly polarized product of this dual inundation, at once the most sentimental *and* the darkest of all Capra's films. What's so amazing about the movie—what separates it from everything else Capra did—is its knife's-edge balance between uplift and loathing, its vision of the community as extended family *and* instrument of suffocation. The parallel world of Potterville is so much more plausible than the "real" one of Bedford Falls (does the town's name end in noun—or verb?). Surely, Capra failed to recognize this—otherwise why risk betraying everything we associate with the word "Capraesque." Or was the shock of recognition there, and so great as to undo him? How else account for the failure of nerve, and abrupt artistic decline, evident in the dwindling number of films he made afterward. Tellingly, there were only five over the course of the next fourteen years—this from a man who had made fifteen films during the 1930s alone.

The shame of it all is that Capra *should* have had one last chance, for what might have been the great opportunity for him to redeem his art and retrieve his reputation came nine years after the release of *Pocketful of Miracles*. It is here that we can discern the richest connection between the maker of *Mr. Smith* and the events that followed in the wake of the Cambodian invasion. Yes, Capra put on the screen a model for Nixon's visit to the memorial, the culminating event of those days of national nervous breakdown. More than that, though, it was Capra who might have best captured the upheaval that the nation experienced during the first week of May in 1970, might have made an updated *American Madness*—one far different in plot, scale, and milieu, but every inch the original in thrust and mood. Why bother with the threat of a bank failure when one could put up on the screen the threat of a government failure, a nation failure? The only problem would have been the lack of a simple plot resolution. Jefferson Smith's visit with Lincoln was an escape that helped provide a remedy. Nixon's was just an escape. Evoking American madness was unthinkable for Capra without then resorting to American sentiment. Dead students on an Ohio campus—let alone the real ending, helicopters atop the Saigon embassy—was not a Capra finish.

No, the idea of his doing such a film is unthinkable—almost as unthinkable as any studio backing it. The aggressive innocence of Capra's earlier work had for twenty years seemed to belong to another world: the crisp blacks and whites of the Depression years (made visible on the screen through the splendid artistry of Joseph Walker, Capra's favorite cameraman) having long since given way to the muddy grays of the '50s and oversaturated colors of the '60s. The Second World War had changed everything, but it had not changed Capra. If anything, it made him all the more entrenched in his sentimentality—and all the warier of the furies that had always lurked beneath it. Trying to rekindle his career, he remade two of his films—*Riding High*, in 1950, based on 1934's *Broadway Bill*, and *Pocketful of Miracles*, based on *Lady for a Day*—and searched for projects that might revitalize his art (one of them, briefly, was *The Best Man*, and Gore Vidal's airily belittling account of his dealings with Capra is almost painful to read). If rekindling the old magic meant cannibalizing his past—or appropriating others' present—so be it. It was as if Capra wasn't so much betraying his talent as now utterly alienated from it.

One script, called "The Gentleman from Tennessee," had for its premise a rock singer turned political demagogue. Capra sought Elvis Presley for the title role. Even as the project stole from *A Face in the Crowd*, it looked back to *Mr. Smith*—as incongruous a pair of titles as one might imagine. Yet it is no more incongruous a combination than that of Capra and Elvis: two such alien talents, almost geologically differentiated, America's great celebrant of secular piety joining forces with its unbuttoned prophet of sanctified appetite. One need look no further for an emblem of how rapidly Capra had come to seem outdated, a hopeless anachronism. The thought of him meeting Elvis is almost as disorienting as that of, say, Nixon meeting Elvis.

Richard Nixon, Elvis Presley, and Egil Krogh

"SUSPICIOUS MINDS"

■ ■

He was flamboyant. . . . But as I talked to him, I sensed that he was a very shy man. The flamboyance was [a] covering up. . . . He wanted to be an example to young people. RICHARD NIXON, ON ELVIS PRESLEY; NIXON LIBRARY AUDIO PRESENTATION

The three best-known Western names in China: Jesus Christ, Richard Nixon, Elvis Presley. USELESS FACTS WEBSITE, MAY 7, 1996

"Suspicious Minds" isn't a movie, but a song: Elvis Presley's seventeenth, and last, number-one record. It topped the charts on November 1, 1969, two days before Richard Nixon went on national television to deliver an address invoking "the great silent majority of Americans." In retrospect, one might detect in that conjunction a fleeting aptness, for that great silent majority harbored countless Elvis fans—the demographic overlap between who voted for Nixon and who listened to Elvis was by no means inconsiderable. While the cautionary tale the lyrics tell is of marital mistrust, the chorus—"We can't go on together, with suspicious minds (suspicious minds); / And we can't build our dreams, on suspicious minds (suspicious minds)"—might just as easily have served as text to a Nixon administration theme song. From enemies lists to wiretaps to illegal break-ins, paranoia was the governing principle of its five and a half years in office. A good deal of that paranoia may have been justified —who have ever hated as muscularly, as self-sustainingly, as Nixon haters have?—but all of it was destructive. Even Nixon came to understand this, albeit far too late. "Those who hate you don't win unless you hate them," he said in his farewell address to his staff on August 9, 1974. "And then you destroy yourself."

Not that Nixon ever appreciated the import of "Suspicious Minds." It's hard to conceive of him even knowing such a song existed, and he was no more aware of its lyrics than he was of its rolling guitar intro or famously extended fade-out. Elvis was not Nixon's sort of thing, not hardly, and he never did quite appreciate the import of that miraculous—and, in hindsight, weirdly fitting—moment on December 21, 1970, when two such mightily Middle American specimens as the president and the King conducted a summit meeting (of sorts) in the Oval Office. There was no shock of recognition on either side: for Nixon, it was just another meet-and-greet with someone he'd barely heard of; for Elvis, simply a last-ditch effort to add a Bureau of Narcotics and Dangerous Drugs badge to an already-bulging collection of law-enforcement memorabilia—but such mutual obliviousness was inevitable. Indeed, it is central to why the meeting remains such a beguilement in the national imagination. Elvis and Nixon stood far closer together than anyone might have reasonably imagined in 1970; it's just that they were standing back to back rather than side by side.

What had been the measure for president-meeting-celebrity incongruity—Lauren Bacall giving Harry Truman a sloe-eyed look as she lay leggily curled atop his piano—didn't even involve a chief executive: Truman was still vice president at the time. So the Nixon-Presley summit had no real competition in setting a new standard. Nor has it been since surpassed. A smilingly ill-at-ease Gerald Ford handing an equally smiling and equally ill-at-ease George Harrison a WIN button at the White House in 1974 or Ronald Reagan's good-humored bafflement a decade later when he and Nancy presented a fully caparisoned Michael Jackson with an award for his work (?) against drug abuse was as nothing by comparison. Elvis and Nixon created a benchmark so far surpassing any similar encounter as to brook comparison with events in almost no other field.

Well, there was Nixon's meeting with James Brown in 1972, but at least the Godfather of Soul took the trouble to wear a tie. No, nothing else really compares, for supreme American weirdness of one sort meeting comparable same of another. Absolute id crashed into absolute superego, supernova encountered black hole, Carnival consorted with Lent, as the uptightest man in America shook hands with just about the loosest. It was incommensurability concentrated, constellated, and completely out of control.

The incongruity begins with it being a BNDD badge that Elvis was seeking. The fact that he had long since turned himself into a pharmaceutical pinball machine didn't keep him from having a sincere, if highly inchoate, desire to help in the war on drugs. However, that was the least of his reasons for wanting a badge. A BNDD credential would also allow him to carry a gun anywhere in the country, and any collector would consider possession of such a hard-to-obtain item a real coup. A badge's seeming unattainability had been but recently brought home to Elvis when he met John Finlator, the deputy head of BNDD, to ask for one. That was impossible, Finlator told him, adding half-jokingly that only the president could grant such a request. This was all Elvis needed to hear: off he went to Washington.

On the plane, Elvis met U.S. Senator George Murphy (he took this to be a good omen) and drafted a letter to Nixon on American Airlines stationery, which he presented at the White House's Northwest Gate early on the morning of December 21. The document is as notable for its appearance as its substance. "The handwriting seemed of grade school quality," recalled Egil Krogh, who as deputy counsel to the president presided over Elvis's Oval Office appearance (this was the same Krogh who, seven months before, had been the White House official shadowing Nixon on his visit to the Lincoln Memorial). Krogh also noted "a rather uninhibited use of capital letters throughout."[1]

"Dear Mr. President," the letter begins.

First I would like to introduce myself. I am Elvis Presley and admire you and Have Great Respect for your office. . . . The Drug Culture, The Hippie Elements, the SDS, Black Panthers, etc do not consider me as their enemy or as they call it The Establishment. I call it America and I love it. Sir I can and will be of any Service that I can to help the country out. I have no concern or Motives other than helping the country out. So I wish not to be given a title or an appointed position. I can and will do more good if I were made a Federal Agent at Large and I will help out by doing it my way through communications with people of all ages. First and foremost I am an entertainer but all I need is the Federal credentials. . . .

. . . I will be here [in Washington] for as long as it takes to get the credentials of a Federal Agent. I have done an in-depth study of drug abuse and Communist brainwashing techniques and I am right in the middle of the whole thing where I can and will do the most good. . . .[2]

Krogh, an Elvis fan, was delighted when asked to meet the King and assess the suitability of a presidential meeting. Two things struck him: Elvis's sincerity, which reassured him, and Elvis's attire, which did not. "Uh-oh," Krogh recalled thinking. "This could get a little dicey."[3] Elvis was wearing a black suede suit with a high-collared white shirt open to the sternum, a wide belt with an elaborate 24-square-inch gold buckle, a purple velvet cloak, and, in the words of Marty Lacker, one of Elvis's "Memphis Mafia," "enough mascara for the Avon Lady."[4] Accessories included silver-plated tinted glasses, a cane, gold medallion and chain, and various other items of jewelry. Small wonder that—even though it is apocryphal—the most frequently cited exchange from the Oval Office meeting is Nixon's saying, "Boy, you sure do dress kind of wild," to which Elvis rejoins, "Well, Mr. President, you got your show, and I got mine." In fact, the most enchanting of the twenty-eight images White House photographer Ollie Atkins recorded of their encounter shows Nixon leaning over, a moue of admiration on his lips, examining Elvis's cufflinks as the singer catches the eye of a bemused Krogh.

His fashion fears notwithstanding, Krogh signed off on the meeting and prepared a set of talking points for the president. They included mention of the drug-related deaths earlier that year of Janis Joplin and Jimi Hendrix—news to Nixon, presumably—and a proposal that Elvis "record an album with the theme 'Get High on Life' at the federal narcotics rehabilitation and research facility at Lexington, Kentucky."[5] There was one minor crisis to surmount before the meeting could take place. Elvis had wanted to personally present the president with a mounted commemorative .45-caliber automatic pistol, but the Secret Service would not allow a gun into the Oval Office. (The gift is now one of the most popular exhibits at the Nixon Library.) And at 12:30 P.M., with Krogh's words "Mr. President, this is Mr. Elvis Presley," celebrity worlds collided.[6]

Nixon, who (inevitably) referred to Elvis as "Mr. Presley," thanked him for wanting to help with the administration's anti-drug efforts, and Elvis began showing Nixon some of his police badges and family snapshots.

After the two men posed for some photographs, Elvis told Nixon, "I've been performing a lot in Las Vegas. Quite a place."

"I know very well how difficult it is to play Las Vegas," replied Nixon, perhaps drawing upon his newfound friendship with Frank Sinatra.

After some more small talk, Elvis finally got around to his real reason for coming, asking outright for a badge (something he had failed to mention to Krogh during their exploratory conversation). A startled Nixon batted the question to Krogh, who batted it back to Nixon, who said, "I'd like to do that. See that he gets one." Thrilled, Elvis gave the president a hug (alas, Atkins did not capture that moment on film). Nonplussed, Nixon patted Elvis on the shoulder. A jubilant Elvis asked if his two bodyguards, Sonny West and Jerry Schilling, who were waiting outside, might be allowed to greet the president. Nixon assented, and so easy had the mood by then become he noted their arrival by finally getting on a first-name basis with his guest: "You've got a couple of big ones here, Elvis." Nixon then moved behind his desk to get some tie clasps to present as mementoes. Elvis followed and, fascinated, joined in examining the contents of the drawer. "Remember, Mr. President," a tactful yet not unemphatic Elvis allowed, "they've got wives." More mementoes offered, and gratefully accepted, the meeting ended on a high note.

At the time, their encounter created no stir. It did not, in fact, become public knowledge until thirteen months later, when Jack Anderson broke the news with an appreciative, if somewhat jocose, account in his syndicated newspaper column. Haldeman didn't even bother to record the meeting in his very lengthy diary entry for that day. Nor did Atkins include any mention of it in his 1977 account of his time at the White House. Yet over the course of time it has earned a rich if narrow niche in American folklore. So many requests began coming in from the general public for copies of the most famous of the Atkins photographs, the one of Nixon and Elvis shaking hands and looking at the camera, that the National Archives had to print up order forms, and it became the most asked-for item in the archives' history.

The meeting also now helps finance the maintenance of Nixon's reputation. Unlike other presidential libraries, which receive money from the federal government, the Nixon Library is supported solely by private funds. Leading moneymakers for the library have turned out to be souvenirs commemorating the meeting: T-shirts, refrigerator magnets, postcards, even a wristwatch. It's only just, perhaps, that the last thing Nixon wrote for publication, completed only eight days before his death, was a blurb addressed "To Fans of the King" for inclusion in *The Day Elvis Met*

Nixon, Krogh's charmingly modest 1994 memoir of the visit. "He gave her class, and she gave him sex appeal," Katharine Hepburn reportedly said of Astaire and Rogers. To be sure, the president and the King were no Fred and Ginger (recall JFK's assessment of Nixon: "No class")—but there is a certain parallel. The two men's mutual strangeness somehow cancels out: the garishness of Elvis in his late phase working to enliven Nixon's dourness, and Nixon's implacable sobriety helping to tone down Elvis's excessiveness.

How Elvis came to be in the Oval Office makes for a wonderfully oddball story, yet its very bizarreness obscures the ways in which there was a higher logic to their meeting. For one thing, the two weren't *completely* incongruous; they had a few things in common: poor boys who'd made good, sons unbounded in their attachment to their mothers, fifties icons (albeit of wildly different provenance). Like Nixon, Elvis was passionate about football and a big fan of *Patton*; he saw it six times and had committed George C. Scott's opening speech to memory.[7] Like Nixon, Elvis was a strong advocate of law enforcement: his lust for that narcotics badge was born of an obsession with police officers and their regalia—*he* was on the right side of the law-and-order issue, Nixon's most effective in 1968. Above all, both men had a large and loyal following in Middle America, a following whose devotion seemed to the cultural elite so inexplicable as to cry out for mockery.

In his own, rather more resplendent way, Elvis was nearly as uncool in 1970 as Nixon was. Middle America still loved him, but *Rolling Stone* America didn't. Barely fifteen years had passed since he had erupted into the national consciousness, and songs like "Hound Dog" and "Jailhouse Rock" retained a bite and thrust far exceeding that of most of what one heard on progressive FM radio in 1970. Of course, "Hound Dog" and "Jailhouse Rock" *weren't* songs one would be hearing on FM radio in 1970. How could they be? Elvis was now an entirely different demographic. A month before Woodstock, he opened in Vegas. In an era that made denim a uniform of individuality, he wore jumpsuits and jewelry. He had become the sort of rock star who would . . . well, who would have a meeting with Nixon. Elvis was yesterday, an oldies act: predictable, stale, of another era. *American Graffiti* (1973) had yet to make "oldies" popular again, to turn them into a highly lucrative property in a record company's catalog. The inspiration behind Sha Na Na, the one contemporary rock group that specialized in oldies—and which, unlike Elvis, *did* appear at Woodstock—was to make fun of fifties music. Oldies were at best a joke in 1970 and at worst just what their name declared them to be: records that were *old* in a youth culture ever more centrifugally oriented toward the new.

The British Invasion of the mid-1960s had made early rock 'n' roll—all that *greaser* music—seem outmoded. "For a long time," Peter Guralnick wrote during what he termed the "Beatles era," "to suggest that you liked Elvis Presley only invited ridicule"[8]—and not from one's elders, but one's juniors and peers. Elvis seemed hardly to matter anymore, and his rare attempts at relevance looked, at best, calculated—or, far worse, just plain lame. How had Elvis made his celebrated "comeback" in 1968? Not with a new album or at a rock festival or by touring, but with a network television special—a network television special sponsored by that paragon of hipness Singer Sewing Machines. The next year his single "In the Ghetto" may have risen to number three on the charts, but you didn't hear it played in too many college dorms (or, for that matter, ghettos). Seemingly rendered superfluous, Elvis had outgrown the fifties—he'd evolved as, say, Chuck Berry or Jerry Lee Lewis clearly had not—but without ever entering into the spirit of the sixties. Not that he much cared. "I like a lot of the new groups," he announced to the audience during the comeback special. "The Beatles. The Byrds [which he pronounces 'Beards']. Whoever." Even without the mispronunciation, the insincerity is patent.

When the Beatles had arrived in America in 1964, all the initial comparisons had been to Elvis. The screaming girls, the sold-out shows, the string of hit records, the appearances on *The Ed Sullivan Show.* Elvis seemed almost to have been a dress rehearsal for the Beatles. "Dress rehearsal," however, carried with it a sense of secondary status—John the Baptist isn't the Son of God—and soon enough the new number one so overshadowed the old that all comparisons ceased. Colonel Parker, Elvis's manager, knew just what he was doing in sending a congratulatory telegram in his and Elvis's name to be read by the host when the Beatles debuted on Sullivan's show. Parker sensed both that the torch was being passed—worse, it was being taken away—and that the best way to disguise that fact was to appear to welcome the passing.

That didn't make it any easier for Elvis, of course, whose attitude toward the Beatles would always be, at best, ambivalent. Parker passed on Elvis's phone number to the Beatles and had invited them to Graceland. When Paul McCartney telephoned to apologize for their inability to schedule a visit, Elvis said, "Tell the other Beatles I think they're doing a great job." Somewhat more ambiguously, he also told McCartney that he liked the cover art on the *With the Beatles* album because it made the band look like the faces in the film *Children of the Damned.*[9]

There was nothing ambiguous about the Beatles' feelings for Elvis, whom they revered. As John Lennon flatly declared, "If there hadn't been Elvis, there would not have been the Beatles."[10] On the California leg of their 1965 U.S. tour, they actively sought to meet their hero. On August 27, while in Los Angeles, they got their wish, and the *other* great Elvis summit meeting occurred. Meeting their idol, the Beatles were at a loss for words. "Hey, I didn't mean for this to be like the subjects coming to the king," Elvis said. "Quite frankly, if you guys are going to stare at me all night, I'm going to bed. I thought we'd talk a little and maybe jam a little."[11] Ice broken, the five of them played music together for an hour, and Elvis's four guests ended up staying till 2 A.M. The following evening Lennon told a friend of Elvis's, "Last night was the greatest night of my life." Elvis's response was less enthusiastic: "I did my duty. I met them, and that's it."[12]

He went on to record a number of Beatles songs, but the lachrymose nature of the selections—"Something," "Yesterday," "Hey Jude"—suggests Elvis's diffident view of his legatees' music. His opinion of their politics was anything but diffident, as he made clear to Nixon when they met. Unprompted, he told the president, "The Beatles, I think, are kind of anti-American. They came over here. Made a lot of money. And then went back to England. And they said some anti-American stuff when they got back."[13] (Though Krogh reports that Nixon looked surprised to hear this, Elvis's words may have registered: a little more than a year later, the Immigration and Naturalization Service began a four-year effort to have Lennon deported.)

Ten days after meeting Nixon, Elvis tried to visit J. Edgar Hoover. Hoover—aware of Nixon's experience?—had Elvis told he was out of town, forcing the singer to settle for a tour of the FBI Building. The agent who conducted the tour noted in a memo that Elvis "indicated that he is of the opinion that the Beatles laid the groundwork for many of the problems we are having with young people by their filthy unkempt appearances and suggestive music while entertaining in the country during the early and middle '60s. He advised that the Smothers Brothers, Jane Fonda and other persons in the entertainment industry of their ilk have a lot to answer for in the hereafter for the way they have poisoned young minds by disparaging the United States in their public statements and unsavory activities."[14]

If the agent exaggerated—and what FBI operative wouldn't relay things the director was sure to want to hear?—he surely did so merely by degree, not kind. Elvis, having done so much to prepare the way for the great youthquake of the sixties, effectively disowned it with the image he presented throughout the decade. Once he got back from the army, it was all over. By the time Nixon entered the White House, Elvis had long since attained respectability. He was squarely on the government's side in what he represented as well as in what he said, for it was the youth revolution that did so much to antagonize the Nixon administration, to force it into a bunker mode. The counterculture, not the media or Eastern establishment, was the most dangerous enemy of the administration, insofar as no other antagonist so drew out its darker side or was so alien to it. There were media people in the Nixon White House (Ray Price, Herb Klein, John Scali). The Eastern elite had its representatives, too (everyone from David Bruce to Elliot Richardson—this *was* a Republican administration, after all). There were no longhairs though, no weekend rock 'n' rollers. So when "a bunch of long-haired college newspaper editors" came by the Oval Office one day in 1971, Nixon hastily summoned the closest approximation he could find on the White House staff: John W. Dean III. As Haldeman told him after the meeting, "The President thinks you look hippie."[15]

Looking at Elvis, the Nixon people could see hope as well as reassurance: *he* had turned out all right (or so it seemed at the time)—why not the rest of the kids, too? Just tough it out, and they'd grow up and come around. It was during the first Nixon administration that those under twenty-one gained the right to vote, and a *CBS News* exit poll found that on Election Day in 1972 Nixon took 48 percent of the youth vote, nearly capturing a majority of the much-vaunted vanguard of George McGovern's antiwar crusade.[16] Apparently, that "great silent majority of Americans" extended across the generations—across both AM and FM dials.

Among the myriad reasons the Nixon administration felt such antagonism toward the media was their failure to acknowledge this fact. Look at any magazine cover, watch any news broadcast, and one would think every American under thirty was smoking a joint and carrying a picket sign. The worst of this misrepresentation came from Hollywood. The real reason "the revolution will not be televised"—as the black poet Gil Scott-Heron chanted on a recording that one *would* have heard on FM radio— was because there wasn't any revolution. But a moviegoer would hardly know that, for the revolution certainly was being filmed. Such cinematic dinosaurs as *Doctor Dolittle* (1967) and *Star!* (1968) having brought the studios to the brink of extinction, it seemed as though "everybody under 30—and his idiot brother" could get backing for a film, or so an amused yet envious Orson Welles wrote in 1970.[17] Catering to the youth market had created an explosion of profits for the recording industry—why not for the movie industry, too? *Easy Rider* (1969) was the textbook case, or so studio executives hoped, of how you could take a shoestring budget and, with a sense of political relevance and enough rock 'n' roll on the sound-track, produce the fourth-biggest gross of the year. If only it were that sim-ple! *Easy Rider* was a financial anomaly—stupendously so. It was the utter failure of *The Last Movie* and *The Hired Hand* (both 1971), the films the studios backed by Dennis Hopper (the director of *Easy Rider*) and Peter Fonda (its producer), that were the norm.

Easy Rider was the great progenitor of youth rebellion movies—not the first, but the most lucrative, the one most perfectly balanced between popular acceptance and calculated outrage—the film that demonstrated just how much material gain there was to be gotten giving a platform to denigrations of material gain. Of course, part of the reason *Easy Rider* was singular, that it *remained* singular, was that it owed so much to more tra-ditional genres: the road picture, the buddy movie, and, above all, the Western. Weren't Billy and Captain America basically a pair of cowboys who'd traded their horses for motorcycles? An updated pair of Pony Ex-press riders whose saddlebags carried not the U.S. mail but cocaine (a fact all too many viewers preferred to overlook)? Three decades later the film's characters seem to have less in common with the Weather Under-ground than they do with the title characters in *Butch Cassidy and the Sun-dance Kid*, itself a modish variant on the traditional Western (and the biggest-grossing film of 1969), which also ended with its pair of outlaw heroes being blown away in a highly violent—and highly romanticized—send-off.

But the youth rebellion movies that came in the wake of *Easy Rider*—a representative sampling would include, from 1969, *Alice's Restaurant*; from 1970, *Getting Straight, R.P.M., The Strawberry Statement*, and *Zabriskie Point*; and from 1971, *Drive, He Said*—seemed to spring full-blown, with-out any identifiable cinematic ancestors, from the fevered brow of the six-ties. There had been youth rebellion movies before *Easy Rider*—ranging from the precious (*The Graduate*, 1967) to the preposterous (*Wild in the Streets*, 1968) to the nearly precognitive (the motorcycle films produced by American International Pictures, which provide the link between *Easy Rider* and *The Wild One*, the 1954 granddaddy of all youth revolution movies, where Marlon Brando answered the question "What are you rebelling against?" with one of his own, "What have you got?"). In these pre–*Easy Rider* works, the youthful threats are either unthreatening in their coats and ties—think of Dustin Hoffman's poor mournful Benjamin ornamenting his parents' cocktail parties—or else rock stars and bikers who are overtly beyond the pale in their studs and leather. After *Easy Rider*, abnormality—membership in the great vocal minority—was presented as the norm. Not only were there now decidedly more youth rebellion movies, but the youthful threats they showed were college students; worse, they weren't even presented as threats, but as heroes.

Well, they weren't heroes to Richard Nixon. As he said in his post–Kent State press conference: "On university campuses the rule of reason is supposed to prevail over the rule of force. And when students on university campuses burn buildings, when they engage in violence, when they break up furniture, when they terrorize their fellow students and terrorize the faculty, then I think 'bums' is perhaps too kind a word to apply to that kind of person." Yet neither were they *necessarily* villains (note the care with which Nixon justified and qualified his original use of "bums"). No, neither heroes nor villains, student protesters were something far more daunting to Richard Nixon, far more rankling: they were a puzzle. Still baffled two decades later, he lamented to an aide in 1992, "My God, I wasn't just from another generation from these people; it was like I was from a different planet."[18]

Nixon had nothing against young persons wanting to "have a good time," "play the field," maybe even stay out late and have a drink or two too many. His notoriously asking David Frost, "Well, did you do any fornicating this weekend?"[19] testified less to an iron morality than a tin ear. However clumsily, the question was meant to indicate that Nixon, like Frost, was a man of the world. Never a swinger, but no prude, either: *he* knew the score (he just didn't know the language of scoring). "If you ever have to say you were working late, I'll cover for you," he once told an all-male gathering of his staff.[20] It was an awareness of the sexual revolution as preached by Hugh Hefner and practiced by (yes) JFK, one that had nothing to do with Norman O. Brown and Mick Jagger, but it *was* an awareness. Sex was the least of Richard Nixon's problems with the counterculture. That prefix "counter"—with all it declared about an oppositional stance toward everything the "culture" stood for—*that* was the problem.

License, more than anything else, was what defined "the sixties" (which lasted well into the '70s—until, let us say, August 9, 1974). License back then took many forms, and so many of them unprecedented for mainstream, middle-class, Nixonian America. Sex was one thing—not Richard Nixon's thing, perhaps, but it was as old and inescapable as human nature; he had no difficulty acknowledging that—it was the other stuff, drugs and long hair and disrespect (disrespect especially), *those* were what bothered him. Disrespect for tradition, disrespect for custom, disrespect for government and patriotism: such actions were the behavior of "bums." Note how old-fashioned the term is, the way it suggests an offense to decorum rather than morality. Sure, live it up, you're only young once—animal high spirits and all—but you're still American. That's what was so touching about Elvis's letter. Okay, he dressed kind of wild, was even a little grabby maybe, but he had his priorities straight. He loved America, dammit.

The irony was that Nixon had come of age in what previously had been the century's most socially turbulent decade. He would revert to the thirties when trying to comprehend the sixties. In London, on his first overseas trip as president, Nixon was asked about youth. He replied that "back in the '30s, the student rebel had a cause, a belief, a religion. Today, the revolt doesn't have that form—it's more negative, against the Establishment. But on the plus side, the student generation is infinitely more knowledgeable about the world than my own generation—and in a way, even more idealistic than we ever were. When a nation is at war, you fight to stay alive; in a depression you fight to make a living. But in a time of peace we have to provide a way to help young people make the world a better place—to provide an outlet for a missionary spirit."[21] A year later he assured the students at the Lincoln Memorial that he "knew that young people today were searching as I was searching forty years ago."[22] Two months after that, he jotted down some marginalia on a *New York Times* editorial on "The Mood of the Campus." "Dissent is not new—method of expressing it [is]—illegal strikes, breaking up meetings by shouting obscenities (shouting down speakers with obscenities)—contrary to university."[23]

It wasn't as if Nixon had been *born* old. Youthfulness had, in fact, propelled his own career. His age had helped get him the Republican nomination against Jerry Voorhis and called all the more attention to his performance in the Hiss affair. Most important, it had put him on the ticket with Ike: the energetic young senator, the youngest in the Eighty-second Congress, complementing the wise old general. The election of the GOP ticket that year made Nixon the second-youngest vice president in U.S. history. (John C. Breckinridge had been four years younger at the time of his inauguration in 1857.) *Six Crises* does not fail to note that JFK—the embodiment of the rise of the postwar generation in politics—"was only four years younger than I, and had begun his career in Washington the same year." Kennedy's victory made him the youngest man to be elected president. Yet if Nixon had won, he would have been the fourth youngest. His preternatural seriousness and avid gloom helped obscure the fact that, compared with every other politician of his eminence, Nixon had been a mere stripling. Nor did he operate in a generational vacuum. Lest we forget, his daughters were in their late teens and twenties while he was president. Tricia briefly had the Jefferson Airplane's Grace Slick for a college classmate, at Finch, and also sponsored the first White House appearance by a rock group (the Turtles). Furthermore, his presidential staff was the youngest in history, something he took great pride in, according to David Gergen.[24]

It was not the *what* of the sixties that bothered Nixon so much, or even the *why*. It was the *how*. The problem was one of style even more than substance. If Elvis was the absolutely right man in the right place at the right time—the vessel in whom white C&W and black R&B, revivalist fervor and sensualist abandon, all came together to irradiate the fifties and declare the arrival of rock 'n' roll—then Nixon (poor put-upon, waiting-in-the-wings Nixon) had to endure the opposite. One could even argue that Nixon's plight might be traced in part to Elvis: it was the Kulturkampf that Elvis, more than any other individual, helped instigate (before stoutly decamping to the other side) that did so much to ensnare, bedevil, and bewilder Richard Nixon. William Safire is very much writing as a partisan when he argues that "Nixon succeeded in focusing the organized hatred of the Sixties on himself,"[25] but that in no way diminishes the truth of his observation. For everything Nixon was, everything he represented, stood in diametrical opposition to the youth culture that was inundating the media and defining the terms of social debate. The sixties could not have come at a worse time, so far as Richard Nixon was concerned. This superbly qualified man, trained as no other had been to assume the presidency, found himself in the acutely uncomfortable position of being the right man in the right place at the wrong time. JFK was the sixties excitingly early; and Nixon, endlessly unfortunate Nixon, was the fifties woefully late.

Nixon's fifties uptightness obscured the fact that he so wanted to be avuncular. It wasn't that he was all that uncomfortable with young people per se; it was that he was uncomfortable with *everybody*. As he said in his first inaugural address, "I know America's youth. I believe in them. We can be proud that they are better educated, more committed, more passionately driven by conscience than any generation in our history." Everything that had been denied him—affluence, self-indulgence, leisure—they had gotten. All well and good, Nixon did not begrudge them that. How could he? Their winning those privileges validated the sacrifices his own generation had had to make. What he did resent—it visibly ate away at him—was their having taken good fortune for granted, their considering it to be a set of so many entitlements that they then (and this was the greatest offense of all) blithely pissed away. Why bathe? Why wear nice clothes? Why lead the good life when you can turn your back on it? It was worse than an insult; it was a mystery. There was Nixon, who as a high school student had won the Harvard Club award and been offered a scholarship to Yale but had been too poor and had to settle for Whittier and live at home—and here were these "bums" given all the privileges he had not even dared dream of. When he apostrophized students in his disastrous 1970 election-eve broadcast—"Hit the books or hit the road"—it was more than just sloganeering. It was his heart speaking. It was his *past* speaking.

Were they grateful, appreciative, did they work hard? No, they listened to loud music, used language containing expletives far worse than any that would be deleted from the White House transcripts, and not only did they take illegal drugs—they flaunted it, as if it were some kind of generational badge of honor (which, of course, it was). They were dirty, they were lazy, and—worst offense, without question—they were *so* self-important. That cringing self-abasement, which displayed Nixon at his most Heepish—but also his most human and unguarded—was nowhere evident in these prideful youth. "In a blundering toward confrontation with each other," Garry Wills noted at the time, "Nixon and the kids are not only masked but blindfolded, opposed twin parodies . . . one the measure of the other's excess. The 'privileged' students, without having the tasks, have some of the attitudes, of an aristocracy—mainly this: they have no doubt of their own worth. They do not feel they must earn dignity. . . . [A]s Nixon told Theodore White, 'They were given too much, too easily; and this weakened them.'" In the Nixon lexicon (the Nixicon?), there is, of course, no more damning term than "weakened."[26] It's even worse than "weak," for those who are weak could have started out that way. You can't blame people for the shortcomings they were born with. Those who have weakened, though, have *surrendered* their strength. What Munich had been to totalitarianism, the sixties generation was to affluence.

Few memos could have better gratified Daniel Patrick Moynihan's boss than the one in which he referred to demonstrators as "rich college f-- cks" (the absurd chasteness of those dashes!). "I do no know," Moynihan went on to say, "but strongly suspect, that especially to working class America, the misbehavior of students is seen as a form of class privilege. Which it is."[27] Nixon could not have put it better himself Even without his own burning bundle of resentments, he was too good a politician to fail to recognize that so much of the turmoil in the sixties had to do with class: that is, upper-middle-class kids bumping up against working-class values. In that regard, one might think Nixon had an advantage over, say, a Mayor Daley or George Wallace, with his own hard-won social standing bringing him a certain affinity with the youthful elite. Indeed, in terms of the sixties Kulturkampf, Wallace is much more of an antipocal figure than Nixon is, which makes all the more striking Nixon's own embattled status. But Wallace (who also had his photo taken with Elvis) played off of, and fed into, the madness of the sixties in a way that Nixon never could. Wallace contributed to the sixties; Nixon was consumed by them. Make no mistake: George Corley Wallace had no small amount of rock 'n' roll snarling in his soul. A more simpatico running mate in 1968 would have been Jerry Lee Lewis, not Curtis LeMay. No, Nixon was the boy who took piano and violin, diligently thumped out the classics, and *enjoyed* thumping them out. It was a Rachmaninoff piano concerto, not some moody after-hours music, that he listened to before heading off to the Lincoln Memorial. His idea of something rousing to put on the hi-fi was *Victory at Sea.*

In his musical tastes, as in his social manner, Nixon was very much a product of the genteel tradition. A January 29, 1973, memo from the White House Communications Agency that lists "the current Presidential music library of stereo 8-track cartridges that have been accumulated since August 1969"[28] gives some sense of just how unhip Richard Nixon was musically. Nixon's collection of recordings, like those of most American music listeners of the time, consisted of LPs (they took up ten feet of shelf space in the Lincoln Sitting Room). Even so the list of tapes is representative—as well as indicative of an easy-listening sensibility that, for a rock fan, would have been tantamount to exile to a sonic Siberia. The most frequently included artists were Mantovani, with twelve selections; the Boston Pops, with eight; 101 Strings, with seven; and Percy Faith, with six. The Nixons also exhibited a particular fondness for motion picture soundtracks—*Gone with the Wind, My Fair Lady* (1964), *Doctor Zhivago* (1965)—that is very much in keeping with the president's moviegoing tastes, as we shall see in chapter 10.

There is also a fair sampling of classical recordings, mostly warhorses from the standard orchestral repertory (Tchaikovsky was a particular favorite). Nixon—who had a sophisticated-enough knowledge of classical music to complain that he "would have chosen a different program" when the Kennedy Center debuted for classical music and to specify that he wanted his second inaugural festivities to include Eugene Ormandy and the Philadelphia Orchestra—was well aware of the retro nature of his musical tastes—and took pride in it. As he said to Haldeman after hearing his aide's firsthand account of the world premiere of Leonard Bernstein's rock-inspired "Mass," "I just want to ask you one favor. If I'm assassinated, I want you to have them play 'Dante's "Inferno"' and have Lawrence Welk produce it."[29]

Nixon knew where his tastes stood—and knew that, politically, they stood him in good stead. "Sometimes our family was called square and as far as we were concerned, that was just fine," he wrote in his memoirs. "In the environment of Washington, 'square' often means rooted in principles that ignore chic, transitory fashion."[30] This is *ur*-Nixon; he is being at once absolutely correct (it was fine with him to be considered square) and breathtakingly disingenuous (in the context of Washington, "square" means votes). Most people are square. Certainly, most people during Nixon's presidency were, and the center of the square is where any good politician wants to be.

Not that Nixon's squareness was the product of calculation—does an ocean have to pretend it's wet? a desert that it's dry?—but calling attention to it most certainly was. "He is not just square," Stewart Alsop noted in 1972—"he is *totally* square."[31] Rebellion, rule breaking, self-indulgence: none of these was in Nixon's character. Neither was any sort of modishness. When Herb Klein took over as Nixon's campaign press secretary in 1968, the first question he fielded came from a UPI reporter who had heard that Nixon would be going after the youth vote by "campaigning in a Nehru jacket." Klein, who quickly assured the reporter that the answer was no, was still marveling at the query's preposterousness a dozen years later. "I would answer hundreds of press questions," he notes in his 1980 memoir, *Making It Perfectly Clear*, "but never one so absurd as this."[32] Most comfortable in a Brooks Brothers suit with flag pin, never a Nehru jacket with love beads (he didn't like *Nehru*, let alone the man's jacket), Nixon was the ultimate buttoned-down man in a supremely unbuttoned age.

With its aggressive informality, the sixties could have found no more antipathetic figure to fasten upon, to scorn and taunt, than Richard Nixon. As Wills presciently noted in 1970, "With other politicians, informality exposes the man behind the office, a range of personality that extends beyond political role. But Nixon does not exist outside his role, apart from politics: take his clothes off, he would be invisible."[33] Woodstock Nation took *its* clothes off and did so with the exact opposite aim: to become visible, as well as liberated—to call attention to itself. Which makes all the more absurd an idea Nixon briefly toyed with on how best to decry the growing immorality in society. As Haldeman described it in his March 28, 1969, diary entry: "P had me in quite a while before NSC, mainly on wanting to take stronger action on obscenity. . . . Even decided he'd go to a play in New York where they take off clothes [*Hair*], and get up and walk out, to dramatize his feelings."[34]

Nixon did no such thing, of course. Dramatizing his feelings was as unlike him as publicly taking his clothes off. Almost as bad was when others dramatized their feelings in his presence. In some ways, it was worse, since Nixon had no control over the situation—other than to flee. Not that he could he get away when Sammy Davis Jr. started hugging him in Miami—on national television, no less—minutes after he'd been renominated at the 1972 convention. Sammy Davis Jr.—who had just had a number-one hit with "Candy Man" and who was following Frank in dragging the tattered remnants of the Rat Pack from Camelot to Key Biscayne—was very, very far, from being of the sixties. Yet even with Sammy, there was the painfully apparent sense of Nixon feeling things were going too far. All these men in gold chains (worse, all these men in gold chains *hugging him*)! Going too far, that more than anything else was what the sixties were all about, license as praxis; and going too far, even with someone as mainstream and passé as Sammy Davis Jr., was simply, utterly, irretrievably alien to who Richard Nixon was.

Going too far, it should be noted, to either extreme: the Young Americans for Freedom never appealed to Nixon, either. The YAF types were, in their way, as unfathomable as the hippies and Yippies: radicals of the Right who differed from radicals of the Left in little more than grooming and choice of stimulants. They were the Goldwater people, after all, the ones who had reviled him at the 1960 convention after he had cut his deal with Nelson Rockefeller. They were a younger, more presentable version of the Birchers who had hounded him in the California gubernatorial race. They were supporters of U.S. Representative John Schmitz, the Orange County Republican who ran as a protest candidate against Nixon in 1972. The YAF types were extremists—and extremists, almost by definition, caused trouble. They especially caused trouble when, like Tom Charles Huston, a former national director of YAF, they managed to find a place on the White House staff. The Huston Plan, with its Constitution-flouting designs on basic guarantees of personal freedom, was political dynamite, as even so complaisant a friend of civil liberties as J. Edgar Hoover recognized. Hoover's objections scuttled the plan, but it would come back to haunt Nixon—another example of all the problems youthful hotheads were presenting him with.

No, a generation of David Eisenhowers—squarely moderate as well as moderately square—that was what Nixon would have wished for, what he could have understood and dealt with. And the feeling was mutual: "He's really easygoing," David said of his future father-in-law during the '68 campaign, "a lot of fun, and has a good sense of humor—the perfect father for a teenage serial."[35] Such a bewitching, if barely imaginable, conceit—Robert Young with a five o'clock shadow (*President Knows Best?*)— is a fifties dream image, yet a dream turned nightmare, for Nixon's curse was to be a sixties president.

It also became the curse of David and his wife. Considered sell-outs, or worse, to all that young people were supposed to oppose, they were treated as laughingstocks in the alternative press (a particularly vile instance was a *National Lampoon* recording that purported to reenact their wedding night). Everything about them was so completely alien to the zeitgeist. They were college sweethearts. He had been her escort when she was presented at the International Debutante Ball. Dr. Norman Vincent Peale officiated at their wedding, and the song they chose for the first dance at the reception was "Edelweiss," from *The Sound of Music*. They married while still in college; and, once David graduated, he went off to serve in the navy. It all made them seem perfect foils to the tenor of the times: class couple in a silent-majority Komsomol. Yet even as they were drawing jeers from their more engagé contemporaries, Julie was lobbying her father to support the Equal Rights Amendment and, during the final days of the Nixon administration, David was quietly urging his father-in-law to resign. Had he ever bothered to ponder it, Nixon could have taken a grim satisfaction in knowing there was far more substance to them—and far more complexity—than those who disdained them ever imagined.

The dislocations of the youth revolt made Nixon depend all the more on David and Julie. She became one of the administration's most popular speakers, and David did everything from collaborating on the all-time all-star team the president compiled in honor of the centennial of professional baseball in 1969 to writing at his father-in-law's request a critique (heavily underscored by Nixon) of the report of the presidential commission on student unrest in 1970. As a Nixon aide once confided to

Wills, "He has great input from David and Julie."[36] Nixon was astute enough to realize they were more suitable in such a role—more palatable, too—than Edward and Tricia Cox. With his Princeton/Harvard Law/Nader's Raiders résumé, Ed had a rather suspect pedigree; and Tricia seemed to combine the worst of both her parents, the father's meanness with the mother's unreality. Worse, Tricia and Ed looked cold and aloof compared with David and Julie. Julie's warmth was patent, and David had a slightly goofy, gee-whiz quality—his forehead too high, his grin too eager—that humanized him in contrast to Ed's preppie blond-beast hauteur.

No, a generation of Davids would have been just fine—or, failing that, even a generation of Elvises. In his memo informing Haldeman of Elvis's desire to meet Nixon, presidential appointments secretary Dwight Chapin argued that "if the President wants to meet some bright young people outside the Government, Presley might be a perfect one to start with." In his prim script, Haldeman wrote in the margin, "You must be kidding."[37] Chapin wasn't—nor should he have been. "The modesty, the deferential charm, the soft-spoken assumption of common-sense virtues,"[38] as Guralnick has termed them, these were as much a part of Elvis as the slicked-back hair and swiveling hips. Even at his most rebellious, Elvis never failed to exhibit these characteristics. They were qualities he'd learned growing up poor, for Elvis was one of the people. No child of privilege he: Elvis and his family were living in public housing when he made his first recordings. He was working for an electrical company when his first record came out, and the reason he grew his sideburns long had nothing to do with any incipient youth revolution; he wanted to look like a truck driver. Best of all, Elvis didn't dodge the draft. Unlike those rich college boys during Vietnam, *he* went into the army. "I'm kinda proud of it," Elvis told reporters on the day of his induction. "It's a duty I've got to fill, and I'm gonna do it."[39] Colin Powell, then a lieutenant commanding a company in Germany, encountered him one day during maneuvers. He could have been speaking for Nixon, whom he later served as a White House Fellow, when he recalled, "What impressed me was that instead of seeking celebrity treatment, Elvis had done his two-year hitch, uncomplainingly, as an ordinary GI, even rising to the responsibility of an NCO."[40]

If it sounds odd to speak of Elvis as a Nixonian archetype for the young, that is because there were three archetypal Elvises—and the most Nixonian, the Elvis visible on the screen in the twenty-seven feature films he made during the '60s, is the one least remembered now: Hollywood

Elvis (the movie star) is dwarfed in popular memory by Memphis Elvis (the singer) and Vegas Elvis (the sacred monster). The Memphis period lasted from 1954, when he made his first recording, until 1958, when he entered the army. The Hollywood period began with his return to civilian life in 1960 and ended in 1969, with the release of his last feature film, *Change of Habit*. That same year Vegas Elvis emerged full-blown with the singer's record-setting engagement on the Strip. The division is more suggestive than exact. Elvis lived in Memphis much of his life, did nearly all of his studio sessions elsewhere, and recorded music right up until his death. He made his first four movies while still in his Memphis phase and played Vegas as early as 1956. Still, this schema conveys the essential trajectory of Elvis's career: from sexy rock 'n' roll revolutionary in the '50s to bloated, bespangled legend in the '70s, with the tame tepidity of his films coming in between. The great paradox of Elvis's career is that the man who did so much to trigger the sixties spent that decade on the sidelines in Hollywood cranking out three movies a year, each and every one of which stood in numbingly flaccid contradistinction to everything the sixties (and, for a time, Elvis) represented.

When the U.S. Postal Service held its contest in 1992 to decide which image to put on its Elvis stamp, Memphis Elvis and Vegas Elvis were the contenders. No Hollywood Elvis, and rightly so: the movie period is the Bermuda Triangle of his career. Even his two years in the army produced the pent-up excitement of awaiting his discharge. Nothing, though, is seen to redeem the Hollywood years. Even the final period, with its Vegas-ized Fat Elvis, had its own garish integrity. There's no comparably resplendent egregiousness to the movies, no thrill of excess. They're flat, mechanical, bored.

As a presence in the American psyche, Elvis has no show-business rival; yet his movie career, while certainly a part of his fame, was more a tribute to his popularity than a major contributor to it. If anything, his movie acting seems like a detour from what being Elvis was all about: a tycoon's investment that barely broke even. Yet his screen presence is such that, clearly, Elvis *could* have been a real movie star. Think of his foremost vocalist predecessor in Hollywood, Bing Crosby. *He* made the transition. For all that Crosby is second only to Louis Armstrong in his influence on popular singing in the twentieth century, he is now remembered more as movie star than crooner. (In 1965's *Girl Happy*, Elvis plays a singer whose band includes Gary Crosby, Bing's son, and one gets the creepy sense of seeing the new king exhibit the old king's heir as vassal.) Given a longer leash by the Colonel, surely Elvis could have had a real movie career.

Consider how much better fared Dean Martin, Elvis's idol when he was starting out. Martin got to work with Howard Hawks, on *Rio Bravo* (1959); Vincente Minnelli, on *Some Came Running* (1958) and *Bells Are Ringing* (1960); and Billy Wilder, on *Kiss Me, Stupid* (1964). The best Elvis ever did was Michael Curtiz, on *King Creole* (1958), and Don Siegel, on *Flaming Star* (1960). Not surprisingly, they are Elvis's two best pictures. Siegel, for one, admired Elvis's "sensitivity as an actor," affirming in his autobiography that Elvis "could have become an acting star, not just a singing star."[41]

Elvis's film persona in the '60s, Ethan Mordden observes, belongs to "Old Cinema in a New Age; it cuts the unique down to acceptable size. Even the most rebellious of kids can be enlisted on the side of the traditions and the pieties and the cautions."[42] In *Jailhouse Rock* (1957), his third film, it's as if Elvis dances on the grave of the movie musical: Pandro Berman, who oversaw the Astaire-Rogers pictures at RKO, produced it, and the studio was MGM, home of the Freed unit that last bastion of all singing, all dancing in Hollywood. Yet a decade later, in *Speedway* (1968), there's Elvis in an honest-to-goodness, old-fashioned production number. No go-go dancers or kids on the dance floor, no attempt to account naturalistically for why these people are singing and dancing (in an IRS office, no less). Suddenly, a roomful of men in suits bursts into song and dance, like a road-show production of *How to Succeed in Business without Really Trying*. After the song, "He's Your Uncle, Not Your Dad," Elvis gives the supreme demonstration of his beyond-Nixonian respect for authority: he agrees with the IRS when it docks him for back taxes and disallows several deductions even before the auditor does It's hard to imagine being more on the side of the cautions.

In his autobiography, *Starmaker*, Hal Wallis, who first signed Elvis to a movie contract and produced nine of his films, nicely illustrates Mordden's Old Cinema/New Age dichotomy. Of Elvis's screen test he wrote: "I felt the same thrill I experienced when I saw Errol Flynn on the screen. Elvis, in a very different, modern way, had exactly the same power, virility, and sexual drive. The camera caressed him." Yet in person, "I knew him only as a happy, modest, clean-cut American boy."[43] It's that latter Elvis we almost exclusively see onscreen. Aside from the occasional karate chop, no hint of Errol Flynn (let alone his wicked, wicked ways) is anywhere to be seen.

In fact, filmgoers got to watch Elvis mature from delinquent, or borderline delinquent, into fine young man—and Nixonian ideal—the sort of screen character who might be, as Elvis was, named one of the Jaycees' Ten Outstanding Young Americans in 1971. In *Jailhouse Rock*, he kills a man and goes to prison. In *King Creole*, he gets involved with a street gang. In *Wild in the Country* (1961), he attacks his brother (albeit with just cause) and is placed on probation. Yet in his fifth film, *G.I. Blues* (1960), he's a soldier; in *Kissin' Cousins* (1964), he's an air force officer; in *Easy Come, Easy Go* (1967), a navy officer; in 1965's *Harum Scarum* (perhaps the worst of all Elvis's movies, and that's really saying something), he's a singer-actor on a State Department goodwill tour; and in *Change of Habit*, he's an inner-city doctor (the sort of sixties idealism—practical, professional, well-groomed—not even Nixon might have objected to).

There is no such thing as a good Elvis movie, but there are differing degrees of badness. The early ones tend to be less bad, the later ones worse (by then, not even Elvis was disguising the extent of his ennui). The early ones—say, up to *Blue Hawaii*, in 1961—at least try to be real movies. Elvis is still raw in these pictures, still rebellious and surly, still (thankfully) undomesticated. Hollywood as yet feels the need to defer to Elvis's Elvisness. In *Loving You* (1957), his performing gets him banned in Texas; Elvis is "the one with the jumpin' beans in his pants," an admiring female fan declares. Yet he's never truly wild in any of these films—not even in *Flaming Star*, a Western in which he plays a half-breed who's *supposed* to be somewhat wild. The sole concession the later films make to Elvis's animal vigor is a general weakness for speed: fast cars (*Viva Las Vegas*, 1964; *Spinout*, 1966; *Speedway*), aircraft (*It Happened at the World's Fair*, 1963; *Kissin' Cousins*; *Paradise, Hawaiian Style*, 1966) fast boats (*Girls! Girls! Girls!*, 1962; *Easy Come, Easy Go*; *Clambake*, 1967), or motorcycles (*Roustabout*, 1964).

It seems to have been unanimous among Elvis scriptwriters that, when not singing, he was good only for girls and cars—or something else with an engine in it—as if he were the ultimate teenage boy. That kind of condescension is there from the very start of his film career. The obverse of his tending to play bad boys early on is that he brings out the maternal instinct, and rather more, in older women. *They* can see that underneath all the loud music and tough-guy posturing, he really is a very nice boy. (He was so good to his mother, after all, and Elvis's love of Gladys makes Nixon's devotion to Hannah seem almost perfunctory.) He appeals to his male elders, too, albeit in an uncomplicatedly filial way. As Wendell Corey, his bandleader-boss in *Loving You*, tells him, "You're the kind of boy any man would be proud to have as a son." He's always careful to address his elders as "Mr." or "ma'am," and "sir" takes precedence over "cars" or even "girls" as Elvis's favorite movie monosyllable (if he used it any more often, he could have auditioned for the lead in a musical version of *Mr. Smith Goes to Washington*).

The Elvis canon has one axiomatic principle: respectful, respectable hedonism—aka good, clean, boys-will-be-boys fun. Yet that principle has a dark (dare one say "Nixonian"?) underside: class resentment. The rebelliousness once displayed toward social mores gets redirected at highbrows and university types. This class consciousness receives its most pointed treatment in *Roustabout*, where Elvis performs a song called "Poison Ivy League," whose words might have sounded perfectly natural on the White House tapes:

Poison Ivy League, poison that Ivy League
Gives me an itch, those sons of the rich

The rah-rah boys will go to bed so early tonight
Before exams they need a lot of rest
They got to make good for Dad, they got to make good so bad
They'll even pay someone to take that test

(Ted Kennedy, as anyone at the Nixon White House could have pointed out, did indeed get someone to take an exam for him at Harvard.)

Only twice does Elvis play a rich boy, in *Blue Hawaii* and *Clambake*. In both cases, he chafes at his wealth, attempting to break free of his affluent background and make it on his own. It's not just his pride; it's also vanity: nearly all the women in the Elvis movies, regardless of age, are his social betters. Independence and disdain are his sole defense against the appearance of being a kept man. Like any hardworking male, Elvis has his self-respect. In *Girls! Girls! Girls!* (such a giddily egregious title), he plays a charter-fishing skipper who dreams of regaining the sailboat his father designed and he helped build. But it's a dream he must pursue without handouts from anyone—either an older woman with a yen for him ("Mrs. Morgan," he tells her, "I don't accept charity from anybody. I have to earn what I get") or even his wealthy girlfriend ("A man has to work for what he wants," he lectures her. "I don't take any handouts"). One of the blunter instances of Elvis's blue-collar stance comes during his dealings with social worker Hope Lange in *Wild in the Country*. Here, as throughout the canon, his character is a sort of Everyman (Elvisman?), average in his behavior and tastes, unusual only in his talent. Inspecting a Paul Klee reproduction hanging in Lange's study, he speaks for good old boys everywhere when he asks the rhetorical question, "Do you think this is art?" He's just as emphatic six years later in *Easy Come, Easy Go*. Pursuing a pretty bohemian, he encounters a bunch of "kooks," as he calls them, conducting a happening. It's "like a smash-up in an Italian restaurant," complains a perplexed Elvis.

Lucky Jackson, Elvis's character in *Viva Las Vegas*, typifies his screen roles. Fun-loving and exuberant, yes, but this race-car driver is also an air force vet who gets on better with his girlfriend's father (William Demarest) than he does with her (Ann-Margret). Indeed, she initially dismisses him as "crazy," but Count Mancini (Cesare Danova), Lucky's Old World rival for her hand, has him pegged far more accurately when he tells Lucky how much he admires the young man's "bravado." He's independent, hardworking, and wants to pay his own way. When he accidentally loses all his money, he takes a job as a waiter to make good on his hotel bill. Facing a similar dilemma, would an Eddie Cox, or even a David Eisenhower, have done the same? Lucky is the Nixon view of young people incarnate: lively and a bit hedonistic, yes; looking for a good time, to be sure; even a little rambunctious (animal high spirits and all that)—but when the day is done, essentially decent, law-abiding, proud to have served his country.

Like most of the characters he played onscreen, Elvis came from just the kind of patriotic, working-class, southern background that Nixon saw as the foundation of the new majority he successfully brought together in 1972, the new majority he hoped would replace the one Franklin Roosevelt had made the dominant factor in presidential politics forty years earlier. This group of voters—the Elvis bloc—had previously served as one of the bases of FDR's grand coalition. It should come as no surprise, then, that Elvis's own affinities tended to be Democratic. That was a legacy of his upbringing in what was still a very solid South. Born in Bilbo's Mississippi, raised in Boss Crump's Memphis, Elvis's bloodlines were pure yellow-dog Democrat. Asked by reporters in 1956 about "Elvis for President" buttons, he took the opportunity to plug his candidate: "I'm strictly for Stevenson. I don't dig the intellectual bit, but I'm telling you, man, he knows the most."[44]

All such statements soon enough ceased. The Colonel saw to that: for every fan pleased by a public stand Elvis took, there could be another offended. So Elvis scrupulously avoided comment on political or social issues. The answer he gave when Mississippi governor J. P. Coleman asked him what he'd run for if he ever got into politics was emblematic: "The city limits."[45] Still, he clearly remained a cultural Democrat, and his kinship with many of the party standard-bearers who followed Stevenson is plain. Kennedy was as sexy (might he and Elvis have slept with some of the same women?); and Elvis, who much admired JFK, was so exercised by the assassination, he expressed a wish to shoot Lee Harvey Oswald.[46] Lyndon Johnson could have been Elvis's father—and, who can say, might have entertained thoughts of being Elvis's father-in-law when his daughter Lynda Bird visited him on a film set during the mid-'60s. (Compared with George Hamilton, whom she had recently been dating, Elvis may not have looked like such a bad match.) Jimmy Carter, who was a fan and visited with Elvis backstage after an Atlanta concert in 1973, could have been his prissy older brother; and in an act worthy of Carter's scapegrace brother Billy, Elvis called the president in 1977 seeking assistance for a friend in trouble with the IRS (Carter politely fobbed him off).

Above all, there is Bill Clinton, for whom Elvis was practically an honorary family member and would one day serve as a campaign prop. Virginia Kelley, Clinton's mother, harbored an enthusiasm for Elvis of near-tabloid intensity. She kept a bust of the King in her dining room and owned a puka-shell necklace once worn by Elvis: "Sometimes I can still smell Elvis's Brut cologne coming from the porous shells."[47] Knowing how much Elvis meant to her, Clinton rushed to the phone when he heard of his death to relay the news himself.[48] Fifteen years later the Elvis connection was underlined not once but twice: when Clinton donned sunglasses and took up his tenor sax to perform a respectable "Heartbreak Hotel" on *Arsenio* and then, six weeks later, when Al Gore began his speech accepting the nomination as Clinton's running mate with the words, "I've been dreaming of this moment since I was a kid growing up in Tennessee: that one day I'd have the chance to come here to Madison Square Garden and be the warm-up act for Elvis."

The young Clinton may have met JFK, but he never met Elvis. Nor did any of the other presidents while in office. Only Nixon did, which is as it should be. He and Elvis were soul mates of a sort—far-fetched though that sounds—and in some strange way they may even have recognized this themselves. Elvis, for all his lack of interest in politics and his Hollywood-bred cynicism about human nature, steadily professed his belief in Nixon's innocence during Watergate. Making this faith all the more notable was his view of Spiro Agnew, whom Elvis had encountered in Palm Springs three weeks before the Oval Office meeting and presented with a pair of gold-plated .45-caliber pistols "I want my goddamn guns back,"[49] Elvis complained when corruption charges forced Agnew's resignation in 1973. No such plaint was heard concerning Agnew's superior, not even when he resigned a year later. Indeed, Elvis called Nixon when he was hospitalized after returning to San Clemente. Nixon reciprocated in August 1975, telephoning his wishes for a speedy recovery (the call was such a surprise, it actually seemed to give Elvis a little boost). After his death, Nixon paid Elvis as high a compliment as he could offer, noting that Presley "had the power over people's imaginations that would [have] enable[d] him to attain high office."[50]

It is each man's overwhelming sense of social isolation, his being an emotional prisoner—Nixon of his own awkwardness and insecurity, Elvis of his astounding popularity and fame—that makes their meeting so fitting, that gives it such a happy glow in memory: for those fifteen minutes, at least, each man could bear the burden of his uncomfortableness in the presence of one who understood what it meant to carry such a weight. Yes, they both appreciated "how difficult it is to play Las Vegas." Self is a prison we all must endure, and fame a prison for any who experience it in an age of mass communication. But who has more punishingly experienced the one than Richard Nixon, and the other than Elvis Presley? Each was trapped in a success of his own making, a success each simultaneously loathed and required. "I watch my audiences and I listen to them," Elvis once said. "I know that we're all getting something out of our system, but none of us knows what it is."[51] If Elvis's tragedy was never to be able to know what it was he and his audiences were getting out of their system, Nixon's was that he was never able to get *anything* out of his system, period. Each man was so radically apart, so disjunct—but Nixon even more so. At least for Elvis there was the consolation that this is in the nature of stardom (what is the close-up but apartness exalted, made socially attractive, and, quite literally, applauded?). Nixon had no such solace, for in a democracy, apartness in a leader amounts to a kind of self-indictment, an implicit acknowledgment of executive inadequacy: that he is not one of the people. That he could reach the highest office in the land despite such a handicap makes Richard Nixon's achievement all the more remarkable. It also makes the rest of his life—who he was rather than what he became—seem all the more tragic. In that tragedy one finds the profoundest, as well as the most moving, connection with Elvis. This is why it is so breathtakingly right that Nixon should have been the only president to have met Elvis in the Oval Office. For of no other president can it be said that, in his deepest, truest self, he was the words of Elvis made flesh, his every gesture and unscripted remark so nakedly crying out, "I feel so lonely, I could die." Even in the Heartbreak Hotel of darkness—no, there especially—one meets the man's sad, absorbing singularity. There above all, solitary and not a little baffled, Nixon's the one.

Dustin Hoffman and Robert Redford

9

ALL THE PRESIDENT'S MEN

■■■■■■■■■■■■■■■■■■■■■■■■■■■■■■■■

"What are scenarios?" says Winifrede.
"They are an art form," says the Abbess of Crewe, "based on facts. A good scenario
is a garble. A bad one is a bungle. They need not be plausible, only hypnotic, like all
good art." MURIEL SPARK, *The Abbess of Crewe*

It would make a funny Goddamn movie. H. R. HALDEMAN, TO RICHARD NIXON, ON
THE WATERGATE BREAK-IN, JUNE 22, 1972

Richard Nixon and Elvis Presley had something else in common:
they were both recording artists. Elvis had all those gold records,
and Nixon—however inadvertent his artistry—had the great and
awful reel-to-reel culmination of his career. Watergate was an
event (or, rather, congeries of events) driven and defined by the
slow-grinding turn of audiotape. The wiretapping of reporters and
National Security Council staffers in 1969 set the Nixon administration on the road of illegality. Watergate derived its name from
the site of the break-ins to install eavesdropping devices at Demo-

cratic National Committee headquarters in 1972. And there was the decisive, determining act in his downfall, Nixon's taping of himself and his associates.

The fallout when the public learned the particulars of the first two enterprises shook his presidency, but it was the taping system that drove him from the White House. For without the tapes, it would have come down to Nixon's word against John Dean's, the president's denial of guilt against his opponents' lack of proof, his immovable object against their constitutionally resistible force. Such a situation would have guaranteed an ugly, stalemated second term—but however diminished in authority, Nixon surely would not have been impeached or forced to resign. The great imponderable of Nixon's presidency isn't how events would have played out had he burned the tapes (destroying evidence *is* a crime, after all). It's how they would have played out had he not put in a taping system.

People forget that it wasn't until February 1971 that Nixon had recording devices installed (two months earlier, and history would now have his meeting with Elvis in audio vérité). Nor do they generally realize he inherited an Oval Office taping system installed by Lyndon Johnson, one technologically superior to his, and had had it removed. Franklin Roosevelt had been the first chief executive to record himself, though neither he nor Dwight Eisenhower, the next president to do so, taped more than a few conversations. John Kennedy recorded some 262 hours of meetings and phone calls, and Lyndon Johnson approximately 9,500 conversations on 643 hours of tape.

Johnson loved gadgets almost as much as he loved power. In the White House alone, besides the taping system, there was his Oval Office news center, with its three-screen television console and pair of news tickers, a telephone with forty-two lines, and the multi-nozzle, high-pressure shower in his bathroom. His successor's first morning as president, the shower nearly knocked him over, and he promptly had it replaced. The other items fared no better. Richard Nixon, who loathed gadgetry of any sort (as one subordinate put it, "He has trouble making a ballpoint pen work"), had declared his intention to get rid of the television and news tickers even before his inauguration, and the number of lines on the Oval Office telephone was reduced by thirty-eight.[1] And when a week after the election Nixon learned from Johnson of the existence of the tape recorders, he ordered Bob Finch, "Get them out of here."[2]

Nixon's distaste for surreptitious taping had less to do with any moral qualms than it did with galling firsthand experience. He knew that Johnson had had the FBI bug his campaign plane the previous fall and, according to Henry Kissinger, "was convinced that wiretapping had been a key weapon in the Kennedy arsenal during the campaign of 1960."[3] Still, it wasn't as if the idea completely lacked appeal. Fifteen years before, a visitor remarked on Nixon's "wistfully" commenting "that he'd love to slip a secret recording gadget in the President's office, to capture some of those warm, offhand, great-hearted things the Man [Eisenhower] says, play 'em back, then get them press-released."[4]

Folksiness and calculation so balletically commingled is unmistakably Nixon. When he reversed his original decision about a White House taping system, it was calculation that dominated his thinking. He was increasingly aware of the need to verify that his administration's foreign policy initiatives were his doing rather than Kissinger's. And while he could not have foreseen the ordeal of Watergate when it did develop, he considered the tapes his trump card. "I had always wondered about the taping equipment," he confided to Haldeman on April 25, 1973, "but I'm damn glad we have it, aren't you?"[5]

More important, however, was a reminder from Johnson about how useful he had found Oval Office tapes in writing his memoirs. That argument carried particular weight with Nixon. "From the very beginning," he later wrote in *RN*, "I had decided that my administration would be the best chronicled in history."[6] This sounds like standard Nixon rhetoric: impressive, inflated, essentially meaningless (what auditing body might validate a presidency's claim of being "best chronicled"?). This was one case, though, where he really did mean what he said, for by serving history, he thought he might best serve his own interests, too.

There is nothing more un-American (that crucial word in the Nixon vocabulary) than "history." Yet it was history that obsessed him. Hungry for its recognition, he wanted not just to appear in its pages but to dominate them. When Richard Nixon looked into the mirror, it wasn't a Herblock cartoon he saw; it was the image of a statesman: a craftier Disraeli, a mightier Metternich. According to Harry Truman's derisive formulation, "A statesman is just a dead politician." No wonder he and Nixon repelled each other. A statesman is a dead politician who *mattered*—who continues to matter—or so Nixon believed . . . no, so Nixon knew. A statesman belongs to history: the big-time, the major leagues, the place where no competitor could best him. For Nixon, someone who made a fetish of pointing out the example of Lot's wife and never looking back (Henry Kissinger was by no means the sole beneficiary of this advice), history wasn't about the past: it was about the future. So he installed the machinery to make the recordings he could one day cite to prove his greatness, which would detail his decision making and be the centerpiece of a presidential archive that would awe historians with an unmatched immediacy and comprehensiveness. This restless man who sprang from the most deracinated region in the most traditionless nation on earth would have his roots planted—magnificently, inextricably—in history's record.

That's what he had envisioned. What he got was the "smoking gun" tape, which would force him from the White House. It was his obsession with history that ruined him and mocked him, too. For the Nixon Library isn't the depository of those tapes, or of his administration's documents. It is instead a kind of Potemkin village for posterity. "The only presidential library run without taxpayer dollars," the library proclaims, leaving unsaid the reason why: Congress didn't trust Nixon with the records of his own presidency. Rather than a monument to Nixon's reputation, the library became its mausoleum: history's revenge on a man without history.

Yet if the tapes were part of Nixon's strategy to shape how he would be seen in the future, they also betrayed a lifetime spent trying not to be seen in the present. From the beginning, his deepest desire had been to be simultaneously renowned and anonymous, a man lionized by millions even as he was truly known by none. Now there was no way even Nixon, a man with so impressive a track record of doing the impossible, could square two such diametrically opposed urges; and their irreconcilability had become plain to everyone (Nixon excepted) long before the existence of an Oval Office taping system was revealed.

It was the tapes that finally, grotesquely, put paid to this wish to have things both ways. There is an almost eerie sense in which the White House taping system functions as a metaphor for a life spent in the pursuit of opacity yet withal so disconcertingly transparent. And now, thanks to the recording apparatus, transparent not just in his public moments but in his private moments as well. There he was, the inner Nixon, warts and so much worse, just waiting to be played over and over again by not only historians but any tourist who might wander into the National Archives.

This is the single most fascinating thing about this endlessly fascinating man: an utter inability to mask his inner self—let alone the restlessness of its motivations and needs—alongside a resolute unwillingness to acknowledge that inner self's existence. Nixon's life was "The Emperor's New Clothes" as psychodrama, his nakedness emotional rather than sartorial. Even on the tapes, where he could assume only history—his future friend and protector—would be there to judge him, he conveys a sense of stumbling in his own person, going against his own grain, and in multiple directions. He will sound elevated and statesmanlike one minute, then profane and posturing the next. Nowhere is more clearly borne out the truth of Kennedy's cutting remark to John Kenneth Galbraith about Nixon's always needing to think about who he is and what a strain that must be. Listening to the tapes is an exhausting experience, and the notoriously poor quality of the audio is the least of it.

A fugitive sense of self could also be a source of strength, however. It allowed Richard Nixon to mean many different things to many different voters. It provided a context—or, perhaps one should say, the lack of a context and the constriction context can bring—for his many comebacks and reconfigurations. To put this another way, Nixon had a unique capacity among U.S. presidents for constructing narratives around himself as he presented for public inspection all those "new Nixons."

Partly, this had to do with sheer longevity. Every political candidate has a product to sell; it's just that Nixon sold himself for so long he ended up doing it so many different ways. "Do you realize," Hugh Sidey remembers Theodore White saying with wonderment at the 1984 Democratic convention, "I have spent the greatest portion of my adult life writing about Richard Nixon?"[7] In one way or another, Nixon figured in every postwar presidential race until 1980: himself on the ticket in five of them and trying to get on the ticket in another (1964); as a source of partisan controversy, with the Hiss case, in 1948; and, in 1976, as the albatross around Gerald Ford's pardon-granting neck. Then for nearly two decades, he was simultaneously America's great elder statesman (Nixon's view) or its political Flying Dutchman. Either way, he was playing a public role as had no ex-president since Teddy Roosevelt.

Contributing even more than duration was Nixon's extraordinary capacity for self-dramatization. We have examined at length one demonstration of his theatrical flair, the Lincoln Memorial visit, but so many more offer themselves up for inspection. We've seen the young Nixon's talent for the stage ("I wouldn't have been surprised if, after college, he had gone to New York or Hollywood looking for a job as an actor," his college drama coach later recalled), and his mastery of stagecraft would stand him in good stead during his HUAC days, let alone during the fund crisis or in the kitchen with Khrushchev.[8] Six Crises could as easily have been called Six Star Turns. Even though it's an autobiography, no details are given of his life prior to the Hiss case. He presents himself throughout as if he were an actor whose only interest for the audience is when he's onstage playing a part.

In addition to the roles enacted there—relentless seeker of truth; calumnied candidate; circumspect Number Two; cool customer in Caracas; tough-guy defender of the West; embattled presidential candidate— we have seen several others: the poor boy who worked hard and lay awake at night listening to the sound of distant train whistles; the crusading moralist who brought down Alger Hiss and harried the corruption of the Truman administration; the selfless supply officer, a before-the-fact Mr. Roberts (the only one of his roles that wasn't self-assigned—and, as it happens, by far the most attractive); the decisive man of action; the blameless victim of the press; the Lincolnesque leader unfairly assailed. Of course, this protean quality is part of what transfixed his admirers, as well as what drove Nixon haters crazy: his ability to contain, or contaminate, multitudes.

Nixon was like a cat, except that by the time of Watergate, he'd used up all but the last of his multiple lives. Not that he knew this, of course. Again and again, one finds him seeking to take control of the situation, trying to make his version of events, his presentation of self, the generally accepted one. Between April 17, 1973, and his resignation sixteen months later, Watergate inspired no fewer than fifteen statements or open letters, eight press conferences, and four television appearances.[9] It did him no good. His repeated attempts to overtake events became "a pattern," as Richard Ben-Veniste and George Frampton Jr. of the Watergate Special Prosecutor's Office put it, as recognizable for its inept execution as its familiarity: "first the bombshell announcement, next the simplistic explanation (sometimes coupled with a salvo against an identifiable Nixon enemy), eventually the proof that the explanation was erroneous."[10] For once, Nixon didn't get to cast any roles in a drama he was participating in, least of all his own, and eventually there was little for him to do but wait and wonder. He was the one doing the wallowing in Watergate, not that he had any real say in the matter. According to William Safire, who had left the White House just before all hell broke loose, Nixon spent his final year in office "playing for time, hoping for a break, delaying as long as he could, always living with the knowledge that his guilt could be established, thinking he was watching a bad movie, and saying to himself, 'Wait—it'll get better,' as it got worse."[11]

So how *would* it all turn out? From at least April 30, 1973, on, with the resignations of Haldeman, Ehrlichman, Dean, and Attorney General Richard Kleindienst, this was the great, all-consuming question of Watergate. Waiting for a resolution became a kind of national blood sport, its drama so compelling that even the most apolitical found themselves caught up in it. The person surest of how the question would be answered was also the person who could least afford to have that answer revealed. "It's all over, Ron, do you know that?" Nixon told an uncomprehending Ziegler after his speech announcing the resignations. "'Well, it is. It's all over."[12] A truth too terrible to act upon, this realization simply compounded Nixon's agony. Having to ignore what he knew to be the inevitable outcome was just one more burden for him to labor under during the next sixteen excruciating months.

So *how* would it all turn out? Watergate resembled a serial, almost, in the way it played: the seemingly inexhaustible string of new developments, each one leading to another, previously unthinkable episode. It was, as Thomas Pynchon approvingly noted a "Byzantine daytime drama."[13] Every month Americans found themselves wondering all over again, this can't go on, can it? It could, it did, in the most protracted denouement in our political history. As an understandably vexed Nixon complained to Kissinger on May 16, 1973, "Christ there's something new every day, you know."[14]

Kissinger certainly did know—by that point everyone on Nixon's staff did. The problem for the White House had been, and continued to be, knowing in a larger sense. "For nine months," a still-incredulous John Connally could write two decades later, "from June 1972 to March 1973— nothing was done that did not deepen the problem."[15] Nixon's failure to control the situation grew out of his underlings' own difficulties. From the beginning, they barely had a clue. These were not criminal masterminds, after all, but distracted apparatchiks—something made painfully clear by the results of their labors. The myth of the cover-up being this carefully plotted, tightly controlled enterprise is just that, a myth. Instead, it was "instinctive and spontaneous," a fact pointed out by an observer as unsympathetic to the Nixon cause as Sam Ervin, chairman of the Senate Watergate committee.[16] No, the central fact about the conspiracy is its having been a series of increasingly desperate afterthoughts: contingent, thrown together, futile. Nixon and his people were reacting to events rather than directing them. "I kept getting information and feedback from three or four different sources," a perplexed Howard Baker told John Ehrlichman, on March 29, 1973, about "the vibration" he was getting from the White House, "and it suddenly dawned on me no one person's in charge."[17]

For much of the time, one person *had* been in charge—in theory— and that was Dean, whose job, in the novelist George V. Higgins's elegant summation, had been "to prevent the inevitable by delaying the immediate."[18] As Dean had reason to know better than anyone else, the cover-up was "ad hoc, developed in small reactions to the flurry of each day's events. There was not time to take stock of the whole case or to plan a careful defense in the meticulous fashion of trial lawyers. Instead, we found ourselves trying to hold a line where we could."[19] The remarkable thing isn't that the cover-up failed. It's that it worked for as long as it did.

Nixon and Haldeman and Ehrlichman were themselves floundering. As amply demonstrated in *The White House Transcripts* and Stanley Kutler's later gathering of Oval Office conversations, *Abuse of Power*, they were endlessly searching for the story—or even *a* story—of what had happened, of what was *happening*, and how best to present it to the public. These men, obsessed with control, were used to being able to take it for granted. To find it denied them, let alone denied under such threatening circumstances, was a profoundly unnerving experience. In their many protestations of bewilderment, they weren't being hypocritical or willfully obtuse. They were genuinely baffled by what was going on.

"I had limited information the entire time, and I was working from all kinds of misleading information from everybody else," Nixon lamented in 1991 to his aide (and putative Eckermann) Monica Crowley in 1991. "I'd make decisions based on what they were telling me, but they all had their own agendas and their own asses to protect. So imagine—I was in the middle of it, not knowing half the things that were going on. I knew what they told me, and I could deduce some things from that, but it was just a mess."[20]

That sounds like Nixon at his most self-servingly exculpatory. Still, no less an authority than Dean, who was not only best situated to refute Nixon on this matter but also had considerable cause to want to do so, concurs. "What is evident to me now," he acknowledged in 1975, "is that Nixon didn't have any damned idea of what was really happening. He couldn't remember from day to day what he was being told, who was involved, or how much they were involved. . . . He was told about it piecemeal, in passing remarks, and he never did get all the necessary details in his head to understand its meaning."[21]

There is a certain aptness in Watergate's central figure having been so confused about what exactly was, or was not, going on. Nixon's confusion reflected the nature of the whole affair. Other than the arrest of the burglars, there was no one trigger event, no sudden breaking of the story, as was the case, say, with Iran-Contra and Attorney General Meese's bombshell announcement. "Watergate" is such a convenient umbrella term, one tends to forget just how many, and diverse, are the elements it comprises: not just the break-in and cover-up, but also the Huston Plan, Nixon's tax difficulties, the enemies list, CREEP's fund-raising practices, Donald Segretti's dirty tricks, the break-in at Daniel Ellsberg's psychiatrist's office, and the other activities of the White House Plumbers Unit—and that doesn't include the ITT scandal or Agnew's resignation.

In retrospect, what's miraculous isn't that an American public long weary of matters political came to follow Watergate so closely—it's that they were able to follow it at all. As William Goldman remarked of his assignment adapting *All the President's Men* for the screen, "Forget, for now, trying to make a screenplay; I was struggling just trying to get the events straight."[22] Nixon could have sympathized. Even with three years to reflect on what had befallen him, he could confess to an aide in 1977 after seeing a day-by-day flow chart of Watergate events, "You know, this is the first time I've really understood everything that happened."[23]

As an exercise in narrative construction, the matrix of scandal, political tragedy, and human interest that came to be known under the general heading of "Watergate" has no rival in our history. There was so much it encompassed, from outrages of the gravest constitutional significance to personal peccadilloes of the utmost triviality, and it went on for such an extended period of time. Nonetheless, the need to make sense of the inherently senseless soon found itself met, and met spectacularly. In that fact, one confronts a fundamental paradox that underlies all the very extensive literature on the subject. The cover-up, the most significant part of the scandal, is always referred to as "unraveling." Yet what the public experienced was these many diverse events coming together with the facture of plot, the cincture of narrative.

This point cannot be emphasized too strongly. The arc of the story was what people found so compelling at the time, as well as what proved ultimately fatal for the Nixon presidency. For all practical purposes, Watergate was as much about the creation of a saga as it was about the creation of a cover-up. The cover-up, haphazardly improvised as the conspirators bumbled along, proved all too implausible. The saga, though, was a thing of beauty and craft: from the first drafts appearing in the *Washington Post* and *Los Angeles Times* to its final definitive redactions in Bob Woodward and Carl Bernstein's *All the President's Men* and Goldman's brilliantly constructed (and even more brilliantly elided) screenplay.

The April 30 resignations had made plain to even the dullest observer that something remarkable was going on, a fact underscored during the second half of May and first half of June by the Senate Watergate Committee hearings. Still, exactly *what* that something consisted of remained murky. The key event in making sense of the narrative was Dean's 245-page opening statement, the reading of which took up his entire first day of testimony. The statement gave a shape and coherence to the whole sprawling mess and did so before tens of millions of rapt television viewers. "Plot," in the sense of conspiracy, was ceding priority to "plot," in the sense of story, and this had enormous consequences. (It's a tribute to Dean's storytelling abilities that he could so successfully structure the narrative even as he unveiled such new plot lines as the Huston Plan and the enemies list.)

Regardless of whether one viewed the former White House counsel as a now-contrite sinner blowing the whistle on high-level corruption (*Meet John Dean?*) or as an ass-covering snitch (*All About Dean?*), the high drama of his five days of testimony was undeniable. Nixon's own people recognized the power of Dean's star turn—not for nothing did Charles Wright, the president's constitutional lawyer, dub the material he assembled to discredit the testimony *Golden Boy*.[24] The one person oblivious to the excitement, seemingly the only one in the entire country, was Wright's client. "I just learned it that they—you know, they carried Dean on three networks for five days straight," or so Nixon told Ziegler—on July 11, nearly two weeks after his nemesis had concluded testifying.[25]

Yet who better than Nixon to understand the kind of impact that might be generated by an opportunity like the one presented Dean? He knew firsthand that when politics and scandal couple before the camera, it can produce high drama—and advance careers. The first televised congressional hearing was the Hiss-Chambers confrontation of August 25, 1948. Four years later there was the Checkers speech, all of which makes the more striking his disparagement of the Senate hearings. Not the least of Nixon's many Watergate miscalculations was his complete failure to reckon with the response the hearings would get from the public. The tapes frequently record him announcing the dulling effect the broadcasts would have on viewers. Nixon was especially dismissive of Ervin, ignoring the appeal to viewers of life imitating art in the form of a flesh-and-blood Seab Cooley. During the Army-McCarthy telecasts, Nixon had explained his failure to watch the hearings with the disdainful comment, "I prefer professionals to amateur actors."[26] That attitude was still on display twenty years later. "Let me tell you," he said to his newly named White House counsel Fred Buzhardt, "they're going to find that they're going to lose their audiences with that stuff. People will be looking for late, late shows."[27]

He couldn't have been more wrong, and nowhere did the Ervin Committee attract a more devoted following than in the movie community, a place where people had a professional interest in vivid characters, outlandish events, and a riveting story. François Truffaut was but one among many devoted viewers in Hollywood (though he had an additional incentive: watching the telecasts helped improve his English). "The big thing now is obviously Watergate," he wrote a friend after watching Dean's testimony. "Even if one didn't completely understand it, it was absolutely fascinating and I read every word about it in the *Los Angeles Times*."[28] The French filmmaker spoke for many, including the screenwriters Paul and Leonard Schrader. Often joined by the director Brian De Palma, they would rise religiously at 6 A.M. to watch each day's telecast.*[29]

Dean's blueprint of the various "White House horrors" resembled a lawyer's brief in its dispassionate laying out of detail. In effect, Dean's statement *was* a lawyer's brief, an obvious attempt to reduce the amount of time he would have to serve behind bars. Whatever color there was in the story, and it was considerable, he carefully deflected from himself. So the Porsche-driving rake who had been the Nixon White House's leading roué made sure to locate his adoring blond bride in a camera-ready position behind him and look sedately professorial in tortoiseshell glasses as he used what Nixon called his "hypnotic monotone" to underscore an image of detached lawyerliness.[30] But where John Dean was trying to make himself look as colorless as possible and emphasize his subsidiary role in the scandal, there was an entire class of Watergate participants eagerly playing up their own role, a group whose daily job just so happened to consist of constructing colorful, plausible narratives: newspaper reporters.

This was another reason Hollywood people responded so keenly to what was going on in Washington. Who better to appreciate the emerging narrative? Once they'd gotten the story straight, Watergate felt familiar to most Americans. They instinctively knew the plot—crusading good-guy underdogs vs. bad-guy boss—and easily recognized the genre

*As it happens, Hollywood was present (almost) the night of the fatal break-in. E. Howard Hunt found himself sharing an elevator in the Watergate Hotel with Alain Delon, who was in Washington filming a thriller in which he played a CIA contract killer. Earlier that evening, Hunt's fellow burglar Frank Sturgis had run into Burt Lancaster ("He's about my favorite actor," Sturgis happily declared. "My wife says I look like him"). Lancaster was Delon's costar in the film *Scorpio*. Nixon had it screened at Camp David on September 22, 1973. Jim Hougan, *Secret Agenda: Watergate, Deep Throat and the CIA* (New York: Random House, 1984), pp. 191, 183.

it belonged to. The scandal was shaping up as, and soon enough would prove to be, the ultimate newspaper movie.

"Even before the outcome of Watergate was clear," Robert Redford told Dean on a visit to the set of *All the President's Men*, "I thought there was a good story in how Carl and Bob were investigating Watergate."[31] It was just a natural. The Old Hollywood's history of infatuation with newspapering met the New Hollywood's detestation of Nixon. Best of all, there was the way the story mirrored—no, demonstrated—the film industry's most cherished beliefs about how happy endings can coexist with, and even triumph over, unhappy realities. The very title *All the President's Men*, while ostensibly alluding to Robert Penn Warren's *All the King's Men* (and, at an additional remove, "Humpty Dumpty"), also communicates a sense of great and powerful forces arrayed against its author heroes. As Alan J. Pakula, the film's director, told one of Woodward and Bernstein's *Post* colleagues, "It's inherent in the story of Carl and Bob that they have become a kind of contemporary myth" whose experience affirms "that American belief that a person or small group can with perseverance and hard work and obsessiveness take on a far more powerful, impersonal body and win—if they have truth on their side."[32]

Omit the last nine words, and the small group Pakula was describing could have been the Nixon White House. (Omit just the last seven, and it could have been a film crew.) The most celebrated shot in *All the President's Men* is the slow reverse zoom showing Redford (as Woodward) and Dustin Hoffman (as Bernstein) sifting through records at the Library of Congress. As the camera draws back to offer a God's-eye view from beneath the library dome, the two reporters get lost among the crowd of researchers in the reading room. The viewer is meant to see the loneliness of Woodward and Bernstein's search for the truth. In fact, the shot might equally well suggest how Woodward and Bernstein were simply two among many pursuing the truth behind Watergate: initially, not many reporters, to be sure, but numerous FBI agents, Justice Department officials, and, later, Senate investigators, members of the Special Prosecutor's Office, and House Judiciary staffers. "How can we enforce a subpoena?" mused a Judiciary member, California Democrat Don Edwards, of Nixon's power. "He has a bigger army than we do."[33] Well, he did and he didn't. Thanks to Defense Secretary James Schlesinger's sub rosa directive to the Joint Chiefs during Nixon's final days that any orders from the White House must be cleared through him, even the U.S. Army wasn't necessarily going to do what its commander in chief told it to. And in more immediate terms, the forces he could command were sadly limited.

Just as the idea of the cover-up as this tightly coiled, carefully plotted enterprise is a myth, so is the image of Nixon immured at 1600 Pennsylvania Avenue in full *Festung* mode.

The White House found itself besieged, all right, but very far from being a fortress. It was the limitations on his power that had gotten Nixon into all this trouble in the first place. Almost from his first day in office, he'd railed in memos to Haldeman of his essential powerlessness. Finally, unable to stop leaks through regular channels, he had approved formation of the Plumbers Unit. Unable to get the CIA to fend off the FBI, he'd had to rely on Dean's improvising a cover-up. Once the legacy of the Plumbers and the cover-up exploded on him, Nixon saw his powers shrink to almost ludicrous proportions. By the spring of 1974, he had all of seven attorneys working on his defense (some of them only part-time), versus 150 employed by the Congress and Special Prosecutor's Office.[34] Archibald Cox mentioned once to Ben-Veniste that he'd been losing sleep worrying about Nixon. "If you think you had a bad night," his deputy reassured him, "imagine what kind of nights he's having."[35] Ben-Veniste was closer to the truth than Representative Edwards. "I *am* the president" was a standard line in the repertoire of every Nixon impersonator, and he was the nation's chief executive all right. Yet from the Saturday Night Massacre on, that fact meant less and less. The most powerful man in the world had ceased to be Dr. Mabuse, capable of making the entire planet do his bidding, and become the Wizard of Oz, hid behind a curtain bearing an increasingly tattered presidential seal.

No one thought so at the time, of course, or at least no one outside the White House. The idea of presidential impotence simply wouldn't play. Hadn't Arthur Schlesinger Jr. just published *The Imperial Presidency*? To have believed that a president was anything other than all-powerful would have been even more subversive than believing this particular president was anything other than all-malevolent. True, Americans did increasingly come to hold the latter belief. But that was the logical obverse of an idea that during Watergate played very well indeed: the ever more widely held belief in the press as public protector.

That that view should become a central tenet of Watergate iconography was all but inevitable. If Dean's statement was what made sense of Watergate for most people, the newspaper version was what made it sexy. Judge John Sirica, he of the Draconian make-them-talk sentencing, was the crucial figure in cracking the cover-up; and Congress, with the power to impeach and remove from office, was Nixon's deadliest opponent. Yet the workings of the judicial and legislative branches were grounded in abstractions and alien to the concerns of the average person—unlike the newspaper that landed by the door every morning or the evening news watched after dinner. Reporters finding out the facts and sharing them with the public—doing their exciting, unrarefied job of blowing the whistle and getting at the truth—this was something the average person not only could relate to but thrill to. Throw in a little cloak-and-dagger (Deep Throat, late-night meetings in parking garages), and the whole thing became irresistible. Ask anyone, they'd tell you: it was the press, and Woodward and Bernstein, above all, who broke open Watergate.

The scandal's very nature worked to the advantage of the press. It wasn't about signing treaties or waging wars or campaigning for votes. It was about testifying, issuing denials, admitting guilt: events whose meanings were not readily discernible to even the most sophisticated news consumer. The fact that so much of Watergate (the Senate hearings, Nixon's press conferences and speeches, the House Judiciary sessions) took place for the benefit of the camera—or tape recorder—obviously aided the press. So much more, though, went unseen or needed explaining, and this benefited the press even more. Watergate cried out for analysis and explanation, for text and explication rather than image and presentation, as, say, the "living-room war" fought in Vietnam had not. When has the word "transcript" seemed so momentous, when have organization charts been gazed at so raptly? Watergate was *the* newspaper story, one that the networks were notably ill suited to deal with. Even during television's greatest moment during Watergate, the Ervin hearings, viewers needed print to distill what they had seen in such vast, unmediated detail the day before.

Never before had print journalism mattered so much, not even in the days before radio and television—yet neither has it mattered anywhere near as much since. Watergate was the glorious last stand of print. Small wonder that newspaper people loved Watergate so and kept dwelling on it long after the fact, celebrating for all it was worth (and perhaps rather more) the story behind the story: the meta-story, *their* story. The press has never lacked for self-esteem, but Watergate raised its traditional self-regard to a new plane. As Katharine Graham, writing with considerable restraint, noted a quarter century after the break-in, "The press after Watergate had to guard against the romantic tendency to picture itself in the role of a heroic and beleaguered champion, defending all virtues against overwhelming odds."[36]

Yet such concerns lay many years, and thousands of editions, in the future. By the time Nixon flew off in disgrace to San Clemente, the legend of the heroic and indispensable role of the press in foiling him was the accepted version of what had happened—a version whose acceptance was helped not a little by the phenomenal response to *All the President's Men*. Published three months before Nixon's resignation, it became the fastest-selling nonfiction hardcover in U.S. history.[37] Two years later the film version was released and went on to become the fifth highest-grossing movie of 1976, win four Academy Awards, and, in the opinion of no less an authority than Ronald Reagan, ensure Gerald Ford's defeat at the hands of Jimmy Carter.[38] Even so well informed an observer as the *New Republic*'s John Osborne, probably the most respected and influential reporter covering the Nixon White House, could describe Woodward and Bernstein as having done more than "any officials did to expose the evil of Watergate and drive Richard Nixon from the presidency."[39]

The *Post* and, to a lesser extent, the *Los Angeles Times* were indeed courageous in their pursuit of the story in the fall and winter following the break-in. Woodward and Bernstein did labor heroically and met with spectacular success. The press acquitted itself admirably. It did not, however, do the hard work of getting Nixon out of office. As a rueful John Dean conceded (the rue coming perhaps because he and Woodward and Bernstein shared the same literary agent), "If the Nixon White House had had to contend only with *The Washington Post*, the Watergate cover-up probably would have succeeded."[40] Sirica still would have sentenced without the *Post*, James McCord still would have written his letter hinting at the existence of a cover-up . . . and, no sooner, and surely no later, the final outcome would have remained the same. Even the many revelations that appeared in the press more often than not came courtesy of Justice Department or FBI leaks. As Edward Jay Epstein has convincingly argued, "It was not the press which exposed Watergate; it was agencies of government itself."[41] The press was the cavalry that rode to glory while the infantry slogged the way to victory.

The point isn't the legend's truth but its persuasiveness. As a newspaper editor tells James Stewart's U.S. senator in *The Man Who Shot Liberty Valance* (1962), "This is the West, sir, and when fact becomes legend, we print the legend!" (Earlier in the movie, Stewart is heard to describe "an honest newspaper" as "the best textbook in the world." Understandably, perhaps, this is one of the very few John Ford films of the Sound Era that Nixon did not have screened while president.) The legend of the crusading reporter was what Nixon had bumped up against, and one of the reasons he could never get ahead on Watergate was precisely this: once it became apparent that the newspapers really were on to something, people instinctively felt they already knew the story—and Nixon had to be the bad guy. Just as Watergate was the logical moral climax to Nixon's career—the man who saw enemies in so many places finally became one to himself—so, too, was it the logical Hollywood climax. The good guys—or at least the likable guys—were the ones behind the typewriters. To Richard Nixon's dark, dour, disingenuous matter, the Hollywood image of journalists was absolute, annihilating antimatter. "Butch Cassidy and the Sundance Kid Bring Down the Government" was the way one *Post* editor described the first draft of Goldman's screenplay, which isn't far off as a description of the final version, either.[42] In real life, as onscreen, how could the public *not* go for something like that?

Yet as can't-miss as the subject might have seemed at first, the actual storytelling mechanics made it, "at best, a dubious project," as Goldman wearily recalls. How *do* you keep an audience interested when "people were sick to fucking death of Watergate" (Goldman again) and literally everyone in the country knows how your story turns out?[43] You do it in three ways—all of them, as it happens, further conducing to the journalistic legend of Watergate. First, you turn the reporters into cops in drag and make a movie that's a police procedural by other means (Warner Bros.' ad campaign billed *All the President's Men* as "The most devastating detective story of the century"). Second, you emphasize mood and technique for all they're worth. Third, you play up the least-familiar part of the story and those particulars they don't already know: the newsroom part of the story and the figure of Deep Throat.

These stratagems proved highly successful. More than just a commercial triumph, *All the President's Men* is a very good film: gripping, meticulous, miraculously lucid. In fact, Goldman may have understood the thrust of the narrative better than even Woodward and Bernstein did. "Follow the money," that definitive Watergate phrase, appears nowhere in the book or the reporters' *Post* stories: it's Goldman's coinage. Yet there's a nagging hollowness to *All the President's Men* that upon repeated viewings becomes all too apparent. Considered apart from the now-distant headlines that inspired its making, the film stands as a rather peculiar achievement: a thriller in which nothing actually happens, a political film devoid of issues or ideology, a marvel of sustained tension in which no true dramatic resolution occurs.

Just as the Senate is the real star of that classic Old Testament Washington movie *Advise and Consent,* so is the real star of this greatest of New Testament Washington movies Watergate itself. It's because *All the Presi-*

dent's Men is so obsessed with skirting the edges of the much-larger narrative that inspires it, trying at once to remain true to the Watergate scenario while also keeping it fresh, that the film remains so much smaller and less resonant than that story. This is one instance where the truth is incalculably stranger than the fiction, and none of its many virtues can keep *All the President's Men* from suffering the consequences.

Enlarging the human element would have been the one obvious way to make the film more artistically ambitious. Yet this model of scrupulous, intelligent filmmaking is as uninterested in the development of its characters—of either good guys or bad—as the cheapest exploitation quickie. With the bad guys, in fact, that approach isn't even an option. The title would seem to imply that *All the President's Men* is about Nixon's side. It's not, of course, and one of Goldman's canniest inspirations is to consistently represent administration figures obliquely: in news footage, in television interviews, or on the telephone. Besides helping simplify what is already a very complicated story, this device makes the Nixon people appear all the more distant and unnatural. It also creates a larger sense of isolation around Woodward and Bernstein as they pursue the story. It's as if they're moving in a vacuum and chasing phantoms. Not only does this make their task seem all the more difficult; it imparts a vague spookiness to their labors (a contributing factor in the film's impressive ability to maintain its atmosphere of low-key paranoia). Even for legends in the making, it's hard to know if you're on to something when the people you're chasing seem to consist only of disembodied voices and video images.

The film is just as put off by the inner workings of its heroes. That axiomatic Hollywood principle, action is character, takes a strange turn in *All the President's Men*. To underscore the objectivity and professionalism of its twin protagonists, action becomes the absence of character. The Woodward and Bernstein we get to see—so dutiful, so *serious*—are Butch and Sundance gelded. From the filmmakers' point of view, they need to be to cast into even greater relief the bad guys' badness. It wasn't as if Woodward and Bernstein and the *Post* were out to get the president and his men (the party line of Nixon apologists). They don't bring down the government out of any animus. They don't even do it because it's fun. (The only person in *All the President's Men* who ever seems to be enjoying himself is Jason Robards's Ben Bradlee.) They bring down the government because it's a great story, and getting great stories is their job.

To be sure, Woodward and Bernstein aren't exactly presented as angels ("I guess I just don't have the sense for the jugular that you guys do," a fellow reporter tells them, and she does not mean it as a compliment). But their very colorlessness emphasizes that their personalities aren't what matters. What's important is their role as America's recording angels. As so hard-headed—if also partisan—an observer as Bradlee tells them, "Nothing's riding on this except the First Amendment to the Constitution, freedom of the press, and maybe the future of the country. Not that any of that matters." When it's put like that, who's to complain? Such sins as Woodward and Bernstein may commit in the course of getting the story are justified by later events. Dwelling on the *whys* of their actions holds no interest for *All the President's Men*, unlike the *whats* and *hows*.

Even bearing in mind what's at stake, there's something just a little *too* intense about this pair. Everything about Woodward and Bernstein in their screen incarnation is so straight and sober, one comes to pine for at least their Mutt & Jeff mismatchedness being played for a laugh. Instead, Redford's Nordic cool gets mixed with Hoffman's Jewish heat to keep things at an unwavering room temperature. Poor Hoffman, even with that gorgeous mane of hair and nifty crooked grin, can only hint at what a rascal his character could be in real life. And it's not as if Redford, far from the most expressive of male stars, needs help in toning down a characterization. Just in case, though, the movie has him driving around in a Volvo—and an early model Volvo, at that—whereas in the book Woodward owns a Karmann Ghia. It's a strange state of affairs when a film's most raffish character, Bradlee, is a Boston Brahmin. Not surprisingly, Robards walks away with the picture. "I hate trusting anybody," he growls at one point, revealing a gleam of the old newspaper movie spirit.

The film simultaneously trades on the image its genre predecessors established and turns the image on its head. On the one hand, we automatically know who the good guys are: the reporters and editors (who else?), with their loosened ties and rolled-up sleeves, set against the Nixonites' telltale button-down neatness. Yet these journalist good guys are light-years away from the lovable-scoundrel reporters of *Front Page* lore: Woodstein and their *Post* colleagues have much more in common with John Dean than they do with Hildy Johnson. Nor can Woodward's derring-do with Deep Throat disguise the fact that Xerox machines and computer printouts advance the story far more than does Hal Holbrook's unnamed White House official.

The heroism of newspapering remains as irresistible on the screen as ever, but it's abstract in *All the President's Men* as it never was in earlier newspaper movies. What's so charismatic about journalism here isn't its practitioners (Bradlee once again excepted); it's the *idea* of journalism.

The epitome of that idea is the film's justly famed opening: a close-up of corrasable bond paper, its overpowering whiteness implicitly contrasted with the darkness in the DNC offices during the burglary we will soon see reenacted. The shot produces an almost unbearable tension. It's held for eighteen seconds before there's any action, a keystroke, its impact resounding like cannon fire. The stage is thus set for the rest of the movie, which ends with actual cannon fire (at Nixon's second inaugural), and a series of close-ups of major Watergate stories being printed out on a teletype machine. What we will see for the next two hours and nineteen minutes is a display of the power of the word and, something utterly new to the newspaper movie genre, the *purity* of the word.

The creamy whiteness of that paper is so different in appearance from the six-ply copy journalists used in the days of hot type. But it's intended to presage the glaring illumination of the *Post* newsroom. Along with Deep Throat's beloved parking garages, it's one of the film's two moral centers: each of them large, open, windowless spaces that are almost unnerving in the artificial brightness of their lighting. These are the outposts of truth under the Nixon dispensation. If anything, the fluorescent-lit newsroom is the scarier looking of the two. It's like a laboratory or hospital ward, always shiny and vaguely antiseptic, almost comically unlike the dim and dusty proto-noir newsrooms of the "Sweetheart, get me rewrite" era. It speaks volumes that the filmmakers made such a fetish of the site, constructing a $450,000 replica on two soundstages at the Warner Bros. studio in Burbank, its wastebaskets filled with tons of trash taken from the actual *Post* newsroom. *All the President's Men* belongs in this setting not just because it's the site of most of the events in the film. It belongs there because so right thinking and public spirited and ultimately unimaginative a work seems utterly at home in such a setting.

The lidless-eye look of the *Post* newsroom lends *All the President's Men* a slightly sinister cast, as if it had started out as a science-fiction movie, then lost its nerve. Such remorseless illumination communicated a far different meaning at the time. Conveying reassurance and fidelity to the truth, it answered the equally unrelieved darkness directed against the Republic by the president and his henchmen. What better antidote for paranoia than glare? It deprives enemies of any shadows to lurk in. And make no mistake, paranoia runs like a black thread throughout the movies of this period. Its unremitting shine makes the *Post* newsroom a lonely island of light in the dark sea of seventies cinema, an environment in which the Nixon administration's mania for suspicion and conspiracy found its mirror image.

When Paul Schrader predicted at the beginning of 1972 that "as the current political mood hardens, filmgoers and filmmakers will find the *film noir* of the late Forties increasingly attractive," even he could not have imagined how accurate he would be.[44] The decade's great contribution to Hollywood genre, the paranoid thriller was noir minus the sex and with substantially more darkness. It drew on the cynicism and sense of menace of the earlier genre, as well as the topicality and shock value of the many disillusioning events culminating in Watergate to proffer an all too plausible vision of modern life as something dominated by a global cartel of conspiracy.

The paranoid thriller also resembles noir in its being so grounded in style and attitude. Each genre owes as much to look as formula, ensuring its influence extended well beyond its own wary confines. In countless ways, the paranoid thriller helped color a generation and more of film-makers who for too many years had seen sinister manipulation revealed and their worst suspicions confirmed. As Warren Beatty tells Paula Prentiss in *The Parallax View*, "People were crazy for any kind of explanation then. Every time you turned around, some nut was knocking off one of the best men in the country." (It was Pakula's direction of *The Parallax View* that convinced Redford to hire him for *All the President's Men*.) The explanation Hollywood offered was presented in such films as *The Anderson Tapes* (1971), *The Day of the Dolphin* (1973), *The Conversation* (1974), *The Killer Elite* (1975), *The Domino Principle* (1977), and *The Fury* (1978).

Obsessed with surveillance and filled with foreboding, the paranoid thriller was *Rear Window* (1954) writ large, taking the film grammar of Hitchcockian suspense and applying it to the many dark lessons learned from the Kennedy assassination, CIA black ops, and, of course, Watergate. It also applied that grammar to *us*, for the first principle of the genre was that our own people were now the ones to watch out for. A decade earlier, in *The Manchurian Candidate*, the film we can now see as the genre's prototype, it was still them out to get us (in this case, a Sino-Soviet them)—and in the end, however bloodily and barely, the good guys *do* win. The idea of a foreign-controlled political candidate and high-level assassin working in tandem seemed so preposterous, it needed to be played as satire. Contrast that with *Executive Action* (1973), in which the idea of an actual plot to assassinate an actual president is played as docudrama.

In its reception as in its very existence, an *Executive Action* is unthinkable at any other moment in Hollywood history. Its portrayal of a group of wealthy Americans arranging to have John F. Kennedy murdered is so matter-of-fact one might think they were planning a Rotary luncheon. Of course, eighteen years later there was *JFK*, a film not exactly circumspect in its positing of conspiratorial threats to the Republic. Yet *JFK* and *Executive Action* differ in two key respects, and they underscore the singularity of the era in which the latter was made. Where even Oliver Stone felt compelled to include an idealist hero (Kevin Costner's Jim Garrison) as a sop to audience sentiment, *Executive Action* disdains the need for any hero—that would have been too much of a concession to optimism. An utterly undistinguished work, *Executive Action* received nothing like the attention *JFK* did. It came and went almost unnoticed, a far cry from Stone's film, which generated huge controversy, attracted a wide audience, and (forgetting for the moment its many mendacities) is an impressive demonstration of filmmaking technique. One of the few people who did see *Executive Action* was Richard Nixon. He had it screened at Camp David in January 1974, and the thought of him watching in the dark while preparations are made to assassinate his great rival is not a little unnerving.

As with the dog in the night in the Sherlock Holmes story, what's most noteworthy about *Executive Action* is the absence of any barking. Remember, what we have here is a film that doesn't just suggest but takes for granted that less than a decade before, a right-wing conspiracy murdered the president of the United States. And this was no avant-garde fringe enterprise like, say, Barbara Garson's off-Broadway play *MacBird* (1966) with its portrayal of Lyndon Johnson conniving in the assassination. "A major motion picture"—produced by National General, starring Burt Lancaster and Robert Ryan, with a script by Dalton Trumbo—this was the kind of mainstream, if provocative, film that could get made in Hollywood during much of the 1970s without raising a stir.

"Do you know the expression 'Let sleeping dogs lie,' Mrs. Mulwray?" Jack Nicholson's J.J. Gittes asks Faye Dunaway in *Chinatown*, the paranoid thriller's greatest achievement. "I *have* to know," she replies, speaking for all her fellow inhabitants of the genre. Unproven paranoia is inherently dissatisfying, and proof was never hard to come by in the paranoid thriller. It's what determines which is crazy, the world or the paranoid's response to it, and that was where Watergate came in. For all those who might look askance at some of the more perfervid displays of suspicion in the paranoid thriller, the genre's enthusiasts had a one-word rebuttal happily available to them. Watergate was conclusive evidence, as if by then any were needed, that paranoids most certainly do have enemies.*

For that reason alone, *All the President's Men* holds a special place among these titles. No other work rivals it for so forthrightly bringing together the paranoid thriller's real-life roots with their reimagining on-screen. This braiding together of fact and fear achieves a kind of apotheosis just before the movie ends. The teletype machines' triumphal clatter just minutes away, *All the President's Men* finally, furiously, surrenders to its underlying paranoia. It's the payoff scene for all those inconclusive meetings between Woodward and Deep Throat. Nixon's evildoing, the reporter learns from his source, "involves the entire U.S. intelligence community: FBI, the CIA, Justice. . . . It leads everywhere. Get out your notebook. There's more. Your lives are in danger." As it happens, Deep Throat grossly exaggerates—not that the actual situation wasn't dire enough—but small matter. Dialogue like that, by placing the audience within the reassuringly familiar confines of the paranoid thriller, helped make miraculous sense of the arcana of Watergate. Just as Watergate helped shape the paranoid thriller, so did the paranoid thriller help shape the public response to Watergate. It was just like all these other narratives of the day, albeit that much more satisfying for being based (more or less) on the truth.

If anything, that *All the President's Men* springs from actual events makes classifying the film as a paranoid thriller slightly problematic. The constraints of truth deny it the wilder shores of hypothesis and dread. This is a considerable shortcoming from a canonical viewpoint, one somewhat compensated for by the profession of the film's heroes. The exploits of Woodward and Bernstein and their colleagues proved a godsend to the paranoid thriller. The genre's embrace of journalists was more than just a rekindling of Hollywood's age-old crush on the newshound. Conspiracies are by definition secret. *Somebody* has to reveal their existence to the audience or else there's no story. Who better than journalists: isn't the most trustworthy person in an environment where no one in authority can be trusted someone whose job it is to question authority? Professional skeptics and truth seekers with immediate access to

*There's even a certain rough justice at work in Nixon and Watergate looming so large in the genre, since he helped pave the way for it. As Carlos Clarens notes, conspiracy films offer "a left-wing paranoia of autocracy to balance the fifties right-wing paranoia of a Communist conspiracy." Carlos Clarens, *Crime Movies: From Griffith to* The Godfather *and Beyond* (New York: W. W. Norton, 1980), p. 329.

vehicles of publicity, journalists provide the genre with an ideal audience surrogate.

Reporters become almost as ubiquitous in seventies movies as they are in thirties movies. Usually they're print journalists, but sometimes they work for television, as Jane Fonda and Michael Douglas do in *The China Syndrome* (1979), or even radio, as Geraldine Chaplin does in *Nashville*. The latter film, while by no means a thriller, enthusiastically partakes of the genre's sense of free-floating anxiety and ends in an assassination. Chaplin shares the paranoid-thriller journalist's essential apartness—that is, the unwillingness to believe what everyone else does—but in this case she's such a fish out of water her character cuts an absurd figure. This makes her all but unique among journalists in seventies movies. Far more typical is Beatty's Joe Frady (a hip Joe Friday?) in *The Parallax View*. There's nothing funny about a reporter so dedicated to getting the story behind the shooting of a U.S. senator and the subsequent deaths of all the killing's witnesses that he ends up murdered himself. The Beatty character might be taken as a reductio ad absurdum of the paranoid reporter. He sees all laypersons as suspect; only a journalist, as fellow member of the priesthood of paranoia, can be trusted. Hence the sole person he confides in is his editor, who, of course, gets murdered, too.

The press's role as deus ex machina of the paranoid thriller receives clearest expression in *Three Days of the Condor* (1975), with Robert Redford, of all people, relying on the fourth estate as a kind of witness-protection program. Redford finds out that there's a rogue CIA operation at work, and it has already seen to the killing of seven agency operatives. Redford seems set to become victim number eight—except he's foreseen that eventuality. He walks CIA man Cliff Robertson to the door of the *New York Times* and announces he's told the paper everything he knows. This is the '70s, though, not the '30s, so Robertson coolly inquires, "How do you know they'll print it?" It's paranoid-thriller id (they're *all* out to get you) vs. paranoid-thriller superego (the press shall make you free).

The genre sends the message that no one's any good anymore—save for the occasional conspiracy theorist or investigative reporter. However unconsciously, the paranoid thriller embodies a populist nihilism that takes Capra's darkest elements—there's a reason his work enjoyed such a revival in the early '70s—and brings them to their illogically logical conclusions. The roots of the paranoid thriller extend well beyond Capra (from whom they got their crabbed idealism) and Hitchcock (from whom they got their storytelling wherewithal), going all the way back to the seventeenth century. It's the Puritan jeremiad, with its bleak and absolute condemnation of contemporary society, that begat the paranoid thriller.*

Visually as well as geographically, the sun-blasted ochers and Spanish Revival luxe of *Chinatown* are far removed from the world of Cotton Mather and Jonathan Edwards. Yet in Huston's Noah Cross (a name that needs only three syllables to subvert both halves of the Judeo-Christian heritage), they could find not just their worst nightmare but also a kind of soul mate from the other side. Blandly declaring to Nicholson, "You see, Mr. Gitz [*sic*], most people never have to face the fact at the right time and the right place they're capable of anything," he announces a truth altogether alien to post-Enlightenment America—and axiomatic to any sinner in, or out of, the hands of an angry God.

With his patriarchal face and a voice that could turn water into wine (which, in a sense, is what Cross does), Huston states these words with an ex cathedra authority. They are at once thrilling and awful—and their utterance constitutes a decisive moment in Hollywood history. It expressed a point of view the movies—that plushest, most accommodating, and complaisant engine of American secular religion—had previously refused to acknowledge, let alone explore. Now Hollywood did—and with a vengeance. How could it not, with a president in the White House who was demonstrating that the truth of Noah Cross's words applied even to the highest office in the land.

Chinatown ends with what may be the grimmest denouement of any major American film: its heroine shot to death, its hero disillusioned, an innocent child returned to the arms of her incestuous father/grandfather. One reason *All the President's Men* remains somewhat outside the paranoid-thriller tradition is the simple fact that it has a happy ending (that it's a happy ending based on actual events makes its genre affiliation that much more dubious). The loosening of moral strictures that Hollywood experienced in the '60s first affected the portrayal of sex, language, and violence. Once the viewer had become accustomed to nudity, obscenity, and gore, a more pernicious immorality began to exhibit itself: virtue was no longer assured of being rewarded.

*In fairness to Hollywood, one should note that the masterpiece of the paranoid style (in any medium), Pynchon's *Gravity's Rainbow*, was published three weeks before Sirica sentenced the Watergate burglars. Among many other things, Pynchon's novel draws a direct line between New England Puritanism and conspiracy theory. It also takes its concluding epigraph ("What?") from none other than Richard Nixon, and one "Richard M. Zhubb" (yes, he's who you think he is) makes a fleeting appearance. Clearly, something was in the air back then, a scent inebriate as well as acrid.

The paranoid thriller was merely the tip of an increasingly dark iceberg. Now recognized for the monstrosity it was, the calculated naïveté and inflexible uplift of Golden Age Hollywood began to give way to an equally grotesque, equally mechanical pessimism. "American movies didn't 'grow up,'" Pauline Kael wrote at the time; "they did a flipover from their prolonged age of innocence to this age of corruption."[45] What Ethan Mordden describes as the very sixties "air of distrusting one's own distrust" now ceases to apply.[46] Again and again in seventies films, distrust becomes a form of reassurance, the one thing a character can have faith in. Popular genres and subgenres sprang up to accommodate this. Revenge movies, such as *Walking Tall* (1973) and *Death Wish* (1974), and disaster movies—such as *The Poseidon Adventure* (1972), *The Towering Inferno* (1974), and *Earthquake* (1974)—shared in, and propagated, the elemental distrust and despair of the paranoid thriller. There was even a paranoid thriller that doubled as a disaster movie, *The Cassandra Crossing* (1976).

Again and again one encounters that favorite seventies formula: a nameless, faceless them vs. a bewildered, powerless us. The bad guys are as bad as ever—if anything, they're worse—it's that they're no longer guys. "You may think you know what you're dealing with," Huston warns Nicholson in *Chinatown*, "but believe me, you don't." How could he, when what he was dealing with—what *we* were dealing with—was less individual evil than that of organizations, processes, the system itself. The fact that Hollywood had had such a long and expert history of providing memorable villains lent a special horror to evil divorced from recognizable human form. (The phenomenon wasn't restricted to theaters: "CREEP" always sounded so much more ominous than "Mitchell," "Magruder," "Liddy," "Hunt.") Wasn't that part of the appeal of *The Godfather*, and why audiences could warm so to Marlon Brando's title character? The feudal authority of a Vito Corleone, a hands-on don in a day and age of full deniability, is an explicit anachronism. Heinous as his acts might be, they offered the paradoxically reassuring sight of evil emanating from an individual rather than a condition. Don Vito represented crime (and control) with a human face.

Among the reasons *Godfather II* had nowhere near the commercial success its predecessor did was that Francis Ford Coppola chose to explore this very theme of the corporatization of evil and did so at the expense of any romanticizing of his protagonist-villain. Cool, calculating, businesslike, Al Pacino's Michael Corleone could have fit right in at CREEP (didn't Nixon frequently point out the GOP's need to appeal to ethnics?). The only possible drawbacks would have been his being a Dartmouth man and possessing far too much intelligence to have fit in at the committee. If only Michael Corleone had been the one overseeing the break-in then Nixon would never have had to . . . Well, some things don't bear dwelling on.

Even as it epitomized the blandness of evil in contemporary U.S. society, Watergate signally contributed to a view of that society as, if not outright evil, then deeply flawed and suspect. The United States has engaged in all too many blameworthy actions, but during Watergate an administration's excesses for once weren't directed against Vietnamese or Chileans or Iranians but against *us*. As such, the break-in and cover-up provided an almost too perfect climax to the string of disillusionments that ran from Dallas to Saigon to Tehran. To be sure, the loss of American innocence in the 1970s would have occurred with or without Watergate. Instead, what Watergate uniquely bequeathed was a cultural legacy whose burden we continue to labor under. Cynicism about Washington waxes and wanes, as does faith in the national might and right (less than four years after the release of the Iranian hostages, once again it was morning in America). Yet that deeper, more amorphous sense of distrust and doubt that Watergate inspired has never quite left us. As a genre, the paranoid thriller lurches on, sustained by the suspicion-soaked likes of *Blow Out* (1981), *Conspiracy Theory* (1997), and *Enemy of the State* (1998)— that draws on the tradition.* The paranoid-thriller *sensibility*, however, thrives. Having percolated throughout the culture, its influence is evident in places as diverse as the novels of Don DeLillo, the militia camps of the mountain West, and the editorial page of the *Wall Street Journal.* What is *The Truman Show* (1998) but the ultimate surveillance movie?

Nowhere is this post-Watergate sense of things more widely disseminated than via the stripped-down doominess of such television series as *Twin Peaks, Millennium,* and *The X-Files.* A trio of characters in the latter are known as "the Lone Gunmen" (they even briefly got their own series), their name a very overt *hommage* to that lodestone of all latter-day conspiracy theorists, the Kennedy assassination. Yet *The X-Files'* spiritual locus resides a decade later: the series could justifiably bear the title *Twisting Slowly, Slowly, in the Wind,* so indebted is it to mid-'70s atmospherics. Mulder and Scully have a lot more in common with Woodward and Bern-

---

Enemy of the State boasts a sly nod to Coppola's *The Conversation.* In the former, Gene Hackman plays a surveillance expert named Harry Caul (he figures prominently in chapter 11). In the latter, he plays a disgruntled former National Security Administration employee. His two-decades-old NSA ID photo shows Hackman as Caul.

stein than they do with Captain Kirk and Mr. Spock or even Napoleon Solo and Ilya Kuryakin. "I was about 15 or 16 years old when Watergate happened," Chris Carter, the series' creator has said, "and I think that ruined me forever as far as my belief in institutions and in authority and agendas of government."[47] It's a ruination passed on to millions of Generation Xers.

Not even Richard Nixon found himself immune to the disquieting effects of what he had helped wrought. The man who'd made a career out of getting his enemies before they could get him soon found himself worrying about their trying to get him all over again—and in a very Watergate way. The first time Charles Colson saw Nixon after the White House taping system had been disclosed, he half-jokingly asked, "Mr. President, is our conversation being recorded?" The question transformed what had been a convivial visit into an interrogation. Nixon "sat upright in his chair, the smile gone, a flash of fear in his face," Colson writes. "What do you mean, 'recorded'? Who would do that to us?" The idea Colson had brought up in jest seemed deadly serious to Nixon. Furthermore, the thrust of the question had been that Nixon himself would be doing any taping. The president took it to mean the exact opposite: *he* was the one being taped (by Jaworski? the Secret Service?). "The tapes," he explained, trying to regain control of the situation, "they were all Haldeman's idea. Stupid, just stupid."[48] The taping *was* stupid, but Nixon's realizing that had come too late, far too late, and so the age of surveillance claimed another victim, one in a singular position to understand its depredations.

Not much more than a year after the Watergate break-in, he was reduced to believing that even as holder of the highest office in the land— the most exposed office in the land?—he was vulnerable. "After the first death," Dylan Thomas wrote, "there is no other." After the first suspicion, there is *every* other, and fifteen years later, his situation considerably changed, Nixon could find himself casually remarking to an interviewer, "Everybody tapped phones, you know. It's going on right now."[49] That "you know" suggests a jaunty tone—but take the truest believer in the existence of black helicopters and he or she would be hard pressed to better the dead, dire certainty of "It's going on right now." The patron saint of the paranoid thriller, as one might say, had taken to seeking sanctuary at his own shrine.

Nixon always said no one in his administration profited from Watergate. He was right about that—unless you count book deals or the payoffs to Howard Hunt—but as was so often the case with Nixon, in observing the letter of the law (barely), he was ignoring its spirit (completely). So much of the reason Watergate retains the imaginative power it does—an imaginative power that Teapot Dome, say, never had—is that the break-in and cover-up and all that followed were never about money and always about power: power and belief. "Follow the money"? "Follow the fear" should be the scandal's motto.

In those three words, one sees how Watergate lives on: not in the ineffective campaign-finance laws it produced or as the bestower of "gate" as an all-purpose suffix for scandal, certainly not in the several shelves of self-serving memoirs it generated. Rather, the most lasting achievement of the scandal lies in the making of fact into fiction and back into fact (if enough people believe strongly enough in something, it becomes a *kind* of fact, doesn't it?). Three decades and more later, Watergate's capacity to intertwine truth and fantasy, fact and legend, still takes one's breath away. There are the fantastical truths and truthful fantasies we have looked at above—of a carefully organized cover-up, of Watergate's having "unraveled," of the press single-handedly doing that unraveling—along with such others as those of secret CIA involvement or the "John Dean did it" scenario of the 1991 best-seller *Silent Coup* or the numerous identifications of Deep Throat, any or all of which might someday (it is not inconceivable) turn out to be true. The transcendent fantasy, though, the only one that still truly matters in the daily life of the Republic, is this comprehensive vision of a world wherein our lives are governed by the workings of machinery kept concealed from all but a select few. The events of September 11, 2001, at once seemed to validate such a view—and beggar it.

Just as politics is the art of the possible, so was Watergate the art of the unthinkable. The indisputable facts of break-in and cover-up metamorphosed into a set of certain peculiarly resonant fantasies of hidden control that in turn metamorphosed into a way of seeing the world that, regardless of whether the facts ultimately justify it or not, has become an ineradicable part of that world. Even in the safest neighborhood in the best-policed community, it's a rare American who doesn't feel at least a little anxious in a parking garage late at night. The legend of Watergate flourishes long after the events that gave rise to it have lost their meaning to any American of less than middle age.

Or perhaps "Print the legend" should take pride of place over following either money or fear as the scandal's first commandment. Indeed, the power of the legend soon reached all the way to where, in a sense, it had all started: the White House. Barely two and a half years after Nixon's resignation ended the scandal's active phase, there took place an otherwise unremarked intersection of political reality and Watergate stagecraft that conveys almost too neatly just how hard it had become to separate where the reality of what had happened ended and where perception began. When Jimmy Carter watched his first film in the White House Theater, all of two days after taking office, it was *All the President's Men.* How could it not have been? Carter was no fool: what more dramatic way to underscore the difference between the administration that now was and the administration that had been. "I felt strange," Carter wrote in his diary after the screening, "occupying the same living quarters and position of responsibility as Richard Nixon."[50] Presumably, he wouldn't have felt quite so strange had he just seen *Sunrise at Campobello* (1960) or *PT 109.*

Would Carter have felt that much stranger, though, had he known he'd just been enjoying in those same living quarters one of his tainted predecessor's favorite leisure-time activities? For as much as Hollywood loved Watergate, Richard Nixon loved Hollywood that much more. Not only were its scenarios ones he could wholeheartedly give himself up to; they made no pretense about being the truth. It was better that way—for all concerned.

Richard Nixon and Jack Benny, San Clemente, August 27, 1972

10

NIXON AT THE MOVIES

■■■■■■■■■■■■■■■■■■■■■■■■■■■■■■■■■■

It's a way he likes to relax. NIXON PRESS SECRETARY RON ZIEGLER, ON HIS BOSS'S
MOVIEGOING

Oh, we sat through some real lemons. Bebe would fall asleep. Mother and Tricia
would tiptoe out, but Daddy would stick with it. JULIE NIXON EISENHOWER[1]

Toward the end of *The Senator Was Indiscreet* (1947), William Powell's title character suddenly gets cold feet about seeking the highest office in the land. Then he's reminded that among the attractions the presidency has to offer is "a projection room right in the White House: run your own pictures!" Learning this, Powell reconsiders. "Lana Turner?" he asks. "All of them," he's told. Powell decides the Oval Office may be worth the effort after all (Henry Kissinger would have understood).

Richard Nixon, who saw but two Lana Turner films while president—*The Postman Always Rings Twice* (1946) and *The Bad and the Beautiful* (1952)[2]—needed no such inducement to seek the presidency. This did not mean that once he reached the White House he wasted much time in taking advantage of this particular presidential perquisite. On January 22, 1969, only his third night in the White House, Nixon screened his first movie there, *The Shoes of the Fisherman* (1968). He didn't even wait for the weekend: January 22 was a Wednesday.

Over the course of the next sixty-seven months at the White House, Camp David, Key Biscayne, San Clemente, and a handful of other locations, Nixon would spend well over five hundred nights at the movies. As Watergate worsened, in 1973, he averaged almost two and a half a week. Of course, few other Americans had the opportunity to screen movies for themselves: at the White House Theater, in the family room at Camp David, at Key Biscayne, or San Clemente in the living room with a projector and screen set up for the occasion. Even fewer "can usually get any picture you want," as Rose Mary Woods explained in a memo to the Nixon family written shortly before they saw *The Shoes of the Fisherman*.[3] Remember, too, this was in the days before VCRs became a mass consumer item; one can hardly imagine the bliss a movie fan might have felt three decades ago presented with Nixon's situation. What movie fan *wouldn't* find him- or herself sitting in the dark as often as Nixon did?

Lest we forget, though, he wasn't just the nation's first film buff but also leader of the Free World. The two positions do not balance out—the call of office rather obviously takes precedence—a fact that Nixon was uncomfortably aware of. He made a point of qualifying his remarks about *Chisum* with a (false) disclaimer that "I don't see too many movies"; and in *RN* writes, "Our favorite relaxation after dinner at Camp David or in Florida or California was to watch a movie,"[4] pointedly omitting the White House, where, in fact, he saw many movies, too. Nixon's awareness that all this moviegoing might call into question how hard he worked— something he took inordinate pride in—makes all the more striking that he should have nonetheless managed to spend so much time watching movies.

For all that the president was unusual in how much he saw, he was much less so in what he saw. Nixon saw at least two of the five top-grossing films for each of the years between 1968 and 1973; more often, he saw three. From 1968, he saw *Funny Girl*, *The Odd Couple*, and *Bullitt*, while missing *2001: A Space Odyssey* and *Romeo and Juliet*. From 1969, *Butch Cassidy and the Sundance Kid* and *Hello, Dolly!*, but not *The Love Bug*, *Midnight Cowboy*, or (surprise) *Easy Rider*. From 1970, *Love Story*, *Airport*, and *Patton*, but not *The Aristocats* or *M*A*S*H* (Julie saw it, though, at the White House Theater, in May 1971). From 1971, *Fiddler on the Roof*, *The French*

Connection, and *Diamonds Are Forever*, but not *Billy Jack* or *Summer of '42*. (*Diamonds*' female lead was Jill St. John, Kissinger's putative girlfriend; did Nixon and Rebozo, with whom he saw it on April 27, 1972, make comments?) From 1972, *The Godfather*, *The Poseidon Adventure*, and *What's Up, Doc?*, but neither *Deliverance* nor *Jeremiah Johnson*. From 1973, *The Sting*, *American Graffiti*, and *The Way We Were*, but not *The Exorcist* or *Papillon*.

That first movie he saw at the White House, *The Shoes of the Fisherman*, did not do anywhere nearly as well at the box office as any of those films. Still, it would prove in several respects indicative of the many presidential nights at the movies to come. Like the average filmgoer, Richard Nixon saw most of his movies on Friday and Saturday nights. But that didn't mean this most disciplined of men ruled out the luxury of an occasional weeknight movie—*Topkapi*, for example, on May 12, 1970, a Tuesday; or, also a Tuesday, *The Sons of Katie Elder* (1965) on October 24, 1972—or let stand in the way of his seeing a movie something so mundane as learning of the Watergate break-in (that night he watched *The Notorious Landlady*, a 1962 Kim Novak comedy), winning reelection (the Wednesday after his landslide victory over George McGovern, Nixon saw *Victory at Sea* in the White House Theater), or the Saturday Night Massacre (having plunged the nation into "what may be," as John Chancellor said on NBC, "the most serious constitutional crisis in its history," Nixon went off to watch *The Searching Wind*, a 1946 drama starring Robert Young). The presidency would mean neither an interruption nor a reduction in Nixon's pursuing his love of the movies; rather, it allowed him to wallow in watching.

The Shoes of the Fisherman not only offered an odd presage of détente (the plot concerns a Russian-born pope, played by Anthony Quinn, trying to stave off World War III); it gives a fair sense of the fundamental fact of Nixon's movie watching: how cheerfully undiscriminating his preferences were. Pauline Kael, in her *New Yorker* review, called *The Shoes of the Fisherman* 1968's "worst-written, worst-directed, worst-photographed, and worst-edited *big* picture."[5] It's not that Nixon necessarily lacked taste in what he saw. As we know, Nixon's favorite director was John Ford, and he would occasionally see such a relatively recherché classic as *Lady from Shanghai* (1947). He was also partial to Oscar winners, and among the films he had screened while president were eighteen of the twenty-four Best Picture winners between 1950 and 1973. The point is that Nixon was open to pretty much anything. He just loved watching a movie, even a piece of bloated hackwork like *The Shoes of the Fisherman*. "I've never seen a play I didn't like," he'd told the *New York Times* in 1963.[6] That's how he felt about the movies, too. It's quite winning, actually, this eagerness on Nixon's part to be entertained, winning precisely because the idea of him wanting to enjoy himself and believe in the make-believe up there on the screen is so alien to our standard conception of the man. Yet from those 530 cinematic nights emerges a spectacle as fabulous as any in the 1,001 Arabian nights: the spectacle of a wide-eyed Richard Nixon.

The movies he saw were a happily magpie miscellany, as varied in genre and date as they were in quality. Consider what Nixon watched during January 1973: *Three Coins in the Fountain*, a 1954 romantic comedy about three American secretaries in Rome; Sam Peckinpah's 1962 Western, *Ride the High Country*; John Huston's 1941 classic, *The Maltese Falcon*; *Mary, Queen of Scots*, a 1971 biopic starring Vanessa Redgrave; George Stevens's 1943 comedy, *The More the Merrier*; Tony Richardson's Oscar-winning adaptation of *Tom Jones* (1963); and *This Gun for Hire*, the 1942 thriller that made Alan Ladd a star.

"My father is patient and loyal to a movie," Tricia Nixon told Allen Drury. "The rest of us keep saying let's go, come on, this is lousy, but he says no, let's wait a bit and maybe it will get better."[7] Her sister told William Safire, "No matter how terrible the first reel is, he always thinks it will get better. 'Give it a chance. . . . Wait—it'll get better.'"[8] It's a sentiment any movie fan can relate to. According to Paul Fisher, the White House projectionist, Nixon did little talking or eating during a movie.[9] He would *concentrate* on what was up there on the screen—it absorbed him. As he told an interviewer in 1980, "I've never gone to sleep in a movie, nor a play. Even as dull as they can be at times."[10] Those hours in the dark, even as dull as they can be at times, demonstrate an attachment to possibility, a pledge to promise: the possibility and promise that at any given moment something might happen up there on the screen to snare one's attention and repay the small amount of effort involved in sitting and looking. It doesn't even matter if the movie gets better: simply being there in the dark is enough.

Richard Nixon just loved going to the movies, and like any other devoted moviegoer, there were those movies he loved going to see even more than others. It's appropriate that *The Shoes of the Fisherman* inaugurated his presidential moviegoing, for Nixon was notably fond of blockbuster narratives and big-budget epics—films with sweep and splash—*movie* movies.

Certainly, his favorite movie qualified. It's widely assumed *Patton* was Nixon's most cherished film. Instead, that honor belongs to another 170-minute spectacular, one that Nixon also saw three times while president,

Around the World in 80 Days. "For some strange reason, he loved that movie," H. R. Haldeman noted in 1993, still bemused at how Nixon cherished the film version of Jules Verne's novel.[11] The reasons really aren't so strange. Mike Todd's extravaganza had lavish production values, gorgeous scenery, and dozens of stars in cameo roles. It had the further advantage of prestige, having won the 1956 Academy Award for Best Picture. Neither artistically venturesome nor emotionally demanding, it was just the sort of leisurely spectacle that Nixon delighted in. In his diary Haldeman relates how, on February 27, 1971, Nixon decided to celebrate John Connally's fifty-fourth birthday at Camp David with a screening of *Around the World.* "He was hysterical through it, as each scene was coming up, he'd say 'you're going to love this particular part,' or 'the scenery is just great, now watch this closely.' . . . He obviously has seen it time after time and knows the whole thing practically by heart."[12]

A less evident reason for *Around the World*'s appeal was its being such a billet-doux to the British empire. Nixon was very much a cinematic Anglophile, especially if—like the very Victorian *Around the World*—the movie had a historical setting. Not surprisingly, he was a fan of the later David Lean. He saw *The Bridge on the River Kwai* (1957) and *Ryan's Daughter* (1970) once, and *Lawrence of Arabia* (1962) and *Doctor Zhivago* (1965) twice. (The incongruity of Nixon's watching a depiction of Bolshevik triumph did not go unremarked. *Newsweek* reported that one guest got so exercised by the revolutionary scenes she walked out;[13] and Haldeman, who was also present, observed in his diary entry for April 20, 1969, "Strange to sit in a room with leader of free world and Commander in Chief of Armed Forces and the pictures of the Russian Revolution, Army overthrow, etc. We all had the same thought."[14])

In many ways, Fred Zinnemann's *A Man for All Seasons* (1966) qualifies as an ideal Nixon feature: British, prestigious (it won six Academy Awards, including Best Picture), historical, a biopic, a thinking-man's spectacular. Nixon saw it in May 1969—the projectionist at Camp David got the reels mixed up—and again in December 1973. That second screening, coming as it became increasingly plain that there was no escaping Watergate, suggests a more specific, and highly personal, attraction for Nixon in this film about a political leader suffering for his beliefs. How could he fail to regard Paul Scofield's More—statesman, lawyer, father of a spirited, intelligent daughter—as a forebear? As Nigel Davenport's Duke of Norfolk says to More, "We've *all* given in! Why must *you* stand out?" No bug-out option for *this* embattled man of conscience. Just as all the elitists and trendies in the sixteenth century wanted to give up on their Catholic faith and flee the church of their fathers, so did their twentieth-century counterparts want to betray their country and clear out of Vietnam—or, later, see a president driven from office. True, More's obduracy lost him his head; it also earned him a sainthood—and Scofield an Oscar. Alas, most viewers are likelier to see Nixon in Leo McKern's Thomas Cromwell: from beetling brow to grinding ambition, he is a beefier, Tudor Tricky Dick. Even his Heepish unction is Nixonian. "Sir Thomas, believe me— no, that's asking too much. But let me tell you all the same, you have no more sincere admirer than myself."

Nixon himself could have addressed that last sentence—and far more truthfully—to John Wayne, the star of two more titles he saw twice: *The Quiet Man*, John Ford's 1952 film about a retired boxer returning to the Irish village of his birth, and *Chisum*. As we know, the Duke was the president's favorite actor. For all that Wayne's politics contributed to Nixon's partiality, he liked movies too much to let purely ideological considerations determine his movie selection. Gregory Peck, with nineteen films the runner-up to Wayne as Nixon's most frequently watched star, was on the White House enemies list, as were Barbra Streisand, Steve McQueen, and Paul Newman (Nixon saw four films starring each). Nixon let neither Streisand's nor Newman's politics stand in the way of his seeing both *The Way We Were* and *The Sting* twice. Other well-known Democrats whose movies Nixon watched included Henry Fonda, twelve; Kirk Douglas, twelve; and Burt Lancaster, ten. (Douglas, at least, might be explained away as mistaken identity: Nixon, in a White House receiving line, greeted the actor as Danny Kaye.)[15]

Gender, far more than ideology, helped shape what Nixon watched: the highest-ranked actress is Audrey Hepburn, with nine films, and he saw only six films with Elizabeth Taylor or Ingrid Bergman, five with Katharine Hepburn or Grace Kelly, four with Bette Davis, three with Barbara Stanwyck or Marilyn Monroe. In art, as in life, women made him uncomfortable; and, not surprisingly for a man who liked action films, he preferred such masculine heroes as James Stewart (sixteen films) and Clint Eastwood (twelve).

Eastwood was the one contemporary star whose work Nixon relished. He appointed him to the National Council on the Arts in 1972 and in 1991 confided to a young associate, "I like Clint Eastwood."[16] Besides seeing *The Good, the Bad, and the Ugly* (1967) twice, he saw four other Westerns, *A Fistful of Dollars* (1964), *High Plains Drifter* (1973), *Hang 'Em High* (1968), *Joe Kidd* (1972); three *policiers*, *Dirty Harry* (1971), *Magnum Force* (1973), and *Coogan's Bluff* (1968); and a pair of World War II movies,

Where Eagles Dare (1968) and *Kelly's Heroes* (1970); as well Eastwood's directorial debut, the psychological thriller *Play Misty for Me* (1971), and his first (and last) singing role, *Paint Your Wagon* (1969).

With its Lerner and Loewe score and California Gold Rush setting, *Paint Your Wagon* was a Nixon three-fer, satisfying his love of Eastwood, Westerns, and musicals. In all, Nixon saw thirty-three musicals; and one of them, *Gigi* (1958), he saw twice. There were patriotic musicals (*Yankee Doodle Dandy*, 1942), sports musicals (*Damn Yankees*, 1958), nostalgic musicals (*By the Light of the Silvery Moon*, 1953), even Disney musicals (*The Happiest Millionaire*, 1967, starring none other than Fred MacMurray—Walter Neff sings).

In his 1963 *New York Times* interview, Nixon confided that he and Pat generally went to the theater or opera weekly. More often than not, what they saw was musicals. A list of facts about her boss that Rose Mary Woods compiled for the press in 1957 states that his favorite play was Rodgers and Hammerstein's *South Pacific* (1958) with *The King and I* (1956) a close second.[17] He saw their movie versions, a week apart in October 1972, as well as those of *Oklahoma!* (1955), *The Sound of Music* (1965), and one other Rodgers and Hammerstein production, *Flower Drum Song* (1961). That Nixon would favor Rodgers makes perfect sense—Rodgers had, after all, composed *Victory at Sea*. But Hammerstein's uplifting, irony-immune lyrics were, if anything, even closer to Nixon's heart. He found Hammerstein vastly more to his taste than the superbly suggestive brilliance of Lorenz Hart, Rodgers's previous lyricist. Nixon saw only one Rodgers and Hart musical, the little-known *Mississippi* (1935); and the main attraction may not have been Rodgers or Hart, but W.C. Fields, who played a riverboat captain in the film (while president, Nixon screened both *My Little Chickadee* [1940] and four Fields shorts).

Nixon had little trouble adjusting to the peculiar forms the musical began to take during the '60s. Scope was what he liked, and scope was what the musical began to provide. He saw *West Side Story* (1961)—the one movie he's recorded as having walked out on (according to Haldeman, the president "couldn't stand the propaganda"),[18] *Funny Girl*, *My Fair Lady* (1964), *Oliver!* (1968), *Hello, Dolly!*, and (ahem) *Camelot* (1967). Of the period's studio-swamping dreadnoughts, he missed only *Doctor Dolittle*.

Musicals could always be counted on to be safe, in subject matter as well as style. That assumption began to be put to the test. *Sweet Charity* (1969), which Nixon saw on January 3, 1970, not only starred Shirley MacLaine, an ardent feminist who would be a leading McGovern supporter; it was quite matter-of-fact in dealing with its heroine's being a prostitute. Far worse was another musical directed by Bob Fosse, *Cabaret* (1972). Nixon saw it on September 8, 1972, one of twenty films he managed to see in the eleven weeks between the Republican convention and Election Day. Clearly, Nixon felt he had little to fear from McGovern. Far more threatening was the "divine decadence" of Liza Minnelli and Joel Grey. Nor need the dubiety of the new musical be solely sexual in nature. *On a Clear Day You Can See Forever* (1970), which Nixon saw on September 11, 1970, finds a way to include a student demonstration (albeit in support of one of the less burning issues of the day, a professor's right to study reincarnation). Far more disconcerting, if only in retrospect, its plot hinges on Barbra Streisand's discovering that Yves Montand has been surreptitiously taping their psychiatric sessions together.

Musicals appealed to Nixon's escapist bent. That he had one, we must concede (no one without an escapist bent sits through *Around the World in 80 Days* more than once). Yet seriousness appealed to him, too; certainly, the appearance of it did. In the eyes of such an incessantly solemn man, it helped justify such an ostensibly frivolous activity as moviegoing. That side of Nixon responded to prestige-treatment adaptations like *War and Peace* (1956) and *The Brothers Karamazov* (1958), to each of which he devoted two separate nights of viewing. Seeing them was *purposeful* moviegoing. Nixon hardly ever read fiction—unlike movies, novels clearly *were* frivolous—but he made an exception for the Russian classics. At the end of his junior year in college, a professor had told him that until he'd read the nineteenth-century Russian masters, his "education would not be complete." No such call to seriousness and purpose Nixon could ignore and "that summer," as he recalled in *RN*, "I read little else."[19] It's an arresting image, that of this graceless young man seeking out—and, as he later acknowledged, being deeply moved by—these great and overwhelming works of the imagination.

As previously noted, it's easy to forget how much a product of the genteel tradition Nixon was: the boy with a quotation from Longfellow hanging over his bed; the music student who practiced away at his violin and piano; the Whittier High senior so sedulous at his Latin he was chosen to play Aeneas in a high school production of the *Aeneid*. The boy was the father to the man who found the time while president to sit through some episodes of Sir Kenneth Clark's *Civilisation* and who, despite a lifetime of political achievement, could wistfully write that his "two great—and still unfulfilled—ambitions" were "to direct a symphony orchestra and to play an organ in a cathedral."[20]

Not "desires," "ambitions": goals to be achieved, attainments to be reached, pursuits of the will rather than the heart. Culture, for someone of Nixon's background, was something to be taken seriously and worked at diligently, like doing chores or getting good grades. In essence, reading the right books and learning about the finer things was another form of getting good grades. What's so striking about Nixon's pursuit of *Bildung*, whether it be in reading Tolstoy and Dostoyevsky or wanting to wield a conductor's baton, is the sense of directedness on display: the aspect of practical application that underlay his cultural aspirations. That he reached a high degree of cultivation one cannot doubt—how many presidents over the past half century could identify who Aeneas was, let alone recite Virgil?—but the joyful wisdom it was not. There was an arduous quality to Nixon's cultivation, as there was not to John F. Kennedy's, the inevitable (inescapable) presidential comparison. As so often in the contrast between them, it was a case of the grind vs. the natural. But that was because Nixon had had to work at culture, to earn it. For Nixon, it was a tool; for JFK, a luxury. *His* cultivation was about as hard earned as his Pulitzer Prize had been. It had its origins as a trapping of power, a form of noblesse oblige. For Nixon, who was all oblige and no noblesse, cultivation was simply one more stamp in his copybook: another proof, like teeing off at Baltusrol, that the poor boy had made it.

"Camelot was the opium of the intellectuals," Garry Wills has written,[21] and anti-Camelot—the Nixon White House—was their cod-liver oil. No one would ever think to name a national center for the performing arts for Nixon. Yet his personal commitment to culture, leaden though it may have been, and so awkwardly worn, was that much more sincere, deeper even, than Kennedy's was. Where JFK could joke that he hadn't been sure what Pablo Casals played when he'd been invited to perform at the White House, Nixon knew the cellist's music well enough to complain to Haldeman that Casals's invitation (for which the Kennedys got such acclaim) came "forty years after his prime."[22] Where Nixon read Robert Blake's *Disraeli*, Kennedy's favorite book was Lord David Cecil's *The Young Melbourne*. (Nixon had the superior taste not just in biographers but prime ministers.) Worse, where Nixon nightly trudged through his histories and biographies upstairs at the White House—taking his reading seriously enough to seek Daniel Patrick Moynihan's "recommendations of the ten best political biographies and histories"[23]—Kennedy was famously enjoying (and drawing inspiration from?) the fiction of Ian Fleming. Making it look so easy, Kennedy could appear cultured with what was mostly just style. Making it look so hard, Nixon never could.

Clearly, he took his movies seriously. Nixon saw at least three movies one can imagine JFK going to see, too—and then ducking out of once the lights went down: Sidney Lumet's 1968 version of Chekhov's *The Sea Gull*, Olivier's *Richard III* (1955), and Nicol Williamson's *Hamlet* (1969). *The Sea Gull* was Nixon with another of his Russians. Far more intriguing are the other two selections. Surely, he must have realized that his crook-backed namesake had long been the favorite Shakespearean analog for Nixon detractors to cite. As for *Hamlet*, its Claudius is Anthony Hopkins. Might Nixon have experienced a premonitory start watching him then or, at a Key Biscayne screening two nights after the Watergate break-in, in *When Eight Bells Toll*, a 1971 adaptation of an Alistair MacLean best-seller? Chances are better for a shock of recognition during Hopkins's turn in *Young Winston* (1972), for at least he was playing another distinguished (if also duplicitous) twentieth-century statesman, David Lloyd George.

Edification had its place, but it was entertainment that prevailed in Nixon's moviegoing. It's important to note that he watched Chekhov and Shakespeare *and* that such films were not typical of what he watched. Sheer omnivorousness was the key ingredient in his moviegoing. The night before screening *The Sea Gull*, Nixon viewed *Seven Brides for Seven Brothers* (1954). The prior movie to *Richard III* was a Jackie Gleason comedy; and to *Hamlet*, a Gregory Peck Western. Nixon's eclecticism could reach high as well as go low. Mostly, it stayed firmly in the middle.

There was one thing, and one thing only, almost all the movies Nixon watched had in common: they were American or, to a far lesser extent, English. As he told his guests at a special campaign reception at San Clemente for entertainment celebrities on August 27, 1972: "I like my movies 'Made in Hollywood.'"[24] He saw only five foreign films while president. One of them, *The Sicilian Clan*, a 1969 French caper film with Jean Gabin, was simply a Hollywood picture by other means: 20th Century–Fox produced it. Two others boasted Hollywood stars: *Dead Run*, a 1961 spy spoof, with Peter Lawford; and *The Master Touch* (1972), starring Kirk Douglas. The final pair may be the most anomalous titles Nixon saw: *The Sky Above, the Mud Below*, a French-Belgian-Dutch coproduction about primitive tribes that won the 1961 Oscar for Best Feature Documentary, and the Marcello Mastroianni comedy *Divorce—Italian Style* (1961).

In all, Nixon saw nearly a hundred comedies, romantic comedies, and comic thrillers. He even saw a Woody Allen movie, *Take the Money and Run* (1969), notwithstanding its brief, unflattering glimpse of him, in newsreel footage, fishing with Eisenhower in 1952. Comedies were an excellent source of diversion, something Nixon needed more than the average moviegoer. Thus the weekend before announcing the mining of Haiphong harbor, which he later described as perhaps the hardest decision of his presidency, the second sentence in his diary entry was "We saw a good comedy with Bob Hope last night," *Critic's Choice* (1963).[25] It's hard to say which is more remarkable: that Nixon would choose to record such a fact at such a momentous occasion or that he'd consider an undistinguished comedy with Hope and Lucille Ball "good."

Then again, compared with some of the things Nixon watched, *Critic's Choice* might not have looked so bad. Nixon saw his share of classics—*Vertigo* (1958), *The Treasure of the Sierra Madre* (1948), *The Lady Eve* (1941), *Citizen Kane*, *The Grapes of Wrath*, *Some Like It Hot* (1959), *All About Eve* (1950)—but he saw even more movies that have been justifiably forgotten. It is one thing to watch famously bad films or outright debacles, such as *Cleopatra* (1963) or *Duel in the Sun* (1946) and quite another to see such unremarked-upon mediocrities as *The Bridge at Remagen* (1969), *What the Peeper Saw* (1972), *The Doctor Takes a Wife* (1940), *To the Ends of the Earth* (1948), *Lady Ice* (1973), *Twisted Nerve* (1968), *How to Commit Marriage* (1969), and *The Iron Petticoat* (1956). Spanning genres and decades, this list is united only by the fact that all the titles on it are movies hardly anyone would recognize—and for good reason. Yet Richard Nixon watched them all and, if his daughters are to be believed, with nary a complaint.

Not surprisingly, Nixon saw a number of political films, such as *Wilson* (about the twenty-eighth president, 1944), *Beau James* (about New York mayor Jimmy Walker, 1957), *Sunrise at Campobello* (about FDR's battle with polio), and *The Last Hurrah* (1958), John Ford's blearily overfond adaptation of Edwin O'Connor's novel. There's some piquancy in the thought of Nixon watching *The Chairman*, an undistinguished 1969 thriller about Gregory Peck infiltrating China to assassinate Mao, or *The Day of the Jackal* (1973), with its semi-documentary account of a very nearly successful assassination attempt on Charles de Gaulle.

Two political films from 1972 hit even closer to home. Nixon surely took a professional interest in *The Man*, a drama concerning the first black president of the United States (James Earl Jones). Writing in his diary, he termed it "interesting." What's off-putting about his response is that, rather than making any observations about race or the presidency, Nixon recorded that "what really struck me about it was the way that they had an American flag in the lapel of the Secretary of State—who was, of course, depicted as a very bad character."[26] Far worse, from Nixon's point of view, was *The Candidate*, with its decidedly jaundiced view of a California Senate campaign. Even though the film's title character, a liberal

Democrat modeled on U.S. Senator John Tunney, is portrayed as, at best, a puppet and, at worst, a fool, Nixon complained to Haldeman "about how [the filmmakers] had really jobbed the conservatives."[27] Nor could he have enjoyed seeing the film's star mock him. Sitting in the backseat of a limousine, Robert Redford recites increasingly nonsensical phrases from his stump speech. He stops finally, frowns, and thrusts his arms up in a double V-for-victory gesture. Clearly, Nixon's the one.

Nixon rarely saw more than seven or eight movies a month during his first administration. The most he saw was thirteen in July 1971 (July or August in San Clemente, when he took a lengthy vacation each summer, tended to see Nixon's biggest moviegoing). That began to change in November 1972 when, safely reelected, he saw twelve. In December, vilified on a global scale for the Christmas bombing of North Vietnam, he again saw twelve. January, with seven, marked a brief return to form. With Watergate becoming more and more of an issue, though, he saw twelve in February and ten in March. That he managed to see eight in April was no small accomplishment, for that was the most important Watergate month since the break-in itself, with Nixon forced to jettison Haldeman, Ehrlichman, Dean, Attorney General Richard Kleindienst, and his FBI director, L. Patrick Gray.

It was then, at the end of April, to his family, that Nixon first broached the possibility of resigning. The departure of Haldeman and Ehrlichman having put the handwriting on the wall, it also put more movies on the screen, and the number of films Nixon saw soared in May to a record fifteen. It went back down in June, but not too far, to eleven, then rose back to fourteen in July, and fifteen in August. By September, with Agnew's resignation imminent and confrontation with the Special Prosecutor's Office looming, he was back down to eleven. In October, even with the Yom Kippur War and the aftermath of Cox's firing, he found time for another ten—one of which, *Fail-Safe*, suggests the mordant state to which Nixon had been brought. He saw the movie, with its mushroom-cloud ending, on October 27, just two days after the United States had gone on nuclear alert in response to threatened Soviet actions in the Middle East.

Bleak though the jest may have been, seeing *Fail-Safe* that weekend was by then about as good a source of relief as Nixon could hope to find. For the first time, he saw sixteen movies in a month, in February 1974. And even with the threat of impeachment hanging over him—or, more likely, in direct response to it—he saw thirteen in July 1974. That last full month in office he sought surcease in his final presidential showing of *Around the*

World in 80 Days, as well as in several films whose titles might have given pause: *The Big Heat* (1953) and *Man without a Star* (1955). That month he also saw *Double Indemnity* (!) and *It's a Wonderful Life* (!!).

Living in the presidential equivalent of Potterville, might Nixon have fantasized about an angelically determined happy ending? One could hardly blame him if he did. A more accurate reflection of Nixon's situation comes in another movie, however, one released the year before and which he never saw while president. If only Nixon had seen Terrence Malick's *Badlands* (1973), he could have experienced what may be the most Nixonian moment in all of film. Martin Sheen's Kit Carruthers bears absolutely no resemblance to Nixon. He's young and impulsive, a misfit and outlaw: the perpetrator of a multistate murder spree across the Great Plains. Yet after finally being apprehended, Kit utters a truth that gets at the very heart of the sad wonder and abiding perplexity of Richard Nixon. "Kit, I got a question for you," a deputy sheriff asks. "Do you like people?" Sheen takes but a moment to ponder this. "They're okay," he shrugs, saying this with the blank, self-deluded politeness of a famished man who claims to lack any appetite.

That's it: "They're okay." It's not exactly the answer the deputy was looking for. "Okay"? *"Okay"?* Of course they're not okay! That's why Kit could go around shooting half a dozen of them and more without suffering the least bit of remorse. And that affirmative Kit chooses for his three-syllable reply—"okay," a word as flat and empty as the Plains themselves—tells us all we need to know. OKAY? People are oppressive and awful and always getting in the way of whatever it is you really want to do. And when they're not getting in the way, it's only because they're too busy asking stupid questions like "Do you like people?"

Nixon has nothing whatsoever in common with a Kit Carruthers except for this: even as he understood—perfectly, painfully, profoundly—the requirement to say that people are okay, he demonstrated with every fiber of his being his utter conviction that, in point of fact, they most certainly are *not* okay. "Politics would be a helluva good business," Nixon lamented to a subordinate, "if it weren't for the goddamned people."[28] Or as he told Theodore H. White, conceding his detestation of pressing the flesh, ". . . and all the while you're smiling you want to kick them in the shins."[29] A politician who shrank from his fellow citizens: this may be the central, the defining, contradiction of this incomparably contradictory man. It's not that this trait he shared with Kit means he could have ended up like him—not hardly—but a politician? One outcome is almost as preposterous as the other. "What I never understood is why he became a politician," a baffled Henry Kissinger admitted in 1975. "He hated to meet new people. Most politicians like crowds. He didn't."[30] (Crowds? They're okay.)

Inward, indwelling, inhibited: such a man needs diversion more than most, and for such a man no diversion rivals the movies. Just walk in as the lights go down and the credits roll, then walk out at the end as they begin to roll again. You're all set, as alone as you want to be. For a man like Nixon, the movies possessed an especial seductiveness: all the vividness and pageantry of life—no, in the sorts of films he particularly prized, a vividness and pageantry exceeding that of life—without any of the human complications. How could Nixon *not* have loved the movies? This was a man who, as president, had the White House staff instructed not to respond to any greeting from him or his wife.[31] Too polite not to acknowledge passersby, yet too uneasy to want any response in turn, he so orders things that he can recognize others, but to them it is as if he does not exist (the emperor's clothes are real; it's the emperor who's imaginary). Sitting in the dark, surrounded solely by family and friends, was as close to informality as so uncomfortably formal a man might ever get. Even walking on the beach, he'd keep his dress shoes on. Yet who's to say if, after the first reel, Richard Nixon didn't kick off his shoes? Regardless of whether he did, he always knew that he *could* have: in the dark, no photographer might ever catch him off guard, ever make him look unpresidential. Nixon could (literally) sit back and, insofar as this was possible, relax. Seated with a projector behind him, Nixon could find what a cinema's darkness so seductively offers: the screen's ability to meet a man's gaze without returning it. Or as Sean Penn replies when asked in another Malick film, *The Thin Red Line* (1998), if he's ever lonely, "Only around people."

The movies were not only larger than life; they were safer than life. That's been part of their appeal at least since that bandit at the end of *The Great Train Robbery* fired into the audience and everyone who ducked was able to get back up again, nonplussed perhaps, but assuredly unscathed. What Joan Didion has written of Californians' love of swimming pools— that they are "a symbol . . . of order, of control over the uncontrollable"— also describes the fundamental reason why Richard Nixon loved movies and their capacity to enclose (and chlorinate) existence. "A pool is water," as a film is life, "made available and useful, and is, as such, infinitely soothing."[32]

Is it any wonder the movies came to influence how he saw the world, how he explained its reality to himself? He soon enough outgrew the dream he had nurtured as a little boy of one day becoming a train engineer. He never outgrew, though, the need to dream, the need *to believe.* "The strength of the movies," Ethan Mordden writes, "is that people must believe in them."[33] Belief is the single, surpassing requirement of moviegoing—that, and the price of a ticket—and it marks the intersection between Nixon's love of the medium and the man's marrow-filling faith in his own ambitions. Whenever the subject of destiny came up in interviews, he would dismiss it. Nixon was far too pragmatic ever to let himself go in for so mystical a concept as fate. Instead, his faith was Emersonian: in who he was, in what he wanted to do, in what he *could* do. Just like those men up on the screen, he would triumph, he would not give up, and somehow, sooner or later, there would be a happy ending. "You won't have Nixon to kick around anymore," he'd told the press in 1962; and, regardless of how mephitic the motivation behind that statement, he'd meant it. As it turned out, they *wouldn't* have Nixon to kick around, but not because he was giving up and going away. Rather, it was because next time he'd *win* and you can't kick around a winner, not in this country, anyway: six years later he was president-elect. It should have been the perfect happy ending, except that the movie still had several reels to go and turned into *All the President's Men.*

The temptation to superimpose a filmic narrative over the events of one's life is something few of us are immune to, and during the past half century there can be only a fraction of the earth's population who have not had their way of looking at reality shaped at least a little by the motion picture. (What prayer and sainthood were to the Middle Ages, a way of trying to elevate one's existence and provide a model of transcendence, montage and stardom are to our own). "The only way to avoid Hollywood is to live there," Stravinsky once remarked.[34]

Yet some people, even presidents, are clearly more shaped than others: Kennedy more than Eisenhower, say, or Clinton more than either Bush, and Nixon more than any of them. The others' linkage to the movies—even that of Ike, a man born before the medium was—is through stardom. Reagan, who was a movie star before he became president, is the clearest example of this. But all the other presidents since 1950 were schooled in how to behave in the spotlight—how to *perform* in it—by what they had spent years seeing onscreen. A Kennedy or Clinton wanted to act like a movie star, to be *treated* like a movie star, to generate the same sort of love, envy, and (most of all?) desire. With Nixon, who loathed the spotlight's capacity to reveal even as he clutched at the warmth and implicit approval its glare conveyed, the linkage is through the audience.

Nixon knew himself too well to think himself capable of inspiring the emotions that an Ike or a Kennedy could. Rather than raising himself to the firmament, he would bring the firmament (as the rest of us do) down to his own level. He would think in movie terms of life rather than of himself.

Thinking this way runs like a thread throughout his career, and twice it got him in trouble: when he used *Patton* to help steel himself to invade Cambodia and, a few months later, when he cited the frontier justice in *Chisum* as a model for American jurisprudence. In both cases—George C. Scott as personification of the American military tradition; John Wayne as embodiment of a nation of men not laws—there is this clear desire on Nixon's part to integrate his fantasy life into policymaking. That desire for congruence between what one sees on the screen and what one feels and does in one's life is almost universal—it's one of the most fundamental appeals of moviegoing—but it's a little unnerving when the desire belongs to someone with such a momentous capacity to act upon it. See enough movies, see them eagerly enough, excitedly enough, and all that seeing can't help but affect how a person comes to see the world around him. Even more than the number of movies he saw—which a skeptic could argue was owing more to convenience than anything else—this movie sense of life is what most clearly marks Richard Nixon as a true lover of motion pictures. And his employment of movies as an explanatory tool need not be as consequential as in 1970. It's the more trivial instances that point out how natural it was for him to think this way.

Recall how, in his 1958 interview with Stewart Alsop, Nixon compared Jerry Voorhis to Jefferson Smith. Telling Jonathan Aitken about the mansion of a wealthy contributor to the '46 campaign, he compared it to "the house in the film *Sunset Boulevard*."[35] Recall how Safire, along with Garment and Kissinger the most acute of Nixon's associates in analyzing their chief, remarked that "he saw his character the way he would like himself to be: the John Ford hero."[36] Or, most explicitly, there was the night of November 14, 1969, when he joined Haldeman and Ehrlichman in the latter's office to watch antiwar demonstrators marching on the Vietnamese embassy. Nixon sat there for two hours, absorbed in the spectacle. "Very relaxed," Haldeman described him in his diary. "Said was like watching an old movie, keep thinking something interesting will happen."[37] It's almost eerie, the sense of detachment—aestheticization even—such a comment suggests. Yes, this was a man who could sit back and have no trouble viewing *Fail-Safe* two days after ordering a nuclear alert. Nixon, who prided himself on his decisiveness, his ability to confront a crisis, on being such a man of action, was in fact the classic watcher, never so happy as when aloof, apart, secluded.

Most often he would watch with family members (though Pat would frequently slip out after the movie had started to go off and read) and such friends as Bebe Rebozo and Robert Abplanalp. Working weekends at Camp David, he would have aides join him in watching. Less often, he would honor some luminary with inclusion in the presidential party, like Connally at that screening of *Around the World in 80 Days*, or J. Edgar Hoover and Clyde Tolson at an April 25, 1969, White House screening of *Where Eagles Dare*. Once, Nixon even watched a movie at Camp David with no one else for company but Haldeman's secretary. Whom he saw a movie with or even what the movie was counted for less than the simple act of seeing. As any true moviegoer knows, being at the movies is only incidentally a social occasion. It's the being there that matters.

Nixon often let others choose the movie—again, it was the act of watching that mattered most to him; the what was almost an afterthought. There would be a rotating list of eight to twelve features available at any given time, with a brief synopsis of each title to aid in making a selection. Tricia was the one who picked *Chisum*; Pat, *Doctor Zhivago*; and when Bebe Rebozo was present, Nixon had him select the movie. This had unforeseen consequences on May 12, 1973, when Rebozo chose *Hammersmith Is Out* (1972) a comedic updating of the Faust legend, with Richard Burton and Elizabeth Taylor. The movie's R-rated goings-on bore little resemblance to what the Nixon family was used to watching. The president teased his friend, "Your kind of movie, Bebe? This is your idea of family entertainment?" When the lights went up, Rebozo confessed that he had misinterpreted the designation in the listing of films available for that night's screening. "I thought R stood for 'Regular.'"[38]

Such confusion isn't all that surprising; R movies were rarely screened at the White House or Camp David. Nixon confided to his guests at the San Clemente reception that while he and Pat had not seen any X-rated movies, "We had seen an R-rated, and 'that's about as far as you can go.'" In fact, Nixon had seen nine R-rated films by then (*The Sterile Cuckoo*, 1969; *Klute*, 1971; *Dirty Harry*, *The Last Picture Show*, 1971; *The French Connection*, *The Music Lovers*, 1971; *The Godfather*, *There Was a Crooked Man*, 1970; *Frenzy*, 1972) and would see another six before his resignation (*Hammersmith*; *High Plains Drifter*; *Play Misty for Me*; *The Long Goodbye*, 1973; *Serpico*, 1973; *Magnum Force*). There were two other films Nixon saw—*The Prime of Miss Jean Brodie* (1969) and *Coogan's Bluff*—that were "Suggested for Mature Audiences," the ratings forerunner to R. Still, those seventeen films constitute barely 3 percent of the movies Nixon had screened. And there was an extenuating circumstance for five of them: they were Clint movies.

Such a low percentage was no small accomplishment. Nixon's time in office coincided with an unprecedented period in film history, one that saw not just the reexamination of American values in such films as *Easy Rider* and *M*A*S*H* and *The Godfather*, but something even more startling: the sexual unburdening of America on the big screen. By 1973 the sixth- and eleventh-biggest-grossing films were X-rated: *The Devil in Miss Jones* and *Deep Throat*. Thanks to Howard Simons, the managing editor of the *Washington Post*, who bestowed the name on Woodward and Bernstein's secret informant, the latter film's title became inextricably linked to the fall of Richard Nixon—but only the title. Nixon was quite vocal in his opposition to the availability of such sexually explicit films. That opposition may have been good politics, but it was also sincere. Barely two months into his presidency, Nixon was privately voicing his distaste for *I Am Curious (Yellow)*, the first X-rated hit, ordering Haldeman "to have John Mitchell do something about the dirty movie from Sweden."[39]

"Hollywood is sick," Nixon wrote in his final book, *Beyond Peace*. "Its values are not those of mainstream America. The depiction of violence and explicit sex sells, and Hollywood is in the business of making money. But by forgoing its responsibility to observe basic standards of decency, Hollywood has accelerated the decline of these standards in the community at large."[40] It was a view utterly consistent with what he had felt a quarter century before and, in fact, that view had its origins in the years of his presidency. On November 1, 1968—four days before Nixon was elected president—the Motion Picture Association of America inaugurated its new classification system of G, M, R, X. (M, sounding too dire, soon became GP; GP sounding not dire enough, later became PG and PG-13.) Where the Academy Award for Best Picture in 1968 had gone to a musical drawn from Dickens, the G-rated *Oliver!*, things had changed so rapidly that the next year's winner was a drama about a male hustler, the X-rated *Midnight Cowboy*.

Not surprisingly, Nixon managed to miss *Midnight Cowboy*—the sole Best Picture winner between 1968 and 1973 he neglected to see. (Pat and Julie saw it, though—did they tell him?) Perhaps it was chagrin, as much as distaste, that accounted for his failure to see it, for Nixon had an indirect role in *Midnight Cowboy*'s having been made. The film's producer, Jerome Hellman, found his career threatened in 1964 when a picture he was overseeing for Warner Bros., *A Fine Madness*, so displeased Jack

Warner, he fired Hellman and banished him from the Warners lot. Hellman was a friend of Garment, one of Nixon's law partners, who brought the matter to the attention of his famous associate. An amused Nixon was glad to see what he could do. A telephone call full of praise for "my brilliant young friend Jerry Hellman," who "I expect will have a large place in my political future" quickly assuaged—and surely surprised—Warner, who immediately rehired the producer.[41] Hellman's career was saved . . . and, five years later, *Midnight Cowboy* got released. Even worse, perhaps, in 1978 Hellman produced the anti-Vietnam film *Coming Home*. With Warner, as with Goldwyn, friendship with a film mogul could have unforeseen consequences.

Midnight Cowboy exemplified the new permissiveness not just in subject matter but also outcome and attitude. Dustin Hoffman's Ratso Rizzo dies a wasting death, and Jon Voight's Joe Buck finds himself far more confused (if also far less innocent) than when he started out: Butch and Sundance they're not. Aggressively downbeat, the film makes such a fetish of sordidness that, for all intents and purposes, it comes to seem as morally unreal as anything from the age of the Production Code. Just as a film back then had to have a happy ending, no matter how implausible, now a film, if it wanted to demonstrate how serious and up to the minute it was, had to have an unhappy ending. It wasn't just those unfortunates inhabiting paranoid thrillers who were ending badly. Lest we forget, even so happy-go-lucky a twosome as Butch and Sundance get gunned down at the end. This was something far more subversive to the ethos of the American cinema than sexual frankness: the good guys no longer always won. The era of the happy ending had ended—or, rather, of the *guaranteed* happy ending. And this may be the best way to categorize Richard Nixon as a filmgoer: he belonged to the era of the guaranteed happy ending. On January 6, 1970, he saw *Those Were the Happy Times*, the truncated version of *Star!*, the 1968 Julie Andrews musical. That title might serve as both touchstone for the Nixons' movie tastes and most fundamental explanation for why they saw so relatively few contemporary movies: the Nixon years were *not* the happy times on American movie screens.

The San Clemente reception can be seen as the last stand of the happy times. The White House strove to make the event, in Haldeman's words, "a very high-level, special occasion," with food from Chasen's, the famed Hollywood eatery, and "the very best brands of Scotch and Bourbon, not the ordinary stuff we've used in the past."[42] Such care was lavished upon a tellingly skewed sampling of the film community. Of the four hundred guests, only two might be considered representatives of the New Hollywood: Peter Bogdanovich, the director of *The Last Picture Show* and *Paper Moon* (1973), both of which Nixon saw, and his then-companion, Cybill Shepherd. Far more typical of the gathering were such guests as Don DeFore, Virginia Mayo, Rhonda Fleming, and Lloyd Nolan. "This looks like a cocktail party at the Hollywood Wax Museum," one guest was heard to complain.[43]

Nixon had wanted it that way. In a memo to Haldeman on November 30, 1970, he was already looking ahead to endorsements from Hollywood celebrities for 1972. While he acknowledges "that we must, of course, go for all the new stars," what predominates is his pride in the celebrities whose support he anticipates getting, "a pretty imposing list: Ruby Keeler[!], Gloria Swanson, Joan Crawford, Ginger Rogers, Bette Davis."[44] Two years later, finding himself a prohibitive favorite to win, he could stick with the people *he* cared about.

Seeking a way "to show how much it means to us" to have such a starry collection of guests, he recalled how during a telephone conversation, U.S. Representative Charles Rangell had confided to him, "If I'd told my Dad when I was growing up as a kid in Harlem I'd be talking to the president someday, he'd have told me I was crazy!" "Well," Nixon added, "when I was growing up as a kid in Yorba Linda, if I'd told my Dad I'd be talking to Jack Benny someday, he'd have told me *I* was crazy."[45] It's pure Nixon: the love of creaky anecdote, the overeagerness to ingratiate himself along with the willingness to twist facts to do so (by the time Frank Nixon might have heard of Jack Benny, the Nixons had been out of Yorba Linda for more than a decade and, for that matter, Nixon had met Benny at least fifteen years before). The story is revealing on two counts. It reminds us how fundamentally starstruck Nixon could be—to what does he equate meeting the leader of the Free World? meeting a superannuated comedian—and it underscores the provenance of the stardom he found most striking. It stemmed, not surprisingly, from Hollywood's Golden Age and belonged to the stars of his youth: a gamut of glamour that ran from his loyal supporter John Wayne to his correspondent Jane Wyman to, yes, Jack Benny, singled out among hundreds of Hollywood luminaries as *primus inter pares*.

It's fair to say that Richard Nixon had some peculiar ideas as to who did and did not matter in Hollywood in 1972. Other than the fact that each was on celluloid, *Buck Benny Rides Again* (1940) or *The Horn Blows at Midnight* (1945) had about as much in common with *Midnight Cowboy* as Everett Dirksen did with Abbie Hoffman. Clearly, Nixon was no man of the seventies so far as the movies were concerned. The products of Hollywood's Silver Age seemed every bit as strange and alienating to him as those of the Golden Age seemed familiar and appealing. The unhappy times were not his times, not at the movies, anyway. Yet across the vast gulf that lay between Nixon and seventies Hollywood, a sort of conversation was taking place. It might be one-sided, it might be fractious, but messages were being received—and, as we shall see, memorably acknowledged.

Watching a movie in the White House Theater or at Camp David or one of his vacation homes, Nixon was largely safe from the subversive onslaught of seventies Hollywood. The reverse did not hold true, however. Much more than anyone might have supposed at the time, Hollywood was far from immune from the differently subversive impact of Richard Nixon. Which was as it should be: the movies had done so much to shape his own way of looking at things, it was only fair that his way should now help shape theirs. His spiritual influence (for lack of a better term) would come to be felt in some of the greatest films of the era. Nixon at the movies would meet with an improbable counterpart: Nixon *within* the movies.

Gene Hackman

11

THE CONVERSATION

▪▪▪▪▪▪▪▪▪▪▪▪▪▪▪▪▪▪▪▪▪▪▪▪▪▪▪▪▪

Reminds me of Washington; just different names, different faces.
HENRY KISSINGER, AFTER ATTENDING THE PREMIERE OF *The Godfather*[1]

Put it like this: two people—Richard Nixon and Travis Bickle—got away with things in the mid-seventies in ways that should not have passed. DAVID THOMSON, *Beneath Mulholland*

On June 23, 1972, Richard Nixon kicked off another Camp David weekend the way he liked best, with an after-dinner Western. *Hang 'Em High* must have seemed made to order for Nixon's tastes: 114 minutes of Clint Eastwood seeking retribution, with lots of action along the way, and a tried-and-true supporting cast boasting the likes of Ed Begley, Ben Johnson, Pat Hingle, and Alan Hale Jr. Yet even in something so otherwise reassuring and familiar, Nixon couldn't altogether escape the great cultural revolution then under way in Hollywood. For there briefly appears in *Hang 'Em High* an actor who would prove a pivotal figure in the seventies movie pantheon, the Mordred of the New Hollywood, Dennis Hopper.

Part of Hopper's significance was that he was no newcomer, but rather a bridge to the Old Hollywood. Besides *Hang 'Em High*, Nixon saw him in *Rebel Without a Cause* (1955); *Giant* (1956), where he played Rock Hudson and Elizabeth Taylor's son (!); *The Sons of Katie Elder*; and *True Grit*, where, appropriately enough, he ran afoul of John Wayne. In those films, Hopper's not as yet the fantastical creature who would spend much of the rest of his career roaming the screen like the ghost of *Walpurgisnacht* past. In *Hang 'Em High*, though, Hopper gives an indication of just how explosively he was about to burst his chrysalis. He has only one, brief scene, but it more than suffices. Hirsute and ravening, Hopper lies in chains, proclaiming that he is a prophet and "they" are "scared of the Wrath of God." The marshal, played by Johnson (something of a seventies icon himself), unshackles Hopper, who knocks him down and tries to flee. Reluctantly, the lawman guns down the escapee, and that's that. Yet the chiliasm of Hopper's rant implies resurrection—and *Easy Rider* was but a year away. A specter was haunting Hollywood, the specter of the seventies, and nothing was safe anymore, not even a Clint Western.

One can argue that the president partly had himself to blame. The wrathful deity whose prophecies Hopper foretold, the avatar of seventies Hollywood, wasn't it Richard Nixon? True, he was by no means attuned to American film's new dispensation. As we have seen, what he preferred was old, and old-fashioned, movies. He was suspicious of hipness and extremism. He shrank from prurience and permissiveness. It's as if everything Nixon feared the New Hollywood embraced: patriotism mocked, radicalism encouraged, immorality made to appear matter-of-fact and mainstream. Depending on where your loyalties lay, seventies Hollywood was the negative of Nixon's positive, or he was the negative of its positive. Either way: they were separated by an immense and Manichaean divide bridged only by mutual distrust.

That, however, is precisely the point. Nixon's diametrical opposition to the values of seventies Hollywood acted both to highlight those values and to shape them. His inescapable, uncomfortable presence helped provide a climate for these movies to occur in. His ideological certitude and uneasiness with himself paralleled the New Hollywood's own ideological certitude and uneasiness with America—and, of course, uneasiness with its president. Like him, so many of those movies were imbued with a tense malevolence that indelibly marks them as being of that time. The experimentation and unpredictability—the very considerable accomplishments—of Hollywood in these years are unmistakably a product of the tumultuous, overwrought America presided over and, in a very real sense, defined by Richard Nixon.

Think of the era's greatest achievement, and one of the greatest of any Hollywood era, Francis Ford Coppola's first two *Godfather* films. Though set in the Truman and Eisenhower years, their spirit patently derives from the era of their making. From each film's being an archetypal revenge tale (Nixon's favorite form of reverie) to their depicting the classic American success story as morally ruinous (akin, say, to a poor boy growing up to become president—and then having to resign the office) to the gorgeous crepuscularity of Gordon Willis's cinematography (its umbrageous palette that of a Nixon daydream), Coppola's films are on intimate terms with the animus of Richard Nixon's presidency. No one would ever mistake him for a Corleone capo—to the extent he recalls any member of the family, it's poor put-upon Fredo—but a grimly discernible affinity obtains.

Norman Mailer, for one, recognized this when he called his book about the 1972 political conventions *St. George and the Godfather*;[2] and when John Dean first told his attorney about the president's boast that he could get a million dollars in hush money, the latter exclaimed, "The P[resident] sounds like the Godfather, for Christ's sake."[3] Even before the drumbeat of damning revelations during his second term, Nixon could be perceived as a version of Don Vito—the ultimate maker of offers that couldn't be refused—for the Corleone worldview and the Nixon worldview coincide considerably. Both esteem loyalty and hard work. Both prize tradition and order. Both revere the family and respect authority (if not the law). Both value ruthlessness, recognize the primacy of power—and understand the utility of fear and suspicion. The primary difference between them, of course, is that the Corleones are criminals and Nixon, president of the United States. Yet was that so much of a difference, after all—a question whose pertinence was underscored during the thirty months that passed between the two films' releases dates. When Kay Adams (Diane Keaton) reproaches her future husband for being naive in equating his family's actions with those of the government—"Presidents and senators don't have men killed," she tells him—Michael Corleone's reply is seventies Hollywood distilled to an acid essence. "Now look who's being naive." One can only imagine how Nixon, who wasted no time in seeing *The Godfather* (he had it screened nine days after it opened), might have chuckled over Michael's retort—or perhaps thrilled at it. "God, Mao," Nixon once remarked with a trace of wistfulness to Murray Kempton. "How many people do you suppose he had killed?"[4]

It's a question equally pertinent to the Corleones, *père et fils*, and one all but asked of Michael in *Godfather II* during his appearance before a Senate investigative panel. While clearly modeled on the 1950–51 Kefauver Committee, what it inevitably recalls is the Senate Watergate hearings, which had riveted the nation eighteen months before the movie's release. As Keaton sits silent and supportive behind her husband as he testifies, she could be Mo Dean's more lifelike, brunette sister. Earlier in the film, Lee Strasberg's Hyman Roth—a gangster modeled on Meyer Lansky—who wants the Corleones to invest in Cuba, waxes lyrical to Michael on the profits available to the Mob there "in partnership with a friendly government." From there, it's "just one small step to looking for a man who wants to be president of the United States and has the cash to make it possible." It was John F. Kennedy who had the real-life ties to the Mafia, but it is Nixon, the beneficiary of CREEP's bulging coffers—and once again jobbed by JFK's memory—we are meant to understand is the man who "has the cash."

A dank, dark Yahweh, he is this pervasive, unspoken presence throughout so many of the era's films. And sometimes the sacred unutterable actually makes it onto a soundtrack. Stacy Keach's butler in *Brewster McCloud* (1970) is named "Milhous." George C. Scott, in *The Hospital* (1971), grouses about "Nixon administration funding cuts" (no doubt the president, who saw the movie at Camp David in January 1974, derived a certain sour satisfaction). In *Sleeper* (1973), Woody Allen remarks that "whenever [Nixon] used to leave the White House, the Secret Service would count the silverware." And even so audience-sensitive a production as *Airport 1975* (1974) has a Nixon joke. When Nixon's name goes unmentioned, his troubles—and troubling presence—can remain discernible, as in *Harry and Tonto* (1974) when Art Carney jauntily asks a newsdealer, "Who's the vice president this week?" Even *Jaws* (1975) includes a Watergate reference—the size of a captured shark moves an onlooker to note, "That's got a deep throat, Frank"—and, lest we forget, it has for a major subplot an attempted cover-up.

Nixon had a way of popping up in the most unexpected places. Set in 1968 on Election Day and the morning after, Hal Ashby's *Shampoo* (1975) might as easily have been called *Smiles of a Nixon Night*. Threading through the film's series of trysts is the victorious candidate. His image, voice, and name constantly recur, employed as a sort of reality principle amid all the luxe and California volupté. At one point, Nixon even assumes the role of Greek chorus: as Jack Warden confronts Warren Beatty over his infidelity with not just Warden's wife but also his mistress and daughter, the television in the room carries that portion of Nixon's victory speech in which he cites the homemade sign he saw in Deshler, Ohio, urging him to "Bring Us Together."

From Richard Nixon, Mob boss manqué, to Richard Nixon, master of the revels—and all these others in between—it's a wildly miscellaneous collection of references and allusions. That it's such a mishmash reminds us just how ubiquitous Nixon was back then. Varied though the range of citations is, it would be far longer if one wanted to be comprehensive. Could one compile a comparable list of Clinton film references, or even Reagan film references? (One could for Franklin D. Roosevelt, as we shall see.)

Even granting the possibility of a similar list being assembled, still it would not resonate as Nixon's does, for his ubiquity coincides with a singular epoch in American movies. These were great times for Hollywood, a Silver Age. The studio system had finally collapsed, and just as the perfecting of that system coincided with the Golden Age of the '30s and early '40s, so did its final dissolution coincide with the Silver Age. For a decade or so—from the release of *Bonnie and Clyde* in 1967 to that of *Taxi Driver*, just in time for the Bicentennial, in 1976—Hollywood became, as Pauline Kael approvingly put it, "a fertile chaos."[5] Pretty much anything went, with results atrocious as well as magnificent, and American movies came to possess a daring and freshness that they'd never had before—or have had since. There was a rush of new directors (Coppola, Robert Altman, Scorsese, Steven Spielberg), new stars (Pacino, Jack Nicholson, Hoffman, Gene Hackman), and landmark films (*M*A*S*H,* the first two *Godfathers, Chinatown, Nashville, Mean Streets, The Wild Bunch*). There was an excitement attached to the movies, a feeling of discovery and innovation. A powerful sense of anticipation surrounded the medium and, even more remarkable, often found itself justified.

The movies mattered, or seemed to, as they had not before and have not since. Films in the first half of the '70s resembled politics in the latter half of the '60s: *anything could happen.* The resemblance to politics wasn't coincidental. Graphic violence, sexual openness, and frank language were the most obvious elements in the new movie environment, but they were also the most superficial. Far more important was what Kael, whose concurrent emergence as America's foremost film critic played a notable supporting role in the making of the Silver Age, termed "a new, open-minded interest in examining American experience."[6] The opening line of *The Godfather* is emblematic: "I believe in America." In the context of both the movie and the period, that assertion conveys no little irony. Previously, the movies had taken the American experience almost entirely for granted—it was simply there, as immutable and sustaining as the sun shining down on the Hollywood Hills—and on those rare occasions when the movies had consciously dwelled on the American experience, they did so in explicitly celebratory terms. From Capraesque idealists to Kissingerian cowboys, Hollywood had provided a seemingly inexhaustible repository of American self-satisfaction. The Silver Age changed that. What is on display in each of the landmark titles cited above (and numerous lesser films besides) is American self-examination.

In such a context, national self-satisfaction is inherently ideological—not least of all, because it never acknowledges itself as such. So, too, with self-examination—except that it explicitly acknowledges its ideological thrust—and seventies movies evinced a free-floating sense of politicization unlike anything Hollywood had previously shown. While it tended to be vaguely leftist in orientation, this particular *politique des auteurs* still left room for such Nixon-friendly films as *Dirty Harry* and *Patton* and such a proudly illiberal sensibility as that of the writer-director John Milius. It's a mark of just how pervasive this attitude was that in their useful study *Hollywood Films of the Seventies* (1984), the all-inclusive term Seth Cagin and Philip Dray employ for what we have been alternately referring to as "seventies Hollywood," "Silver Age Hollywood," and "the New Hollywood" is "Political Hollywood."

In ways both subtle and overt, Political Hollywood was about nothing so much as a bittersweet disgust with America. "You know—this used to be a helluva good country," Nicholson's George Hanson laments to Hopper's Billy and Peter Fonda's Captain America in *Easy Rider*. That statement, with its veneration of an Edenic American past and contempt for a brutish American present, is one of the founding principles of the Silver Age. In the eyes of the New Hollywood, the clearest proof of our national devolution was the identity of the man currently occupying the Oval Office. Richard Nixon was both symptom and agent: a sign of how far we had descended *and* of what (or who) had helped bring us to such a pass. Nixon was everything, just about, that was wrong with America, the glum, graceless personification of meanness and sanctimony, hypocrisy and greed, racism and warmongering. Trad and square, he personified the dead hand of the fifties refusing to acknowledge its time was up. (True, the not-so-Edenic fifties belonged to America's past; but logic has never much concerned Hollywood, Old or New.)

More specifically, Nixon was the war—far worse, he was its continuation long after everyone realized what a debacle the war had become—

and, of course, he was Watergate. Watergate was the too perfect denouement, at once dreadful and exhilarating, of all the assumptions the New Hollywood had about Nixon: dreadful because it proved America really had ceased to be a helluva good country, and exhilarating for the same reason. It's only fitting that on the day Nixon saw *Hang 'Em High*, he had had his "smoking gun" conversation with H. R. Haldeman, wherein the president ordered his chief of staff to use the CIA to hinder the FBI's investigation of the break-in. It was that conversation that originated the cover-up, and a little more than two years later, it was the release of the tape of that conversation that forced Nixon's resignation.

Nixon's relation to the Silver Age went beyond politicization and mutual paranoia, though. It extended to the nature of celebrity. As the embodiment of anti-charisma, he was the perfect president for an age that was redefining stardom. Where Nicholson's Bobby Dupea in *Five Easy Pieces* wanted a chicken salad sandwich on whole-wheat toast, Nixon asked only for his daily cottage cheese with a slice of pineapple—but in their ruthless devotion to apartness, as in their plebeian palates, they shared certain preferences. If the sixties had taken their stand with the antihero—who was simply the standard Hollywood hero, only in reverse: just as sexy, but now he sneered where he used to smile—the seventies took it one step further, to the nonhero. Stars no longer needed to be good-looking (George C. Scott, good-looking?), or glamorous (Gene Hackman, glamorous?) or larger than life (Dustin Hoffman, larger than life?).

Wasn't it his looks that had contributed to Nixon's defeat at the hands of the matinee-idol candidate, JFK—the same JFK who slept with movie stars and found himself played by Cliff Robertson onscreen? Kennedy's first choice had been Warren Beatty, an unnervingly astute selection. Hollywood was in JFK's blood, after all, what with old Joe's days spent assembling RKO and nights spent sleeping with Gloria Swanson. Who during Nixon's incumbency might imagine a movie made about his wartime exploits—or about *anything* concerning him? So what if *PT 109* wasn't a hit: JFK was big box office regardless. No one would ever accuse Nixon of being big box office. In the one period when Hollywood turned away from its classic verities—prettiness and heroism and the good guys always winning—here was that rejection made flesh and put in the Oval Office.

Nixon mouthed all the old pieties, to be sure. Yet the truth about him was revealed, as John Mitchell would say, not in what he said but in what he *did*. He was, of course, the first president to have to declare he wasn't a crook, to turn out to be an unindicted co-conspirator, to end up roaming the White House during his final days in office all but unhinged. All of which made Nixon both unique among our chief executives and all the better suited to preside over the Silver Age. What plainer demonstration could there be of the movies' new moral dispensation: that the good guys no longer always won and, even worse, the good guys were now often bad guys? As James Caan—playing a CIA hit man, no less—laments to his handler in Peckinpah's *The Killer Elite* (1975), "The cleft chins and true hearts are out."*

The most memorable film protagonists of the era were nuts or crooks or a little bit of both: Redford and Newman's Butch and Sundance; Hoffman and Jon Voight's Ratso and Joe Buck in *Midnight Cowboy*; Donald Sutherland and Elliott Gould's Hawkeye and Trapper John in *M*A*S*H*; Scott's megalomaniacal Patton; Hackman's bend-the-rules cop in *The French Connection*; Eastwood's break-the-rules cop in *Dirty Harry*; Malcolm McDowell's Alex the droog in *A Clockwork Orange* (1971); Brando and Pacino in the *Godfather* films; Redford and Newman's swindlers in *The Sting*; Nicholson's sociopathic Randall McMurphy in *One Flew Over the Cuckoo's Nest* (1975); Pacino's gay bank robber in *Dog Day Afternoon* (1976); Peter Finch's psychotic anchorman in *Network* (1976); Robert De Niro's murderous isolato in *Taxi Driver*. And none of them, not even McDowell's Alex or De Niro's Travis Bickle, was a mere cult figure. These were protagonists of highly popular films and figures of public fascination. If one wanted to include films that were more successful critically than at the box office, there were such equally memorable, and morally problematic, figures such as Beatty and Julie Christie's title characters in *McCabe and Mrs. Miller* (1971), Harvey Keitel and De Niro's aspirant Mafiosi in *Mean Streets*, Martin Sheen's Kit Carruthers in *Badlands*.

It's not that Hollywood had previously failed to put forward heroes who were criminals or outcasts. It had—but never in such numbers as during the Silver Age, never with such approval of their actions. More telling still, when these latter-day criminals suffered retribution, as they sometimes did, it was seldom intended as a condemnation of them but rather of society. The Old Hollywood may have offered Little Caesar or Scarface as a hero, but it made sure to kill him off before the closing credits and, in killing him off, turn him into a cautionary tale. The New Hollywood simply abandoned any pretense of exacting death as the price an outlaw hero must pay. And when such a hero does die, like Butch and Sundance

---

*Caan's costar, and the film's villain, Robert Duvall, recalls Peckinpah yelling at him during a scene, "HE'S NIXON. YOU HATE HIM." An annoyed Duvall replied, "How'd you know how I vote?" Gavin Smith, "A Lifetime in the Moment: Robert Duvall Interviewed," *Film Comment*, November–December 1997, p. 31.

or McMurphy, death serves to enhance his heroic status and add to his luster.

Of all the bonds between Nixon and the Silver Age, this may have been the most fundamental. He broke the rules. Wasn't that what the New Hollywood was all about? Even better, he got away with it—found out, yes, but in the end unpunished, thanks to the intercession of Gerald Ford—and getting away with breaking all the rules was what the New Hollywood *wanted* to be all about. Neither party, as is painfully apparent, may have been listening to the other consciously, but a conversation was being conducted, a curious kind of discourse, to be sure, one consisting of equal and opposite harangues—and, on the West Coast, at least, lessons were being learned. It's not too much to say that Richard Nixon was the tutelary deity of Hollywood's Silver Age.*

In that role, he had a precursor, for as RN was to Hollywood's Silver Age so was FDR to its Golden Age. Franklin Delano Roosevelt's smiling, clear-eyed vigor—the positive of Hollywood's positive—perfectly expressed the fundamental ethos of American movies during the '30s and the war years, and the twelve years of his presidency almost exactly coincided with the glory days of the Studio Age. It was within a year of his inauguration that the motion picture industry, after disastrous losses in the wake of the Crash, began to turn a profit again. Those profits would continue to grow, reaching a peak in 1946, a year after the president's death, when weekly movie attendance in the United States reached its all-time high.

It was more than just a rising Rooseveltian tide lifting all boats, the studios' included. There were specific ties between the New Deal and the Golden Age. What were the studios but the corporatist, managerial ideal of the National Recovery Administration (the centerpiece of the early New Deal) perfected and institutionalized, their assembly-line output put up on a screen for an eager public to enjoy and admire? It was the National Industrial Recovery Act, which took effect in June 1933, that essentially sanctioned the collusive practices of the major studios. Moreover, the industry's own trade group, the Motion Picture Producers and Distributors Association, was allowed to write the Code of Fair Competi-

---

*Nixon's role as muse is as impressive as it is surprising. What other president has inspired so many creative imaginations? They include John Adams (*Nixon in China*, 1987), Philip Guston (*Poor Richard*, 2001), Robert Coover (*The Public Burning*, 1977), Philip Roth (*Our Gang*, 1971), Philip K. Dick (*Radio Free Albemuth*, 1985), Muriel Spark (*The Abbess of Crewe*, 1974)— all the way to Neil Young ("Even Richard Nixon has got soul" goes the refrain to his 1975 song "Campaigner").

tion the law required. That code, which the government singled out as a model, was the only one among a total of more than six hundred promulgated that permitted manufacturing, wholesaling, and retailing within the same body of regulations.[7] More significant in the long run, the act ushered in the unionization of the studios, establishing the guild system that has been a mainstay of Hollywood production ever since. The Golden Age of Hollywood not only coincided with the Age of Roosevelt. It owed its very existence to the Age of Roosevelt. When the studios all shut down production on the day of the president's funeral, it was to acknowledge a debt as well as to pay respects.

Yet FDR's influence on Hollywood transcended economics and organization. In numerous ways, what was on the screen reflected the personality of the man in the White House. From Roosevelt's confidence and optimism to his sunniness and gentility, from his all-embracing vision of America to his absolute moral assurance, the movies of the Golden Age were the products of his climate. As ubiquitous as relief or the draft, as *efficacious* as relief or the draft, Roosevelt simply dominated the country—and Hollywood, too. Partly, that was attributable to sheer longevity. For many Americans, he was the sole president in living memory, a leader who very nearly seemed immortal. He was also a different *kind* of president: not even Lincoln or Wilson, in the role of wartime commander in chief, had had the impact on U.S. society that Roosevelt did. It was as if all roads led from Washington almost from the moment of his first inaugural address. We have so come to take for granted that a Roosevelt-style presidency is what the office is *supposed* to be that we can barely appreciate how novel such a presidency once seemed and what an astonishing impact that novelty had.

More than that, FDR was the first superstar president. No previous president could have had the impact he did because none had had access to newsreels, network radio, glossy magazines. While these media had certainly existed before Roosevelt took office, they were still being absorbed into the culture. Even if Herbert Hoover had been disposed to give them, a series of pre-Roosevelt radio talks could not have comparably affected public opinion simply because broadcasting had not yet become so well integrated into daily life. Just as important, no previous president had appreciated the media's importance, as Roosevelt did. His cultivation of political reporters is legend, as are his Fireside Chats. But he was fully aware of the power of Hollywood, too, and acted accordingly. When, for example, the NIRA threatened to reduce the salaries of Hollywood's top stars, Roosevelt personally intervened to suspend the provisions as they applied to Hollywood.

FDR was aware of the power of the movies because he felt it himself: so far as its holder was concerned, the office of presiding deity was by no means ex officio. Given his way, he'd have been involved in the movies himself: during the early '20s, he went so far as to peddle a film treatment he'd written on the life of John Paul Jones.[8] It was never produced, but in 1938 FDR became the only president ever to receive a "story by" credit. It was for *The President's Mystery*, a 1936 drama based on an idea Roosevelt had shared with an editor of *Liberty* magazine, who had then assigned it to be written as a serial, which inspired the film.[9]

Roosevelt liked to see two to three movies a week, with each feature preceded if at all possible by a Mickey Mouse cartoon.[10] He had a favorite movie star, Myrna Loy, and they exchanged fan mail during the war years. It should come as no surprise that such a dedicated moviegoer was the president who had the White House Theater put in, ordering in July 1942 that a large cloakroom in the East Wing, "the Hat Box," as it was called, be converted into a presidential screening room.[11]

Roosevelt's passion for the movies was by no means unrequited. Gore Vidal means to mock both FDR and academe when he writes, "It is worth at least a doctoral thesis for some scholar to count how often in films of the thirties and forties a portrait of Franklin Roosevelt can be found."[12] Vidal is on to something, though, and it's the most direct indication of how thoroughly Roosevelt pervaded the Golden Age. Like God, he was everywhere—from a stripper's makeup mirror, to which his photo is taped, during the credit sequence of *Lady of Burlesque* (1943) to the Acme Book Shop in *The Big Sleep* (1946), where another FDR portrait looks down on Bogart's badinage with Dorothy Malone—and why not? "The greatest man in the United States played by the greatest actor," Joan Leslie, as Mrs. George M. Cohan in *Yankee Doodle Dandy*, says to her husband (James Cagney), about his portraying FDR in the Rodgers and Hart musical *I'd Rather Be Right*, "nothing wrong with that." What's most telling is the matter-of-factness with which she states it. Of course her husband is the greatest actor—and *of course* Roosevelt is the greatest man.

Such an opinion was company policy at Warner Bros., the studio that made *Yankee Doodle Dandy*. Warners was the studio with a chip on its shoulder, the home of Cagney and Edward G. Robinson, of Bogart and Bette Davis. The moviegoers it sought to reach were the voters FDR already had. Cracking wise, talking tough, patrolling mean streets, the classic

Warners movies, even when eschewing ideology (as was usually the case), consistently demonstrated a profound affinity with Rooseveltian politics. True, it professed his politics in a world, and certainly in a manner, far removed from the president's own. The world as seen by, say, MGM—unhurried, refined, comfortable—was far closer to FDR's Hudson Valley background than the highly urban, thoroughly up-to-the-minute world of Warners. But that's the point: anything up to the minute in the United States between 1933 and 1945 was perforce Rooseveltian.

It was simply good business to be allied with so popular a figure, and Warners made every effort to emphasize its affiliation. The studio even went so far as to make him a character in *Mission to Moscow* (1943) and, yes, *Yankee Doodle Dandy*. Perhaps the most striking instance of Warners' FDR idolatry comes in the 1933 musical *Footlight Parade*. It's so telling precisely because a Busby Berkeley movie is the last place one would expect to find Roosevelt, and it comes at the very beginning of his presidency. In the movie's concluding production number, hundreds of sailors hold up placards to form a U.S. flag. Then, as if it's nothing remarkable, they shift the cards to reveal first FDR's face, then the NRA eagle. Equating the president's image with Old Glory is presented as routine. (The studio promoted another of its hit musicals from that year, *42nd Street*, as "A New Deal in Entertainment.")

It's but the most striking example of FDR's connection to the Golden Age that he should be the one president who could boast of having a favorite studio—or, more accurately, of being a studio's favorite president. The grandest of the moguls, Louis B. Mayer, gloried in his friendship with Hoover and his overnight visits to the White House, but MGM never became associated with Hoover as Warners did with Roosevelt. It couldn't have, even if Mayer had tried. The studios weren't yet important enough, the president wasn't yet important enough, and each one's defining principle—stardom as power, power as stardom—had yet to assert themselves clearly enough for a symbiosis to emerge. With the coming of FDR, all the conditions were met.

No one recognized that truth more clearly than Jack Warner, the president's preferred mogul. Mayer may have gotten mileage out of his friendship with Hoover, but Warner made movies out of it. Nor was his fealty a product of mere party loyalty. In his autobiography, Warner declares that he and his brother Harry (who headed the studio's East Coast operations) "had always been faithful Republicans"—until meeting FDR. Soon Jack was Los Angeles chairman of the NRA and boasting how he "virtually commuted to the White House." FDR "enjoyed having me around," he later explained, "because I was an amusing fellow who wanted nothing in exchange."[13]

The mutual duplicities and self-deceptions in such a statement are breathtaking to contemplate. Yet even factoring out the inevitable exaggerations, there was genuine affection between the two men and a real sense of trust. Roosevelt successfully prevailed upon Warner to make a movie of *Mission to Moscow*, Joseph E. Davies's account of his time as ambassador to the Soviet Union, to boost Allied relations. (Four years later it was a decision the mogul would very publicly regret when the House Committee on Un-American Activities, at its Hollywood Ten hearings, cited the film as a particularly subversive example of pro-Soviet propaganda.) Conversely, a cherished project of Warner's was "to make a picture which, for want of a better title, I called *The Roosevelt Story*."[14]

It was a movie he never made. Instead, Warner came back to the GOP fold. (He hadn't even waited for FDR's death, having supported Wendell Willkie in 1940.) Within a few years, if he were cherishing the thought of a political biopic, it could have been called—for want of a grander title—*The Nixon Story*. After all, the only thing Nixon needed to get Jerome Hellman rehired was a brief phone call. That's the kind of sway he held with Warner, who, according to one biographer, "was in awe of Richard Nixon."[15]

Their relationship dated from the Hollywood Ten hearings, where the one bright spot for Warner had been Nixon's questioning. The congressman made sure to absent himself after the first day of testimony, but what questions he asked before then included a selection of softballs lobbed in the direction of a grateful Warner. When Nixon ran for president thirteen years later, Warner supported him as fervently as he had Roosevelt, personally paying for full-page ads in the *New York Times* and other newspapers to boost his candidate.[16] Warner remained a supporter in 1968 and enjoyed the fruits of their friendship after his victory. Where FDR had asked him to make a movie, Nixon helped Warner reedit one. He had taken the president a preview version of the musical *1776* for showing at the White House, and Nixon suggested eliminating an antiwar song and antibusiness song that had appeared in the stage version. Warner happily complied.[17]

By then, Warner was in no position to put his studio at the disposal of the president. For one thing, it was no longer his studio: he had sold his holdings in 1967. For another, the culture of both Hollywood and the country had changed far too much for a president's politics to be reflected in a studio's output. The centralized, top-down organization of the Studio Age had long since given way to a vastly more diffuse environment in which scores of boutique operations flourished and the grand old names—Warners, Universal, 20th Century–Fox, MGM, Paramount, Columbia—increasingly concerned themselves with distribution rather than production. And even as the imperial presidency that had begun with Roosevelt grew vastly in power and influence, the office lost the unique hold on the national imagination that it had held during FDR's twelve years in office. There hadn't been another president like him, and no one was more conscious of it than Richard Nixon.

Ike may have been his presidential father, and JFK his fabled nemesis, but of all those who preceded Richard Nixon as chief executive, "the ghost that did most to shape his presidency was that of Franklin Delano Roosevelt," or so felt Raymond Price, his chief speechwriter and one of the few subordinates the president considered an intellectual peer. "It was the Roosevelt pattern in domestic policy that Nixon sought to reverse, the Roosevelt coalition he sought to replace, the Roosevelt legacy he sought to supplant."[18] Theodore H. White agreed, stating that "anyone who has talked to Richard Nixon, over a period of years and privately, knows that, without ever avowing it, he has been running against Franklin D. Roosevelt since he began campaigning for office. He speaks of Roosevelt not with bitterness or disrespect or anger—but in a way that makes clear in all conversation that his own measure of himself is a measure against Franklin Roosevelt."[19]

How could it have been otherwise? Nixon was nineteen when Roosevelt was first elected president, too young to vote but old enough for his political consciousness to be lastingly affected, and it was under FDR that he came of political age. During a 1981 interview, Nixon dismissed the idea that Roosevelt had influenced his political thinking. "You must understand that in the thirties, of course, I was in school, in law school."[20] Yet it was as a law student that Nixon most directly experienced the New Deal: he helped support himself at Duke with a research stipend from the National Youth Administration. He listened to the Fireside Chats ("very effective"),[21] strongly supported the Social Security Act, but very much opposed Roosevelt's running for a third term. That opposition inspired his first political speeches, as he stumped for Willkie. During the war, he even got to experience the Roosevelt star power at firsthand—though it was in the person of Eleanor, whom he saw on New Caledonia, in 1943.

The most tangible influence Roosevelt had on Nixon was in invoking a cocker spaniel. The reference to Checkers in the 1952 fund speech originated in Roosevelt's celebrated ridicule of the Republicans for criticizing his dog Fala in the 1944 presidential campaign. "I got kind of a malicious pleasure out of it," Nixon later told Stewart Alsop. "'I'll needle them on this one,' I said to myself."[22] A decade later Nixon had an opportunity to go after another Roosevelt when, having moved back to California after losing the presidential election in 1960, he found himself living in the congressional district represented by FDR's son James. Urged to run against him in 1962, Nixon instead took on Pat Brown. (Roosevelt would be one of the more prominent Democrats to endorse Nixon over McGovern in 1972 and after Nixon resigned the presidency visited him in exile in San Clemente.)

Once in the White House, one of Nixon's first acts was to have the Fish Room, a conference room across the hall from the Oval Office, renamed the Roosevelt Room for TR and FDR. Nixon was heard to boast of his staff having "the highest IQs since FDR's Brains Trust,"[23] a jab at JFK's New Frontiersmen as well as a compliment to Roosevelt. In April 1970 Nixon watched *Sunrise at Campobello*, the film adaptation of Dore Schary's hagiographic account of FDR coming to terms with his polio. It made enough of an impression that, two years later, just prior to the Republican convention, Nixon ordered Haldeman to have a print taken to a wheelchair-bound George Wallace "as a way of giving him a big lift."[24]

For months Nixon had been cultivating the Alabama governor, eager to ensure Wallace would not be running against him as a third-party candidate for president as he had in 1968. With McGovern for an opponent, Nixon saw the makings of a landslide victory and wanted nothing to stand in its way. He wanted his own version of 1936, the election that demonstrated the coalition that had elected Roosevelt four years before was a force that would dominate U.S. politics. That year even Frank Nixon voted for FDR. That's how resounding a triumph it had been. Lyndon Johnson's landslide in 1964 had been a freak, a one-of-a-kind lining-up of the political planets, with Goldwater's ineptitude only strengthening Johnson's invincibility in the wake of JFK's murder. Johnson's reelection was as much JFK's reelection and Goldwater's rejection. But '36 had been all about FDR—a landslide reelection of an incumbent by acclamation—as Nixon hoped '72 would be all about Nixon. Just as Johnson had hungered to better FDR's victory margin, so did Nixon. Only FDR had a better electoral record at the national level than he did; this was his chance to draw even with the champion.

Of course, Nixon wanted more than just a landslide to rival FDR's in 1936. He wanted to create a sea change in American politics. What the FDR coalition had been to the middle third of the twentieth century his—*his*—"New American Majority" would be to the final third. That's why it was so crucial that 1972 prove to be not 1964 (which had produced no realignment) but 1936. Nixon saw his role as decisively reorienting his party and, in reorienting it, redefining what it stood for and whom it represented. As Patrick Buchanan declared in a memo to Nixon on November 10, 1972, "Our primary objective in the second term should be making of the President, the Republican FDR, founder and first magistrate of a political dynasty."[25] It's not insignificant that the gravamen of Buchanan's memo is his desire to be named director of communication, a request that comes after many hundreds of words of similar flattery. He knew just what his boss wanted to hear. Right down to the grandiose rhetoric and referring to Nixon by title rather than name, Buchanan was parroting his boss's thoughts. FDR, not JFK, was the set of initials that mattered most to him: JFK he'd wanted to beat, but FDR he wanted to *be*. "Franklin Roosevelt was a titan," Nixon remarked to an aide in 1992, if also "a superb manipulator. . . . He had it all: the ability to take risks, balance pragmatism and idealism, make the hard decisions, and use power for a supreme cause."[26] The wistfulness in those words is not hard to hear, the sense of identification painfully close to the surface.

For Roosevelt presented more than just an ideal of presidential success to which Nixon might aspire. FDR could also be seen to offer a degree of fellowship as a brother in contumely. The most hated presidents of the twentieth century, Roosevelt and Nixon found themselves incessantly scorned, reviled, ridiculed. The *reasons* for each man's inspiring such hatred differed, to be sure, but not the degree of hatred or the extent to which it was personal. To his enemies, FDR was simply "that man," the two syllables dripping with equal parts venom and bile. "Tricky Dick" never mustered quite the same level of outrage—it was too jocose, too dismissive—but any deficiencies in contempt were more than balanced by the ardor with which the epithet was employed.

No, Nixon had to suffer the singular ignominy of having even his own surname turned against him. Pronouncing *Nixon*—the flatness of the *n*'s repetition, the hiss of the *x*—all too easily lent itself to a sneer. *Roosevelt* was too ungainly for any such purpose; it sounded the way Queen Victoria looked: off-putting, irreproachable. Not *Nixon*, alas: those five five-o'clock-shadowed letters would sit there and sigh—stop a moment to linger over the sound of them—like sullen poetry on the page. It's such a simple, abrupt name (almost a palindrome): the symmetrical *n*'s, a pair of glowering bookends; that sinister, axial *x*, poised in the middle, neat as a cross; and the two vowels, so close but in the end not, with that notness violating the perfection of the lexical arrangement and, in the intractable opposition it comprises, representing the man's own insurmountably divided nature: the *echt*-anti-Communist who went to Beijing; the self-styled man of the people who shrank from the company of others; the embodiment of propriety whose mere presence could set off paroxysms of rude, irrational, even outrageous behavior in everyone from student to senior statesmen.

There was, for example, the unpleasantness at a soigné Georgetown dinner in 1950 to which both Nixon and Averell Harriman had been invited. "I will not eat dinner with that man," the future governor of New York declared for all to hear.[27] So Nixon, too, could be "that man" on occasion (Henry Kissinger had used the same term, and even more dismissively, prior to the press conference in 1974 when he threatened to resign)—but with a crucial difference. FDR was "that man" as viewed from below: an aristocrat whom even Wall Street and the country club set lacked enough lineage to look down upon—detest, yes, but only from an inferior position. Nixon was "that man" looked down on from above: the classic parvenu who, no matter how far he rises, retains his inferior status and remains open to detestation from all.

What is so striking about Nixon is his ineluctable apartness. The sense of loneliness conveyed by everything about him, from the furtiveness of his look to the awkwardness of his gait, is absolute. No matter how many people are in the room, Nixon is always somehow separate from them. Even with Pat—no, especially with Pat—he would seem distanced: isolated in his own gloom. The emotional moat is perpetually there. Nor is this impression just a quirk of the television camera or public platform. Up close and personal, he would look, if anything, even further away and more impersonal. As Jules Witcover noted after spending two weeks accompanying Nixon in 1966, "This man never seemed, even in a crowded room, to really be *with* anybody—and much preferred it that way."[28] In nearly everything he did, Nixon appears so uncomfortable. He manages to look out of place nearly everywhere, a kind of Zelig in reverse. No other public figure can match him in this peculiar capacity to seem incongruous in almost all situations.

The contrast with Roosevelt could not be greater. In his own way, FDR also communicates a consistent sense of being apart, but in an altogether different manner. For all his smiling affability, he is utterly aloof; nonetheless, even with his aristocratic distance, the man seems so deeply rooted in others' lives, so *connected*: a democratic Sun King ceaselessly shining down on his citizen-subject satellites. He gives the impression of fitting in anywhere, equally at ease at a Harvard commencement or a migrant labor camp, because his every action and gesture declares that whomever he is with exists as an extension of himself. When Stewart Alsop, who was a distant relation, mentioned to Nixon that FDR "wasn't really a warm personality" and described him as "essentially a cold man," Nixon was surprised. "Was he? I never met him. But he projected warmth."[29] That is the key: even someone so politically ill disposed toward FDR as Nixon might pick up on that warmth.

There was also this sense of unanimity about Roosevelt, as if he remained in the White House by acclamation or birthright. It drew on several sources—his regal bearing, the name shared with his cousin, his being a president in wartime, the unprecedented length of his time in office, the sheer tidal pull of his popularity—and it was also, of course, an illusion. Even at the zenith of his popularity, in the first few months of the New Deal, there were the likes of Louis B. Mayer waiting for him to fail. And in 1936, in his greatest triumph, almost 40 percent of the electorate voted against him. Still, the illusion was there. He *projected* consensus (as Nixon might have put it) and gave the impression of representing the American public in its entirety as no one else in the twentieth century did.

Of all the many differences between him and Nixon—the wealthy populist Democrat and the poor conservative Republican: light vs. dark, connection vs. separation, presence vs. absence, even (apparent) warmth vs. (transparent) cold—this may be the greatest of all. Nixon, the man who pledged to "bring us together," was all about divisiveness: not uniting people but splitting them apart. He was the dark prince of America's disorder. While Nixon did not create the climate of dislocation that marked his years in office, he both enlarged and profited by it. Roosevelt, the foremost presidential embodiment of "one out of many," built the great unifying coalition Nixon wanted to supersede. Nixon, the exploiter of faction and stirrer up of resentments, failed to make anything of his "New American Majority." How could he have? Such a political entity was inimical to everything he had stood for.

In that contrast, one finds each man reflecting "his" Hollywood. During the Rooseveltian Golden Age, Robert Sklar writes in *Movie-Made America*, "Hollywood directed its enormous powers of persuasion to preserving the basic moral, social and economic tenets of traditional American culture."[30] Indeed, that very congruence between Hollywood's images and the upholding of America's image underlay the goldenness of the age. The Silver Age was the exact opposite. Not only did it neglect to uphold those selfsame tenets of traditional American culture; it chose to deride them when not dismissing them outright. Ethan Mordden, writing of such proto-seventies movies as *Psycho* (1960) and *The Manchurian Candidate*, suggests they forced "upon Americans a new relationship with their movies, one of challenge rather than flattery, of doubt rather than certainty."[31] The New Hollywood took that evolution a decisive step further: going beyond challenge to condemnation, leaving behind doubt to achieve outright certainty of one's suspicions.

Where an abiding strength of the Golden Age had been its complete identification with the common culture, the Silver Age preferred detachment from that culture. By the late '60s, television had assumed the role that Hollywood had enjoyed during the Roosevelt years: the primary vehicle for popular entertainment and (through strict censorship practices and an implicit emphasis on moral uplift) custodian of middle-class values. Television's coming to the fore helped free Hollywood not just from Victorian sexual mores but also its hortatory, even evangelical posture toward society. The movies, in effect, were able to "marginalize" themselves and in so doing reap enormous aesthetic benefits. (Economic benefits, too: in 1972 gross box-office receipts for the first time exceeded those in what had been Hollywood's all-time record year, 1946—though inflation played no small part in that.) Hollywood did not become part of the counterculture exactly, the popularity of recreational drug use at Beverly Hills parties notwithstanding, but a significant aspect of it *did* assume a stance that lay athwart mainstream American culture.

In this sense, too, Richard Nixon—that great polarizing force, that studied sower of dissension—was the perfect figure to preside over the multiple-personality Hollywood of the late '60s and early '70s. For the New Hollywood by no means meant the death of the Old Hollywood, simply the loss of its monopoly. The Nixon years were the years of *Easy Rider* AND *Hello, Dolly!*, *Harold and Maude* AND *Love Story*, *Mean Streets* AND *The Sting*. The lumbering success of the likes of *Airport* (1970), *The Poseidon Adventure* (1972), and *The Sting*—massive hits, all—reminds us that canonical seventies movies were a minority. There were many more Nixon-type movies than Nixon-era movies. The former had gone out of fashion only critically. They were still doing well at the box office, still winning most Academy Awards. As Nixon, ever alert to majority preferences, lamented in 1971 to Nancy Hanks, of the National Endowment for the Arts, "They are still making the weird pictures, whereas the kinds of pictures people like to see are stories, they want to see a story! . . . Like

Charlton Heston, he always plays in story movies. We just gotta make some movies that do tell stories. Why is it for example that people still go see John Wayne?"[32]

Yet even the most anachronistic white elephants of the period—the disaster movies, say, with their underlying paranoia, or *The Sting*, with its celebration of criminality, or the willed nostalgia of *That's Entertainment* (1974), with its slogan of "Boy, do we need it now"—either betray traces of New Hollywood influence or are conscious reactions against it. No less of a dinosaur than *Airport* boasts split screens—like *Woodstock* (1970), for heaven's sakes—and *Love Story* was notorious for its smattering of off-color language.

Or notorious in the Nixon household. The president publicly praised the movie (which he had seen on Christmas Eve, no less). However, when he gave the film his presidential seal of approval, Nixon pointedly qualified his praise. All three Nixon women had read the book and experienced "shock" over "the dialogue they put in the girl's mouth," Nixon told reporters. "I wasn't shocked. I know these words, I know they use them. It's the 'in' thing to do." Swearing "has its place, but if it is used it should be used to punctuate."[33] Little did Nixon realize how ludicrously chaste the movie's one "bullshit" and occasional "goddamn's" would seem a few years later when his own failure to delete expletives from his private conversations became public.

Nixon saw *Love Story* just six days after it opened. Among other current releases he wasted little time in seeing were *The Poseidon Adventure* (the day it premiered), *Chisum* (the day after), *Hello, Dolly!* (eight days), and *Plaza Suite* (1971, two weeks). He was quick to fasten upon such safely staid titles, and that quickness underscores how relatively few of the movies he saw were current or recent releases, and of those current or recent releases almost none were seventies movies. Nixon's presidential moviegoing took place in the Silver Age, but it was very rarely *of* the Silver Age.

He saw only one film with Nicholson, as close as the period has to a defining actor, and that movie, *On a Clear Day You Can See Forever*, was highly atypical of the actor's career. Nixon saw nothing with Faye Dunaway or Warren Beatty or Jon Voight or Karen Black. He did see one film with Elliott Gould and two with Pacino, but none with Hoffman—Nicholson's nearest rival as the era's touchstone performer. There were no films directed by Arthur Penn, Paul Mazursky, Hal Ashby, Martin Scorsese, Bob Rafelson, Roman Polanski, or Brian De Palma. He did see a pair of Peckinpah Westerns (*Ride the High Country* and *Major Dundee*, 1965), but they safely predate *The Wild Bunch*. Among contemporary filmmakers, Nixon gravitated to such unthreatening, even anachronistic, talents as Arthur Hiller (five films), Norman Jewison (four), Gene Saks (three), and Sydney Pollack (two). He saw but one film directed by Mike Nichols (*The Day of the Dolphin*) and one by Ken Russell (*The Music Lovers*).

Nixon also saw but one movie directed by Robert Altman, arguably the foremost filmmaker of seventies Hollywood—certainly, the most *seventies* seventies filmmaker. That film, *The Long Goodbye,* is an example of the sort of trouble he could get himself into screening something contemporary. What would have seemed a safe-enough bet—the film version of Raymond Chandler's penultimate novel—instead fits out Philip Marlowe with neighbors who do their yoga exercises topless, sadistic cops, and a general atmosphere of dope-haze looseness. There's even a reference to Nixon. A gangster proudly informs Marlowe: "I live in Trousdale, three acres, across the street from where the president lived" (Trousdale Estates, as previously noted, was the Beverly Hills development where the Nixons moved in 1962).

Joan Tewkesbury, who's credited with the screenplay for *Nashville,* has said that part of that film's motivation was the director's hate for "what Nixon was doing to the country."[34] Yet fascination underlay Altman's disgust, and he would proudly display a letter Nixon sent him after resigning from office in which the former president confided that *Nashville* was Julie's "favorite movie" and inquired as to the possibility of obtaining a print for her.*

Later, he sent the director an inscribed copy of *RN.*[35] Altman no doubt kept it close at hand while filming *Secret Honor* (1984), Donald Freed and Arnold M. Stone's excoriating one-man play about Nixon's final days. In *Prêt-à-Porter* (1994), he includes a winningly uninflected joke about a character named Anne Eisenhower (Julia Roberts) having a brief affair with a journalist who, fumbling for her last name, refers to her as, what else, Anne Nixon—and the paper he works for is, of course, the *Washington Post.*

Nixon saw only three movies that were *echt*–Silver Age: *The Godfather, The Last Picture Show,* and *Klute.* The first can be seen as a simple concession to popular taste, and the second was so pallid a specimen of the genre that in her *New Yorker* review, Kael allowed as how "even Nixon could like *The Last Picture Show*"[36] (Safire reports that he did). But *Klute!* Yes, it's a well-made thriller, not a little in the Hitchcock vein. Indeed, it has certain affinities with *Frenzy,* the director's 1972 "comeback" film,

*Her having such a preference is surprising not least of all because her father is referred to in the film as "the asshole."

which Nixon saw in August of that year. There was also no way for him to know that the film's director, Alan J. Pakula, would later make something called *All the President's Men*. But the linked mysteries that drive the movie—what happened to the missing man from Pennsylvania who was Donald Sutherland's friend? and who is it stalking a New York call girl?—are merely devices to inspire anxieties far deeper than those of the "don't go in that room" variety. *Klute* is a movie meant to unsettle, and few viewers could have been more unsettled by it than Richard Nixon.

The movie opens with spools turning on a tape recorder—shades of the Oval Office?—and surreptitious taping is a recurring motif. Awash in kinky sexuality, it also boasts pimps, junkies, and that call girl, who turns out to be the heroine. It gets worse, for playing her is Jane Fonda—Hanoi Jane, a member in good standing of the White House enemies list—who, with a shag haircut, flauntingly braless, smoking dope, reading *Linda Goodman's Sun Signs*, is the very model of early '70s rebelliousness. If all that isn't bad enough, a portrait of JFK hangs (however improbably) in her bathroom. She tells one of her customers, "I think the only way any of us can be happy is to let it all hang out. You know, do it all and—fuck it." No, Nixon did not know. More his speed was Donald Sutherland as the title character—honorably stiff, a bit beleaguered, and more than a little out of his element. In his own way, Sutherland was very much a Silver Age figure. But the other movies of his Nixon saw weren't *M*A*S*H* or Mazursky's *Alex in Wonderland* (1970) or Dalton Trumbo's *Johnny Got His Gun* (1971), but a pair of World War II movies: *The Dirty Dozen* (1967) and *Kelly's Heroes* (1970).

Outright products of the New Hollywood were generally easy to recognize. A greater threat to Nixon's viewing enjoyment was what could be termed "genre infiltration." What better way for Nixon to seek ninety minutes of distraction in April 1974, as the dissolution of his presidency became increasingly inevitable, than to watch Peter Bogdanovich's updated screwball comedy, *What's Up, Doc?* Yet setting the story in motion—indeed, the first character we see—is a Daniel Ellsberg manqué (Michael Murphy) who has stolen a briefcase full of top-secret government documents. Just what Nixon would want to see: Ellsberg as laff riot.

Even something as Old Hollywood as *The Way We Were*, ostensibly a can't-miss, hopelessly retro star vehicle, turns out to be a paean to the Hollywood Ten. Not only is the film's heroine, Barbra Streisand, a communist, her marriage to Robert Redford founders on his choosing to remain apolitical (the ultimate seventies movie sin). There's a reference to bugging (the favorite seventies movie crime), as a film director discovers his screening room conceals a listening device. Worse, Nixon himself—albeit not by name—receives a dig. A left-wing scriptwriter complains at a cocktail party, "We can't even write our congressman. He's on the committee." As no other California representative sat on HUAC, it had to be Nixon. The jab couldn't have bothered him much: he saw the movie twice.

Just as an old-fashioned women's picture like *The Way We Were* could prove subversive, not even a Clint Eastwood Western could be completely relied upon—and the occasional irruption of a Dennis Hopper was the least of it. *Joe Kidd*, the last movie Nixon saw before the 1972 Republican convention, promised to be a simple tale of bounty hunter (Clint) and hunted. Instead, it turns into a tract on Hispanic rights and the evils of capitalism. Seeing his people's property claims being disallowed, a reformer named Luis Chama (John Saxon) protests, which leads a Southwestern land baron (Robert Duvall) to try to enlist Clint's title character in Saxon's murder. "I got claim to . . . nearly 600,000 acres," the magnate says. "I'm not going to permit some sheepherder by the name of Luis Chama to get away with cutting fences and stirring up the Mexican population with talk about land reform." "Louis CHAY-ma," Duvall says, anglicizing the name even as he demonizes it. Clint pronounces it correctly, of course. Which of them the movie favors—and why—is as plain as the fact that the white hats here have a distinctly reddish tinge.

Duvall also figures as a sinister rich man in Francis Ford Coppola's *The Conversation*, which exemplifies not genre infiltration but rather what one might call genre inauguration. As we've seen, the paranoid thriller is both the key seventies genre and the most explicit example of Nixon's impact on contemporary Hollywood. *The Conversation* is the subtlest of these films—and so, in some ways, the most troubling. No other seventies film is so *atmospherically* Nixonian, so spiritually blanched, or given to such a tightly held anguish; and its external particulars—the plot concerns a professional wiretapper inadvertently uncovering a conspiracy—provide the most overt instance of Nixon's unspoken yet manifest presence in movies of the period.

The Conversation opens in San Francisco's Union Square, where a pair of lovers are meeting clandestinely. Their conversation is being secretly taped by Harry Caul (Gene Hackman), a renowned surveillance expert who has been hired by a business executive (Duvall) to investigate the couple. In the maze of ambient noise he gets on tape, Caul picks out one of the lovers saying, "He'd kill us if he got the chance." Or what if it's "He'd kill *us* if he got the chance"? Caul assumes the former and finds himself plunged into a moral quagmire. Several years before, his eaves-dropping led to the murder of three people. Can Caul, still consumed with guilt, let the same thing happen again? Yet even more problematic than the question of how he might intervene is the fact that intervention of any kind is utterly inimical to a man like Caul, someone who predicates his existence on maintaining an insurmountable distance toward all other people.

The Conversation owes an obvious debt to *Blow-Up* (1966), using audio-tape to do for ambiguity what Antonioni's film did with photography, and to a more European approach generally. This is another reason it's a key film in the seventies pantheon: just as the French New Wave could not have happened without the influence of Hollywood's Golden Age, so was the Silver Age unthinkable without the example of the leading European filmmakers of the early '6os: Fellini, Bergman, Truffaut, Godard, and, of course, Antonioni. In no other film is this quite so apparent as *The Conversation*. It's not too much to say that Coppola's film—so reified and ea-gerly peripheral—is the most European film ever made on this side of the Atlantic. It's what *Zabriskie Point* might have been had Antonioni set up shop in the Bay Area rather than Death Valley.

With its concerns about privacy and illegal taping, *The Conversation* would seem even more influenced by Watergate. In fact, its origins pre-date the break-in—yet further proof of how much Nixon was simply in the cinematic air, superseding actual occurrence to become a source of inspiration unto himself. He even figures in the film as a job credential: Harry's chief professional rival (Allen Garfield) implies he once bugged Tricky Dick himself. He announces that a bugging job he did may have helped ensure a presidential candidate's defeat "a dozen years ago"— that is, 1960, an election in which, as we have seen, the losing candidate harbored similar suspicions. Nixon is also mentioned, by name this time, during a television news broadcast, when Harry desperately turns on a tel-evision to drown out the sounds of the murder.

Coppola says the inspiration for the movie came from a conversation he had in 1966 about the existence of a microphone that could be used to eavesdrop from a distance on individuals in a crowd.* He wrote his first draft of the script in 1968 and claims to have finished two-thirds of the filming by June 17, 1972.[37] "I never meant it to be so relevant," Coppola

*In his book *An American Life,* Jeb Magruder recounts how G. Gordon Liddy, on his second day at CREEP, ordered Magruder to turn on the radio in his room before he'd talk to him. He pointed across the street. "There's a new honing [*sic*] device that can pick up vibrations across a street and through a window."

lamented. "I almost think the picture would have been better received had Watergate not happened."[38] He may be right. Harry's profession makes *The Conversation* now seem like a period piece: an illustration in a 35-mm textbook on "the Watergate era." In point of fact, Coppola's film is far less an exposé of wiretapping than it is a character study. What is truly remarkable about the film, what transcends any allusion to Watergate, is Hackman's Harry Caul. Hackman is brilliantly cast against type: such a vigorous, forthright actor bringing an undertow of tension, a reined-in quality, to someone so aggressively recessive. A man most vivid in his inhibitions, Harry is unlike the protagonist of any other Hollywood movie. Blank, colorless, evasive, he wears a plastic rain shell whenever outdoors and can announce in all sincerity, "I have nothing personal" except "my keys." He also wears a pair of off-puttingly ugly eyeglasses that could have been passed on to him by J.J. Hunsecker (a onetime client?) and that serve the same purpose the columnist's did: to wall off their wearer, to shield him from the gaze of others even as they enhance his own ability to scrutinize.

Harry is frequently shown behind glass blocks, scrims, screens, or in mist: a man in hiding even when out in the open—no, especially when out in the open. Lurching, lugubrious, ardently opaque, he could be the son Nixon never had. Certainly, he's capable of remarking (as Nixon once did), "I must build a wall around me."[39] Maybe you just want nothing so much as to disappear into your own discomfort, to become as invisible as—in Harry's case—the sounds you record. Both men make of introversion something aesthetic. They are hunger artists of emotion, presenting their loneliness for others' inspection as a wrought artifact: the alienated sublime. Harry, in fact, goes so far as to declare artistic status. "I'm a kind of musician," he tells his girlfriend just before she leaves him, "a freelance musician." And it's true, in a way: moving meaning from air to magnetic tape, he's a sonic maestro, manipulating the impalpable at his soundboard, sitting before it with all the assurance and skill of an Art Tatum at the keyboard.

The musical analogy may be just figurative for Harry's vocation, but it applies literally to his avocation. The one personal pastime we see him indulge in is playing the saxophone. Even that emphasizes his isolation: he sits alone in his apartment playing along with a record (technology is the sole companion he's comfortable with). One thinks of Nixon, after the firing of Archibald Cox led to the first wave of calls for his impeachment, banging away at the piano well after midnight in the White House. "Sometimes all alone at night," Julie Nixon Eisenhower confided to a reporter, "you'll hear this music in the hallways."[40] The image conjured up, of a president so besieged he can seek solace only in sound, is as haunting as that with which *The Conversation* ends: Harry, having torn up his apartment in an unsuccessful search for a listening device, sits in the now completely emptied space, mournfully playing his saxophone. This time, though, he's playing for an audience: the person (or persons) who have bugged *him*.

Not a great film, *The Conversation* is something rarer, actually: a troubling and persistent film, one whose sense of internalized confinement and hermetic despair match Harry's own. It's studied and schematic, but also possessed of an intelligence and moral concern unusual in any Hollywood era. It is at once a mark of the film's quality and a tribute to the special character of seventies Hollywood that *The Conversation* was one of the Best Picture nominees at the 1974 Academy Awards ceremony. A particular significance attaches to that ceremony, for on that night the revolution not only reached but finally overran the most sacred precinct of the Old Hollywood, the Academy of Motion Picture Arts and Sciences. Three of that year's Best Picture nominees, *Godfather II*, *Chinatown*, and *Lenny*, Bob Fosse's adaptation of the play about comedian Lenny Bruce, were pure products of the seventies imagination. Each also subverted a classic Golden Age genre: the gangster picture, the crime film, and the biopic. As for *The Conversation*, it was, if anything, even purer seventies, exemplifying the paranoid thriller. The idea of a major studio (in this case, Paramount) backing such a film would have seemed unthinkable as recently as five years before.

The fifth nominee, *The Towering Inferno*, was so hackneyed a throwback to the empty old days that its presence simply underscores the sea change Hollywood had undergone. It even bears traces, faint though they may be, of the new dispensation. As a disaster movie, it belongs to the other genre developed during the Silver Age. Also marking it as being of its time is the occupation assigned its primary villains: Richard Chamberlain and William Holden play wealthy businessmen, a type whose capacity for evil is second only to faceless government officials in Silver Age demonology. Yet the nomination of such a crowd-pleasing blunderbuss as *The Towering Inferno* also showed the staying power, and hinted at the eventual restoration, of the ancien régime. Ironically enough, for all its overindulgence in Old Hollywood values—star and spectacle and budget doing the work of what might even remotely resemble art—Irwin Allen's burning-building blockbuster is the one nominated film to betray contempt for the Golden Age. How else to describe so shabby an act of movieland lèse-majesté as revealing to the audience that the tux worn by Fred Astaire's gentleman con artist is a rental?

The Towering Inferno won for Best Cinematography (Gordon Willis, the decade's most influential cinematographer, wasn't even nominated for *Godfather II*); and, in an even greater travesty, Walter Murch and Arthur Rochester's work on *The Conversation*—the most innovative use of film's sonic properties since *Citizen Kane*—lost the Best Sound award to Ronald Pierce and Melvin Metcalfe Sr. for *Earthquake* and its Cinerama-for-the-ears gimmick, Sensurround. Clearly, the Old Hollywood wasn't giving up without a fight. Just as clearly, however, this was the New Hollywood's night. The Best Actress prize went to Ellen Burstyn for her feminist title role in *Alice Doesn't Live Here Anymore* (Martin Scorsese's second film for a major studio). Even so plain a concession to nostalgia as the Best Actor award to Art Carney for his cat-loving retiree in *Harry and Tonto* was a nod to the Silver Age. True, Carney's recognition came at the expense of performances by Pacino in *Godfather II* and Nicholson in *Chinatown* that helped define the era—but in its far sunnier way, *Harry and Tonto* was as much a product of the New Hollywood as those films were, having been written and directed by Mazursky, who was to the Silver Age what Leo McCarey had been to the Golden. Nor did *Chinatown* or *Godfather II* go unrecognized. Robert Towne's classic script for the former won the Best Original Screenplay award, and *Godfather II* dominated the evening. Though far darker than *The Godfather*, and nowhere near as successful at the box office, it still won Best Picture, as well as Best Director, Best Adapted Screenplay, Best Score, and Best Art Direction. Most telling of all, Robert De Niro won for Best Supporting Actor—this despite the fact that the film's admirers had two other nominees, Lee Strasberg and Michael V. Gazzo, to choose from in the category; and De Niro also had to contend with a clear sentimental favorite, *The Towering Inferno*'s Astaire. (Could it have been the tux?)

The most startling demonstration of the New Hollywood's domination of the Old came in a lesser category, Best Documentary Feature. The winner was *Hearts and Minds*, a tendentious and (in hindsight, at least) painfully superficial critique of U.S. involvement in Indochina Accepting the award, coproducer Bert Schneider told the audience, "It is ironic that we're here at a time just before Vietnam is about to be liberated," and then read a telegram of congratulation from the National Liberation Front. Later in the ceremonies, Bob Hope had Frank Sinatra read a hastily written disclaimer. It was too late. The final bastion had fallen. Hollywood had not only ceased to love America. Saluting the imminent victory of North Vietnam and the NLF, it had announced it loved America's enemies. Short of putting Dennis Hopper in the White House, it's hard to imagine a starker symbol of Political Hollywood triumphant.

Five years later a Hollywood actor did get elected president—but his name wasn't Hopper. It was, in fact, hard on the heels of the 1974 Oscars that one could discern the first clear-cut sign of the coming of Reagan-era Hollywood—the Hollywood dominated by George Lucas and Steven Spielberg's magic-industrial complex; the Hollywood of *Star Wars* and *E.T.* (1982); the Hollywood that once again abjured controversy and prided itself on providing escapism; the Hollywood whose loss of nerve would be most apparent in its mania for sequels, the Hollywood of Rocky and Rambo, of Superman and Indiana Jones, of even, alas, *Godfather III* (1990); the Hollywood that reorganized itself as part of a new world entertainment order that dwarfed anything even the most visionary mogul of the Studio Age might have imagined; and, above all, the Hollywood that began to generate more income, and from more sources, than anyone could have previously thought possible. From the outset, of course, Hollywood had been about money—but never before so grandly, so globally. The Silver Age, one can now see, was a kind of interregnum between dynasties, the studio system and the synergies system. Even as Saigon fell (and Bert Schneider rejoiced), the restoration of the Old Hollywood was getting under way.

When the interregnum began to end can be dated as precisely as its high-water mark. On June 22, 1975, Spielberg's *Jaws* opened. The film was a sensation, the likes of which Hollywood had never seen. It made $7.1 million that first weekend, helped to the biggest opening in Hollywood history by $700,000 worth of television advertising. Its success beggared that of *The Godfather*, which had required ten months to become the top-grossing film of all time. *Jaws* took only eighty days to surpass it in gross receipts. Far more than just an expert entertainment (which it certainly is), *Jaws* unveiled a brave new world in the marketing of American movies. It had three basic elements: building up audience interest in advance through the use of television advertising, exploiting the film's opening as fully as possible through saturation booking, and aiming the film primarily at the teenage audience. This new dynamic put a premium on artistic predictability (the formulaic being a far easier sell than the innovative or difficult) and, by substantially increasing marketing costs, worked to raise the cost of filmmaking generally, thus making it substantially harder for the work of unestablished or provocative directors to get studio backing.

The undoing of the New Hollywood came at the hands of two of its own. Spielberg's first theatrical release was *The Sugarland Express* (1974)—Nixon saw it at Key Biscayne four months before he resigned—a small, offbeat work recognizably in the Silver Age mode, as was George Lucas's first film, *THX 1138* (1971), a chilly dystopian fantasy. It was Lucas's *Star Wars* that completed the restoration. It opened almost exactly two years after *Jaws* had—and earned no less than $63 million more (back when that was real money). The empire had struck back, with a vengeance, and between those two openings sealed the fate of the Silver Age. True, it was a somewhat slow fade to black. *Nashville* opened one week before *Jaws* did. *One Flew Over the Cuckoo's Nest* took every major award at the 1975 Academy Awards. The next year *Taxi Driver*, *Network*, and *All the President's Men* received Oscar nominations for Best Picture (only to lose to, of all things, *Rocky*). *Days of Heaven* was released in 1978, *Apocalypse Now* (the Götterdämmerung of seventies movies) in 1979, and as late as 1980 there was *Raging Bull*. But these were stragglers refusing to surrender long after their army had disbanded. The Silver Age now belonged to history as much as the Golden Age did.

All this, one can be sure, was a matter of complete indifference to the nemesis/muse of the New Hollywood. Even if seventies movies had been more like *Around the World in 80 Days*—and they hadn't—Richard Nixon had other things on his mind by the time *Jaws* opened. He'd been back in San Clemente for ten months, a president forced to resign, a tutelary deity dispatched into exile. Just as those gleaming sharky teeth had snapped shut on the New Hollywood, so had the "smoking gun" tape done in the man who had presided over it. Their oblique, charged relationship was no more, rendered moot by the course of events. The conversation between them had been concluded, and it's no exaggeration to say neither our movies nor our politics have been as interesting since.

Oliver Stone, left, *directs Joan Allen, as Pat Nixon, and Anthony Hopkins, as Richard Nixon*

Epilogue

Nixon in the Movies

Why would you give Oliver Stone seven dollars of your money? RICHARD NIXON TO AN AIDE, UPON HEARING SHE'D SEEN *JFK*, DECEMBER 23, 1991[1]

Nixon arrived on the national stage just as television did, in the late '40s, and stayed there for almost fifty years, longer than any figure of comparable stature in our history. Such ubiquity in the mass media made it impossible for Hollywood to ignore him. More important, his spectacularly peculiar personality made him impossible to resist. Shakespeare couldn't keep from writing about Iago, Malvolio, Richard III. With Nixon, you get all three. Is it any wonder so many filmmakers have found him irresistible?*

To his dying day, he was a work in progress, a flesh-and-blood story arc, forever in search of an uplifting ending and never finding one. There were all those "new Nixons" so arduously emerging from a man who kept trying to reinvent himself. Fatiguing though such an internal process must have been, its incessant unease and constant novelty are an artist's mother lode. The very traits that made Nixon so ill suited to politics—the sense of inauthenticity, the personal uncomfortableness—endow him with even more possibilities onscreen than off-.

*Anyone pursuing the intersection of Nixon and popular culture owes a debt to Thomas Monsell's *Nixon on Stage and Screen: The Thirty-seventh President as Depicted in Films, Television, Plays and Opera.*

Among other things, the endless discrepancy between who Nixon was and how he wanted to be seen makes him a walking punch line. Just the sound of his name or sight of his face is enough to provide a comic pay off. As Robin Williams laments in *Good Morning, Vietnam* (1987), "I can't even make fun of Richard Nixon, and there's a man who's screaming out to be made fun of." One of the funniest sight gags in *The Big Lebowski* (1998) is the poster that hangs in Jeff Bridges's apartment of Nixon bowling. (It must be said, though, that 1991's *Barton Fink* is the Coen brothers movie where Nixon most belongs.) To see Beavis encountering a White House portrait of Nixon in *Beavis and Butt-Head Do America* (1996) is a joke unto itself. And in *Caddyshack* (1980), all Cindy Morgan has to do to dismiss Chevy Chase's love of the links is say, "Nixon plays golf."

When the man's sheer incongruity isn't employed to supply a laugh, there's his darkness to draw on as a kind of existential shorthand. Bob Dole called a photo of Gerald Ford, Jimmy Carter, and Nixon, "See No Evil, Hear No Evil, and Evil." His being the sole president to have resigned ensures his villain status transcends partisanship and endures long after the heat of political combat has cooled. A less heinous Benedict Arnold, Nixon remains an American archetype of moral failure.

Certainly, Hollywood has exploited that aspect of his image. In *Misery* (1990), James Caan discovers an "Elect Nixon" pennant in Kathy Bates's scrapbook. Forget the news clippings about mysterious deaths in her vicinity. Forget even the clipping about her being sent to prison. *Here* is proof positive of how scary she is. In *Fear and Loathing in Las Vegas* (1998), we glimpse Nixon wearing a Hitler mustache on a poster in Benicio Del Toro's office. Later, after he's seen delivering the Silent Majority speech on three televisions in the hotel suite of a severely drug-addled Johnny Depp, each talking head comes off the screen to float through the room. Do bad trips get any worse?

Sometimes Nixon just happens. He has an unnerving capacity to crop up in the interstices of movies—even interstellar interstices (he's an uncredited Voice through Space in *Contact*, 1997). One of the first things seen in Leon Gast's 1996 documentary, *When We Were Kings*, about the 1974 heavyweight championship fight between Muhammad Ali and George Foreman, is a close-up of Ali announcing at a press conference, "If you think the world was surprised when Nixon resigned, / Wait until I kick Foreman's behind." A Nixon bobblehead doll appears in *The Buena Vista Social Club* (1999). Inevitably, he figures in *Forrest Gump* (1994). That appearance required a good deal of computer-generated help. It's through undoctored archival footage that he makes cameos in everything from Steven Seagal action features (*Above the Law*, 1988) to Dennis Quaid male weepies (*Frequency*, 2000) to rock-star biopics (*The Doors*, 1991).

The director of *The Doors* is, of course, Oliver Stone. His *Nixon* is only the most notable of many instances of a film with the thirty-seventh president as protagonist or leading character. On the face of it, it makes no sense. Wouldn't a Washington or Lincoln make a better presidential muse? Each has a luster that Nixon (drab, dreary Nixon) so achingly lacks. That's just the point, though. A Lincoln or a Washington is a monumental presence and overwhelms the imagination. Think of how the reverential treatment in even such highly regarded films as *Young Mr. Lincoln* or *Abe Lincoln in Illinois* stunts portrayal of the protagonist.

Or what about Kennedy? He would seem ideal casting for the part of Hollywood president: so handsome, so perfect for the part, all white teeth and never-fading tan. Yet his very perfection as a celebrity personage undercuts Kennedy artistically. James Ellroy knew just what he was doing when he called his 1995 novel about the assassination *American Tabloid*. A tabloid dream, JFK seduces the imagination. Indeed, his image is so potent that just invoking the name conjures up his presence. It makes perfect sense no actor plays him in Stone's *JFK*. The title—no, that set of initials—is more than enough.

Conversely, the title character appears in nearly every frame of Stone's *Nixon*—all 192 minutes of it. How could it be otherwise? Nixon, in all his sweaty darkling splendor, challenges the imagination. He has to be seen to be believed—and then reimagined to be understood. Where a Lincoln appeals to our aspirations, a Kennedy to our fantasies, Nixon just is. He meets us face-to-face (even if he refuses to meet our gaze), neither his virtues nor even his vices outsize.

On the few occasions Nixon was willing to sit for an official portrait, John Ehrlichman recalls, he'd invariably joke "about the hard job an artist had in making him look good."[2] A far harder job is to make him look convincing.

Who could have done him justice? Even before the question of skill, there's the matter of physical resemblance. Warren Oates? Dean Stockwell? Zachary Scott? A degraded Dirk Bogarde? An exalted Harry Dean Stanton? Any actor playing Nixon faces two fundamental problems. First, there is familiarity: imitate him too closely, the performance falls into mere mimicry; fail to imitate him enough, and the performance lacks verisimilitude. Even more challenging is the issue of plausibility: how to take a star turn as a character so utterly lacking in star power?

What is surely the richest flesh-and-blood rendering of Nixon, James Maddalena's performance of the title role in the Houston Grand Opera production of John Adams's *Nixon in China* and on the subsequent Nonesuch recording (1988), has the great advantage of being sung as well as acted. Adams's music enormously enhances Maddalena's ability to convey the constant battle in Nixon between the banal and the epic: his plodding delivery and awkward manner versus his overarching vision of world affairs.

Others who have attempted Nixon have fared less well. In *Nasty Habits* (1977), Glenda Jackson has the benefit of being doubly unique. Not only is Jackson the sole actress to play a Nixon-based character. She gets to play him as Nixon would have liked to be: decisive, commanding, unflappable (that, and she has Ehrlichman's eyebrows). Hollywood, which loves to show Nixon as a pawn or buffoon, for once goes to the other extreme.

Bob Gunton, who was Juan Perón in the original Broadway production of *Evita*, is perhaps the least plausible of all movie Nixons, in *Elvis Meets Nixon* (1997). He doesn't look like him, sound like him, or move like him. He plays the character strictly for burlesque: scribbling up an enemies list, which he hides behind his family Christmas list; watching a football game with a San Diego Chargers jersey over his dress shirt and tie. The most memorable thing about the film, from a Nixonian perspective, is a documentary-style cameo from Alexander Butterfield Jr., the Haldeman aide who revealed the existence of the White House taping system. He proves to have a surprisingly relaxed and engaging camera presence.

Almost as risible as Gunton is Beau Bridges in that TNT movie *Kissinger and Nixon*. He's always using football jargon and proffering cocktails—preferably bourbon—even to the teetotaling Haldeman. He keeps calling Chuck Colson "Charlie" and generally behaves with a manic oafishness that makes Ron Silver's Kissinger look suave by comparison.

In *Concealed Enemies* (1984), a PBS drama about Alger Hiss and Whittaker Chambers, Peter Riegert enjoys the considerable benefit of playing Nixon before he's recognizably *Nixon*. He's still a work in behavioral progress. Other than a noticeable thickening of his brows, there's no attempt to make Riegert look like Nixon, and the only actorly suggestions of him are a tightness in the shoulders and the mechanical hand gestures while speaking in public—chopping the air, punching fist into palm—that became as much a part of his physical demeanor as the upthrust V-for-victory.

Rip Torn, in *Blind Ambition* (1979), the CBS miniseries based on John Dean's memoir, is also good at Nixon's body language, and there's a fair physical resemblance. Overall, it's a surprisingly restrained performance from one of the great Hollywood scenery-chewers. In contrast, Jason Robards's Richard Monckton in the ABC miniseries *Washington: Behind Closed Doors* (1977) always seems to be shouting, as if noise were the sole cure for his perpetual dyspepsia. In profile, Robards can look a bit like Nixon's Watergate lawyer, James St. Clair. Worse, there's the association with Ben Bradlee, from his Oscar-winning work in *All the President's Men*. The idea of casting Robards must have gotten a good laugh when it first came up (once again, Nixon is his own punch line), but this time the joke's on the viewer.

For sheer explosiveness, no Nixon performance matches Philip Baker Hall's tour de force in Robert Altman's *Secret Honor*. If Torn captures Nixon's tortured body language, Hall inhabits it. In our first shadowy glimpse of him, on a television monitor, the resemblance is eerie. Hall's ability to communicate the sense of cramp that afflicted Nixon's every movement verges on the physically painful—for viewer as well as actor. It's as if each appendage is only a spasm away from starting to move of its own free will. Hall's voice barely recalls Nixon's (he has instead the gargly timbre of George C. Scott), but who notices when he roars out a declaration like "The prisoner in the dock is guilty of one crime only, and that crime is being *Richard . . . Milhous . . . N IXON!*"

Hall's Nixon is a malevolent clown, an angry puppet. The film's constant agitation becomes tiresome, as does the supposed humor of Hall's eruptive obscenity and the sniggery bark of his laughter. Alternately the occasion of laughter and disgust, contempt and perplexity, this Nixon is a sot, a mama's boy, delusional, physically inept, morally negligible. It's so extreme a portrait that a furtive, feral sympathy keeps slipping out from the dense disdain that otherwise characterizes the film.

It must be said, Altman does keep things moving—no small feat for a filmed one-man play. Stone's *Nixon* barrels along, too, and that despite working on a vastly larger canvas. But Stone's gift for narrative velocity derives from the inherent pulpiness of his sensibility, which does not exactly conduce to his stated aim of achieving the cinematic equivalent of Shakespeare's history plays. There's something very nearly psychotic about Stone's moviemaking. This keeps it exciting, unpredictable, electric—but also, well, nutty. The narrator of the newsreel about Nixon's career that Stone uses as a movie within a movie says of the Checkers speech, "It was shameless. It was manipulative. It was a huge success." Other than "huge success," he could be talking about *Nixon*.

It's *Citizen Kane* without Rosebud. The voice-overs and documentary clearly echo Welles. The way Stone has his cinematographer, Robert Richardson, shoot the White House—angled up, through the Pennsylvania Avenue fence, in wild wind and rain—declares it an alabaster Xanadu. Mary Steenburgen's Hannah Nixon is a prettier—and even more severe!—Agnes Moorehead. Joan Allen's Pat Nixon is Dorothy Comingore with more spine but just as beleaguered.

Anthony Hopkins's is the most famous Nixon screen impersonation. Unfortunately, it's just that, an impersonation—and not necessarily all that good. The accent keeps floating away from Southern California to head off in the general direction of Cardiff (the plumminess of those rounded vowels!). Hopkins does have the body language down—the hunched shoulders, the cemented-in elbows, the spastic thrusts—but that just emphasizes how much of a caricature his performance is.

The best thing about *Nixon* is its teeming gallery of supporting players: James Woods's Haldeman, David Hyde Pierce's Dean, Paul Sorvino's Kissinger, J. T. Walsh's Ehrlichman, Fyvush Finkel's Murray Chotiner, David Paymer's Ron Ziegler, Dan Hedaya's "Trini Cardoza" (Bebe Rebozo in all but name). Four years later Hedaya moved up to play the title character in what might appear to be one of the more negligible Nixon offerings, *Dick* (1999). In fact, this ebulliently shallow comedy comes closer to getting to its title character's dire essence than perhaps any other film has.

It's a teenybopper retelling of the Watergate story, with two adolescents girls, Arlene (Michelle Williams) and Betsy (Kirsten Dunst), proving the crucial actors in the scandal. After inadvertently helping foil the Watergate burglars, they become Nixon's dog walkers. (In a gag that soon pales, he follows their lead and starts calling his Irish setter, King Timahoe, "Checkers.") They then witness various incidents in the cover-up and contact Woodward and Bernstein. Yes, Arlene and Betsy are also Deep Throat.

The jokes, starting with the title's double entendre, tire pretty quickly. Admittedly, getting to see Hedaya riding a white horse on the beach to the soaring strains of Barry White's "Love's Theme" in a fantasy sequence approaches pop-cultural sublimity, but even pop-cultural sublimity will take a movie only so far. Ultimately, *Dick* cares less about Nixon than his era. It's an almost-perfervid exercise in seventies nostalgia. The soundtrack doubles as a pre-disco jukebox. The sets and costumes are an orgy of synthetic fibers and even more synthetic color schemes. Yet it's precisely this emphasis on a cheerfully lightweight context—the way it makes Nixon seem at once peripheral and diminished—that lets us see him in so revealing a light. The only thing he's central to is Arlene's romantic fantasies. We're able for once to view him not as he saw himself or even as his enemies did, but on something like a human scale.

The freshest, most authentic thing in the movie is the relationship between Arlene and Betsy. These girls are friends, not as senators are friends, but as friends are friends. Their mutual fondness and devotion are patent and utterly charming. Whatever its makers' intent, *Dick* isn't really a movie about bad music or bad decor or even bad politicians. It's a movie about friendship.

As such, despite all its knowing irony and reflexive referentiality, *Dick* casts into almost heartbreaking relief the implacable isolation of its title character, a man who can't even get the name of his own dog right. "If you want a friend," Harry Truman once said of politics, "get a dog." No wonder Nixon had it in for Truman. The joke, once again, was on him—although this time with the saddest of implications. Even with man's best friend, he remains apart, disconnected, trapped in a self of his own making. Maybe that's why the old Nixon kept coming up with all those new Nixons. Otherwise whom else would he have had? He was alone, so absolutely alone.

Acknowledgments

This book began the morning after Richard Nixon died. David Thomson called from San Francisco, where he'd spent much of the night watching Nixon footage on CNN. "You should write something about Nixon and movies," I told him. "No *you* should," he replied.

Pat's being an extra, Nixon's having been on HUAC during the time of the Hollywood Ten hearings, the multiple screenings of *Patton* at the time of Cambodia, his publicly stated enthusiasm for *Love Story* and *Chisum*: there must be an essay in bringing these associations together and drawing some sort of larger conclusions about how antithetical (or not) this dour man was to all that the movies stand for.

That summer would mark the twentieth anniversary of Nixon's resignation. I now can't remember whether it was my *Boston Globe* colleague Louise Kennedy or I who suggested doing a roundup of Watergate-related books. Either way, I thank her for viewing the enterprise favorably, for among the titles was *The Haldeman Diaries*, that numbing, engrossing, and indispensable account of the first fifty-two months of the Nixon administration. I proposed including the CD-ROM version, rather than the book, which edits the text down to a length both more manageable and less revelatory. The CD-ROM also includes the president's daily diary. Consulting the latter, I kept discovering how frequent an entry "Movie" was at the end of the day.

A few months before all this, I had bought my first computer, with the assistance of George Booz, who insisted I include a CD-

ROM drive in my purchase. On several other occasions, George provided technical support, as did Michael Kosowsky. Michael deserves additional thanks, as does Jennifer Drawbridge, for sitting through an extremely didactic viewing of *Sweet Smell of Success* with nary a complaint—and providing the VCR, to boot. By then, intended essay had become projected book.

Mark Horan and Martha Sheehan were kind enough to put me up during research trips to the National Archives. Poor Mark has had to spend more years listening to me go on about Nixon than anyone outside my family. Indeed, as teenagers, we watched Nixon's resignation speech together in his parents' living room.

I'd like to thank the staff of the National Archives' Nixon Presidential Materials Project, in College Park, Maryland, and in particular Allen Rice; the staff of the Museum of Broadcasting, in New York City; the staff of the Frank Capra Collection at the Wesleyan Cinema Archive; Dorinda Hartmann, of the Wisconsin Center for Film and Theater Research; Faye Thompson, Kristine Krueger, Alexandra Batiste, and Jonathan Wahl, of the Academy of Motion Picture Arts and Sciences' Margaret Herrick Library; and Kathy Struss of the Dwight D. Eisenhower Library.

Various colleagues, friends, acquaintances, and, in a few cases, absolute strangers made the writing of this book considerably easier. They offered words of encouragement, provided assistance in various forms, read portions of the manuscript, or simply expressed an interest at times when that was very welcome indeed. A few qualify on all counts.

Among those I wish to thank are Daniel Aaron, Don Aucoin, Alex Beam, Jack Beatty, Fred Biddle (who scared up a tape of *Kissinger and Nixon*), Viki Bok, Howard Boyer, Justin Broackes, Marcia Campbell and her late husband, Dick Campbell, my late uncle Bill Carney (whose love of golf was such that, despite never having played Baltusrol, he could immediately indicate which was the best-known hole there), Richard Carpenter (who was kind enough to loan me, unasked, a copy of *Elvis Meets Nixon*), Jeff Danziger, D. C. Denison, Richard Dyer (who may be the only person in North America with an authorized videotape of *Nixon in China*), Richard Eder, Anne Fadiman, Agnes Feeney, Jan Freeman, Nick and Caroline Friend, Ivan Gaskell and Jane Whitehead, Bob and Margie Gibbons, Suzanne Gluck (does Cameron Diaz have an older sister?), Rachel Gorlin, Wil Haygood, Scott Heller, John Hoberman, Cindy Hoffman, Gerry Howard, Margo Howard, James Isaacs and Ande Zellman, Richard T. Jameson (who provided a then-much-needed copy of *American Madness*), Neal Karlen, John Keegan, Rick Kot, Suzanne Kreiter, Michael

Larkin, the late Eppie Lederer, Irv Letofsky, Fiona Luis, Elaine Markson, Eileen McNamara, David Mehegan, Jack Miles, Greg Moore, Mary Murrell, Holly Nixholm, Tim Noah, David and Olivia Nyhan, Richard Pennington, Rick Perlstein, Katherine Anne Powers, William H. Pritchard, Susan Ralston, William Rawn, Richard Reeves, Richard Rodriguez, Geoff Shandler, David Shribman, Anna Simons, Peter Sis, Alex Star, Paige Tolbert and Jim Mulholland (not just picking up, but dropping off, too—*and* the Indian food), Lisa Tuite, Larry Tye, David Warsh (than whom one could have no more dedicated advocate), Ralph Whitehead, Mary Jane Wilkinson, and the late Tom Winship.

When I told Matt Storin, who was then editor of the *Boston Globe*, I wanted to go on leave to work on this book, he said, "Well, I'm not the person you ask—but I'll make sure he says yes."

Margaret Manning died almost a decade before this project began, and Kirk Scharfenberg almost two years before. Yet without their professional support, inspiration, and example, it's unlikely I would ever have been in a position to undertake it. As for Martin F. Nolan, he is not only my favorite member of the White House enemies list but a teacher, guide, and journalist's journalist.

It seems presumptuous to cite Pauline Kael and Murray Kempton as models, but I can't imagine having done this book without having read them. Their work has done so much to enrich my understanding of the movies and Nixon. And for all that I suspect she found the whole thing a bit baffling, I cherish the encouragement Pauline offered when I described this project to her.

At the University of Chicago Press, I have been fortunate to work with Susan Bielstein, Anthony Burton (I promise Anthony to keep working on my Jerry Lewis imitation), Erin Hogan, and Erin DeWitt, whose thoroughness and professionalism are every bit as Haldemanesque as her wit, charm, and good cheer are not.

Peter Guralnick (by letter), Paul Fisher (by telephone), and Leonard Garment (in person) kindly responded to questions and helpfully gave of their time. In addition, Len intervened to help with a publisher; that intervention, it so happened, went for naught, but I am no less grateful for the vote of confidence it represented. Particular thanks are owed Peter. Every time we would be in touch, he would ask after the project, always offering encouragement and good advice.

A special debt is owed Jay Cantor and Melinda Marble. Jay and Melinda were the first persons I described this project to. As it happened, it was while we were driving to a movie (*Eat Drink Man Woman*, in case you were wondering). They greeted my description with silence. Unnerved, I allowed as to how the project must sound crazy and maybe wasn't right for a book. "Oh, it's crazy, all right," Jay said, "but it *is* a book." A year later Grace Cantor entered the picture, about six weeks before William Feeney did, and in her estimable way she pitched in, too. (William and Grace see to it the Acme Tape Company is always on call.)

"Ni-ni" was one of the first words uttered by William, who'd pronounce it whenever he saw a photograph of the thirty-seventh president of the United States. His presence made the writing of this book considerably more difficult and the life of its author inexpressibly more worthwhile.

No one believed in this project more than Claire Silvers did—and to think she was once in SDS and got thrown in the can for demonstrating when Spiro Agnew gave his famous speech in Des Moines attacking the media! It's one thing to support a husband's undertakings, but to support those undertakings when they involve Richard Nixon is truly above and beyond. It's no exaggeration to say her commitment to this project surpassed even its author's.

This book is dedicated to Joan Feeney and Bruce Phillips because of the unstinting support—intellectual, emotional, even financial—they have extended over far too many years to both book and author. If that isn't reason enough, he's the finest person I know (and she's right up there, too).

Appendix

What the President Saw and When He Saw It

This list of Nixon screenings is primarily drawn from the President's Daily Diary, which was kept by the Secret Service throughout his presidency. During much of 1969, the diary was kept in a sketchier fashion than during 1970–73. In December 1973, the White House became increasingly anxious about leaks as Watergate worsened and directed the Secret Service to keep a less detailed record of the president's daily schedule.

Citations that do not list a date, site, or both, are drawn from one of three sources: *The Haldeman Diaries*; a 1970 memorandum Rose Mary Woods prepared in response to a *Newsweek* query as to what films Nixon had seen while president; or, from the second half of December 1973 until August 1974, the personal logs kept by White House projectionist Paul Fisher. I am very grateful to Mr. Fisher for sharing that information, as well as to Irv Letofsky for putting me in touch with him.

Screening sites: White House (WH); Camp David (CD); Key Biscayne (KB); San Clemente (SC); Walter Annenberg's Palm Springs estate (PS); Robert Abplanalp's Grand Cay home (GC); Caneel Bay Plantation (CB); Minot Island, Maine (MI); Thomas McCabe's residence on Assateague Island, Maryland (AI)

	FILM	Date	Site
1969	The Shoes of the Fisherman	1/22	WH
	The Sound of Music	2/14	WH
	The Sand Pebbles	2/15	CD
	*	3/29	CD
	Play Dirty	4/12	CD
	Doctor Zhivago	4/19	CD
	Where Eagles Dare	4/25	CD
	Camelot	5/17	KB
	A Man for All Seasons	5/23	CD
	Mayerling	5/29	KB
	Twisted Nerve	5/30	KB
	Bullitt	5/31	KB
	The Prime of Miss Jean Brodie	6/4	SC
	Shalako	6/5	SC
	Support Your Local Sheriff	6/20	CD
	True Grit	6/28	WH
	The Bridge on the River Kwai	7/2	KB
	My Side of the Mountain	7/5	KB
	The Sound of Anger	7/11	CD
	My Little Chickadee	7/17	CD
	West Side Story	7/18	CD
	The Odd Couple	7/26	CD
	Gigi	8/?	SC
	The Happiest Millionaire	8/?	SC
	Dead Run	8/?	SC
	The Guns of Navarone	8/?	SC
	The Longest Day	8/?	SC
	The Dirty Dozen	8/13	CD
	Their Finest Hour	8/14	WH
	Born Free	9/19	CD
	How to Commit Marriage	10/11	CD
	Hard Contract	10/17	WH
	Roman Holiday	10/18	WH
	The Scalphunters	10/24	CD

*Haldeman mentions "a lousy movie" after dinner.

	FILM	Date	Site
1969 (cont.)	Oliver!	11/1	CD
	The Bridge at Remagen	11/5	CD
	The Russians Are Coming, the Russians Are Coming	11/15	CD
	If It's Tuesday, This Must Be Belgium	11/22	CD
	Cat Ballou	11/27	KB
	The Great Bank Robbery	11/28	KB
	The Undefeated	11/29	KB
	The Pink Jungle	12/13	CD
	P.J.	12/14	CD
	Marooned	12/20	WH
	Hello, Dolly	12/26	WH
	Seven Brides for Seven Brothers	12/31	SC
1970	The Sea Gull	1/1	SC
	Sweet Charity	1/3	SC
	The Robe	1/4	PS
	Around the World in 80 Days	1/5	PS
	Those Were the Happy Times	1/6	SC
	The Sterile Cuckoo	1/7	CD
	Civilisation	1/?	WH
	Paint Your Wagon	1/24	CD
	Cactus Flower	1/31	CD
	The Secret of Santa Vittoria	2/7	CD
	No Time for Sergeants	2/12	KB
	Hawaii	2/13	KB
	Anne of the Thousand Days	2/?	CD
	Quo Vadis	3/6	KB
	To Catch a Thief	3/13	CD
	Paper Lion	3/26	KB
	Funny Girl	3/28	KB
	The Stalking Moon	3/29	KB
	Hamlet	4/3	CD
	Patton	4/4	WH
	The Caine Mutiny	4/6	WH

FILM	Date	Site
1970 (cont.)		
My Fair Lady	4/14	CD
The Cincinnati Kid	4/24	CD
Patton	4/25	WH
The Last Hurrah	5/1	CD
The Blue Max	5/2	CD
Sunrise at Campobello	5/6	WH
Topkapi	5/12	WH
A Big Hand for the Little Lady	5/13	WH
Oklahoma!	5/14	KB
Before Winter Comes	5/15	KB
Butch Cassidy and the Sundance Kid	5/17	KB
Ice Station Zebra	5/22	CD
The Cardinal	5/23	CD
The Train	5/29	WH
How the West Was Won	5/30	KB
Smith	6/6	CD
Patton	6/12	KB
The Battle of Britain	6/13	KB
War and Peace	6/19	CD
The Man in the Gray Flannel Suit	6/21	CD
The Egg and I	6/25	SC
Flower Drum Song	6/26	SC
Auntie Mame	7/1	SC
Father Goose	7/3	SC
The Professionals	7/5	SC
Our Man in Havana	7/?	CD
The Out-of-Towners	7/25	SC
Bell, Book and Candle	7/26	SC
Chisum	7/31	SC
Swiss Family Robinson	8/2	SC
Cromwell	8/7	CD
The Cross and the Switchblade	8/8	CD
The Sicilian Clan	8/15	CD
Dial M for Murder	8/22	SC
Born Yesterday	8/23	SC

	FILM	Date	Site
1970 (cont.)	Tell Them Willie Boy Is Here	8/24	SC
	Mister Roberts	8/25	SC
	The Treasure of the Sierra Madre	8/28	SC
	Wilson	8/30	SC
	Chisum	8/31	SC
	The Roaring Twenties	9/4	SC
	The Big Country	9/5	SC
	On a Clear Day You Can See Forever	9/11	CD
	McCloud	9/12	CD
	Operation Cross Eagles	9/?	CD
	The Chairman	9/?	WH
	A Place in History	9/?	WH
	The Unsinkable Molly Brown	9/?	WH
	Giant	10/8	KB
	The Country Girl	10/9	KB
	Mildred Pierce	10/10	KB
	The Americanization of Emily	11/2	SC
	Khartoum	11/5	KB
	The African Queen	11/7	KB
	Walk, Don't Run	11/9	GC
	Goodbye, Mr. Chips	11/13	WH
	How Do I Love Thee?	11/14	CD
	Richard III	11/20	CD
	Tora! Tora! Tora!	11/26	WH
	It's a Mad Mad Mad Mad World	11/27	WH
	The Greatest Show on Earth	11/28	CD
	Good Sam	12/5	CD
	Stagecoach	12/19	WH
	Love Story	12/24	WH
	You Can't Take It with You	12/25	WH
	Pursuit of the Graf Spee	12/26	CD
1971	Anatomy of a Murder	1/1	CD
	Barabbas	1/2	CD
	Citizen Kane	1/5	WH

	FILM	Date	Site
1971 (cont.)	**All About Eve**	1/7	SC
	Mississippi	1/8	SC
	Gigi	1/9	SC
	Torn Curtain	1/11	SC
	Doctor Zhivago	1/15	CD
	Sitting Pretty	1/16	CD
	Song of Norway	1/25	WH
	Spartacus	1/29	CB
	High Society	1/30	CB
	The Iron Petticoat	1/31	CB
	Dr. Day Revisited *and* **A Man Named Lombardi**	2/6	CD
	Four W. C. Fields shorts	2/11	KB
	The Great Chase	2/12	GC
	Gone with the Wind	2/13–14	KB
	Friendly Persuasion	2/20	CD
	Around the World in 80 Days	2/27	CD
	Lawrence of Arabia	3/3	CD
	Lawrence of Arabia, part 2	3/6	CD
	In Harm's Way	3/12	KB
	The Sundowners	3/13	KB
	The Flight of the Phoenix	3/14	GC
	Arabesque	3/27	SC
	A Man Could Get Killed	3/29	SC
	Sahara	4/2	SC
	The List of Adrian Messenger	4/3	SC
	Rio Lobo	4/4	SC
	Ryan's Daughter	4/10	CD
	A New Leaf	4/?	WH
	O'Hara, U.S. Treasury	4/?	CD
	Captain Horatio Hornblower	4/30	SC
	Houseboat	5/1	SC
	The High Commissioner	5/2	SC
	The Egyptian	5/14	KB
	Ship of Fools	5/16	KB
	The Lady from Shanghai	5/21	WH

	FILM	Date	Site
1971 (cont.)	Take the Money and Run	5/22	KB
	Red Sky at Morning	5/23	KB
	Red Ball Express	5/24	KB
	Waterloo	5/29	CD
	Plaza Suite	5/30	CD
	Rose-Marie	6/5	CD
	The Cheyenne Social Club	6/6	CD
	Broken Lance	6/18	KB
	Donovan's Reef	6/19	KB
	Zeppelin	6/25	CD
	Shane	6/26	CD
	Proudly They Came and Valdez Is Coming	7/4	CD
	All the Brothers Were Valiant	7/7	SC
	Breakfast at Tiffany's	7/8	SC
	The Apartment	7/9	SC
	The Quiet Man	7/11	SC
	Diamond Head	7/13	SC
	They Might Be Giants	7/14	SC
	Raid on Rommel	7/16	SC
	Damn Yankees	7/17	SC
	The Last Valley	7/24	CD
	That Touch of Mink	7/25	CD
	The Barbarian and the Geisha	7/31	CD
	A Fistful of Dollars	8/6	MI
	The Conqueror	8/7	MI
	Heaven Knows, Mr. Allison	8/9	SC
	The Virginian	8/17	SC
	The Good, the Bad, and the Ugly	8/21	SC
	The Bridges at Toko-Ri	8/22	SC
	El Cid	8/23	SC
	The Fortune Cookie	8/24	SC
	The Ipcress File	8/27	SC
	Shanghai Express	8/29	SC
	Send Me No Flowers	8/30	SC
	The Alamo	9/5	CD

	FILM	Date	Site
1971 (cont.)	**Big Jake**	9/11	CD
	Hud	9/17	CD
	Cleopatra	9/18–19	CD
	The Sheepman	9/20	WH
	Wild Rovers	9/24	WH
	The Grass Is Greener	10/1	KB
	To Kill a Mockingbird	10/3	KB
	The Red Tent	10/9	CD
	The Bravados	10/10	WH
	Beau James	10/15	CD
	Klute	10/24	CD
	Under the Yum Yum Tree	11/5	KB
	Wait Until Dark	11/7	KB
	San Francisco	11/12	CD
	The Bad and the Beautiful	11/13	CD
	Suspicion	11/20	CD
	Gaslight	11/25	SC
	Cannon for Cordoba	12/3	KB
	The Badlanders	12/16	KB
	The Last Run	12/17	KB
	The Strange Love of Martha Ivers	12/19	WH
	The Night Visitor	12/22	CD
	Brian's Song	12/23	CD
	Nicholas and Alexandra	12/25	WH
	Love in the Afternoon	12/29	KB
	The Lonely Profession	12/30	KB
1972	**The Brothers Karamazov**	1/7	SC
	Hotel	1/13	CD
	Papa's Delicate Condition	1/14	CD
	Lawman	1/15	CD
	The Brothers Karamazov	1/29	CD
	Romance of a Horsethief	2/4	KB
	The Good, the Bad, and the Ugly	2/11–12	GC

	FILM	Date	Site
1972 (cont.)	Kotch	3/1	WH
	Nine Hours to Rama	3/2	KB
	Dr. No	3/3	KB
	Dirty Harry	3/10	CD
	The Last Picture Show	3/11	CD
	The Music Lovers	3/17	WH
	Paris When It Sizzles	3/18	WH
	The Grapes of Wrath	3/24	CD
	The French Connection	3/25	CD
	Lord Jim	4/1	CD
	Duel in the Sun	4/2	CD
	Bachelor in Paradise	4/6	KB
	Boomerang	4/7	KB
	The Godfather	4/21	CD
	There Was a Crooked Man	4/22	CD
	Diamonds Are Forever	4/27	KB
	Pendulum	4/29	KB
	Critic's Choice	5/5	CD
	Kidnapped	5/6	CD
	Funeral in Berlin	5/7	CD
	Goldfinger	5/11	CD
	The Carpetbaggers	5/12	CD
	Good Neighbor Sam	5/13	CD
	From Russia with Love*	5/18	CD
	Move Over, Darling	5/19	WH
	The Prince and the Showgirl	6/2	KB
	Elmer Gantry	6/3	KB
	The Four Horsemen of the Apocalypse	6/4	KB
	Take Her, She's Mine	6/8	CD
	The Skin Game	6/16	GC
	The Notorious Landlady	6/17	GC
	When Eight Bells Toll	6/18	KB
	The Cardinal	6/21	WH
	Hang 'Em High	6/23	CD

*Seen two days before leaving for the first Moscow summit.

FILM	Date	Site
1972 (cont.)		
The Hot Rock	6/24	CD
Harlow	7/1	SC
The V.I.P.s	7/3	SC
Reap the Wild Wind	7/4	SC
Coogan's Bluff	7/5	SC
Irma La Douce	7/9	SC
Gambit	7/11	SC
Two documentaries (on Pat's visit to Africa and the Washington Redskins)	7/12	SC
Skyjacked	7/19	WH
She Wore a Yellow Ribbon	7/22	CD
Fort Apache	7/24	WH
Lady Liberty	7/29	CD
The Mouse that Roared	7/30	CD
Frenzy	8/4	AI
The War Between Men and Women	8/5	AI
Bend of the River	8/11	CD
Joe Kidd	8/12	CD
Kelly's Heroes	9/3	SC
Crusade in Europe	9/6	WH
Cabaret	9/8	CD
The Groundstar Conspiracy	9/9	CD
The Great Northfield, Minnesota Raid	9/16	CD
The Man	9/19	CD
Yankee Doodle Dandy	9/23	CD
Their Finest Hour	9/24	CD
Thirty Seconds Over Tokyo	9/26	CD
War and Peace	9/30	CD
Fiddler on the Roof	10/1	CD
Major Dundee	10/5	WH
The King and I	10/7	CD
South Pacific	10/14	CD
Love Is a Many-Splendored Thing	10/20	CD
The Sons of Katie Elder	10/24	WH
Midnight Lace	10/?	CD

	FILM	Date	Site
1972 (cont.)	Cancel My Reservation	10/29	CD
	Crusade in Europe	10/31	WH
	Civilisation	11/5	SC
	Victory at Sea	11/8	KB
	The Great Escape	11/9	KB
	Boys' Night Out	11/10	KB
	Fuzz	11/12	CD
	John Paul Jones	11/16	CD
	Man with a Million	11/19	CD
	Young Winston	11/22	CD
	The Emigrants	11/23	CD
	The Carey Treatment	11/26	CD
	Pancho Villa	11/27	CD
	Rio Bravo	11/28	CD
	The Heroes of Telemark	12/3	KB
	What the Peeper Saw	12/7	CD
	The Candidate	12/8	CD
	Sounder	12/9	CD
	The Poseidon Adventure	12/12	WH
	The Hanging Tree	12/17	WH
	Charade	12/20	KB
	The Inn of the Sixth Happiness	12/21	KB
	The Lady Eve	12/22	KB
	Butterfield 8	12/24	KB
	The Big Clock	12/28	CD
	The General Died at Dawn	12/29	CD
1973	Three Coins in the Fountain	1/6	CD
	Ride the High Country	1/7	WH
	The Maltese Falcon	1/9	WH
	Mary, Queen of Scots	1/12	KB
	The More the Merrier	1/26	KB
	Tom Jones	1/27	KB
	This Gun for Hire	1/28	KB
	The Accused	2/3	CD

FILM	Date	Site
1973 (cont.)		
So Big	2/4	CD
A Double Life	2/8	SC
On the Waterfront	2/9	SC
The Last Voyage	2/10	SC
Undercurrent	2/11	SC
The Man Who Knew Too Much	2/13	SC
Some Like It Hot	2/16	KB
Keeper of the Flame	2/17	KB
Boom Town	2/18	KB
Vertigo	2/23	CD
The Doctor Takes a Wife	2/24	CD
Viva Zapata!	3/4	CD
Picnic	3/9	CD
Owen Marshall	3/10	CD
To the Ends of the Earth	3/11	WH
Texas	3/15	WH
Sleuth	3/18	CD
Frenchman's Creek	3/24	KB
Anne of the Thousand Days	3/25	KB
The Shepherd of the Hills	3/26	KB
Three Little Words	3/30	SC
Two Rode Together	4/1	SC
Gideon of Scotland Yard	4/3	SC
Meet Me in St. Louis	4/4	SC
Kind Hearts and Coronets	4/5	SC
Forever and a Day	4/7	SC
Some Came Running	4/20	KB
The Seven Year Itch	4/21	KB
The Quiet Man	4/23	GC
Ocean's 11	5/3	KB
What Price Glory	5/4	KB
Inherit the Wind	5/6	KB
Notorious	5/10	WH
The Long Voyage Home	5/11	CD
Hammersmith Is Out	5/12	CD

	FILM	Date	Site
1973 (cont.)	The War Wagon	5/13	CD
	The Searchers	5/17	WH
	A Hole in the Head	5/19	CD
	High Plains Drifter	5/20	CD
	The Wreck of the Mary Deare	5/22	WH
	Tea and Sympathy	5/23	CD
	Indiscreet	5/25	KB
	Proud Rebel	5/26	KB
	Twelve O'Clock High	5/27	GC
	Night People	6/2	CD
	Separate Tables	6/8	KB
	A Tree Grows in Brooklyn	6/9	KB
	Stage Fright	6/15	KB
	The Ladykillers	6/16	KB
	A Letter to Three Wives	6/25	SC
	Love Me or Leave Me	6/26	SC
	Never Let Me Go	6/27	SC
	Pat and Mike	6/28	SC
	The Gazebo	6/29	SC
	The Citadel	6/30	SC
	Daisy Kenyon	7/1	SC
	The Railway Children	7/2	SC
	North to Alaska	7/4	SC
	Alexander the Great	7/5	SC
	Tom Sawyer	7/6	SC
	His Majesty O'Keefe	7/7	SC
	The Far Country	7/8	SC
	Rebel Without a Cause	7/?	SC
	Detective Story	7/?	CD
	The Iron Duke	7/21	CD
	Life with Father	7/22	CD
	The Day of the Jackal	7/23	CD
	Centennial Summer	7/28	CD
	Vera Cruz	7/29	CD
	A Touch of Class	8/3	CD

	FILM	Date	Site
1973 (cont.)	The Sky Above, the Mud Below	8/4	CD
	Man on a String	8/5	CD
	Run for Cover	8/8	CD
	The Nelson Affair	8/9	CD
	The Light that Failed	8/17	KB
	You Gotta Stay Happy	8/18	KB
	Lawrence of Arabia	8/23–24	SC
	Please Don't Eat the Daisies	8/25	SC
	Ivanhoe	8/26	SC
	Kentucky	8/27	SC
	On the Town	8/28	SC
	Dark Victory*	8/29	SC
	All This, and Heaven Too	8/30	SC
	The Postman Always Rings Twice	9/1	SC
	The Blue Dahlia	9/2	SC
	David and Bathsheba	9/8	CD
	I'd Climb the Highest Mountain	9/9	CD
	Lady Ice	9/14	CD
	Paper Moon	9/15	CD
	A King's Story	9/16	CD
	Scorpio	9/22	CD
	Key Largo	9/23	CD
	Bang the Drum Slowly	9/29	CD
	Lonely Are the Brave	9/30	CD
	Play Misty for Me	10/4	KB
	Khartoum	10/6	KB
	Zulu	10/13	CD
	Suez	10/16	CD
	The Sting	10/19	WH
	The Searching Wind	10/20	WH
	The World in His Arms	10/23	CD
	Fail-Safe	10/27	CD
	Hitler: The Last Ten Days	10/29	CD
	Live and Let Die	10/31	WH

*"Silly old Alec!"

	FILM	Date	Site
1973 (cont.)	The Master Touch	11/3	KB
	Heaven Can Wait	11/?	KB
	The Way We Were	11/9	CD
	The Long Gray Line	11/10	CD
	The Snows of Kilimanjaro	11/22	CD
	My Darling Clementine	11/23	CD
	A Foreign Affair	11/24	CD
	The Last of Sheila	12/1	WH
	A Man for All Seasons	12/2	CD
	Western Union	12/7	WH
	From the Mixed-Up Files of Mrs. Basil E. Frankweiler	12/8	WH
	The Flim-Flam Man	12/?	WH
	Travels with My Aunt	12/?	WH
	Drums Along the Mohawk	12/?	CD
	Anastasia	12/?	SC
	The House of Rothschild	12/?	SC
	Jane Eyre	12/?	SC
1974	Garden of Evil	Jan.	SC
	Buffalo Bill	↓	SC
	Cahill: U.S. Marshal		SC
	Passage to Marseilles		SC
	Henry VIII and His Six Wives		SC
	They Came to Cordura		SC
	The Whole Town's Talking		PS
	An Affair to Remember		WH
	American Graffiti		WH
	Executive Action		CD
	The Long Goodbye		CD
	The Hospital		CD
	Charley Varrick	Feb.	CD
	The New Land	↓	CD
	Serpico		CD
	The Clouded Yellow		KB

	FILM	Date	Site
1974 (cont.)	A Kiss Before Dying	Feb.	KB
	Harry in Your Pocket	↓	KB
	The Sting		KB
	The Collector		WH
	England Made Me		WH
	Mame		WH
	The Day of the Dolphin		WH
	Pony Express		WH
	Destination Gobi		WH
	The Omega Man		WH
	Butterflies Are Free		WH
	Cheyenne Autumn		KB
	Von Ryan's Express	Mar.	KB
	Friendly Persuasion	↓	WH
	A Place in History		CD
	The Way We Were		CD
	Sunset Boulevard		CD
	Magnum Force		CD
	Becket	Apr.	CD
	The Great Gatsby	↓	CD
	Mr. Deeds Goes to Town		CD
	Call of the Wild		KB
	What's Up, Doc?		KB
	The Solid Gold Cadillac		KB
	The Sugarland Express		KB
	The Long, Hot Summer	May	KB
	The Paper Chase	↓	KB
	Rio Conchos		KB
	The Seven-Ups		KB
	On the Beach		WH
	Shenandoah		WH
	The Wrong Box		WH
	Zandy's Bride	June	WH
	Holiday	↓	CD
	Divorce—Italian Style		CD

	FILM	Date	Site
1974 (cont.)	Kitty	June	CD
	The Big Sleep	↓	CD
	The Big Heat	July	KB
	Dead Heat on a Merry-Go-Round	↓	KB
	McQ		KB
	By the Light of the Silvery Moon		SC
	Chad Hanna		SC
	Come Next Spring		SC
	Man on a Swing		SC
	Man Without a Star		SC
	Double Indemnity		SC
	Two for the Seesaw		SC
	The Train Robbers		SC
	It's a Wonderful Life		SC
	Around the World in 80 Days		SC

Notes

Documents from the National Archives and Records Administration's Nixon Presidential Materials Project are preceded by the designation "NPMP."

INTRODUCTION

1. Stanley Cavell, *Pursuits of Happiness: The Hollywood Comedy of Remarriage* (Cambridge: Harvard University Press, 1981), p. 20.

2. John Kenneth Galbraith, *A Life in Our Times: Memoirs* (New York: Ballantine, 1982), p. 288.

3. Arthur M. Schlesinger Jr., *A Thousand Days: John F. Kennedy in the White House* (Boston: Houghton Mifflin, 1965), p. 666.

4. Jules Witcover, *The Resurrection of Richard Nixon* (New York: G. P. Putnam's, 1970), p. 202.

5. Connie Bruck, *When Hollywood Had a King: The Reign of Lew Wasserman, Who Leveraged Talent into Power and Influence* (New York: Random House, 2003), p. 283.

6. Larry Martz, with Thomas M. DeFrank, Howard Fineman et al., "The Road Back," *Newsweek*, May 19, 1986, p. 42.

7. Gary Taylor, *Cultural Selection* (New York: Basic Books, 1996), p. 279. Emphasis in original.

8. Garry Wills, *Nixon Agonistes: The Crisis of the Self-Made Man* (New York: Signet, 1971), p. 31.

9. John Osborne, *The Nixon Watch* (New York: Liveright, 1970), p. 79.

10. Murray Kempton, *Rebellions, Perversities, and Main Events* (New York: Times Books, 1994), p. 418.

11. Henry Kissinger, *Years of Upheaval* (Boston: Little, Brown, 1982), p. 111.

CHAPTER ONE

1. Jessamyn West, *To See the Dream* (New York: Harcourt, Brace, 1956), p. 82.

2. Renee K. Schulte, ed., *The Young Nixon: An Oral Inquiry* (Fullerton: California State University Oral History Program, 1978), pp. 25, 20.

3. Jessamyn West, *Hide and Seek: A Continuing Journey* (New York: Harcourt Brace Jovanovich, 1973), p. 226.

4. Ibid., p. 106.

5. Schulte, *Young Nixon*, p. 85.

6. Stewart Alsop, *Nixon & Rockefeller: A Double Portrait* (Garden City, NY: Doubleday, 1960), p. 195.

7. Stephen E. Ambrose, *Nixon: The Education of a Politician, 1913–1962* (New York: Simon & Schuster, 1987), p. 15.

8. Bela Kornitzer, *The Real Nixon: An Intimate Biography* (Chicago: Rand McNally, 1960), p. 78.

9. Ambrose, *Nixon: The Education*, p. 25.

10. Schulte, *Young Nixon*, p. 78.

11. Richard M. Nixon, *In the Arena: A Memoir of Victory, Defeat and Renewal* (New York: Simon & Schuster, 1990), p. 87.

12. William Safire, *Before the Fall: An Inside View of the Pre-Watergate White House* (Garden City, NY: Doubleday, 1975), p. 8.

13. Stephen E. Ambrose, *Nixon: Ruin and Recovery, 1973–1990* (New York: Simon & Schuster, 1991), p. 329.

14. West, *To See the Dream*, p. 131.

15. Richard M. Nixon, *RN: The Memoirs of Richard Nixon* (New York: Touchstone, 1990), p. 14.

16. M. F. K. Fisher, *Among Friends* (New York: North Point Press, 1983), p. 42.

17. Benjamin F. Arnold and Arilissa Dorland Clark, *History of Whittier* (Whittier, CA: Western Publishing, 1933), p. 50.

18. Schulte, *Young Nixon*, p. 214.

19. Roger Morris, *Richard Milhous Nixon: The Rise of an American Politician* (New York: Henry Holt, 1989), p. 138.

20. Ibid., pp. 77–78.

21. Ambrose, *Nixon: The Education*, p. 522.

22. Joan Didion, *Slouching Towards Bethlehem* (New York: Noonday Press, 1990), p. 171.

23. Morris, *Richard Milhous Nixon*, p. 49.

24. Schulte, *Young Nixon*, p. 78.

25. Joe McGinniss, *The Selling of the President, 1968* (New York: Trident Press, 1969), p. 103.

26. Earl Mazo and Stephen Hess, *Nixon: A Political Portrait* (New York: Harper & Row, 1968), p. 10.

27. Nixon, *RN*, p. 9.

28. Alsop, *Nixon & Rockefeller*, pp. 185–86.

29. Schulte, *Young Nixon*, pp. 241–42.

30. Kornitzer, *The Real Nixon*, p. 81.

31. Jonathan Aitken, *Nixon: A Life* (Washington, DC: Regnery, 1994), p. 60.

32. Ibid., p. 70.

33. Nixon, *RN*, pp. 24–25.

34. Mazo and Hess, *Nixon*, pp. 29–30.

35. Julie Nixon Eisenhower, *Pat Nixon: The Untold Story* (New York: Simon & Schuster, 1986), p. 66.

36. NPMP, PPF, President's Special File, box 79.

37. Eisenhower, *Pat Nixon*, p. 77.

38. NPMP, PPF, box 17.

39. Ralph de Toledano, *One Man Alone: Richard Nixon* (New York: Funk & Wagnalls, 1969), p. 115.

40. Peter Kihss, "Nixon, Happy as New Yorker, Says Job Is Law, Not Politics," *New York Times*, December 29, 1963, p. 1.

41. Morris, *Richard Milhous Nixon*, pp. 646–47.

42. Ronald Brownstein, *The Power and the Glitter: The Washington-Hollywood Connection* (New York: Pantheon, 1991), pp. 133–34.

43. A. Scott Berg, *Goldwyn: A Biography* (New York: Alfred A. Knopf, 1989), pp. 494–95, 506.

44. Thomas P. O'Neill Jr. and William Novak, *Man of the House. The Life and Political Memoirs of Speaker Tip O'Neill* (New York: Random House, 1987), pp. 306–7.

45. Irwin F. Gellman, *The Contender: Richard Nixon, the Congress Years, 1946–1952* (New York: Free Press, 1999), p. 117; Nixon, *In the Arena*, p. 190.

46. Ronald Reagan, *An American Life: The Autobiography* (New York: Simon & Schuster, 1990), pp. 133–34.

47. Lou Cannon, *Reagan* (New York: G. P. Putnam's, 1982), p. 406; Monica Crowley, *Nixon Off the Record: His Candid Commentary on People and Politics* (New York: Random House, 1996), p. 24.

48. Tom Wicker, *One of Us: Richard Nixon and the American Dream* (New York: Random House, 1991), p. 329.

49. Robert Sam Anson, *Exile: The Unquiet Oblivion of Richard M. Nixon* (New York: Simon & Schuster, 1984), p. 226.

50. John Sears, "With Nixon: 'Politics Is Great—Except for People,'" *Los Angeles Times*, April 24, 1994, M2.

51. Crowley, *Nixon Off the Record*, p. 28.

52. Theodore H. White, *The Making of the President, 1968* (New York: Atheneum, 1969), p. 251.

53. Lou Cannon, *President Reagan: The Role of a Lifetime* (New York: Simon & Schuster, 1991), pp. 73–74.

54. Kenneth W. Thompson, ed., *The Nixon Presidency: Twenty-two Intimate Perspectives of Richard M. Nixon* (Lanham, MD: University Press of America, 1987), p. 189.

55. Cannon, *President Reagan*, pp. 73–74.

56. Morris, *Richard Milhous Nixon*, p. 126.

57. Jonathan Aitken, "The Nixon Character," *Presidential Studies Quarterly*, Winter 1996, p. 239.

58. "We in the U.S. Are Suckers for Style," *Time*, April 22, 1985, p. 14.

59. Garry Wills, *Reagan's America: Innocents at Home* (Garden City, NY: Doubleday, 1987), p. 158.

60. Kempton, *Rebellions*, p. 437.

61. Ken W. Clawson, "5 Years Later: A Loyalist Relives the Nixon Resignation," *Washington Post*, August 12, 1979, D1.

62. David Frost, *"I Gave Them a Sword": Behind the Scenes of the Nixon Interviews* (New York: William Morrow, 1978), p. 304.

63. Nixon, *RN*, p. 926.

64. Carey McWilliams, *California: The Great Exception* (New York: Current Books, 1949), p. 61.

65. Ronald Reagan with Richard G. Hubler, *Where's the Rest of Me?* (New York: Duell, Sloan and Pearce, 1965), p. 76.

66. Cannon, *President Reagan*, p. 527; Ambrose, *Nixon: The Education*, p. 27.

67. Christopher Matthews, "Reagan as Narrator of America's Dream," *Boston Globe*, February 8, 1987, A11.

68. Godfrey Hodgson, *The Gentleman from New York: Daniel Patrick Moynihan, a Biography* (Boston: Houghton Mifflin, 2000), p. 173.

69. Theodore H. White, *Breach of Faith: The Fall of Richard Nixon* (New York: Atheneum, 1975), p. 22.

70. Stanley I. Kutler, *The Wars of Watergate: The Last Crisis of Richard Nixon* (New York: Alfred A. Knopf, 1990), p. 433.

71. Robert J. Donovan, "Over-Nominated, Under-Elected, Still a Promising Candidate," *New York Times Magazine*, April 25, 1965, p. 76.

72. Thompson, *The Nixon Presidency*, p. 364.

73. David Greenberg, *Nixon's Shadow: The History of an Image* (New York: W. W. Norton, 2003), p. 101.

74. Morris, *Richard Milhous Nixon*, p. 68.

CHAPTER TWO

1. Nixon, *RN*, p. 22.

2. Maurice Zolotow, *Billy Wilder in Hollywood* (New York: Limelight Editions, 1987), p. 117.

3. Alsop, *Nixon & Rockefeller*, p. 195.

4. Nixon, *RN*, p. 22.

5. Reagan, *Where's the Rest of Me?*, p. 89.

6. Carey McWilliams, *Southern California Country: An Island on the Land* (Freeport, NY: Books for Libraries Press, 1970), p. 242.

7. James M. Cain, *60 Years of Journalism* (Bowling Green, OH: Bowling Green University Press, 1985), p. 167.

8. Wicker, *One of Us*, p. 48.

9. Kornitzer, *The Real Nixon*, p. 47.

10. Ambrose, *Nixon: The Education*, p. 52.

11. Cabell Phillips, "Nixon in '58—and Nixon in '60," *New York Times Magazine*, October 26, 1958, p. 72.

12. Nixon, *RN*, p. 272.

13. McWilliams, *Southern California Country*, p. 207.

14. See Morris, *Richard Milhous Nixon*, pp. 195–97, for the Bewley quote and a full account of the Citra-Frost episode.

15. Gerald S. Strober and Deborah Hart Strober, *Nixon: An Oral History of His Presidency* (New York: HarperCollins, 1994), p. 353.

16. Christopher J. Matthews, *Kennedy and Nixon: The Rivalry that Shaped Postwar America* (New York: Simon & Schuster, 1996), p. 212.

17. Nixon, *RN*, p. 832.

18. Crowley, *Nixon Off the Record*, p. 215.

19. Bobby Baker, with Larry L. King, *Wheeling and Dealing: Confessions of a Capitol Hill Operator* (New York: W. W. Norton, 1978), p. 112.

20. Aitken, *Nixon*, p. 296.

21. White, *Breach of Faith*, p. 73.

22. McGinniss, *Selling of the President*, p. 127.

23. Eisenhower, *Pat Nixon*, p. 111.

24. Ambrose, *Nixon: The Education*, p. 271.

25. Richard M. Nixon, *Six Crises* (New York: Touchstone, 1990), p. 74.

26. Morris, *Richard Milhous Nixon*, pp. 845, 839.

27. Ronald Steel, *Walter Lippmann and the American Century* (New York: Vintage, 1981), p. 483.

28. Nixon, *RN*, p. 957.

29. Crowley, *Nixon Off the Record*, p. 33.

30. De Toledano, *One Man Alone*, p. 41.

31. Morris, *Richard Milhous Nixon*, p. 564.

32. Stephen J. Whitfield, "Richard Nixon as Comic Figure," *American Quarterly*, Spring 1985, p. 126.

33. Barry M. Goldwater, with Jack Casserly, *Goldwater* (Garden City, NY: Doubleday, 1988), p. 255.

34. Leonard Garment, "The Guns of Watergate," *Commentary*, April 1987, p. 20.

35. Sears, "With Nixon," M2.

36. Kornitzer, *The Real Nixon*, p. 19.

37. De Toledano, *One Man Alone*, p. 71.

38. D. B. Hardeman and Donald C. Bacon, *Rayburn: A Biography* (Austin: Texas Monthly Press, 1987), p. 382.

39. Helen Gahagan Douglas, *A Full Life* (Garden City, NY: Doubleday, 1982), p. 303.

40. Matthews, *Kennedy and Nixon*, p. 145.

41. Nixon, *RN*, p. 952.

42. White, *Breach of Faith*, p. 73.

43. Greg Mitchell, *Tricky Dick and the Pink Lady: Richard Nixon vs. Helen Gahagan Douglas—Sexual Politics and the Red Scare, 1950* (New York: Random House, 1998), p. 6.

44. William Costello, *The Facts about Nixon: An Unauthorized Biography* (New York: Viking, 1960), p. 215.

45. Nixon, *RN*, p. 1073.

46. Merle Miller, *Plain Speaking: An Oral Biography of Harry S Truman* (New York: G. P. Putnam's, 1974), pp. 178, 135.

47. Murray Kempton, *America Comes of Middle Age: Columns, 1950–1962* (Boston: Little, Brown, 1963), p. 299.

48. Gore Vidal, *Palimpsest: A Memoir* (New York: Random House, 1995), p. 337.

49. Gore Vidal, *The Best Man: A Play about Politics* (Boston: Little Brown, 1960), p. 134.

50. Paul Bullock, *Jerry Voorhis: The Idealist as Politician* (New York: Vantage, 1978), p. 280.

51. Howard Teichman, *Fonda: My Life* (New York: NAL Books, 1981), p. 305.

52. Whitfield, "Richard Nixon as Comic Figure," p. 116.

53. William Safire, *Safire's New Political Dictionary* (New York: Random House, 1993), p. 837.

54. John Weaver, *Los Angeles: The Enormous Village* (Santa Barbara, CA: Capra Press, 1980), p. 212.

55. Cain, *60 Years*, p. 167.

56. W. W. Robinson, *What They Say about the Angels* (Pasadena, CA: Val Trefz Press, 1942), p. 64.

57. Nixon, *RN*, p. 14.

58. Morris, *Richard Milhous Nixon*, p. 863.

59. Reyner Banham, *Los Angeles: The Architecture of Four Ecologies* (London: Pelican Books, 1973), p. 235.

60. Richard Schickel, *Double Indemnity* (London: British Film Institute, 1992), p. 10.

61. Morris, *Richard Milhous Nixon*, p. 195.

62. Raymond Chandler, *Selected Letters of Raymond Chandler*, edited by Frank Mac-Shane (New York: Columbia University Press, 1981), p. 28.

63. Ibid., p. 405.

CHAPTER THREE

1. Richard Reeves, *President Nixon: Alone in the White House* (New York: Simon & Schuster, 2001), p. 307.

2. Bill Gulley, with Mary Ellen Reese, *Breaking Cover* (New York: Simon & Schuster, 1980), p. 121.

3. Kevin Starr, *Embattled Dreams: California in War and Peace, 1940–1950* (New York: Oxford University Press, 2002), p. 69.

4. Henry Kissinger, *White House Years* (Boston: Little, Brown, 1979), p. 780.

5. Morris, *Richard Milhous Nixon*, p. 273.

6. Carlo d'Este, *Patton: A Genius for War* (New York: HarperCollins, 1995), p. 741.

7. H. R. Haldeman, *The Haldeman Diaries: Inside the Nixon White House. The Complete Multimedia Edition* (Santa Monica, CA: Sony Imagesoft, 1994), entries for April 26, 1969; May 18, 1969; and November 10, 1969.

8. Kissinger, *White House Years*, p. 498.

9. Hugh Sidey, "Anybody Seen *Patton?*" *Life*, June 19, 1970, 2B.

10. Nixon, *RN*, p. 400.

11. D'Este, *Patton*, p. 568.

12. Dwight D. Eisenhower, *Crusade in Europe* (Garden City, NY: Doubleday, 1948), p. 82.

13. Seth Cagin and Philip Dray, *Hollywood Films of the Seventies: Sex, Drugs, Violence, Rock 'n' Roll & Politics* (New York: Harper & Row, 1984), p. 150.

14. Pauline Kael, *Deeper into Movies* (Boston: Little, Brown, 1973), p. 99.

15. Clawson, "5 Years Later," p. 1.

16. Kissinger, *Years of Upheaval*, pp. 103, 1186.

17. Richard M. Nixon, *Six Crises* (New York: Touchstone, 1990), p. 204.

18. Ibid., pp. 265, 271.

19. Dimitri K. Simes, *After the Collapse: Russia Seeks Its Place as a Great Power* (New York: Simon & Schuster, 1999), p. 20; David Remnick, "Gary Hart in Exile," *New Yorker*, April 19, 1993, p. 43.

20. Garry Wills, *The Kennedy Imprisonment: A Meditation on Power* (Boston: Little, Brown, 1992), p. 194.

21. D'Este, *Patton*, pp. 612, 801.

22. Ibid., p. 755.

23. Kissinger, *White House Years*, p. 1200.

24. Nixon, *Six Crises*, p. 152.

25. Ibid., p. 76.

26. Stephen E. Ambrose, *Eisenhower: Soldier and President* (New York: Simon & Schuster, 1990), p. 413.

27. Ibid., p. 527.

28. Paul H. Nitze, with Ann M. Smith and Steven L. Rearden, *From Hiroshima to Glasnost: At the Center of Decision: A Memoir* (New York: Grove Weidenfeld, 1989), p. 296.

29. Benjamin C. Bradlee, *Conversations with Kennedy* (New York: W. W. Norton, 1975), p. 225.

30. Costello, *Facts about Nixon*, p. 230.

31. Nixon, *Six Crises*, pp. 184–85.

32. Nixon, *RN*, p. 377.

33. Crowley, *Nixon Off the Record*, p. 16.

34. Nixon, *RN*, p. 376.

35. Nixon, *Six Crises*, p. 161.

36. Richard H. Rovere, *Affairs of State: The Eisenhower Years* (New York: Farrar, Straus & Cudahy, 1956), p. 294; Milton Eisenhower, *The President Is Calling* (Garden City, NY: Doubleday, 1974), p. 325.

37. De Toledano, *One Man Alone*, p. 162.

38. Kutler, *Wars of Watergate*, p. 56.

39. Theodore H. White, *The Making of the President, 1972* (New York: Atheneum, 1973), p. 57.

40. Haldeman, *Haldeman Diaries*, March 28, 1969.

41. Anthony Holden, *Prince Charles* (New York: Atheneum, 1979), pp. 261–62.

42. J. B. West, *Upstairs at the White House: My Life with the First Ladies* (New York: Coward, McCann, Geoghagen, 1973), p. 358.

43. Herbert S. Parmet, *Richard Nixon and His America* (Boston: Little, Brown, 1990), p. 233.

44. Roger Morris, *Haig: The General's Progress* (New York: Playboy Press, 1982), p. xxi.

45. Elmo R. Zumwalt Jr., *On Watch: A Memoir* (New York: Quadrangle, 1976), p. 412.

46. Nixon, *RN*, p. 532.

47. Richard M. Nixon, *No More Vietnams* (New York: Arbor House, 1985), pp. 120–21. Emphasis in original.

48. Nixon, *RN*, p. 589.

49. Ibid., p. 737.

50. Ibid., p. 356.

51. Stephen E. Ambrose, *Nixon: The Triumph of a Politician, 1962–1972* (New York: Simon & Schuster, 1989), p. 417.

52. W. Scott Thompson, *National Security in the 1980s: From Weakness to Strength* (San Francisco: Institute for Contemporary Studies, 1980), pp. 385–86.

53. Eric Bentley, "The Political Theatre of John Wayne," in *Theatre of War: Comments on 32 Occasions* (New York: Viking, 1972), pp. 308, 309–10, 311.

54. Kissinger, *Years of Upheaval*, p. 294.

55. Garry Wills, *John Wayne's America: The Politics of Celebrity* (New York: Simon & Schuster, 1997), p. 27. Emphasis in original.

56. Ambrose, *Nixon: The Triumph*, p. 323.

57. Mason Wiley and Damien Bona, *Inside Oscar: The Unofficial History of the Academy Awards* (New York: Ballantine, 1993), p. 441.

58. "Nixon's Remarks on Manson and Statement in Washington," *New York Times*, August 4, 1970, p. 16.

59. Nixon, *RN*, p. 867.

60. Morris, *Richard Milhous Nixon*, p. 646.

61. Wills, *John Wayne's America*, p. 185.

62. Kutler, *Wars of Watergate*, p. 10.

63. Ambrose, *Nixon: The Triumph*, p. 480; Melvin Small, *The Presidency of Richard Nixon* (Lawrence: University Press of Kansas, 1999), p. 242.

64. Unless otherwise cited, Wayne references are from Randy Roberts and James S. Olson, *John Wayne, American* (New York: Free Press, 1995), pp. 472, 546, 606.

65. Ambrose, *Nixon: The Education*, p. 108.

66. Nixon, *RN*, p. 28.

67. Mazo and Hess, *Nixon*, p. 40.

68. Wills, *Nixon Agonistes*, p. 86.

69. Mark C. Carnes, ed., *Past Imperfect: History According to the Movies* (New York: Henry Holt, 1995), p. 235.

70. Nixon, *In the Arena*, p. 186.

71. Safire, *Before the Fall*, p. 114.

72. Bradlee, *Conversations with Kennedy*, p. 74.

73. Ambrose, *Nixon: The Triumph*, p. 105.

74. Ambrose, *Nixon: The Education*, p. 111.

75. Ibid., p. 109.

76. Morris, *Richard Milhous Nixon*, p. 252.

77. John Leggett, *Ross and Tom: Two American Tragedies* (New York: Simon & Schuster, 1974), p. 346.

CHAPTER FOUR

1. Mazo and Hess, *Nixon*, p. 296.

2. Morris, *Richard Milhous Nixon*, p. 356.

3. De Toledano, *One Man Alone*, p. 8.

4. Joseph Martin, as told to Robert J. Donovan, *My First Fifty Years in Politics* (New York: McGraw-Hill, 1960), p. 194.

5. Morris, *Richard Milhous Nixon*, p. 358.

6. Stewart Alsop, *Nixon & Rockefeller*, p. 200.

7. Morris, *Richard Milhous Nixon*, p. 356.

8. Aitken, *Nixon*, p. 33.

9. William "Fishbait" Miller and Frances Spatz Leighton, *Fishbait: The Memoirs of the Congressional Doorkeeper* (Englewood, NJ: Prentice-Hall, 1977) p. 305.

10. William S. White, *Home Place: The Story of the U.S. House of Representatives* (Boston: Houghton Mifflin, 1965), p. 24.

11. Nixon, *RN*, p. 72.

12. Wicker, *One of Us*, p. 79.

13. Small, *The Presidency of Richard Nixon*, p. 13.

14. William S. White, *Citadel: The Story of the U.S. Senate* (New York: Harper & Brothers, 1956), p. 82.

15. Nixon, *Six Crises*, p. 260.

16. Costello, *Facts about Nixon*, p. 239.

17. Clinton P. Anderson, with Milton Viorst, *Outsider in the Senate: Senator Clinton Anderson's Memoirs* (New York: World Publishing, 1970), p. 125.

18. Richard H. Rovere, *Senator Joe McCarthy* (New York: Harcourt, Brace and Company, 1959), p. 55.

19. Ralph Flanders, *Senator from Vermont* (Boston: Little, Brown, 1961), p. 268.

20. Donald R. Matthews, *U.S. Senators and Their World* (Chapel Hill: University of North Carolina Press, 1960), p. 99.

21. Norris Cotton, *In the Senate: Amidst the Conflict and the Turmoil* (New York: Dodd, Mead, 1978), p. 117.

22. White, *The Making of the President, 1972*, p. 197.

23. Roger K. Newman, *Hugo Black: A Biography* (New York: Pantheon, 1994), p. 235.

24. Matthews, *U.S. Senators*, p. 137.

25. Robert Coughlan, "Success Story of a Vice President," *Life*, December 14, 1953, p. 154.

26. Kempton, *Rebellions*, p. 262.

27. Goldwater, *Goldwater*, p. 256.

28. Wills, *Nixon Agonistes*, p. 22.

29. Morris, *Richard Milhous Nixon*, p. 654.

30. O'Neill, *Man of the House*, p. 157.

31. Louis Hurst, as told to Frances Leighton Spatz, *The Sweetest Little Club in the World: The U.S. Senate* (Englewood Cliffs, NJ: Prentice-Hall, 1980), p. 166.

32. Morris, *Richard Milhous Nixon*, p. 559.

33. Ibid., p. 655.

34. Matthews, *U.S. Senators*, p. 58.

35. Morris, *Richard Milhous Nixon*, p. 864.

36. White, *Citadel*, pp. 84–85. Emphasis in original.

37. Morris, *Richard Milhous Nixon*, p. 727.

38. Nixon, *RN*, p. 619.

39. Tony Hiss, *Laughing Last: Alger Hiss by Tony Hiss* (Boston: Houghton Mifflin, 1977), p. 159.

40. Curtis Prendergast, with Geoffrey Colvin, *The World of Time Inc.: The Intimate History of a Changing Enterprise, 1960–1980* (New York: Atheneum, 1986), p. 439.

41. Leslie Wayne, "A Hollywood Product: Political Money," *New York Times*, September 12, 1996, A1.

42. Nixon, *RN*, p. 503.

43. O'Neill, *Man of the House*, p. 239.

44. Wicker, *One of Us*, p. 21.

45. Theodore H. White, *The Making of the President, 1964* (New York: Signet, 1966), p. 90.

46. Paul F. Healy, "The Busiest Vice-President We Ever Had!" *Saturday Evening Post*, September 19, 1953, p. 84.

47. Costello, *Facts about Nixon*, p. 237.

48. Sherman Adams, *Firsthand Report: The Story of the Eisenhower Administration* (New York: Harper & Brothers, 1961), p. 139.

49. Hardeman and Bacon, *Rayburn*, p. 382.

50. Wicker, *One of Us*, p. 167.

51. De Toledano, *One Man Alone*, p. 178.

52. Nixon, *RN*, p. 141.

53. Ambrose, *Nixon: The Education*, p. 338.

54. Richard Langham Riedel, *Halls of the Mighty: My 47 Years at the Senate* (Washington, DC: Robert Luce, 1969), p. 194.

55. Thompson, *The Nixon Presidency*, p. 301.

56. Nixon, *RN*, p. 770.

57. Jimmy Breslin, *How the Good Guys Finally Won: Notes from an Impeachment Summer* (New York: Viking, 1975), p. 171.

58. Alsop, *Nixon & Rockefeller*, p. 188.

59. Reeves, *President Nixon*, p. 570.

60. White, *The Making of the President, 1968*, p. 100.

61. Strober and Strober, *Nixon*, p. 89.

62. Ambrose, *Nixon: Ruin and Recovery*, p. 239.

63. Ambrose, *Nixon: The Education*, p. 234.

CHAPTER FIVE

1. Witcover, *Resurrection of Richard Nixon*, p. 170.

2. Mazo and Hess, *Nixon*, pp. 262–63.

3. David Halberstam, *The Powers that Be* (New York: Alfred A. Knopf, 1979), p. 122.

4. Gladwin Hill, *Dancing Bear: An Inside Look at California Politics* (Cleveland: World Publishing, 1968), p. 271.

5. Robert Gottlieb and Irene Wolt, *Thinking Big: The Story of the Los Angeles Times, Its Publishers, and Their Influence on Southern California* (New York: G. P. Putnam's, 1977), p. 271.

6. Marshall Berges, *The Life and Times of Los Angeles* (New York: Atheneum, 1984), p. 112.

7. White, *Breach of Faith*, p. 67.

8. Witcover, *Resurrection of Richard Nixon*, p. 151.

9. Marvin Kalb, *The Nixon Memo: Political Respectability, Russia, and the Press* (Chicago: University of Chicago Press, 1994), p. 8.

10. Richard Kluger, *The Paper: The Life and Death of the* New York Herald Tribune (New York: Alfred A. Knopf, 1986), p. 410.

11. Nixon, *In the Arena*, p. 257.

12. Richard M. Nixon, *Beyond Peace* (New York: Random House, 1994), p. 257.

13. Henry James, *Novels, 1881–1886* (New York: Library of America, 1985), p. 916.

14. Pauline Kael, *The Citizen Kane Book* (New York: Limelight Editions, 1984), p. 19.
15. Ibid., p. 20.
16. Neal Gabler, *Winchell: Gossip, Power and the Culture of Celebrity* (New York: Alfred A. Knopf, 1994), p. 411.
17. Jackson Lears, "Gutter Populist," *New Republic,* January 9 & 16, 1995, p. 42.
18. Gabler, *Winchell,* pp. 449–50, 511.
19. Ibid., p. 511.
20. Philip Kemp, *Lethal Innocence: The Cinema of Alexander Mackendrick* (London: Methuen, 1991), p. 161.
21. Ibid., p. 151.
22. Ibid., p. 148.
23. David Thomson, *A Biographical Dictionary of Film,* 3rd ed. (New York: Alfred A. Knopf, 1994), p. 163.
24. Kemp, *Lethal Innocence,* p. 144.
25. Todd Rainsberger, *James Wong Howe: Cinematographer* (San Diego: A. S. Barnes, 1981), p. 224.
26. Joseph McBride, *Hawks on Hawks* (Berkeley: University of California Press,1982), p. 45.
27. David Denby, untitled, *New York,* December 23–30, 1985, p. 85.
28. Nixon, *RN,* p. 21.
29. Aitken, *Nixon,* p. 75.
30. Ibid., p. 76.
31. Andy Warhol, *The Warhol Diaries,* edited by Pat Hackett (New York: Warner Books, 1991), p. 445.
32. Donovan, "Over-Nominated," p. 14.
33. White, *Breach of Faith,* p. 75.
34. Katharine Graham, *Personal History* (New York: Alfred A. Knopf, 1997), p. 433.
35. Gottlieb and Wolt, *Thinking Big,* p. 364.

CHAPTER SIX

1. Henry Kissinger, "With Faint Praise," *New York Times Book Review,* July 16, 1995, p. 7.
2. John G. Stoessinger, *Henry Kissinger: The Anguish of Power* (New York: W. W. Norton, 1976), p. 208.
3. Walter Isaacson, *Kissinger: A Biography* (New York: Simon & Schuster, 1992), pp. 134–35.
4. Kissinger, *White House Years,* p. 3.
5. Nixon, *RN,* pp. 341, 340.
6. Ibid., p. 341.
7. Marvin Kalb and Bernard Kalb, *Kissinger* (Boston: Little, Brown, 1974), p. 92.
8. Nixon, *RN,* p. 457.

9. John Ehrlichman, *Witness to Power: The Nixon Years* (New York: Simon & Schuster, 1982), p. 311.

10. Bob Woodward and Carl Bernstein, *The Final Days* (New York: Touchstone, 1987), pp. 29–30.

11. Isaacson, *Kissinger*, p. 394.

12. Nixon, *RN*, p. 552.

13. Seymour M. Hersh, *The Price of Power: Kissinger in the Nixon White House* (New York: Summit Books, 1983), p. 110.

14. Wicker, *One of Us*, p. 435.

15. Roger Morris, *Uncertain Greatness: Henry Kissinger and American Foreign Policy* (New York: Harper & Row, 1977), p. 52.

16. Ibid., p. 174.

17. Kissinger, *White House Years*, pp. 13–14.

18. Ibid., p. 942.

19. Woodward and Bernstein, *The Final Days*, p. 188.

20. Daniel Patrick Moynihan, with Suzanne Weaver, *A Dangerous Place* (Boston: Little, Brown, 1975), pp. 8–9.

21. Kissinger, *White House Years*, p. 747.

22. Ibid., p. 3.

23. Ibid., p. 74.

24. Ibid., p. 917.

25. Ibid., p. 1179.

26. Ibid., p. 93.

27. Henry Kissinger, "The 37th President: 'Courage in the Face of Wrenching Domestic Controversy,'" *New York Times*, April 28, 1994, A19.

28. Richard M. Nixon, *Leaders* (New York: Warner Books, 1982), p. 218.

29. Eisenhower, *Pat Nixon*, p. 446.

30. Aitken, *Nixon*, p. 462.

31. Kissinger, *White House Years*, p. 918.

32. Kissinger, *Years of Upheaval*, p. 7.

33. Isaacson, *Kissinger*, p. 396.

34. Kissinger, *White House Years*, p. 1054.

35. Isaacson, *Kissinger*, p. 479.

36. H. R. Haldeman, with Joseph DiMona, *The Ends of Power* (New York: Dell, 1978), pp. 123–24.

37. Isaacson, *Kissinger*, p. 364.

38. Bruce Oudes, ed., *From: The President: Richard Nixon's Secret Files* (New York: Harper & Row, 1989), p. 215.

39. Isaacson, *Kissinger*, p. 362.

40. Liv Ullmann, *Changing* (New York: Alfred A. Knopf, 1976), p. 173.

41. Kissinger, *Years of Upheaval*, p. 4.

42. Candice Bergen, *Knock Wood* (New York: Linden Press/Simon & Schuster, 1984), pp. 235–37.

43. Robert Evans, *The Kid Stays in the Picture* (New York: Hyperion, 1994), p. 209.

44. Ibid., p. 208.

45. Henry Kissinger, *Years of Renewal* (New York: Simon & Schuster, 1999), p. 542.

46. Evans, *The Kid*, pp. 6–7.

47. Ibid., p. 247.

48. Oriana Fallaci, *Interview with History* (New York: Liveright, 1976), pp. 40–41.

49. Kissinger, *White House Years*, p. 1409.

50. Jeb Stuart Magruder, *An American Life: One Man's Road to Watergate* (New York: Pocket Books, 1975), p. 80; Kissinger, *White House Years*, p. 1399.

51. Woodward and Bernstein, *The Final Days*, p. 189.

52. NPMP, PPF, RMW Files, box 18.

53. Andrew Sarris, *The American Cinema: Directors and Directions, 1929–1968* (Chicago: University of Chicago Press, 1985), p. 48.

54. Safire, *Before the Fall*, p. 600.

55. Joseph McBride, *Searching for John Ford: A Life* (New York: St. Martin's, 2001), pp. 708, 712.

56. Andrew Sinclair, *John Ford* (New York: Dial Press, 1979), p. 210.

57. Lindsay Anderson, *About John Ford . . .* (New York: McGraw-Hill, 1983), p. 188.

58. Nixon, *RN*, p. 812.

59. Haldeman, *Haldeman Diaries*, March 31, 1973.

60. Anderson, *About John Ford*, p. 171; Jean-Luc Godard, *Godard on Godard: Critical Writings by Jean-Luc Godard* (New York: Da Capo, 1986), p. 171.

61. Kissinger, *Years of Upheaval*, p. 414.

62. Ambrose, *Nixon: Ruin and Recovery*, p. 348.

63. Charles W. Colson, *Born Again* (Old Tappan, NJ: Chosen Books, 1976), p. 179.

64. Fallaci, *Interview with History*, p. 39.

65. Safire, *Before the Fall*, pp. 390–91.

66. Nixon, *RN*, p. 1076.

67. Kissinger, *Years of Upheaval*, p. 1207.

68. Morris, *Uncertain Greatness*, p. 69.

69. Ibid., p. 56.

CHAPTER SEVEN

1. Haldeman made the remark during the course of the Hofstra University conference whose proceedings have been gathered in Kenneth Thompson's *The Nixon Presidency*, p. 47.

2. Haldeman, *Haldeman Diaries*, April 29, 1970.

3. Safire, *Before the Fall*, p. 202.

4. Alsop, *Nixon & Rockefeller*, p. 187.

5. Kissinger, *White House Years*, p. 514.

6. Nixon, *RN*, pp. 457, 458.

7. *New York Times*, "A Crisis of Leadership," May 10, 1970, sec. 4, p. 16.

8. Haldeman, *Haldeman Diaries*, May 7 and 8, 1970.

9. Nixon, *RN*, p. 459.

10. Safire, *Before the Fall*, p. 203.

11. Aitken, *Nixon*, p. 406.

12. Nixon, *RN*, p. 462.

13. Safire, *Before the Fall*, pp. 205–6.

14. Aitken, *Nixon*, p. 407.

15. Nixon, *RN*, p. 465.

16. Aitken, *Nixon*, p. 408.

17. Haldeman, *Haldeman Diaries*, May 9, 1970.

18. Kalb, *The Nixon Memo*, p. 77.

19. Richard Glatzer and John Raeburn, eds., *Frank Capra: The Man and His Films* (Ann Arbor: University of Michigan Press, 1975), dust jacket.

20. Frank Capra, *The Name Above the Title: An Autobiography* (New York: Belvedere, 1982), pp. xiii, 550, 265, 339.

21. Ibid., p. 374.

22. John W. Dean III, *Blind Ambition: The White House Years* (New York: Simon & Schuster, 1976), p. 298.

23. James Harvey, *Romantic Comedy in Hollywood from Lubitsch to Sturges* (New York: Knopf, 1987), p. 165.

24. Joseph McBride, *Frank Capra: The Catastrophe of Success* (New York: Simon & Schuster, 1992), p. 238.

25. Ibid., p. 637.

26. Greil Marcus, *Mystery Train: Images of America in Rock 'n' Roll Music*, rev. ed. (New York: Dutton, 1982), p. 143.

27. Graham Greene, *The Graham Greene Film Reader: Reviews, Essays, Interviews & Film Stories*, edited by David Parkinson (New York: Applause, 1995), p. 270.

28. McBride, *Frank Capra*, p. 141.

29. Ibid., p. 635.

30. Ibid., p. 432.

31. Capra, *Name Above the Title*, p. xi.

32. McBride, *Frank Capra*, p. 168.

33. Victor Scherle and William Turner Levy, *The Films of Frank Capra* (Secaucus, NJ: Citadel Press, 1977), p. 1.

34. Capra, *Name Above the Title*, pp. 311–12.

35. Nixon, *RN*, p. 6.

36. Kornitzer, *The Real Nixon*, p. 40.

37. Nixon, *RN*, p. 13.

38. Aitken, *Nixon*, p. 406.

39. Taylor Branch, *Pillar of Fire: America in the King Years, 1963–65* (New York: Simon & Schuster, 1998), p. 248.

40. Capra, *Name Above the Title*, p. 291.

41. Nixon, *RN*, p. 577.

42. Jerry Voorhis, *The Strange Case of Richard Milhous Nixon* (New York: Paul S. Eriksson, 1972), dust jacket.

43. Alsop, *Nixon & Rockefeller*, pp. 187–88.

44. Nixon, *In the Arena*, p. 185.

45. Alsop, *Nixon & Rockefeller*, p. 187.

46. Scherle and Levy, *Films of Frank Capra*, p. 168.

47. Capra, *Name Above the Title*, p. 321.

48. Scherle and Levy, *Films of Frank Capra*, p. 15.

49. Ibid., p. 2.

50. Nixon, *RN*, p. 265.

51. Safire, *Before the Fall*, p. 600.

52. Nixon, *Six Crises*, p. 426.

CHAPTER EIGHT

1. Egil Krogh, *The Day Elvis Met Nixon* (Bellevue, WA: Pejama Press, 1994), p. 12.

2. Ibid., p. 10.

3. Ibid., p. 17.

4. Alanna Nash, with Billy Smith, Marty Lacker, and Lamar Fike, *Elvis Aaron Presley: Revelations from the Memphis Mafia* (New York: HarperCollins, 1995), p. 78.

5. Krogh, *The Day Elvis Met Nixon*, p. 23.

6. This account draws on Krogh, *The Day Elvis Met Nixon*, pp. 31–40.

7. Peter Guralnick, *Careless Love: The Unmaking of Elvis Presley* (Boston: Little, Brown, 1999), p. 411.

8. Peter Guralnick, *Lost Highway: Journeys & Arrivals of American Musicians* (New York: Vintage, 1982), p. 142.

9. Bill Harry, *The Ultimate Beatles Encyclopedia* (London: Virgin Books, 1992), p. 532.

10. Ibid., p. 531.

11. Nash, *Elvis Aaron Presley*, pp. 359–60.

12. Ibid., p. 361.

13. Krogh, *The Day Elvis Met Nixon*, p. 35.

14. Nash, *Elvis Aaron Presley*, p. 134.

15. Dean, *Blind Ambition*, p. 134.

16. *Congressional Quarterly Almanac 1972* (Washington, DC: Congressional Quarterly, 1972), p. 1013.

17. Orson Welles, "But Where Are We Going?" *Look*, November 11, 1970, p. 34.

18. Monica Crowley, *Nixon in Winter* (New York: Random House, 1998), p. 254.

19. Frost, *"I Gave Them a Sword,"* p. 171.

20. Safire, *Before the Fall*, p. 150.

21. Ibid., p. 127.

22. Nixon, *RN*, p. 465.

23. NPMP, PPF, box 8, Julie and David Eisenhower folder.

24. Nixon, *Six Crises*, p. 306; David Gergen, *Eyewitness to Power: The Essence of Leadership, Nixon to Clinton* (New York: Simon & Schuster, 2000), p. 96.

25. Safire, *Before the Fall*, p. 294.

26. Wills, *Nixon Agonistes*, p. 371.

27. Parmet, *Richard Nixon*, p. 544.

28. NPMP, PPF, box 36, Movies and Books folder.

29. Haldeman, *Haldeman Diaries*, September 8, 1971.

30. Nixon, *RN*, p. 538.

31. Stewart Alsop, "Nixon and the Square Majority," *Atlantic Monthly*, February 1972, p. 42.

32. Herbert G. Klein, *Making It Perfectly Clear* (Garden City, NY: Doubleday, 1980), p. 13.

33. Wills, *Nixon Agonistes*, p. 372.

34. Haldeman, *Haldeman Diaries*, March 28, 1969.

35. Wills, *Nixon Agonistes*, p. 349.

36. Ibid.

37. Oudes, *From: The President*, p. 193.

38. Guralnick, *Lost Highway*, pp. 119–20.

39. Pauline Bartel, *Reel Elvis: The Ultimate Trivia Guide to the King's Movies* (Dallas: Taylor, 1994), p. 8.

40. Colin Powell, with Joseph E. Persico, *My American Journey* (New York: Random House, 1995), pp. 54–55.

41. Don Siegel, *A Siegel Film: An Autobiography* (London: Faber & Faber, 1993), p. 227.

42. Ethan Mordden, *Medium Cool: The Movies of the 1960s* (New York: Alfred A. Knopf, 1990), p. 107.

43. Hal Wallis, with Charles Highham, *Starmaker: The Autobiography of Hal Wallis* (New York: Macmillan, 1980), pp. 149, 153.

44. Peter Guralnick, *Last Train to Memphis: The Rise of Elvis Presley* (Boston: Little, Brown, 1994), p. 327.

45. Ibid., p. 342.

46. Nash, *Elvis Aaron Presley*, p. 278.

47. Virginia Kelley, with James Morgan, *Leading with My Heart* (New York: Simon & Schuster, 1994), p. 129.

48. *New York Times*, August 13, 1992, C1.

49. Nash, *Elvis Aaron Presley*, p. 500.

50. Guralnick, *Careless Love*, p. 581; John Strausbaugh, *Alone with the President* (New York: Blast Books, 1993), p. 73; Jerry Hopkins, *Elvis: The Final Years* (New York: St. Martin's, 1980), p. 170.

51. Charles Hirshberg and the editors of *Life*, *Elvis: A Celebration in Pictures* (New York: Warner Books, 1995), p. 22.

CHAPTER NINE

1. Gulley, *Breaking Cover*, p. 224; Reeves, *President Nixon*, p. 27.

2. Michael Beschloss, ed., *Taking Charge: The Johnson White House Tapes, 1963–1964* (New York: Simon & Schuster, 1997), pp. 549–50; Aitken, *Nixon*, p. 495.

3. Kissinger, *Years of Upheaval*, p. 1182.

4. White, *Breach of Faith*, p. 189.

5. Nixon, *RN*, p. 843.

6. Ibid., p. 500.

7. Leon Friedman and William F. Levantrosser, *Richard M. Nixon: Politician, President, Administrator* (Westport, CT: Greenwood Press, 1991), p. 9.

8. Morris, *Richard Milhous Nixon*, p. 126.

9. White, *Breach of Faith*, p. 215.

10. Richard Ben-Veniste and George Frampton Jr., *Stonewall: The Real Story of the Watergate Prosecution* (New York: Simon & Schuster, 1977), p. 159.

11. Safire, *Before the Fall*, p. 664.

12. Nixon, *RN*, p. 848.

13. Donald Barthelme, *The Teachings of Don B.: The Satires, Parodies, Fables, Illustrated Stories, and Plays of Donald Barthelme*, edited by Kim Herzinger, with an introduction by Thomas Pynchon (New York: Turtle Bay Books, 1992), p. xv.

14. Stanley I. Kutler, ed., *Abuse of Power: The New Nixon Tapes* (New York: Free Press, 1997), p. 503.

15. John Connally, with Mickey Herskowitz, *In History's Shadow: An American Odyssey* (New York: Hyperion, 1993), p. 253.

16. Sam J. Ervin Jr., *The Whole Truth: The Watergate Conspiracy* (New York: Random House, 1980), p. 5.

17. Kutler, *Abuse of Power*, p. 286.

18. George V. Higgins, *The Friends of Richard Nixon* (Boston: Atlantic Monthly Press/Little, Brown, 1975), p. 95.

19. Dean, *Blind Ambition*, p. 121.

20. Crowley, *Nixon in Winter*, p. 296.

21. John W. Dean III, *Lost Honor* (Los Angeles: Stratford Press, 1982), p. 65.

22. William Goldman, *Adventures in the Screen Trade: A Personal View of Hollywood and Screenwriting* (New York: Warner Books, 1983), p. 235.

23. Anson, *Exile*, p. 180.

24. Leonard Garment, *Crazy Rhythm: My Journey from Brooklyn, Jazz, and Wall Street to Nixon's White House, Watergate, and Beyond . . .* (New York: Times Books, 1997), p. 274.

25. Kutler, *Abuse of Power*, p. 622.

26. Mazo and Hess, *Nixon*, pp. 137–38.

27. Kutler, *Abuse of Power*, p. 524.

28. Antoine De Baecque and Serge Toubiana, *Truffaut: A Biography* (New York: Alfred A. Knopf, 1999), p. 309; Gilles Jacob and Claude de Givray, *François*

Truffaut: Correspondence, 1945–1984 (New York: Farrar, Straus & Giroux, 1989), p. 395.

29. Peter Biskind, *Easy Riders, Raging Bulls: How the Sex-Drugs-and-Rock 'n' Roll Generation Saved Hollywood* (New York: Simon & Schuster, 1998), p. 293.

30. Nixon, *RN*, p. 889.

31. Dean, *Lost Honor*, p. 79.

32. Leonard Downie Jr., *The New Muckrakers* (Washington, DC: New Republic Book Company, 1976), p. 6.

33. J. Anthony Lukas, *Nightmare: The Underside of the Nixon Years* (New York: Viking, 1976), p. 493.

34. Haig, *Inner Circles*, p. 468.

35. James Doyle, *Not Above the Law: The Battles of Watergate Prosecutors Cox and Jaworski* (New York: William Morrow, 1977), p. 82.

36. Graham, *Personal History*, p. 508.

37. Michael Schudson, *Watergate in American Memory: How We Remember, Forget, and Reconstruct the Past* (New York: Basic Books, 1993), p. 112.

38. Goldman, *Adventures in the Screen Trade*, p. 146.

39. John Osborne, *White House Watch: The Ford Years* (Washington, DC: New Republic, 1977), p. 308.

40. Dean, *Lost Honor*, p. 34.

41. Edward Jay Epstein, *Between Fact and Fiction: The Problem of Journalism* (New York: Vintage, 1975), p. 10.

42. Downie, *New Muckrakers*, p. 47.

43. Goldman, *Adventures in the Screen Trade*, p. 115.

44. Paul Schrader, "Notes on *Film Noir*," *Film Comment*, Spring 1972, p. 8.

45. Pauline Kael, *Reeling* (New York: Warner Books, 1976), p. 228.

46. Mordden, *Medium Cool*, p. 68.

47. Beth Carney and Maureen Dezell, "Nixon's Role in *X-Files*," *Boston Globe*, June 15, 1998, D8.

48. Colson, *Born Again*, pp. 175–76.

49. Roger Rosenblatt, "The Dark Comedian," *Time*, April 25, 1988, p. 56.

50. Jimmy Carter, *Keeping Faith: Memoirs of a President* (New York: Bantam, 1982), p. 27.

CHAPTER TEN

1. Ziegler is quoted in "Richard Nixon, Moviegoer," *Newsweek*, August 17, 1970, p. 25; Eisenhower in Safire, *Before the Fall*, p. 621.

2. Unless otherwise specified, information on titles and dates of films Nixon had screened and location of screenings is taken from either NPMP, WHCF (OPPA), Daily Diary, FC 21–43; the personal logs kept by White House projectionist Paul Fisher; *The Haldeman Diaries*; or Rose Mary Woods's response to a 1970 inquiry from *Newsweek* about which films Nixon had seen as president, which is found in her papers among the President's Personal Files (PPF).

3. NPMP, PPF RMW, box 36.

4. Nixon, *RN*, p. 539.

5. Pauline Kael, *Going Steady* (New York: Warner Books, 1979), p. 223. Emphasis in original.

6. Kihss, "Nixon," p. 1.

7. Allen Drury and Fred Maroon, *Courage and Hesitation: Notes and Photographs of the Nixon Administration* (Garden City, NY: Doubleday, 1971), p. 241.

8. Safire, *Before the Fall*, p. 615.

9. Interview with author, November 19, 1996.

10. Bob Greene, "Nixon on Nixon," in *Cheeseburgers: The Best of Bob Greene* (New York: Atheneum, 1985), p. 157.

11. Strober and Strober, *Nixon*, p. 35.

12. Haldeman, *Haldeman Diaries*, February 27, 1971.

13. "Richard Nixon, Moviegoer," *Newsweek*, August 17, 1970, p. 25.

14. Haldeman, *Haldeman Diaries*, April 20, 1969.

15. Kirk Douglas, *The Ragman's Son: An Autobiography* (New York: Simon & Schuster, 1988), p. 431.

16. Crowley, *Nixon Off the Record*, p. 10.

17. Vice-Presidential Papers, VPP "Favorites," April 6, 1957, Rose Mary Woods memo.

18. Haldeman, *Haldeman Diaries*, July 18, 1969.

19. Nixon, *RN*, p. 15.

20. Ibid., p. 9.

21. Wills, *Kennedy Imprisonment*, p. 149.

22. Matthews, *Kennedy and Nixon*, p. 192; Oudes, *From: The President*, p. 421.

23. Oudes, *From: The President*, p. 179.

24. NPMP, PPF, President's Special File, box 79.

25. Nixon, *RN*, p. 602.

26. Ibid., p. 763.

27. Haldeman, *Haldeman Diaries*, December 8, 1972.

28. Sears, "With Nixon," M2.

29. Theodore H. White, *America in Search of Itself: The Making of the President, 1956–1980* (New York: Harper & Row, 1982), p. 2.

30. Ambrose, *Nixon: Ruin and Recovery*, p. 488.

31. Gerald R. Ford, *A Time to Heal: The Autobiography of Gerald R. Ford* (New York: Harper & Row/Reader's Digest, 1979), p. 205.

32. Joan Didion, *The White Album* (New York: Noonday Press, 1990), p. 64.

33. Ethan Mordden, *The Hollywood Studios: House Style in the Golden Age of the Movies* (New York: Alfred A. Knopf, 1988), p. 364.

34. Otto Friedrich, *City of Nets: A Portrait of Hollywood in the 1940's* (New York: Harper & Row, 1986), p. xii.

35. Aitken, *Nixon*, p. 124.

36. Safire, *Before the Fall*, p. 600.

37. Haldeman, *Haldeman Diaries*, November 14, 1969.

38. Safire, *Before the Fall*, pp. 615–16.

39. Haldeman, *Haldeman Diaries*, March 26, 1969.

40. Nixon, *Beyond Peace*, p. 229.

41. Garment, *Crazy Rhythm*, p. 68.

42. Oudes, *From: The President*, pp. 540–41.

43. Bruck, *When Hollywood*, p. 310.

44. Oudes, *From: The President*, p. 178.

45. NPMP, PPF, President's Special File, box 79.

CHAPTER ELEVEN

1. Evans, *The Kid*, p. 10.

2. Carlos Clarens points this out in his *Crime Movies: From Griffith to* The Godfather *and Beyond* (New York: W. W. Norton, 1980), p. 289.

3. Dean, *Blind Ambition*, p. 279.

4. Murray Kempton, "Looking for the Real RN," *Newsday*, April 22, 1994, A7.

5. Kael, *Reeling*, p. 227.

6. Ibid., pp. 16–17.

7. Robert Sklar, *Movie-Made America: A Cultural History of American Movies*, 2nd ed. (New York: Vintage, 1995), p. 168.

8. Brownstein, *The Power and the Glitter*, p. 75.

9. Irv Letofsky, "All the Presidents' Movies," *San Francisco Sunday Examiner & Chronicle*, November 3, 1996, p. 52.

10. Kenneth W. Leish, *The White House* (New York: Newsweek Book Division, 1972), p. 111.

11. William Seale, *The President's House: A History* (Washington, DC: White House Historical Association/Harry M. Abrams, 1986), vol. 2, p. 983.

12. Gore Vidal, *Screening History* (Cambridge: Harvard University Press, 1992), pp. 26–27.

13. Jack L. Warner, with Dean Jennings, *My First Hundred Years in Hollywood* (New York: Random House, 1964), pp. 208, 223.

14. Ibid., p. 285.

15. Bob Thomas, *Clown Prince of Hollywood: The Antic Life and Times of Jack L. Warner* (New York: McGraw-Hill, 1990), p. 207.

16. Ibid., p. 237.

17. Ibid., p. 299.

18. Raymond Price, *With Nixon* (New York: Viking, 1977), pp. 51, 64.

19. White, *The Making of the President, 1972*, p. 15.

20. William E. Leuchtenburg, *In the Shadow of FDR: From Harry Truman to Ronald Reagan* (Ithaca, NY: Cornell University Press, 1989), pp. 160–61.

21. Aitken, *Nixon*, p. 73.

22. Alsop, *Nixon & Rockefeller*, p. 194.

23. Drury and Maroon, *Courage and Hesitation*, p. 245.

24. Haldeman, *Haldeman Diaries,* July 30, 1972.

25. Oudes, *From: The President,* p. 560.

26. Crowley, *Nixon Off the Record,* pp. 11, 12.

27. Walter Isaacson and Evan Thomas, *The Wise Men: Six Friends and the World They Made: Acheson, Bohlen, Harriman, Kennan, Lovett, McCloy* (New York: Simon & Schuster, 1986), p. 547.

28. Witcover, *Resurrection of Richard Nixon,* p. 134.

29. Alsop, *Nixon & Rockefeller,* p. 200.

30. Sklar, *Movie-Made America,* p. 175.

31. Mordden, *Medium Cool,* p. 28.

32. Bruck, *When Hollywood,* p. 280.

33. "The Film 'Love Story' Is Given Presidential Seal of Approval," *New York Times,* January 23, 1971, p. 17.

34. Patrick McGilligan, *Robert Altman: Jumping Off the Cliff* (New York: St. Martin's, 1989), p. 400.

35. Ibid., p. 535.

36. Kael, *Deeper into Movies,* p. 299.

37. Diane Jacobs, *Hollywood Renaissance* (South Brunswick: A. S. Barnes, 1977), pp. 114, 113.

38. Michael Pye and Lynda Myles, *The Movie Brats: How the Film Generation Took Over Hollywood* (New York: Holt, Rinehart and Winston, 1979), p. 98.

39. White, *Breach of Faith,* p. 63.

40. "Julie Eisenhower Says She Proposes, 'Fight. Fight. Fight,'" *New York Times,* November 4, 1973, p. 1.

EPILOGUE

1. The aide was Crowley, who recounts the remark in *Nixon Off the Record,* p. 33.

2. John Ehrlichman, "Art in the Nixon White House," *ARTnews,* May 1982, p. 79.

Bibliography

Aaron, Daniel. "Nixon as Literary Artifact." *Raritan*, Autumn 1995.

Adams, Sherman. *Firsthand Report: The Story of the Eisenhower Administration.* New York: Harper & Brothers, 1961.

Agee, James. *Agee on Film.* Vol. 1. New York: Perigee, 1983.

Agnew, Spiro T. *Go Quietly . . . or Else.* New York: William Morrow, 1980.

Aitken, Jonathan. *Nixon: A Life.* Washington, DC: Regnery, 1994.

———. "The Nixon Character." *Presidential Studies Quarterly,* Winter 1996.

Alsop, Stewart. "The Mystery of Richard Nixon" and "Nixon on Nixon." *Saturday Evening Post,* July 12, 1958.

———. *Nixon & Rockefeller: A Double Portrait.* Garden City, NY: Doubleday, 1960.

———. "Nixon and the Square Majority." *Atlantic Monthly,* February 1972.

Ambrose, Stephen E. *Eisenhower: Soldier and President.* New York: Simon & Schuster, 1990.

———. *Nixon: The Education of a Politician, 1913–1962.* New York: Simon & Schuster, 1987.

———. *Nixon: Ruin and Recovery, 1973–1990.* New York: Simon & Schuster, 1991.

———. *Nixon: The Triumph of a Politician, 1962–1972.* New York: Simon & Schuster, 1989.

Anderson, Clinton P., with Milton Viorst. *Outsider in the Senate: Senator Clinton Anderson's Memoirs.* New York: World Publishing, 1970.

Anderson, Lindsay. *About John Ford . . .* New York: McGraw-Hill, 1983.

Anson, Robert Sam. *Exile: The Unquiet Oblivion of Richard M. Nixon.* New York: Simon & Schuster, 1984.

Arnold, Benjamin F., and Arilissa Dorland Clark. *History of Whittier.* Whittier, CA: Western Publishing, 1933.

Arthur, Paul. "Los Angeles as Scene of the Crime." *Film Comment,* July–August 1996.

Atkins, Ollie. *The White House Years: Triumph and Tragedy.* Chicago: Playboy Press, 1977.

Baecque, Antoine de, and Serge Toubiana. *Truffaut: A Biography.* New York: Alfred A. Knopf, 1999.

Baker, Bobby, with Larry L. King. *Wheeling and Dealing: Confessions of a Capitol Hill Operator.* New York: W. W. Norton, 1978.

Baker, Ross K. *Friend and Foe in the U.S. Senate.* New York: Free Press, 1980.

Banham, Reyner. *Los Angeles: The Architecture of Four Ecologies.* London: Pelican Books, 1973.

Barkley, Alben. *That Reminds Me: The Autobiography of the Veep.* Garden City, NY: Doubleday, 1954.

Bartel, Pauline. *Reel Elvis: The Ultimate Trivia Guide to the King's Movies.* Dallas: Taylor, 1994.

Barthelme, Donald. *The Teachings of Don B.: The Satires, Parodies, Fables, Illustrated Stories, and Plays of Donald Barthelme.* Edited by Kim Herzinger, with an introduction by Thomas Pynchon. New York: Turtle Bay Books, 1992.

Baumgold, Julie. "Nixon's New Life in New York." *New York,* June 9, 1980.

Baxter, Charles. "Dysfunctional Narratives, or: 'Mistakes Were Made.'" In *Burning Down the House: Essays on Fiction.* St. Paul, MN: Graywolf Press, 1997.

Bentley, Eric. "The Political Theatre of John Wayne." In *Theatre of War: Comments on 32 Occasions.* New York: Viking, 1972.

———, ed. *Thirty Years of Treason: Excerpts from Hearings Before the House Committee on Un-American Activities, 1938–1968.* New York: Viking, 1971.

Ben-Veniste, Richard, and George Frampton Jr. *Stonewall: The Real Story of the Watergate Prosecution.* New York: Simon & Schuster, 1977.

Bercovitch, Sacvan. *The American Jeremiad.* Madison: University of Wisconsin Press, 1978.

Berg, A. Scott. *Goldwyn: A Biography.* New York: Alfred A. Knopf, 1989.

Bergen, Candice. *Knock Wood.* New York: Linden Press/Simon & Schuster, 1984.

Berges, Marshall. *The Life and* Times *of Los Angeles.* New York: Atheneum, 1984.

Berman, Larry. *No Peace, No Honor: Nixon, Kissinger, and Betrayal in Vietnam.* New York: Free Press, 2001.

Beschloss, Michael, ed. *Taking Charge: The Johnson White House Tapes, 1963–1964.* New York: Simon & Schuster, 1997.

Biskind, Peter. *Easy Riders, Raging Bulls: How the Sex-Drugs-and-Rock 'n' Roll Generation Saved Hollywood.* New York: Simon & Schuster, 1998.

Bogdanovich, Peter. *John Ford.* Berkeley: University of California Press, 1968.

Bradlee, Benjamin C. *Conversations with Kennedy.* New York: W. W. Norton, 1975.

———. *A Good Life: Newspapering and Other Adventures.* New York: Simon & Schuster, 1995.

Branch, Taylor. *Parting the Waters: America in the King Years, 1954–63.* New York: Simon & Schuster, 1988.

————. *Pillar of Fire: America in the King Years, 1963–65.* New York: Simon & Schuster, 1998.

Breslin, Jimmy. *How the Good Guys Finally Won: Notes from an Impeachment Summer.* New York: Viking, 1975.

Brodie, Fawn M. *Richard Nixon: The Shaping of His Character.* New York: W. W. Norton, 1981.

Brownell, Herbert, with John P. Burke. *Advising Ike: The Memoirs of Attorney General Herbert Brownell.* Lawrence: University Press of Kansas, 1993.

Brownstein, Ronald. *The Power and the Glitter: The Washington-Hollywood Connection.* New York: Pantheon, 1991.

Bruck, Connie. *When Hollywood Had a King: The Reign of Lew Wasserman, Who Leveraged Talent into Power and Influence.* New York: Random House, 2003.

Buford, Kate. *Burt Lancaster: An American Life.* New York: Alfred A. Knopf, 2000.

Bullock, Paul. *Jerry Voorhis: The Idealist as Politician.* New York: Vantage, 1978.

Bundy, William. *A Tangled Web: The Making of Foreign Policy in the Nixon Presidency.* New York: Hill and Wang, 1998.

Cagin, Seth, and Philip Dray. *Hollywood Films of the Seventies: Sex, Drugs, Violence, Rock 'n' Roll & Politics.* New York: Harper & Row, 1984.

Cain, James M. *Double Indemnity.* New York: Vintage, 1978.

————. *60 Years of Journalism.* Bowling Green, OH: Bowling Green University Press, 1985.

Cannon, James. *Time and Chance: Gerald Ford's Appointment with History.* New York: HarperCollins, 1994.

Cannon, Lou. *President Reagan: The Role of a Lifetime.* New York: Simon & Schuster, 1991.

————. *Reagan.* New York: G. P. Putnam's, 1982.

Capra, Frank. *The Name Above the Title: An Autobiography.* New York: Belvedere, 1982.

Carnes, Mark C., ed. *Past Imperfect: History According to the Movies.* New York: Henry Holt, 1995.

Carney, Beth, and Maureen Dezell. "Nixon's Role in *X-Files*." *Boston Globe*, June 15, 1998.

Carney, Raymond. *American Vision: The Films of Frank Capra.* New York: Cambridge University Press, 1986.

Caro, Robert A. *The Years of Lyndon Johnson: Master of the Senate.* New York: Alfred A. Knopf, 2002.

Carter, Jimmy. *Keeping Faith: Memoirs of a President.* New York: Bantam, 1982.

Cavell, Stanley. *Pursuits of Happiness: The Hollywood Comedy of Remarriage.* Cambridge: Harvard University Press, 1981.

Ceplair, Larry, and Steven Englund. *The Inquisition in Hollywood: Politics in the Film Community, 1930–1960.* Berkeley: University of California Press, 1983.

Chandler, Raymond. *The Raymond Chandler Omnibus.* New York: Alfred A. Knopf, 1964.

———. *Raymond Chandler Speaking*. Edited by Dorothy Gardiner and Kathrine Mc-
  Sorley Walker. Boston: Houghton Mifflin, 1962.
———. *Selected Letters of Raymond Chandler*. Edited by Frank MacShane. New York:
  Columbia University Press, 1981.
Clarens, Carlos. *Crime Movies: From Griffith to* The Godfather *and Beyond*. New York:
  W. W. Norton, 1980.
Clawson, Ken W. "5 Years Later: A Loyalist Relives the Nixon Resignation." *Wash-
  ington Post*, August 12, 1979.
Colodny, Len, and Robert Gettlin. *Silent Coup: The Removal of a President*. New York:
  St. Martin's, 1991.
Colson, Charles W. *Born Again*. Old Tappan, NJ: Chosen Books, 1976.
Congressional Quarterly Almanac 1972. Washington, DC: Congressional Quarterly,
  1972.
Connally, John, with Mickey Herskowitz. *In History's Shadow: An American Odyssey*.
  New York: Hyperion, 1993.
Costello, William. *The Facts about Nixon: An Unauthorized Biography*. New York:
  Viking, 1960.
Cotton, Norris. *In the Senate: Amidst the Conflict and the Turmoil*. New York: Dodd,
  Mead, 1978.
Coughlan, Robert. "Success Story of a Vice President." *Life*, December 14, 1953.
"Crisis of Leadership." *New York Times*, May 10, 1970.
Crowe, Cameron. *Conversations with Wilder*. New York: Alfred A. Knopf, 1999.
Crowley, Monica. *Nixon in Winter*. New York: Random House, 1998.
———. *Nixon Off the Record: His Candid Commentary on People and Politics*. New York:
  Random House, 1996.
Curtis, Tony, and Barry Paris. *Tony Curtis: The Autobiography*. New York: William
  Morrow, 1993.
Dash, Samuel. *Chief Counsel: Inside the Ervin Committee—The Untold Story of
  Watergate*. New York: Random House, 1976.
Davis, Mike. *City of Quartz: Excavating the Future in Los Angeles*. London: Verso,
  1990.
Dean, John W., III. *Blind Ambition: The White House Years*. New York: Simon &
  Schuster, 1976.
———. *Lost Honor*. Los Angeles: Stratford Press, 1982.
D'Este, Carlo. *Patton: A Genius for War*. New York: HarperCollins, 1995.
Denby, David. "Stolen Privacy: Coppola's *The Conversation*." In *Sight and Sound: A
  Fiftieth Anniversary Selection*. London: Faber and Faber, 1982.
———. Untitled. *New York*, December 23–30, 1985.
Dick, Bernard F., ed. *Dark Victory*. Madison: University of Wisconsin Press, 1981.
Didion, Joan. *Slouching Towards Bethlehem*. New York: Noonday Press, 1990.
———. *The White Album*. New York: Noonday Press, 1990.
Dmohowski, Joseph. "From a Common Ground: The Quaker Heritage of Jes-
  samyn West and Richard Nixon." *California History*, Fall 1994.

Dobrynin, Anatoly. *In Confidence: Moscow's Ambassador to America's Six Cold War Presidents (1962–1986)*. New York: Times Books, 1995.

Doherty, Thomas. *Projections of War: Hollywood, American Culture and World War II*. New York: Columbia University Press, 1993.

Donovan, Robert J. "Over-Nominated, Under-Elected, Still a Promising Candidate." *New York Times Magazine*, April 25, 1965.

Douglas, Helen Gahagan. *A Full Life*. Garden City, NY: Doubleday, 1982.

Douglas, Kirk. *The Ragman's Son: An Autobiography*. New York: Simon & Schuster, 1988.

Douglas, Melvyn, and Tom Arthur. *See You at the Movies: The Autobiography of Melvyn Douglas*. Lanham, MD: University Press of America, 1986.

Douglas, Paul H. *In the Fullness of Time: The Memoirs of Paul H. Douglas*. New York: Harcourt Brace Jovanovich, 1971.

Downie, Leonard, Jr. *The New Muckrakers*. Washington, DC: New Republic Book Company, 1976.

Doyle, James. *Not Above the Law: The Battles of Watergate Prosecutors Cox and Jaworski*. New York: William Morrow, 1977.

Drury, Allen. *Advise and Consent*. Garden City, NY: Doubleday, 1959.

Drury, Allen, and Fred Maroon. *Courage and Hesitation: Notes and Photographs of the Nixon Administration*. Garden City, NY: Doubleday, 1971.

Dunne, Philip. *Take Two: A Life in Movies and Politics*. New York: McGraw-Hill, 1980.

Edwards, Anne. *Early Reagan*. New York: William Morrow, 1987.

Ehrlichman, John. "Art in the Nixon White House." *ARTnews*, May 1982.

———. *Witness to Power: The Nixon Years*. New York: Simon & Schuster, 1982.

Eisenhower, Dwight D. *At Ease: Stories I Tell to Friends*. Garden City, NY: Doubleday, 1967.

———. *Crusade in Europe*. Garden City, NY: Doubleday, 1948.

———. *Mandate for Change*. Garden City, NY: Doubleday, 1963.

———. *Waging Peace*. Garden City, NY: Doubleday, 1965.

Eisenhower, Julie Nixon, ed. *Eye on Nixon: A Photographic Study of the President and the Man*. New York: Hawthorn Books, 1972.

———. *Pat Nixon: The Untold Story*. New York: Simon & Schuster, 1986.

Eisenhower, Milton. *The President Is Calling*. Garden City, NY: Doubleday, 1974.

Emery, Fred. *Watergate: The Corruption of American Politics and the Fall of Richard Nixon*. New York: Times Books, 1994.

Epstein, Edward Jay. *Between Fact and Fiction: The Problem of Journalism*. New York: Vintage, 1975.

Ervin, Sam J., Jr. *The Whole Truth: The Watergate Conspiracy*. New York: Random House, 1980.

Evans, Robert. *The Kid Stays in the Picture*. New York: Hyperion, 1994.

Evans, Rowland, Jr., and Robert D. Novak. *Nixon in the White House. The Frustration of Power*. New York: Vintage, 1972.

Eyman, Scott. *Print the Legend: The Life and Times of John Ford.* New York: Simon & Schuster: 1999.

Fagen, Herb. *Duke, We're Glad We Knew You: John Wayne's Friends and Colleagues Remember His Remarkable Life.* New York: Birch Lane Press, 1996.

Fallaci, Oriana. *Interview with History.* New York: Liveright, 1976.

Ferrell, Robert H., ed. *Off the Record: The Private Papers of Harry S. Truman.* New York: Harper & Row, 1980.

"The Film 'Love Story' Is Given Presidential Seal of Approval." *New York Times,* January 23, 1971.

Fisher, M. F. K. *Among Friends.* New York: North Point Press, 1983.

Flanders, Ralph. *Senator from Vermont.* Boston: Little, Brown, 1961.

Ford, Dan. *Pappy: The Life of John Ford.* Englewood Cliffs, NJ: Prentice-Hall, 1979.

Ford, Gerald R. *A Time to Heal: The Autobiography of Gerald R. Ford.* New York: Harper & Row/Reader's Digest, 1979.

Frady, Marshall. *Billy Graham: A Parable of American Righteousness.* Boston: Little, Brown, 1979.

Frankel, Max. *The Times of My Life, and My Life with the* Times. New York: Random House, 1999.

French, Philip. *Westerns: Aspects of a Movie Genre.* New York: Viking, 1974.

Friedman, Leon, and William F. Levantrosser. *Richard M. Nixon: Politician, President, Administrator.* Westport, CT: Greenwood Press, 1991.

———. *Watergate and Afterward: The Legacy of Richard M. Nixon.* Westport, CT: Greenwood Press, 1992.

Friedrich, Otto. *City of Nets: A Portrait of Hollywood in the 1940's.* New York: Harper & Row, 1986.

Frischauer, Willi. *Behind the Scenes of Otto Preminger: An Unauthorized Biography.* New York: William Morrow, 1974.

Frost, David. *"I Gave Them a Sword": Behind the Scenes of the Nixon Interviews.* New York: William Morrow, 1978.

Gabler, Neal. *Winchell: Gossip, Power and the Culture of Celebrity.* New York: Alfred A. Knopf, 1994.

Galbraith, John Kenneth. *A Life in Our Times: Memoirs.* New York: Ballantine, 1982.

Gallagher, Tag. *John Ford: The Man and His Films.* Berkeley: University of California Press, 1986.

Garment, Leonard. *Crazy Rhythm: My Journey from Brooklyn, Jazz, and Wall Street to Nixon's White House, Watergate, and Beyond . . .* New York: Times Books, 1997.

———. "The Guns of Watergate." *Commentary,* April 1987.

———. *In Search of Deep Throat: The Greatest Political Mystery of Our Time.* New York: Basic Books, 2000.

Gellman, Irwin F. *The Contender: Richard Nixon, the Congress Years, 1946–1952.* New York: Free Press, 1999.

Gergen, David. *Eyewitness to Power: The Essence of Leadership, Nixon to Clinton.* New York: Simon & Schuster, 2000.

Glatzer, Richard, and John Raeburn, eds. *Frank Capra: The Man and His Films.* Ann Arbor: University of Michigan Press, 1975.

Godard, Jean-Luc. *Godard on Godard: Critical Writings by Jean-Luc Godard.* New York: Da Capo, 1986.

Goldman, William. *Adventures in the Screen Trade: A Personal View of Hollywood and Screenwriting.* New York: Warner Books, 1983.

Goldwater, Barry M., with Jack Casserly. *Goldwater.* Garden City NY: Doubleday, 1988.

Goodman, Walter. *The Committee: The Extraordinary Career of the House Committee on Un-American Activities.* New York: Farrar, Straus & Giroux, 1968.

Gottlieb, Robert, and Irene Wolt. *Thinking Big: The Story of the* Los Angeles Times, *Its Publishers, and Their Influence on Southern California.* New York: G. P. Putnam's, 1977.

Graham, Billy. *Just As I Am: The Autobiography of Billy Graham.* San Francisco: HarperSanFrancisco/Zondervan, 1997.

Graham, Katharine. *Personal History.* New York: Alfred A. Knopf, 1997.

Graubard, Stephen R. *Kissinger: Portrait of a Mind.* New York: W. W. Norton, 1973.

Greenberg, David. *Nixon's Shadow: The History of an Image.* New York: W. W. Norton, 2003.

Greene, Bob. "Nixon on Nixon." In *Cheeseburgers: The Best of Bob Greene.* New York: Atheneum, 1985.

Greene, Graham. *The Graham Greene Film Reader: Reviews, Essays, Interviews & Film Stories.* Edited by David Parkinson. New York: Applause, 1995.

Greenstein, Fred I. *The Hidden-Hand Presidency: Eisenhower as Leader.* New York: Basic Books, 1982.

Gregory, Neal, and Janice Gregory. *When Elvis Died.* Washington, DC: Communications Press, 1980.

Griffith, Robert. *The Politics of Fear: Joseph R. McCarthy and the Senate,* 2nd ed. Amherst: University of Massachusetts Press, 1987.

Gulley, Bill, with Mary Ellen Reese. *Breaking Cover.* New York: Simon & Schuster, 1980.

Guralnick, Peter. *Careless Love: The Unmaking of Elvis Presley.* Boston: Little, Brown, 1999.

———. *Last Train to Memphis: The Rise of Elvis Presley.* Boston: Little, Brown, 1994.

———. *Lost Highway: Journeys & Arrivals of American Musicians.* New York: Vintage, 1982.

Gussow, Mel. *Don't Say Yes Until I Finish Talking: A Biography of Darryl F. Zanuck.* Garden City, NY: Doubleday, 1971.

Haig, Alexander M., Jr. *Caveat. Realism, Reagan, and Foreign Policy.* New York: Macmillan, 1984.

Haig, Alexander M., Jr., with Charles McCarry. *Inner Circles: How America Changed the World: A Memoir.* New York: Warner Books, 1992.

Halberstam, David. *The Powers that Be.* New York: Alfred A. Knopf, 1979.

Haldeman, H. R., with Joseph DiMona. *The Ends of Power.* New York: Dell, 1978.

———. *The Haldeman Diaries: Inside the Nixon White House. The Complete Multimedia Edition.* Santa Monica, CA: Sony Imagesoft, 1994.

Haldeman, Peter. "Growing Up a Haldeman." *New York Times Magazine,* April 3, 1994.

Hamburg, Eric, ed. *Nixon: An Oliver Stone Film.* New York: Hyperion, 1995.

Hardeman, D. B., and Donald C. Bacon. *Rayburn: A Biography.* Austin: Texas Monthly Press, 1987.

Harris, Mark. *Mark the Glove Boy, or, The Last Days of Richard Nixon.* New York: Macmillan, 1964.

Harry, Bill. *The Ultimate Beatles Encyclopedia.* London: Virgin Books, 1992.

Harvey, James. *Romantic Comedy in Hollywood from Lubitsch to Sturges.* New York: Alfred A. Knopf, 1987.

Havill, Adrian. *Deep Truth: The Lives of Bob Woodward and Carl Bernstein.* New York: Birch Lane Press, 1993.

Healy, Paul F. "The Busiest Vice-President We Ever Had!" *Saturday Evening Post,* September 19, 1953.

Heggen, Thomas. *Mister Roberts.* Boston: Houghton Mifflin, 1946.

Herbers, John. *No Thank You, Mr. President.* New York: W. W. Norton, 1976.

Herman, Jan. *A Talent for Trouble: The Life of Hollywood's Most Acclaimed Director, William Wyler.* New York: G. P. Putnam's, 1995.

Hersh, Seymour M. *The Price of Power: Kissinger in the Nixon White House.* New York: Summit Books, 1983.

Hickel, Walter J. *Who Owns America?* Englewood Cliffs, NJ: Prentice-Hall, 1971.

Higgins, George V. *The Friends of Richard Nixon.* Boston: Atlantic Monthly Press/Little, Brown, 1975.

Hill, Gladwin. *Dancing Bear: An Inside Look at California Politics.* Cleveland: World Publishing, 1968.

———. "Nixons' New Home in California Hills Has Austere Decor." *New York Times,* May 9, 1962.

Hirshberg, Charles, and the editors of *Life. Elvis: A Celebration in Pictures.* New York: Warner Books, 1995.

Hiss, Alger. *Recollections of a Life.* New York: Seaver Books, 1988.

Hiss, Tony. *Laughing Last: Alger Hiss by Tony Hiss.* Boston: Houghton Mifflin, 1977.

Hitchens, Christopher. *The Trial of Henry Kissinger.* London: Verso, 2001.

Hodgson, Godfrey. *The Gentleman from New York: Daniel Patrick Moynihan, a Biography.* Boston: Houghton Mifflin, 2000.

Hoff, Joan. *Nixon Reconsidered.* New York: Basic Books, 1994.

Holden, Anthony. *Prince Charles.* New York: Atheneum, 1979.

Hoopes, Roy. *Cain: The Biography of James M. Cain.* 2nd ed. Carbondale: Southern Illinois University Press, 1987.

Hopkins, Jerry. *Elvis: A Biography.* New York: Simon & Schuster, 1971.

————. *Elvis: The Final Years*. New York: St. Martin's, 1980.

Hougan, Jim. *Secret Agenda: Watergate, Deep Throat and the CIA*. New York: Random House, 1984.

Hoyt, Edwin P. *The Nixons: An American Family*. New York: Random House, 1972.

Hughes, Emmet John. *The Ordeal of Power: A Political Memoir of the Eisenhower Years*. New York: Atheneum, 1963.

Humes, James C. *Nixon's Ten Commandments of Statecraft*. New York: Scribner, 1997.

Humphrey, Hubert H. *The Education of a Public Man: My Life and Politics*. Minneapolis: University of Minnesota Press, 1991.

Hurst, Louis, as told to Frances Leighton Spatz. *The Sweetest Little Club in the World: The U.S. Senate*. Englewood Cliffs, NJ: Prentice-Hall, 1980.

Isaacson, Walter. *Kissinger: A Biography*. New York: Simon & Schuster, 1992.

Isaacson, Walter, and Evan Thomas. *The Wise Men: Six Friends and the World They Made: Acheson, Bohlen, Harriman, Kennan, Lovett, McCloy*. New York: Simon & Schuster, 1986.

Jacob, Gilles, and Claude de Givray. *François Truffaut: Correspondence, 1945–1984*. New York: Farrar, Straus & Giroux, 1989.

Jacobs, Diane. *Hollywood Renaissance*. South Brunswick: A. S. Barnes, 1977.

James, Henry. *Novels, 1881–1886*. New York: Library of America, 1985.

Jaworski, Leon. *The Right and the Power: The Prosecution of Watergate*. New York: Reader's Digest Press, 1976.

Jeffries, John C., Jr. *Justice Lewis F. Powell, Jr.: A Biography*. New York: Charles Scribner's Sons, 1994.

"Julie Eisenhower Says She Proposes, 'Fight. Fight. Fight.'" *New York Times*, November 4, 1973.

Kael, Pauline. *The Citizen Kane Book*. New York: Limelight Editions, 1984.

————. *Deeper into Movies*. Boston: Little, Brown, 1973.

————. *5001 Nights at the Movies: A Guide from A to Z*. New York: Holt, Rinehart & Winston, 1982.

————. *Going Steady*. New York: Warner Books, 1979.

————. *Kiss Kiss Bang Bang*. Boston: Little, Brown, 1968.

————. *Reeling*. New York: Warner Books, 1976.

Kalb, Marvin. *The Nixon Memo: Political Respectability, Russia, and the Press*. Chicago: University of Chicago Press, 1994.

Kalb, Marvin, and Bernard Kalb. *Kissinger*. Boston: Little, Brown, 1974.

Kazin, Alfred. "The President and Other Intellectuals." In *Contemporaries*. Boston: Little, Brown, 1962.

Kelley, Virginia, with James Morgan. *Leading with My Heart*. New York: Simon & Schuster, 1994.

Kemp, Philip. *Lethal Innocence: The Cinema of Alexander Mackendrick*. London: Methuen, 1991.

Kempton, Murray. *America Comes of Middle Age: Columns, 1950–1962*. Boston: Little, Brown, 1963.

————. "Looking for the Real RN." *Newsday*, April 22, 1994.

————. *Rebellions, Perversities, and Main Events.* New York: Times Books, 1994.

Keogh, James. *President Nixon and the Press.* New York: Funk & Wagnalls, 1972.

————. *This Is Nixon.* New York: G. P. Putnam's, 1956.

Kessler, Ronald. *Inside the White House: The Hidden Lives of the Modern Presidents and the Secrets of the World's Most Powerful Institution.* New York: Pocket Books, 1995.

Kihss, Peter. "Nixon, Happy as New Yorker, Says Job Is Law, Not Politics." *New York Times*, December 29, 1963.

Kissinger, Henry. *Diplomacy.* New York: Simon & Schuster, 1994.

————. *Does America Need a Foreign Policy? Toward a Diplomacy for the 21st Century.* New York: Simon & Schuster, 2001.

————. *Nuclear Weapons and Foreign Policy.* New York: Harper & Row, 1957.

————. "The 37th President: 'Courage in the Face of Wrenching Domestic Controversy.'" *New York Times*, April 28, 1994.

————. *White House Years.* Boston: Little, Brown, 1979.

————. "With Faint Praise." *New York Times Book Review*, July 16, 1995.

————. *Years of Renewal.* New York: Simon & Schuster, 1999.

————. *Years of Upheaval.* Boston: Little, Brown, 1982.

Klein, Herbert G. *Making It Perfectly Clear.* Garden City, NY: Doubleday, 1980.

Kluger, Richard. *The Paper: The Life and Death of the New York* Herald Tribune. New York: Alfred A. Knopf, 1986.

Korda, Michael. *Another Life: A Memoir of Other People.* New York: Random House, 1999.

Korff, Baruch. *The President and I: Richard Nixon's Rabbi Reveals His Role in the Saga that Traumatized the Nation.* Providence, RI: Baruch Korff Foundation, 1995.

Kornitzer, Bela. *The Real Nixon: An Intimate Biography.* Chicago: Rand McNally, 1960.

Kotsilibas-Davis, James, and Myrna Loy. *Myrna Loy: Being and Becoming.* New York: Alfred A. Knopf, 1987.

Krogh, Egil. *The Day Elvis Met Nixon.* Bellevue, WA: Pejama Press, 1994.

Kutler, Stanley I. *The Wars of Watergate: The Last Crisis of Richard Nixon.* New York: Alfred A. Knopf, 1990.

————, ed. *Abuse of Power: The New Nixon Tapes.* New York: Free Press, 1997.

Lears, Jackson. "Gutter Populist." *New Republic*, January 9 & 16, 1995.

Leff, Leonard J., and Jerold L. Simmons, *The Dame in the Kimono: Hollywood, Censorship, and the Production Code from the 1920s to the 1960s.* New York: Anchor Books, 1991.

Leggett, John. *Ross and Tom: Two American Tragedies.* New York: Simon & Schuster, 1974.

Lehman, Ernest. *Screening Sickness, and Other Tales of Tinsel Town.* New York: Perigee, 1982.

Leish, Kenneth W. *The White House.* New York: Newsweek Book Division, 1972.

Le Shana, David C. *Quakers in California: The Effects of 19th Century Revivalism on Western Quakerism.* Newberg, OR: Barclay Press, 1969.

Letofsky, Irv. "All the Presidents' Movies." *San Francisco Sunday Examiner & Chronicle*, November 3, 1996.

Leuchtenburg, William E. *In the Shadow of FDR: From Harry Truman to Ronald Reagan.* Ithaca, NY: Cornell University Press, 1989.

Liddy, G. Gordon. *Will: The Autobiography of G. Gordon Liddy.* New York: St. Martin's, 1980.

Lodge, Henry Cabot. *The Storm Has Many Eyes: A Personal Narrative.* New York: W. W. Norton, 1973.

Lukas, J. Anthony. *Nightmare: The Underside of the Nixon Years.* New York: Viking, 1976.

Lungren, John C., and John C. Lungren Jr. *Healing Richard Nixon: A Doctor's Memoir.* Lexington: University of Kentucky Press, 2003.

MacNeil, Neil. *Dirksen: Portrait of a Public Man.* New York: World Publishing, 1970.

MacShane, Frank. *The Life of Raymond Chandler.* New York: Penguin, 1978.

Madsen, Axel. *Stanwyck.* New York: HarperCollins, 1994.

Magruder, Jeb Stuart. *An American Life: One Man's Road to Watergate.* New York: Pocket Books, 1975.

Mailer, Norman. *St. George and the Godfather.* New York: Arbor House, 1972.

Mann, James. "Deep Throat: An Institutional Analysis." *Atlantic Monthly*, May 1992.

Maraniss, David. *First Class in His Class: A Biography of Bill Clinton.* New York: Simon & Schuster, 1995.

Marcus, Greil. *Dead Elvis: A Chronicle of a Cultural Obsession.* Garden City, NY: Doubleday, 1991.

———. *Mystery Train: Images of America in Rock 'n' Roll Music.* Rev. ed. New York: Dutton, 1982.

Martin, Joseph, as told to Robert J. Donovan. *My First Fifty Years in Politics.* New York: McGraw-Hill, 1960.

Martz, Larry, with Thomas M. DeFrank, Howard Fineman et al., "The Road Back." *Newsweek*, May 19, 1986.

Matthews, Christopher J. *Kennedy and Nixon: The Rivalry that Shaped Postwar America.* New York: Simon & Schuster, 1996.

———. "Reagan as Narrator of America's Dream." *Boston Globe*, February 8, 1987.

Matthews, Donald R. *U.S. Senators and Their World.* Chapel Hill: University of North Carolina Press, 1960.

Mazo, Earl. "The Nixons Now." *Good Housekeeping*, March 1962.

Mazo, Earl, and Stephen Hess. *Nixon: A Political Portrait.* New York: Harper & Row, 1968.

McBride, Joseph. *Frank Capra: The Catastrophe of Success.* New York: Simon & Schuster, 1992.

———. *Hawks on Hawks.* Berkeley: University of California Press, 1982.

————. *Searching for John Ford: A Life.* New York: St. Martin's, 2001.

McCullough, David. *Truman.* New York: Simon & Schuster, 1992.

McDougal, Dennis. *The Last Mogul: Lew Wasserman, MCA, and the Hidden History of Hollywood.* New York: Crown, 1998.

————. *Privileged Son: Otis Chandler and the Rise and Fall of the* L.A. Times *Dynasty.* Cambridge, MA: Perseus, 2001.

McGilligan, Patrick. *Jack's Life: A Biography of Jack Nicholson.* New York: W. W. Norton, 1994.

————. *Robert Altman: Jumping Off the Cliff.* New York: St. Martin's, 1989.

McGinniss, Joe. *The Selling of the President, 1968.* New York: Trident Press, 1969.

McGovern, George. *Grassroots: The Autobiography of George McGovern.* New York: Random House, 1977.

McWilliams, Carey. *California: The Great Exception.* New York: Current Books, 1949.

————. *Southern California Country: An Island on the Land.* Freeport, NY: Books for Libraries Press, 1970.

Meredith, Scott. "Richard the Actor." *Ladies' Home Journal,* September 1975.

Miller, Merle. *Plain Speaking: An Oral Biography of Harry S Truman.* New York: G. P. Putnam's, 1974.

Miller, William "Fishbait," and Frances Spatz Leighton. *Fishbait: The Memoirs of the Congressional Doorkeeper.* Englewood, NJ: Prentice-Hall, 1977.

Mitchell, Greg. *Tricky Dick and the Pink Lady: Richard Nixon vs. Helen Gahagan Douglas—Sexual Politics and the Red Scare, 1950.* New York: Random House, 1998.

Mollenhoff, Clark R. *Game Plan for Disaster: An Ombudsman's Report on the Nixon Years.* New York: W. W. Norton, 1976.

Monaco, James. *American Film Now: The People, the Power, the Money, the Movies.* 2nd ed. New York: Zoetrope, 1984.

Monsell, Thomas. *Nixon on Stage and Screen: The Thirty-Seventh President as Depicted in Films, Television, Plays and Opera.* Jefferson, NC: McFarland & Company, 1998.

Montgomery, Gayle B., and James W. Johnson. *One Step from the White House: The Rise and Fall of Senator William F. Knowland.* Berkeley: University of California Press, 1998.

Mordden, Ethan. *The Hollywood Studios: House Style in the Golden Age of the Movies.* New York: Alfred A. Knopf, 1988.

————. *Medium Cool: The Movies of the 1960s.* New York: Alfred A. Knopf, 1990.

Morris, Edmund. *Dutch: A Memoir of Ronald Reagan.* New York: Random House, 1999.

Morris, Roger. *Haig: The General's Progress.* New York: Playboy Press, 1982.

————. *Richard Milhous Nixon: The Rise of an American Politician.* New York: Henry Holt, 1989.

————. *Uncertain Greatness: Henry Kissinger and American Foreign Policy.* New York: Harper & Row, 1977.

Moynihan, Daniel Patrick, with Suzanne Weaver. *A Dangerous Place.* Boston: Little, Brown, 1975.

Muzzio, Douglas. *Watergate Games: Strategies, Choices, Outcomes.* New York: New York University Press, 1982.

Nash, Alanna, with Billy Smith, Marty Lacker, and Lamar Fike. *Elvis Aaron Presley: Revelations from the Memphis Mafia.* New York: HarperCollins, 1995.

Newman, Roger K. *Hugo Black: A Biography.* New York: Pantheon, 1994.

New York Times staff. *The Watergate Hearings: Break-in and Cover-up: Proceedings of the Senate Select Committee on Presidential Campaign Activities.* New York: Viking, 1973.

Nitze, Paul H., with Ann M. Smith and Steven L. Rearden. *From Hiroshima to Glasnost: At the Center of Decision: A Memoir.* New York: Grove Weidenfeld, 1989.

Nixon, Hannah, as told to Flora Rheata Schreiber. "A Mother's Story." *Good Housekeeping,* June 1960.

Nixon, Richard M. *Beyond Peace.* New York: Random House, 1994.

———. *The Challenges We Face.* New York: McGraw-Hill, 1960.

———. *In the Arena: A Memoir of Victory, Defeat and Renewal.* New York: Simon & Schuster, 1990.

———. *Leaders.* New York: Warner Books, 1982.

———. *1999: Victory without War.* New York: Pocket Books, 1989.

———. *No More Vietnams.* New York: Arbor House, 1985.

———. *Real Peace.* Boston: Little, Brown, 1984.

———. *The Real War.* New York: Warner Books, 1980.

———. *RN: The Memoirs of Richard Nixon.* New York: Touchstone, 1990.

———. *Seize the Moment: America's Challenge in a One-Superpower World.* New York: Simon & Schuster, 1992.

———. *Six Crises.* New York: Touchstone, 1990.

"Nixon's Remarks on Manson and Statement in Washington." *New York Times,* August 4, 1970.

O'Brien, Geoffrey. *The Phantom Empire.* New York: W. W. Norton, 1993.

Ogden, Christopher. *Legacy: A Biography of Moses and Walter Annenberg.* Boston: Little, Brown, 1999.

O'Neill, Thomas P., Jr., and William Novak. *Man of the House: The Life and Political Memoirs of Speaker Tip O'Neill.* New York: Random House, 1987.

Osborne, John. *The Fifth Year of the Nixon Watch.* New York: Liveright, 1974.

———. *The Fourth Year of the Nixon Watch.* New York: Liveright, 1973.

———. *The Last Nixon Watch.* Washington, DC: New Republic Book Company, 1975.

———. *The Nixon Watch.* New York: Liveright, 1970.

———. *The Second Year of the Nixon Watch.* New York: Liveright, 1971.

———. *The Third Year of the Nixon Watch.* New York: Liveright, 1972.

———. *White House Watch: The Ford Years.* Washington, DC: New Republic Book Company, 1977.

Oshinsky, David M. *A Conspiracy So Vast: The World of Joe McCarthy.* New York: Free Press, 1983.

Oudes, Bruce, ed. *From: The President: Richard Nixon's Secret Files.* New York: Harper & Row, 1989.

Parmet, Herbert S. *Richard Nixon and His America.* Boston: Little, Brown, 1990.

Patterson, James T. *Mr. Republican: A Biography of Robert A. Taft.* Boston: Houghton Mifflin, 1972.

Perlstein, Rick. *Before the Storm: Barry Goldwater and the Unmaking of the American Consensus.* New York: Hill and Wang, 2001.

Persico, Joseph E. *The Imperial Rockefeller: A Biography of Nelson A. Rockefeller.* New York: Simon & Schuster, 1982.

Peterson, Merrill D. *Lincoln in American Memory.* New York: Oxford University Press, 1994.

Peyser, Marc. "On Top of the World." *Stanford,* September–October 1999.

Phillips, Cabell. "Nixon in '58—and Nixon in '60." *New York Times Magazine,* October 26, 1958.

Phillips, Herbert L. *Big Wayward Girl: An Informal Political History of California.* Garden City, NY: Doubleday, 1968.

Phillips, Kevin P. *The Emerging Republican Majority.* New Rochelle, NY: Arlington House, 1969.

Pipes, Daniel. *Conspiracy: How the Paranoid Style Flourishes and Where It Comes From.* New York: Free Press, 1997.

Powell, Colin, with Joseph E. Persico. *My American Journey.* New York: Random House, 1995.

Preminger, Otto. *Preminger: An Autobiography.* Garden City, NY: Doubleday, 1977.

Prendergast, Curtis, with Geoffrey Colvin. *The World of Time Inc.: The Intimate History of a Changing Enterprise, 1960–1980.* New York: Atheneum, 1986.

Price, Raymond. *With Nixon.* New York: Viking, 1977.

Pye, Michael, and Lynda Myles. *The Movie Brats: How the Film Generation Took Over Hollywood.* New York: Holt, Rinehart and Winston, 1979.

Rainsberger, Todd. *James Wong Howe: Cinematographer.* San Diego: A. S. Barnes, 1981.

Rather, Dan, and Gary Paul Gates. *The Palace Guard.* New York: Harper & Row, 1974.

Reagan, Ronald. *An American Life: The Autobiography.* New York: Simon & Schuster, 1990.

Reagan, Ronald, with Richard G. Hubler. *Where's the Rest of Me?* New York: Duell, Sloan and Pearce, 1965.

Reedy, George. *The U.S. Senate: Paralysis or a Search for Consensus?* New York: Crown, 1986.

Reeves, Richard. *President Kennedy: Profile of Power.* New York: Simon & Schuster, 1993.

————. *President Nixon: Alone in the White House*. New York: Simon & Schuster, 2001.

Reich, Cary. *The Life of Nelson A. Rockefeller: Worlds to Conquer, 1908–1958*. New York: Doubleday, 1996.

Remnick, David. "Gary Hart in Exile." *New Yorker*, April 19, 1993.

Reston, James. *Deadline: A Memoir*. New York: Times Books, 1992.

"Richard Nixon, Moviegoer." *Newsweek*, August 17, 1970.

Richardson, Elliott. *The Creative Balance: Government, Politics, and the Individual in America's Third Century*. London: Hamish Hamilton, 1976.

Riedel, Richard Langham. *Halls of the Mighty: My 47 Years at the Senate*. Washington, DC: Robert Luce, 1969.

Roberts, Randy, and James S. Olson. *John Wayne, American*. New York: Free Press, 1995.

Robinson, W. W. *What They Say about the Angels*. Pasadena, CA: Val Trefz Press, 1942.

Roddick, Nick. *A New Deal in Entertainment: Warner Brothers in the 1930s*. London: British Film Institute, 1983.

Rosenblatt, Roger. "The Dark Comedian." *Time*, April 25, 1988.

Rosten, Leo C. *Hollywood: The Movie Colony: The Movie Makers*. New York: Arno Press, 1970.

Rovere, Richard H. *Affairs of State: The Eisenhower Years*. New York: Farrar, Straus & Cudahy, 1956.

————. *The American Establishment and Other Reports, Opinions, and Speculations*. New York: Harcourt, Brace & World, 1962.

————. *Senator Joe McCarthy*. New York: Harcourt, Brace and Company, 1959.

Safire, William. *Before the Fall: An Inside View of the Pre-Watergate White House*. Garden City, NY: Doubleday, 1975.

————. "Report from Elba." *New York Times*, May 5, 1975.

————. *Safire's New Political Dictionary*. New York: Random House, 1993.

Sarris, Andrew. *The American Cinema: Directors and Directions, 1929–1968*. Chicago: University of Chicago Press, 1985.

Sayre, Nora. *Running Time: Films of the Cold War*. New York: Dial Press, 1982.

Schatz, Thomas. *The Genius of the System: Hollywood Filmmaking in the Studio Era*. New York: Pantheon, 1988.

Scherle, Victor, and William Turner Levy. *The Films of Frank Capra*. Secaucus, NJ: Citadel Press, 1977.

Schickel, Richard. *Clint Eastwood. A Biography*. New York: Alfred A. Knopf, 1996.

————. *Double Indemnity*. London: British Film Institute, 1992.

Schlesinger, Arthur M., Jr. *The Imperial Presidency*. Boston: Houghton Mifflin, 1973.

————. *A Thousand Days: John F. Kennedy in the White House*. Boston: Houghton Mifflin, 1965.

Schrader, Paul. "Notes on Film Noir." *Film Comment*, Spring 1972.

Schreiber, Flora Rheata. "'I Didn't Want Dick to Run Again'" (interview with the Nixon family). *Good Housekeeping,* July 1968.

Schudson, Michael. *Watergate in American Memory: How We Remember, Forget, and Reconstruct the Past.* New York: Basic Books, 1993.

Schulte, Renee K., ed. *The Young Nixon: An Oral Inquiry.* Fullerton: California State University Oral History Program, 1978.

Schwartz, Bernard. *Super Chief: Earl Warren and His Supreme Court—A Judicial Biography.* New York: New York University Press, 1983.

Scobie, Ingrid Winther. *Center Stage: Helen Gahagan Douglas: A Life.* New York: Oxford University Press, 1992.

Seale, William. *The President's House: A History.* 2 vols. Washington, DC: White House Historical Association/Harry M. Abrams, 1986.

Sears, John. "With Nixon: 'Politics Is Great—Except for People." *Los Angeles Times,* April 24, 1994.

Semple, Robert, Jr. "Nixons Entertain Their Hollywood Backers." *New York Times,* August 28, 1972.

Sidey, Hugh. "Anybody Seen *Patton?*" *Life,* June 19, 1970.

Siegel, Don. *A Siegel Film: An Autobiography.* London: Faber & Faber, 1993.

Simes, Dimitri K. *After the Collapse: Russia Seeks Its Place as a Great Power.* New York: Simon & Schuster, 1999.

Sinclair, Andrew. *John Ford.* New York: Dial Press, 1979.

Sirica, John J. *To Set the Record Straight: The Break-in, the Tapes, the Conspirators, the Pardon.* New York: W. W. Norton, 1979.

Sklar, Robert. *Movie-Made America: A Cultural History of American Movies.* 2nd ed. New York: Vintage, 1995.

Slotkin, Richard. *Gunfighter Nation: The Myth of the Frontier in Twentieth-Century America.* New York: Atheneum, 1992.

Small, Melvin. *The Presidency of Richard Nixon.* Lawrence: University Press of Kansas, 1999.

Smith, Gavin. "A Lifetime in the Moment: Robert Duvall Interviewed." *Film Comment,* November–December 1997.

Smith, Richard Norton. *Thomas E. Dewey and His Times.* New York: Simon & Schuster, 1982.

———. *An Uncommon Man: The Triumph of Herbert Hoover.* New York: Simon & Schuster, 1984.

Spark, Muriel. *The Abbess of Crewe.* New York: Viking, 1974.

Stans, Maurice H. *One of the Presidents' Men: Twenty Years with Eisenhower and Nixon.* Washington, DC: Brassey's, 1995.

———. *The Terrors of Justice: The Untold Side of Watergate.* Chicago: Regnery, 1984.

Starr, Kevin. *Americans and the California Dream, 1850–1915.* New York: Oxford University Press, 1973.

———. *The Dream Endures: California Enters the 1940s.* New York: Oxford University Press, 1997.

————. *Embattled Dreams: California in War and Peace, 1940–1950.* New York: Oxford University Press, 2002.

————. *Endangered Dreams: The Great Depression in California.* New York: Oxford University Press, 1996.

————. *Inventing the Dream: California through the Progressive Era.* New York: Oxford University Press, 1985.

————. *Material Dreams: Southern California through the 1920s.* New York: Oxford University Press, 1990.

Steel, Ronald. *Walter Lippmann and the American Century.* New York: Vintage, 1981.

Steinberg, Cobbett S. *Film Facts.* New York: Facts on File, 1980.

Stoessinger, John G. *Henry Kissinger: The Anguish of Power.* New York: W. W. Norton, 1976.

Strausbaugh, John. *Alone with the President.* New York: Blast Books, 1993.

Strober, Gerald S., and Deborah Hart Strober. *Nixon: An Oral History of His Presidency.* New York: HarperCollins, 1994.

Stuart, Jan. *The "Nashville" Chronicles: The Making of Robert Altman's Masterpiece.* New York: Simon & Schuster, 2001.

Summers, Anthony. *The Arrogance of Power: The Secret World of Richard Nixon.* New York: Viking, 2000.

Sussman, Barry. *The Great Coverup: Nixon and the Scandal of Watergate.* New York: Thomas Y. Crowell, 1974.

Taylor, Gary. *Cultural Selection.* New York: Basic Books, 1996.

Teichman, Howard. *Fonda: My Life.* New York: NAL Books, 1981.

Tesier, Ruth. *Remembering William F. Knowland.* Berkeley: University of California, Regional Oral History Office, 1981.

Thomas, Bob. *Clown Prince of Hollywood: The Antic Life and Times of Jack L. Warner.* New York: McGraw-Hill, 1990.

————. *King Cohn: The Life and Times of Harry Cohn.* New York: G. P. Putnam's, 1967.

Thompson, Fred D. *At that Point in Time: The Inside Story of the Senate Watergate Committee.* New York: Quadrangle, 1975.

Thompson, Kenneth W., ed. *The Nixon Presidency: Twenty-two Intimate Perspectives of Richard M. Nixon.* Lanham, MD: University Press of America, 1987.

Thompson, W. Scott, ed. *National Security in the 1980s: From Weakness to Strength.* San Francisco: Institute for Contemporary Studies, 1980.

Thomson, David. *Beneath Mulholland: Thoughts on Hollywood and Its Ghosts.* New York: Alfred A. Knopf, 1997.

————. *A Biographical Dictionary of Film.* 3rd ed. New York: Alfred A. Knopf, 1994.

————. "Our Process (Our Show)." *Film Comment,* January–February 1992.

Toledano, Ralph de. *One Man Alone: Richard Nixon.* New York: Funk & Wagnalls, 1969.

Tompkins, Jane. *West of Everything: The Inner Life of Westerns.* New York: Oxford University Press, 1992.

Ullmann, Liv. *Changing.* New York: Alfred A. Knopf, 1976.

Valeriani, Richard. *Travels with Henry.* Boston: Houghton Mifflin, 1979.

Vidal, Gore. *The Best Man: A Play about Politics.* Boston: Little, Brown, 1960.

———. *An Evening with Richard Nixon.* New York: Random House, 1972.

———. *Palimpsest: A Memoir.* New York: Random House, 1995.

———. *Screening History.* Cambridge: Harvard University Press, 1992.

Voorhis, Jerry. *Confessions of a Congressman.* Garden City, NY: Doubleday, 1947.

———. *The Strange Case of Richard Milhous Nixon.* New York: Paul S. Eriksson, 1972.

Wallis, Hal, with Charles Highham. *Starmaker: The Autobiography of Hal Wallis.* New York: Macmillan, 1980.

Walters, Vernon A. *Silent Missions.* Garden City, NY: Doubleday, 1978.

Ward, Elizabeth, and Alain Silver. *Raymond Chandler's Los Angeles.* Woodstock, NY: Overlook Press, 1987.

Warhol, Andy. *The Warhol Diaries,* edited by Pat Hackett. New York: Warner Books, 1991.

Warner, Jack L., with Dean Jennings. *My First Hundred Years in Hollywood.* New York: Random House, 1964.

Washington Post. *The Presidential Transcripts.* New York: Dell, 1974.

Wayne, Leslie. "A Hollywood Product: Political Money." *New York Times,* September 12, 1996.

Weales, Gerald. *Clifford Odets: Playwright.* New York: Pegasus, 1971.

"We in the U.S. Are Suckers for Style." *Time,* April 22, 1985.

Weaver, John. *Los Angeles: The Enormous Village.* Santa Barbara, CA: Capra Press, 1980.

Weigley, Russell F. *The American Way of War: A History of United States Military Strategy and Policy.* Bloomington: Indiana University Press, 1973.

Weinstein, Allen. "Nixon vs. Hiss." *Esquire,* November 1975.

———. *Perjury: The Hiss-Chambers Case.* New York: Alfred A. Knopf, 1978.

Welles, Orson. "But Where Are We Going?" *Look,* November 11, 1970.

West, J. B. *Upstairs at the White House: My Life with the First Ladies.* New York: Coward, McCann, Geoghagen, 1973.

West, Jessamyn. *The Friendly Persuasion.* New York: Harcourt, Brace, 1943.

———. *Hide and Seek: A Continuing Journey.* New York: Harcourt Brace Jovanovich, 1973.

———. "The Real Pat Nixon: An Intimate View." *Good Housekeeping,* February 1971.

———. *To See the Dream.* New York: Harcourt, Brace, 1956.

Whalen, Richard J. *Catch the Falling Flag: A Republican's Challenge to His Party.* Boston: Houghton Mifflin, 1972.

"What the President Saw: A Nation Coming into Its Own Time." *Time,* July 29, 1985.

White, Theodore H. *America in Search of Itself: The Making of the President, 1956–1980.* New York: Harper & Row, 1982.

———. *Breach of Faith: The Fall of Richard Nixon.* New York: Atheneum, 1975.

————. *The Making of the President, 1960*. New York: Atheneum, 1961.

————. *The Making of the President, 1964*. New York: Signet, 1966.

————. *The Making of the President, 1968*. New York: Atheneum, 1969.

————. *The Making of the President, 1972*. New York: Atheneum, 1973.

White, William S. *Citadel: The Story of the U.S. Senate*. New York: Harper & Brothers, 1956.

————. *Home Place: The Story of the U.S. House of Representatives*. Boston: Houghton Mifflin, 1965.

————. "What Bill Knowland Stands For." *New Republic*, February 27, 1956.

Whitfield, Stephen J. "Richard Nixon as Comic Figure." *American Quarterly*, Spring 1985.

Wicker, Tom. *One of Us: Richard Nixon and the American Dream*. New York: Random House, 1991.

Wiley, Mason, and Damien Bona. *Inside Oscar: The Unofficial History of the Academy Awards*. New York: Ballantine, 1993.

Wills, Garry. "The Hiss Connection through Nixon's Life." *New York Times Magazine*, August 25, 1974.

————. *John Wayne's America: The Politics of Celebrity*. New York: Simon & Schuster, 1997.

————. *The Kennedy Imprisonment: A Meditation on Power*. Boston: Little, Brown, 1992.

————. *Nixon Agonistes: The Crisis of the Self-Made Man*. New York: Signet, 1971.

————. *Reagan's America: Innocents at Home*. Garden City, NY: Doubleday, 1987.

Wilson, James Q. "A Guide to Reagan Country: The Political Culture of Southern California." *Commentary*, May 1967.

Witcover, Jules. *The Resurrection of Richard Nixon*. New York: G. P. Putnam's, 1970.

Woods, Rose Mary. "Nixon's My Boss." *Saturday Evening Post*, December 28, 1957.

Woodward, Bob. *Shadow: Five Presidents and the Legacy of Watergate*. New York: Simon & Schuster, 1999.

Woodward, Bob, and Carl Bernstein. *All the President's Men*. New York: Touchstone, 1987.

————. *The Final Days*. New York: Touchstone, 1987.

Zolotow, Maurice. *Billy Wilder in Hollywood*. New York: Limelight Editions, 1987.

Zumwalt, Elmo R., Jr. *On Watch: A Memoir*. New York: Quadrangle, 1976.

Index

Page number for illustrations are in boldface. Book titles are followed by the author's name in parentheses. Other titles, unless otherwise indicated, refer to films.

Bundy, William, 160
Burdick, Eugene, 170
Bureau of Narcotics and Dangerous Drugs, 218, 219
Burstyn, Ellen, 323
Burton, Richard, 291
Bush, George H. W., 22, 87, 289
Bush, George W., x, 289
Bush, Prescott, 104
Butch Cassidy and the Sundance Kid, 226, 276, 342
Butterfield, Alexander, Jr., 330
Butterfield 8, 349
Butterflies Are Free, 354
Buzhardt, Fred, 254
By the Light of the Silvery Moon, 281, 355
Byington, Spring, 201
Byrds, the, 145, 223

Caan, James, 59, 328, 304
Cabaret, 281, 348
Cactus Flower, 341
Caddyshack, 328
Cagin, Seth, 302
Cagney, James, 42, 93, 307
Cahill: U.S. Marshal, 353
Cain, James M., 32, 35, 56, 57, 60
Caine Mutiny, The, 341
Calley, William, 84
Call of the Wild, 354
Cambodia, invasion of, 68, 72, 73, 158, 181, 183–86, 290
Camelot, 281, 340
"Campaigner," 305n
Campbell, Glen, 172
Cancel My Reservation, 349
Candidate, The, xii, 53, 113, 118, 119, 285, 349
"Candy Man," 233
Cannon, Lou, 19
Cannon for Cordoba, 346
Capone, Al, 138
Capra, Frank, x, 136, 184, 205, 206, 267; Capra hero, 193–95; and Ford and Hawks, 199–200; *Meet John Doe*, 200–202; *Mr. Smith Goes to Washington*, 201–2, 208–9; and Nixon, 190–91, 195–96; as

political filmmaker, 197–99; and Presley, 214–15; and Reagan, 193–95
Captain Horatio Hornblower, 344
Cardinal, The, 114, 342, 347
Carey Treatment, The, 349
Carey, Harry, Jr., 173
Carlyle, Thomas, 134
Carney, Art, 300, 323
Carousel, 20
Carpetbaggers, The, 347
Carson, Jack, 21
Carson, Johnny, 45
Carter, Billy, 241
Carter, Chris, 271
Carter, Jimmy, 171, 259, 272, 328; and Presley, 241
Casals, Pablo, 283
Cassandra Crossing, The, 269
Cassavetes, John, 190
Cat Ballou, 341
Catch-22 (Heller), 94
Cavell, Stanley, x
Cecil, David, xi, 283
Centennial Summer, 351
Chad Hanna, 355
Chairman, The, 285, 343
Chamberlain, Richard, 322
Chambers, Whittaker, 90, 101, 126, 133, 254, 330
Champagne Waltz, 33
Chancellor, John, 277
Chandler, Raymond, 55, 57, 59–62; Philip Marlowe (character), 59–62, 65, 317
Change of Habit, 236, 238
Chapin, Dwight, 189, 235
Chaplin, Charlie, 193
Chaplin, Geraldine, 267
Charade, 14, 349
Charles, Prince, 81
Charley Varrick, 353
Chase, Chevy, 328
Chasen's (restaurant), 293
"Checkers speech," 37, 39, 41–42, 48, 76, 132, 145, 188, 195, 204, 254, 310, 331
Chekhov, Anton, 284
Cheyenne Autumn, 173, 354
Cheyenne Social Club, The, 345